THE TEXAS SENATE

THE SENATE OF TEXAS

THE TEXAS SENATE

VOLUME II

Civil War to the Eve of Reform, 1861–1889

EDITED BY

Patsy McDonald Spaw

Texas A&M University Press
College Station

First edition

The paper used in this book meets the minimum requirements
of the American National Standard for Permanence
of Paper for Printed Library Materials, Z39.48–1984.
Binding materials have been chosen for durability.
∞

LIBRARY OF CONGRESS CATALOGING-IN-PUBLICATION DATA

The Texas Senate / edited by Patsy McDonald Spaw.—1st ed.
p. cm.
Includes bibliographical references (p.) and index.
Contents: v. 2. Civil War to the Eve of Reform, 1861–1889.
ISBN 0-89096-857-8 (v. 2 : alk. paper)
1. Texas. Legislature. Senate—History. I. Spaw, Patsy McDonald, 1945– .
JK4876T.48 1991
328.764′071—dc20 90-10988
CIP

TO ROBERT ELLIS JOHNSON

State Representative, 1957–63
House Parliamentarian, 1963–80
Senate Parliamentarian, 1991–95

•

A Texan in size and heart
who faithfully served
the state he loved

Contents

Illustrations

Preface

It is the purpose of this book to continue the history of the Texas Senate and its members and specifically to cover the turbulent years from 1861 through 1889. The book begins during a time of great excitement and optimism over a string of Confederate victories and quickly progresses to the somber days of defeat for the state and its way of life. The story continues with the hateful response of the defeated in enacting the infamous Black Codes, followed by a period of repression and reconstruction and a subsequent resurgence of the Democratic party, and ends with the emergence of the Progressive movement long before that movement took hold in the rest of the nation.

Like the first volume, the book is an informal reference work giving biographical information about members of the Senate and describing issues of the day and Senate procedures used to address those issues. We have attempted to present the facts in an evenhanded manner and with minimal editorial comment, letting the facts speak for themselves. We have tried not to be judgmental but have reported the stated beliefs of participants during the period. While a desire for revenge and feelings of hatred were shared by some of the defeated and some of the victors, a desire for healing and rebuilding was shared by some of the defeated and some of the victors as well. Others adopted a pragmatic approach of doing whatever it took to rise from the ravages of the Civil War, and it is hard to identify concretely their feelings for their fellowman. Nevertheless, both good and evil deeds were committed during the Reconstruction period, and we leave to the reader the interpretation of the participants' words and acts.

A word of caution. When reading the biographical sketches of the senators, the reader should bear in mind that primary sources were often lacking or not readily available. Many of the facts lie buried in courthouse, church, or college records in other states where the senators were born, married, attended college, and so forth. In many cases, the compilers of this book had to rely on secondary sources such as family histories and published legislative personnel manuals, and in the course of the book's preparation, a number of errors were discovered with regard to dates or the spelling of personal names or place names. Even the spelling and form of senators' names in the *Senate Journal* were often inconsistent. We have attempted to reconcile inconsistencies using the resources available.

To the staff members of the Eugene C. Barker Texas History Center at the University of Texas at Austin, the Texas State Library and Archives Commission in Austin, the Texas Legislative Reference Library, and the Austin History Center of the Austin Public Library, I offer special thanks. Others have been gracious and helpful in our research. Dr. Carl H. Moneyhon generously allowed the use of his personal notes on several senators. Dr. Alwyn Barr and Dr. Merline Pitre provided advice on useful readings. Thanks are due to the Alabama Department of Archives and History in Montgomery, Alabama; the Historic New Orleans Collection; and the Steen Library, Stephen F. Austin State University, Nacogdoches, Texas.

Dr. Richard B. McCaslin, although not an employee of the Engrossing and Enrolling Department, performed much of the research for the book and contributed greatly as one of the principal writers.

I offer a special thank-you to the entire staff of the Engrossing and Enrolling Department, who have provided yeomen service on this project. Principal researchers and writers for the project, in addition to Dr. McCaslin, were Mardi Alexander, Patty Michels-Anderson, Mary Hobart Key, Carolyn Maisel, and John Slavik. Special research work was led by Susan Bailey and Bob Edwards, who were assisted by Nancy Alliegro, Sam Menon, Bill Neale, Sandra Lebeyka, and Patience Worrel. The tasks of selecting illustrations and indexing were performed by Virginia Townsend. Typing, copying, and proofreading chores were handled by Betty Jo Bettersworth, Nancy Brown, Sara Day, Debbie Dodds, Diana Fisher, Tommy Gandy, Mike Heffley, Frances Hill, Kelley Humphrey, Ellie Hutcheson, Nanci Longoria, Gay Oden, Loretta Patschke, Sharon Rowlett, Marjorie Sylvester, Frances Tate, Heather White, and Kathryn Williams.

The continued support and encouragement of Betty King, secretary of the Senate, and Lt. Gov. Bob Bullock has given me and my staff the determination to complete this daunting task. Their love for Texas and the Texas Senate has been an inspiration for all who have worked on the project.

Of special importance to me personally is the dedication of this volume to Robert Ellis (Bob) Johnson—former state legislator, former House parliamentarian, former Senate parliamentarian, friend and counselor to all who knew him, and special friend to me. A true expert on legislative procedure and the use and "misuse" of legislative rules, Bob Johnson loved his state and the legislative bodies it elected. He served his state and those legislative bodies his entire life, and it is with love and respect that we dedicate this work in his memory.

Patsy McDonald Spaw
Austin, Texas

Introduction

Some of you laugh to scorn the idea of bloodshed as a result of secession, and jocularly propose to drink all the blood that will ever flow in consequence of it! But let me tell you what is coming on the heels of secession. The time will come when your fathers and husbands, your sons and brothers, will be herded together like sheep and cattle at the point of the bayonet; and your mothers and wives, and sisters and daughters, will ask, Where are they? and echo will answer, where?

You may after the sacrifice of countless millions of treasure, and hundreds of thousands of precious lives, as a bare possibility, win Southern independence . . . but I doubt it. I tell you that, while I believe with you in the doctrines of State rights, the North is determined to preserve this Union. They are not a fiery impulsive people as you are, for they live in cooler climates. But when they begin to move in a given direction, where great interests are involved, such as the present issues before the country, they move with the steady momentum and perseverance of a mighty avalanche, and what I fear is they will overwhelm the South with ignoble defeat.

—*Sam Houston, 1859*

Little heed was paid to this dire warning Sam Houston uttered during his campaign for governor in 1859, yet its prophetic accuracy would in time be apparent to all.

Houston won the 1859 election overwhelmingly despite his strong antisecession views and held firm throughout the regular session of the Eighth Legislature in his refusal to call a state convention to consider secession. The governor had apparently interpreted his election as an endorsement by the people of his views on secession. He was wrong.

Though bombarded with harassing editorials and fiery speeches by ardent secessionists insisting that he call the legislature into special session or call a secession convention, Houston was in late 1860 still steadfastly refusing to do either. The secessionists were not deterred by his refusal, and on November 13, 1860, just days after Lincoln's election, a small group of secessionist leaders met in the state attorney general's office to plan a meeting of interested citizens to discuss the secession issue. The result of that citizens meeting was the call for an election in each representative district on January 8, 1861, for two delegates to a state convention to be held on January 28.

Realizing that he would not be able to prevent the legally unauthorized convention from assembling, Houston, in a preemptive move, on December 17 issued a call for the legislature to meet in special session on January 21, one week before the scheduled secession convention. When the Eighth Legislature convened in special session, the members were not disposed to listen to Houston's arguments either against secession or about the illegality of the proposed convention. Instead, it immediately legalized the convention by resolution.

Although Houston refused to sign the resolution until February 4, the convention assembled on January 28 and quickly set to work. The convention handily adopted an ordinance of secession and annulled the ordinance of annexation, calling for approval by the voters in a special election on February 23. Having completed its task, the convention adjourned on February 5 to campaign for voter approval. It planned to reconvene on March 2 to canvass the votes.

The convention reconvened on Saturday, March 2, but, lacking a quorum, postponed action until Monday, March 5. With a quorum present on March 5, the convention canvassed the votes—76 percent of the votes cast were in favor—and declared March 2 as the official date of Texas' secession from the Union and the same day voted to join the Confederate States of America.

Houston was angered at the convention's usurpation of power. He argued that the legislature's resolution had authorized the convention to address the issue of secession and the submission of the question of secession to the voters, nothing more. The governor further argued that it was the legislature's constitutional responsibility to call a constitutional convention, if necessary, to make changes in the constitution and that the convention clearly overstepped its authority by acting alone to join the Confederacy.

Confident of public support, the convention ignored Houston's protests and proceeded rapidly to take bold steps in exercise of its self-proclaimed power. One such move was an ordinance requiring all state officers to take an oath of loyalty. All state executive officers were required by the convention to take the oath by noon on March 16, and by that date all except Governor Houston and Secretary of State E. W. Cave had complied. The convention removed Houston from office that day and replaced him with Lieutenant Governor Edward Clark.

The Eighth Legislature reconvened for the last time on March 18 for an adjourned session. After the loyalty oath was amended, all the senators took it, even those who opposed secession—the antisecessionist Senate minority and the secessionist Senate majority were not divided in their love for Texas, only in their opinion as to the direction in which the state should go. Shortly thereafter Houston retired to his farm in Huntsville after refusing President Lincoln's offer of Union troops, declaring, "I love Texas too well to bring strife and bloodshed upon her."

As Texas entered the great Civil War on the side of the South, Texans were eager to join the fray. It has been estimated by historians that between seventy and ninety thousand Texans saw military service in the war. Texans stood out for their bravery, leadership, and determination. President Jefferson Davis is recorded as having welcomed Texas troops as follows: "Texans! The troops from other States have their reputation to gain, but the sons of the defenders of the Alamo have theirs to maintain. I am sure you will be faithful to the trust." And faithful they were. Texas troops lived up to their reputation and achieved great distinction on the battlefields of the Civil War.

The costs of the war would be enormous for Texas. Her sons would be sacrificed on distant battlefields, while women and children were left to till the fields and care for the homestead, enduring severe shortages of medicine, clothing, shoes, and farm implements and suffering exhaustion, fear, and loneliness. But when the Ninth Legislature convened in November, 1861, following numerous Confederate successes, there was no inkling of the somber days that lay ahead, only exultant predictions of a quick victory over the enemy to the north. Houston's warning had been quickly forgotten.

THE TEXAS SENATE

CIVIL WAR

CHAPTER 1

The Senate of the Ninth Legislature, 1861–63

On November 4, 1861, the Senate of the Ninth Legislature convened in Austin for a regular session that would last until January 14, 1862, a period of just over ten weeks, making this the shortest session since the early days of the Republic. It was a time of great excitement as men from Texas participated in an almost unbroken string of Confederate victories. Although the senators of the Eighth Legislature had been divided on the secession ordinance, those serving in the Ninth shared a common devotion to the Confederate cause. After Texas had left the Union, they had subordinated their partisan interests to the war effort and closed ranks in pursuit of a Southern victory. Recurring legislative issues, such as land claims and education, were displaced by the need for a sustained war effort. Legislation was passed to spur industrial development as well as military preparations for defense against the increasing number of Indian raids in the west and for participation in the great national struggle in the east. The war effort had not yet reached its zenith when the senators met in special session from February 2 to March 7, 1863.

Of the forty-six senators elected to the Ninth Legislature, only five were not from states belonging to the Confederacy. One was Austrian-born George B. Erath, who had been elected to the House of the Eighth, Ninth, and Tenth congresses of the Republic of Texas; the House of the First Legislature; and the Senate of the Seventh and Eighth legislatures. The others were Lewis F. Casey, from Illinois; Rufus K. Hartley, from Pennsylvania; and the Maxeys, Samuel B. and Rice, from Kentucky. The personal loyalty of many senators to the Confederacy caused the absence of several from the legislative chambers after the regular session. For example, Anthony Martin Branch of Huntsville (who had served in the House during the Eighth Legislature) resigned from the Senate in 1862 to become captain of Company A of the 21st Texas Cavalry Regiment. A distant relative of Robert E. Lee, Branch originally was from Virginia. After graduation from Hampden-Sidney College in Virginia, he practiced law in Huntsville and became an intimate friend of Sam Houston, serving as executor of his will and guardian of his children. Branch was succeeded by David C. Dickson of Montgomery.

Dickson's arrival in the Senate as a replacement for Branch signaled the return of a seasoned legislative veteran. Dickson had served not only as lieutenant governor during the Fifth Legislature, but also as speaker of the House in the Fourth and as a member of the House in the First, Third, Sixth, and Eighth. He had also been a candidate for governor in 1855, when he chose to run on the Know-Nothing, or American, party ticket, rather than campaign as the incumbent candidate for lieutenant governor on the Democratic slate. His decision forced the Democrats into the so-called "Bomb Shell Convention" to replace him. Born in Mississippi in 1818, Dickson graduated from medical school in Kentucky before moving to Texas in 1841 and accepting an appointment as surgeon of the Texas Army. During the Civil War he served as a captain of Texas militia. Following the war, Dickson served as financial agent for the state penitentiary at Huntsville.

Stephen H. Darden of Gonzales had opposed secession, but soon after Texas left the Union he enlisted as a lieutenant with Company A, Hood's Regiment, 4th Texas Brigade, and was actually on furlough from the army during the regular session, leaving thereafter for active duty. Darden and Branch both served in the Confederate Congress. Following the war, Darden was active during Reconstruction and held various state offices; he was elected comptroller of public accounts in 1873. As comptroller he recommended, and as a member of the Constitutional Convention of 1875 eventually sponsored, the proposition that changed "the organic laws by which U.S. bonds in which the school fund was invested should be sold, and the proceeds converted into Texas State bonds, bearing a higher rate of interest, and thus applying the interest paid on the public debt to the maintenance of the public schools." The proposition was passed

David Catchings Dickson, lieutenant governor of Texas, 1853–54, in Fifth Legislature, senator in Ninth and Tenth legislatures. Reproduced from holdings of Texas State Archives.

by the convention. In 1884 Governor Ireland appointed him superintendent of public buildings and grounds. He was also a trustee of the State Lunatic Asylum.

Darden was replaced by Spencer Ford of Lockhart, a former member of the Secession Convention of 1861, for the called session of the Ninth Legislature. Ford returned for the Tenth Legislature. He was a lawyer by profession and after the war served as district judge for Brazos County.

John H. Burnett of Crockett resigned from the Senate in February, 1862 to command the 13th Texas Cavalry, and Anderson F. Crawford, the senator from Jasper, resigned to become his lieutenant colonel. War was not new to Burnett, as he had enlisted at age sixteen as a private soldier in Colonel Calhoun's regiment during the Mexican War and had returned home to Georgia a colonel. He later moved to Crockett and began farming and merchandising. In 1866 Burnett moved to Galveston, where he formed the business partnership Burnett and Wall. He later revived the famous Tremont Hotel in Galveston, invested in valuable properties in the city and along the coast, and became involved in Texas railroads. The vacancies created by the resignations of Burnett and Crawford were filled by Leroy W. Cooper of Crockett and James W. Andres of Livingston.

As successor to Burnett's Eleventh District senatorial seat, Cooper was a novice to the political process when he joined the Senate on February 2, 1863, for service in the called session. He returned for a portion of the Twelfth Legislature as a member of the House. Born in Georgia in 1822 and licensed to practice law in 1845, he moved his family to Crockett in November, 1856. A prominent jurist, Cooper served as a state district court judge during the governorships of both Hamilton and Davis but declined the offer of an appointment as an associate justice of the Texas Supreme Court.

George P. Finlay, born in Perry County, Mississippi, on November 16, 1829, came to the Senate from Lavaca, Calhoun County. Nicknamed "Tall Sycamore" because of his six feet, four inches of height, Finlay was an imposing figure, which probably gave him a special advantage in his roles as both teacher and lawyer. Finlay was at various times a prominent member of the judiciary committees of the Senate and the House and was chairman of that committee in the Senate of the Thirteenth Legislature. He also served in the

Sixteenth, Seventeenth, and Twenty-third legislatures in the House, representing Galveston. Perhaps the achievement that has kept his name longest before the public was his coediting of the *Index to Gammel's Laws of Texas, 1822–1905*, published in 1906 and still very much in use. Finlay enlisted in the 6th Texas Infantry and left public service after the regular session of the Ninth Legislature.

S. Addison White of Victoria succeeded to the senatorial seat left vacant by Finlay's departure. Arriving in Texas from Tennessee in 1830, White was first employed as an overseer on the plantation of Judge Edwin Waller. Later he read law under William and John Wharton and represented Jackson County in the House of the First Congress of the Republic. Twenty years later, he represented the Twenty-sixth District in the Senate of the Sixth Legislature. In 1857, White purchased the *Victoria Advocate*, which he edited until his death in 1869. As mayor of Victoria, he was exempt from Confederate conscription and did not serve in the Confederate military. Sworn into Senate service for the called session of the Ninth Legislature, White returned to serve throughout the Tenth Legislature and was also reelected mayor.

Alfred T. Obenchain of Weatherford resigned from the Senate on February 15, 1862; became a lieutenant colonel in the Frontier Regiment Texas Cavalry (later designated the 46th Texas Cavalry); and rode with Colonel Norris from the Red River to the Rio Grande, selecting campsites for the Rangers. Obenchain was murdered that same year, allegedly by his escort, two privates of the regiment. Obenchain's successor was William Quayle of Norton's Grove.

Although elected to fill the unexpired term of Eggleston D. Townes in the Eighth Legislature, Nathan G. Shelley of Austin was not sworn into office until the Ninth Legislature. He resigned from the Senate on April 1, 1862, to become attorney general of Texas under the Confederacy, as well as to accept an appointment as a brigadier general of Texas state troops. He returned to serve in the Senate during the Eleventh and Thirteenth legislatures. Shelley was born in Hawkins County, Tennessee, in 1825. The family moved to Talladega County, Alabama, in 1837, and Nathan attended Emory and Henry College in Virginia. In 1845, he interrupted his law studies to serve in the Mexican War and participated in several major battles of that conflict. After his return from Mexico, Shelley resumed his law studies, was admitted to the bar in 1849, and became an editor of the *Alabama Reporter*. He was elected to the Alabama Legislature in 1851 and 1853. In 1855, Shelley moved to Austin, where he practiced law with prominent local attorneys George F. Moore and John Hancock. A. W. Moore of Bastrop was elected from the Twenty-sixth District to fill Shelley's unexpired term, taking the oath of office in the called session on February 2, 1863.

Perhaps the most distinguished Confederate elected to the Senate of the Ninth Legislature never attended a single session: Samuel Bell Maxey of Paris, a graduate of the U.S. Military Academy who had fought in the Mexican War before retiring to practice law, initially in Kentucky and then in Texas. Maxey favored the secession of Texas from the Union and was elected to the Texas Senate in 1861 by a large majority, but he declined to serve. Instead, he raised the 9th Texas Infantry Regiment under General Albert Sidney Johnston, and his father, Rice Maxey, was elected to his Senate seat. Samuel Maxey later became one of only three Confederate major generals from Texas and in 1863 was ordered by President Davis to take command of the Indian Territory. After his election to the U.S. Senate in 1874, Maxey took an active part in debates on the tariff commission bill, contending that the government had no constitutional power to levy and collect taxes for any purpose other than the support of government. He strongly favored liberal appropriations to improve rivers and harbors and supported subsidies for steamship lines so as to encourage foreign trade. Maxey is credited with establishing the longest stage line in the world, from Fort Worth to Fort Yuma.

Failure to chronicle the original winner in the race to represent the Sixth Senatorial District (Harrison and Upshur counties) in the Ninth Legislature is due in part to the unsettled times created by war. Almost all information about the August 5, 1861, general election for the Senate seat of the Sixth Senatorial District and about the special election that belatedly followed appears not in the usual sources but rather in the *Texas Republican*, the correspondence of Governor Clark, and miscellaneous minor records. Because the usual sources, such as the *Senate Journal*, fail to indicate that anything is missing, events and persons have inadvertently been left out of later accounts drawing on them. Such is the case with Matthew Fielding Locke.

Samuel Bell Maxey. Reproduced from holdings of Texas State Archives.

Locke was a prosperous planter from Lafayette, Louisiana, and represented Upshur County in the Sixth Texas Legislature. He was reelected and served as speaker of the House for the last twenty-eight days of the Seventh. Born in Rutherford County, Tennessee, on July 10, 1824, he moved with his family in 1836 to Marshall, Mississippi. In 1846, he enlisted in the 1st Mississippi Regiment of Volunteers and saw combat in the Mexican War under Jefferson Davis. He returned to Mississippi and married and in 1850 moved to Upshur County. After his legislative service, he was elected to the Secession Convention of 1861 and was appointed to the committee to notify Governor Sam Houston of his deposition. At that point in Texas history, a number of men in circumstances similar to Locke's felt they had to choose between politics and the military. For the time being, at least, Locke seemed to choose both, for it is almost certain that even while campaigning for the Senate he was attempting to raise a regiment of his own. He would not give up the one effort until he had succeeded in the other.

Of the election itself, the *Republican* said on August 10, "The vote was unusually meagre." It would turn out that all votes in Texas during the war were meager, at least in comparison with the Secession Referendum. Not only were there fewer men of voting age, but also people had little trust or interest in government. On the same date, five days after the election, the paper had more to say: "The returns being incomplete and the race close, it is impossible to determine whether [E. A.] Blanch or Locke is elected to the State Senate from Upshur and Harrison."

It turns out that Locke had won the seat, as the official returns announced on August 24, but he had also made progress with his regiment, which he valued even more than his place in the Senate. Locke was in correspondence with Governor Clark, who might be expected to take an interest in the election, having himself been senator from Harrison County in 1847–48. The several letters from Locke found in Clark's files are brisk and usually have two sections: the first concerning financing, equipment, commissions, and the like for his regiment; the second urging the governor to set the special election for a successor to follow Locke's resignation. Governor Clark, however, issued no proclamation at that time, and the only reason would seem to be that he received no resignation from Locke, despite the governor's urging. Eventually, aspirants to the succession were willing to behave as if Locke had resigned, as evidenced by the *Republican* of September 28: "We are authorized to announce C. C. Coppedge as a candidate for the State Senate, from the counties of Upshur and Harrison, to fill the vacancy occasioned by the resignation of Colonel M. F. Locke."

On October 5, the *Republican* announced the full slate of candidates: Coppedge, S. W. Beazley (later corrected to Beasley), and S. C. Newman. Coppedge was from Marshall, Beasley was from Gilmer, and Newman was of unknown origin. There was no announcement of the election date and, presumably, no news from the colonel.

A proclamation was at last issued on November 5 calling the election, oddly enough, for no earlier than five days from that date and no later than ten days after it, which might mean that Clark still did not have a Locke resignation in hand and was hoping by publication to shame him into sending one. There is no way of knowing for sure whether it arrived, but well after the time the election should have been held, the Gilmer *Patriot*, as reported in the *Republican*, complained that the election was delayed until the week of November 23 for lack of that resignation. The *Republican* wearily noted on December 7 that "Major S. W. Beasley" had won; Coppedge would have to wait until the Eleventh Legislature to be a senator. On December 16, 1861, Beasley took the oath and was seated.

Colonel Locke did have his regiment, the 10th Texas Cavalry, and it fought with great distinction; it was said he was offered a battlefield promotion to general but declined because of his health. The war over, he moved to Van Buren, Arkansas, where he was elected the first commissioner of agriculture of the state. In 1890 he moved to Little Rock; and in 1909, to relieve his third wife's ill health, he made his last move, to El Paso, and died there June 4, 1911, at the age of eighty-six.

Personal tragedy rather than military service caused one vacancy before the special session. Senator Edwin B. Scarborough of Brownsville, after having served in the Senate in the Fifth, Sixth, Seventh, and Eighth legislatures and the regular session of the Ninth, was murdered on October 7, 1862. The circumstances of his death remain obscure. Scarborough is best known as the owner and editor of Brownsville's *American Flag*.

Scarborough was succeeded in the special session by Edward R.

Hord, who took the oath of office on February 11, 1863. Hord was born in 1826 to a prominent Virginia family. Although there are claims of large Texas landholdings by his older brother Richard prior to 1846, Edward is the first member of his immediate family definitely known to have come to Texas, where he was mustered into the Mabry B. (Mustang) Gray Company of Texas Mounted Volunteers on July 21, 1846. He was mustered out in 1847, and in 1848, at the age of twenty-two, he was elected the first clerk of the district court in the newly created Starr County. His legislative experience began in the House of the Fourth and Fifth legislatures and ripened with his advancement to the Senate for the Sixth, but he did not seek election again until the Ninth. Hord returned again for the Tenth Legislature but resigned on the last day, November 15, 1864, to take the important post of collector of customs at the Port of Brownsville and to engage in cotton trading. The Union victory, however, brought an end to those endeavors, and he reportedly practiced law on both sides of the border until his death in 1869.

Eight freshman senators—William C. Batte, John Boyd (who had served in the House during the First and Second congresses), Henry C. Cook, John F. Crawford, Robert H. Graham, John N. Houston, Erastus Reed, and M. W. Wheeler—served only one term in the Senate. Seven other freshmen—S. W. Beasley, James B. Davis, John W. Durant, John T. Harcourt, A. N. Jordan, Pryor Lea, and N. A. Mitchell—returned to complete their Senate careers in the Tenth Legislature. Freshman senator Benjamin T. Selman also served two terms, but his second term was in the Eleventh Legislature. Although George E. Burney was a newcomer to the Senate, legislative service was not new to him, as he had served in the House in the Third and Fifth legislatures; Burney returned to serve in the Senate in the Tenth and Eleventh legislatures. A newcomer to both Texas and the Texas Legislature, William D. Lair was no neophyte to politics, having served four years in the legislature in his native Kentucky before moving to Texas in 1859. After serving in the Ninth Legislature, Lair would not return to the Senate until the Sixteenth and Seventeenth legislatures.

Veteran senator Robert H. Guinn of Rusk previously had served in the Senate during the Fifth, Sixth, Seventh, and Eighth legislatures and would return for the Tenth and Eleventh. The careers of three other returning members would collectively span twelve legislative sessions: Jesse H. Parsons of Henderson served in the House in the Sixth Legislature and in the Senate in the Eighth, Ninth, and Tenth; Chauncy B. Shepard of Long Point served in the Senate in the Seventh, Eighth, Ninth, and Tenth legislatures; and Jefferson Weatherford of Pleasant Run served in the Senate in the Fifth, Sixth, Ninth, and Tenth legislatures.

The senators of the Ninth Legislature who answered the roll in 1861 were no less enthusiastic in their support of the Confederacy than those who joined the army. Indeed, the belligerent tone of many of their resolutions and the great volume of legislation they passed indicate that they considered themselves to be as responsible as any soldier for the fortunes of the Confederacy. One zealous senator, John T. Harcourt, went to the Texas coast at the call of Major General John Bankhead Magruder, commanding general of the District of Texas, to defend the state from invasion by Union forces in 1863. Harcourt was elected captain of an ad hoc company of militia, but the danger soon passed, and the company was disbanded before Harcourt saw any action.

The Senate, despite pressure from the governor for financial retrenchment, elected a full slate of officers: Phineas de Cordova, secretary; A. H. Castile, first assistant secretary; George W. Breeding, second assistant secretary; David C. Burleson, sergeant-at-arms; John W. Murphy, doorkeeper; Flavius Everett, enrolling clerk; and J. Q. St. Clair, engrossing clerk. For the extra session, William Hamby was elected assistant doorkeeper and Castile was replaced by Nathaniel C. Raymond; Burleson by R. H. Clements; Everett by William M. Gilleland; and St. Clair by Henry Thomas, who later succeeded Breeding as second assistant secretary and held both offices. Rev. William A. Smith served as chaplain for both sessions, an office which was opposed by many of the senators but was again created by resolution. Senator Guinn was elected president pro tempore.

Executive leadership during the first two years of the war was provided by Francis R. Lubbock, an ardent Confederate who won a close race for governor in 1861 against former senator and incumbent governor Edward Clark, and by John M. Crockett, former mayor of Dallas, the new lieutenant governor. Lubbock was one of the few Confederate leaders who foresaw a long and bitter war. In his state of the state address to the assembled legislators on Novem-

Francis R. Lubbock, governor of Texas, 1861–63.
Reproduced from holdings of Texas State Archives.

ber 16, 1861, he openly confessed that "no Legislature of any State has ever been called upon to act under more embarrassing circumstances than those which surround you." Texas was in immediate danger of invasion by a new enemy, the Union, at a time when it had not yet settled scores with its old enemies, Mexico and the Indians, and had no funds with which to provide for defense. Lubbock

John McClannahan Crockett, lieutenant governor, 1861–63, in Ninth Legislature. Reproduced from holdings of Texas State Archives.

exaggerated only slightly when he declared that "the State Government is absolutely without a dollar subject to appropriation for the purpose of carrying on the civil affairs, or placing the State in a condition of security against the invasion of the enemy." The first priority of the Senate of the Ninth Legislature would be to provide for financial expansion in both the public and private sectors.

Fiscal retrenchment became a hotly debated issue in the regular session when Governor Lubbock vetoed legislation providing for the salaries and expenses of the legislators. Early in the Ninth Legislature, House Bill 60, an act for payment of twelve thousand dollars in legislative per diem to members and officers, was introduced, passed, and signed. The entire procedure required only six days, November 16 through November 21, perhaps because it was standard policy at the beginning of each session to set the per diem of members or perhaps because there was a commonality of interest in the subject. The per diem was to be paid from "money in the Treasury not otherwise appropriated." One month later, however, on December 18, a second act to pay both mileage and per diem was read for the first time in the House. It passed both the House and the Senate and was on the governor's desk by December 28. The second act allocated "$80,000, or so much as may be necessary . . . out of any money in the Treasury not otherwise appropriated." Supposing, reasonably enough, that there probably were not eighty thousand unappropriated dollars in the treasury, the legislators specified just where the treasurer should find the funds: "university land sales, the settlement of successions [i.e., inheritances], escheated property, and sinking fund [*sic*] on Railroad bonds," to be repaid with state bonds. Of course, the object of these peculiar commands was to lay their hands on specie. If those sources were exhausted, recourse could be had to drafts on the tax assessor and collector of the home county of the member or officer or, in a real pinch, to warrants drawn on the treasurer "receivable for taxes and other public uses," which unfortunately were not specie.

Governor Lubbock was extremely displeased with the second act and on December 31 sent the bill back to the House with a stern and reproachful veto, pointing out that the specified payments would place the members and their employees above all the creditors of the state and that the money taken would deprive schools, widows, and orphans of their due. Worst of all, he wrote, "While I

Edward Clark, governor of Texas, 1861. Reproduced from holdings of Texas State Archives.

believe that the State should pay to the utmost of its abilities, all its officials, both civil and military, yet under the present critical condition of our beloved state and Confederacy, I confess I would witness with feelings of the deepest sorrow the last dollar drawn from the Treasury unless it were to furnish arms, ammunition and clothing to her gallant sons who are now proudly vindicating the old fame of the Texan soldier."

That same evening in the Senate, Weatherford offered a joint resolution as a sarcastic reply threatening adjournment in two days and cessation of pay to all government officials, including the governor:

> WHEREAS, it has become apparent that the Governor has very properly determined that this Legislature shall not receive any compensation for their services, and
>
> WHEREAS, the 9th Legislature heartily approves of this economical policy and desires to extend it to all the functionaries of the Government, therefore,
>
> RESOLVED, *the House concurring*, That this Legislature adjourn *sine die* on the 2nd day of January next at 9 o'clock A.M.

Senator Erath countered with a substitute:

> RESOLVED, That it is the sense of this Senate that the members thereof receive no pay or mileage for the present session and the next two years.

Both the original resolution and the substitute were tabled by a vote of eighteen to nine, Erath voting yea and Weatherford nay.

On the morning of January 3, 1862, the House passed the bill over the governor's veto, fifty-two to twenty-four; and on January 4, the House and Senate agreed to a joint committee to deal with the now all-too-public issue.

Before the committee could report, the Senate, on January 6, refused to override the veto by sixteen to ten, voted to reconsider by twenty-two to five, and again refused to override by seventeen to eleven. A period of confusion followed. A Senate bill on the same subject was engrossed on January 7; the House reported passage of what presumably was the same Senate bill on January 10; and then, on the same day, Weatherford suddenly introduced what may have been a new bill (but possibly a House bill) that was passed by suspending all rules and sent to the governor, who on January 13 signed a modified bill which called for an appropriation of seventy-five thousand dollars and left the comptroller in charge of payment with treasury warrants, to be used when needed. The majority and minority reports of the joint committee were read and voted on after the bill had passed. The majority report attacked the governor vigorously for misstatements that put the legislature in a bad light. The minority report, signed for the Senate only by Erath, stoutly defended the governor and even admitted some possibility of legislative error. The majority report, adopted by a vote of fourteen to thirteen, ended with a request that the "Houston *Telegraph*, Galveston *News, The Civilian and Gazette* and other papers in this State" publish the report. This seems to have been done, but on the same day the *Texas State Gazette* gave the legislature some quite unwelcome attention, not merely defending the governor and the minority report but also pursuing the governor's critics without mercy, all under the stark epigraph "And for his vesture they cast lots." On the same page, the editors of the *Gazette* complained that the legislature, enraged by the publication of the veto message and other unpleasant news, had tried to exclude the paper from competition for the public printing contract. It was true that an attempt was made in the House to amend Senate Bill 39 on the public printing so as to keep the *Gazette* out, but the amendment was tabled by a vote of twenty-eight to thirty-four.

Public printing somehow had disappeared with secession, and Lubbock complained in his first message that without it the government was awash in "a mass of manuscript"; he urged the legislature to do something about the lack of public printing. But nothing was done except for one amendment to existing law governing public printing and a rather forlorn-sounding joint resolution, approved on January 14, 1862, directing the secretary of state, the comptroller, and the treasurer, or a majority of the three, to proceed immediately after adjournment to contract for public printing in accordance with existing law. However, the journals of the Ninth and Tenth legislatures were not published, some of the manuscripts have vanished, and those now in use are modern attempts to arrange the principal sources as a coherent whole.

The primary effort of the wartime legislatures in Texas, as in the rest of the South, was directed toward winning the war. The exact number of Texans who fought for the Confederacy cannot be determined, but the roll of names that can be counted is truly astonishing. Roughly two-thirds of the eligible male population in 1860 appear to have taken part in the conflict. These men needed a vast array of supplies and equipment and required even more support in the way of munitions, clothing, and hospital care once they faced the enemy. Their families at home, struggling to survive without a male head of household, also needed support and looked to the state and to private organizations for funds.

In an act approved on December 9, 1861, the Ninth Legislature at first tried to deal with the crescendo of demands for money by such devices as a "war tax" to be assessed and collected by counties on real and personal property, at no more than twenty-five cents on each hundred dollars of valuation, the funds raised to go largely to military costs within the county and to families of county residents whose men were away at war. The report of the Senate Finance Committee of January 8, 1862, together with recommendations from the comptroller, pointed inexorably to the need for a revision of the basic sources of revenue if the goal "to liquidate the positive indebtedness without interest" within three years—thought by many to be the extreme possible limit of the war—was to be achieved.

The laws to raise revenues by taxation were changed by more than a simple increase in the Ninth Legislature; although the Constitution of 1861 required that these bills originate in the House, the Senate had much to say—and often the final say—about the resulting statute. The striking differences between the actions of the Eighth Legislature and the regular session of the Ninth illustrate the economic effects of the war and the sometimes rather frantic attempts to deal with them. Whereas the Eighth Legislature left unchanged the direct ad valorem tax of "twelve and a half cents upon each hundred dollars value of property, real and personal," the regular session of the Ninth doubled the tax and made four cents of it apply to interest and principal of a war loan. The called session of the Ninth doubled the amount again to fifty cents, specified that personal and real property included "all cotton, wheat, flour, corn, and all other products of the soil, not in the hands of the producer," and made sure that "the tax shall be levied and collected on the assessment of extras for 1863." Similarly, the poll tax went unamended in the Eighth Legislature, but the Ninth doubled the amount of the tax to one dollar and changed its applicability from "free male persons" aged twenty-one to fifty to an open-ended "over the age of twenty-one." In the omnibus tax act, the Ninth Legislature greatly expanded the miscellaneous occupation tax provision and included more lines of work. And in order to free more grain for the starving South—and perhaps in response to prohibitionist sentiments—an exorbitant annual fee of one thousand dollars was levied on "each and every still used . . . in the distillation of spirituous liquors from any kind of grain."

Some of the anticipated new tax revenue was allocated to the maintenance of soldiers in the field. On November 22, 1861, Senator Hartley introduced a bill creating a hospital fund for Texas soldiers in the Confederate Army and, as chairman of the committee to which it was referred, delivered a favorable report on it bound up with a supportive message from Lubbock. Sent next to the powerful Committee on Military Affairs, the bill was favorably reported, passed, and signed by the governor on January 8, 1862, the day of the finance report. It appropriated one hundred fifty thousand dollars, of which fifteen thousand dollars came from the school fund through an act signed on January 13—only the first in a series of raids on that fund. On March 5, 1863, a bill was signed that appropriated an additional two hundred thousand dollars for hospital supplies.

Probably the most effective measure to further the conduct of the war was the creation of the State Military Board, with broad powers to manage money and supplies for the armed forces. The seminal act was signed on January 11, 1862, appropriating five hundred thousand dollars in bonds for the purchase of arms and ammunition and appointing the governor, comptroller, and treasurer as the members of a board to oversee disbursement. A separate act required that all state-owned arms not in use be returned to the government. When these acts proved insufficient, another one million dollars was appropriated in an act signed on January 14, 1862, for the support of state troops called into active service. As specie became increasingly scarce, the board was expected to cope with that as well, and, in an act signed on March 3, 1863, during the special session, the board was authorized to buy cotton and transport it to Mexico for sale in return for hard money to be placed in a sinking fund for the redemption of cotton bonds. The major drawback involved in granting the board so much authority over the transaction was that the board was beset by profiteers.

Another act of January 11, 1862, required all payments of principal and interest on loans from the state to be paid in specie, but treasury warrants or notes from either the state or the Confederate government could be accepted as payment on lands, officer fees, and taxes. At the same time, the law required the treasurer and other state or county officers to accept and disburse Confederate treasury notes and warrants as a circulating medium at par.

The Military Board was also empowered to establish foundries and other industries to further the war effort. The South, and Texas in particular, was a completely agrarian economy and lacked even basic wartime manufactures; guns, munitions, powder—all had come from the North. This critical lack of manufactured goods was never overcome, but Texas tried her best: a state foundry was opened in Austin in July, 1862, along with a plant to manufacture percussion caps, and the Senate endorsed charters for many new private enterprises in response to the demand for munitions. The Texas Powder Company was incorporated to build in Bexar County, or elsewhere in the state, buildings, machinery, and improvements for the manufacture of gunpowder and mining or blasting powder "or such other similar compounds as the Company may at any time manúfacture for sale." The Texas Lead Mine Company also received a charter, as did the Texas Lead and Copper Mine Company and the Texas Iron Company, the latter empowered to operate a foundry in either Marion or Davis County. Attempts at industrial development in Texas would accelerate with the decline of the South's fortunes, especially after control of the Mississippi River passed to the Union in the summer of 1863 with the fall of Vicksburg.

Salt became a particularly scarce staple, vital to the preservation of meat processed for shipment to distant points. On January 10, 1862, the Senate passed a joint resolution authorizing the governor to appoint an agent to take possession of and operate the salt lake in Hidalgo County known as El Sal del Rey. This salt would be sold to the public at the customary rates, with some exceptions. Scarborough, the senator from the district embracing Hidalgo County, introduced the bill into the legislature which would actually implement the plan. Similarly, the legislature, in a joint resolution of March 6, 1863, instructed the Military Board to investigate the expediency of using the salines and salt mines near Double Mountain on the northwestern frontier and made available five thousand dollars to provide for their successful operation under the supervision of state authorities. Private ventures for supplying salt were also encouraged. The Aransas Salt Works Company received a charter as a joint-stock corporation.

The senators proved willing to experiment with new ways to attack the enemy by sea. They appropriated five hundred dollars to Robert Creuzbaur, a clerk in the General Land Office, to assist him in presenting his invention, the *Sea King*, to the Confederate War Department for consideration. Governor Lubbock enthusiastically endorsed the experimental vessel after receiving a glowing report from an investigative committee. Patterned after a submarine vessel designed by Ross and Thomas De Kay Winans during the 1850s, the *Sea King* was a cigar-shaped, armor-plated, propeller-driven craft with very little superstructure visible above the water. Creuzbaur's vessel differed from the Winans submarine in that it had the propeller at the stern rather than in the center, was elliptical instead of circular in cross-section, and used hot air rather than steam for propulsion. It was intended to be a ram, was armed with one breech-loading submarine cannon facing forward, and had a third "mode of destruction" which the investigators said "prudence forbids to mention . . . in a written communication." Judging from similar craft launched by the South, the unmentionable mode of destruction was probably a mine attached to a long boom which could be pushed under the waterline of an anchored enemy ship.

The excitement generated by the *Sea King* was infectious. One of the investigators declared that "one such vessel constructed on the plan proposed will more effectively raise the blockade than a small fleet which could have no advantage over the enemy," and another insisted that "one such vessel carefully constructed could annihilate the fleet of the enemy in a short time." The joint committee on the subject reported that the vessel, even if it could not destroy entire fleets, might at least raise the blockade along the Texas coast. Shelley signed the report for the Senate, and Creuzbaur got his funding, but apparently nothing more came of the idea.

The public sector needed more stimulation than that provided by new incorporations and the spending of the Military Board. In an act signed December 7, 1861, the legislature suspended the operation of all laws for the collection of debts and liabilities on bonds, promissory notes, bills of exchange, and contracts for the payment of money until January 1, 1864, or until six months after the close of the war, should it terminate before that date. The most important exceptions were official liabilities on the part of public officers, indebtedness to the state, and money held in escrow or in trust. The statute would not prevent the initiation of writs of attachment, sequestration, or injunction; settlement would simply have to await the end of the war. The suspension of debt collections did not apply to demands or claims against alien enemies, and a second act, signed on January 10, 1862, provided that those debts due from citizens of Texas to alien enemies that were sequestered under the act of the Confederate Congress could still be collected by southern officials.

A vocal minority of senators, led by Harcourt, chairman of the Committee on the Judiciary, which reported in favor of the bill for suspension of debts, actively opposed the measure, but to no avail. The action was viewed as necessary to encourage the investment of large amounts of capital and to protect both state and private enterprise from the fluctuations of business in the turmoil of civil war. As a political palliative, the act specially stipulated that "no property of any soldier, seaman, or marine, now or hereafter engaged in the military service of the Confederate States of America, or the State of Texas, shall, during such service, be levied on under execution, or sold by virtue of any levy heretofore made." The soldiers who fought for Texas during the Confederacy did not receive land grants or money for their service, but at least the government would protect their property from foreclosure while they were away. During the Tenth Legislature, all sections of the act for suspension of debts were extended for the duration of the war.

The suspension of debts, a desperate action, was accompanied by a series of less radical fiscal measures. All public contracts for internal improvements were extended indefinitely because of the war; through an amendment proposed by Senator Crawford, time limits for contract performance, which had been written into many agreements, would be adjusted taking this extension into consideration. A separate act provided for the relief of Texas railroad companies: failure to complete a specified length of track as provided in the contracts would not result in forfeiture as long as the provisions were met within two years after the end of the war. Previously, the legislature had required the completion of twenty-five miles of track each year; after the passage of this act, if the company did succeed in laying that much track in a year during the war, it would earn additional land grants as a reward.

Time extensions were also given to those settlers with debts due on preempted lands, but the Court of Claims, which was assigned to settle claims filed against the state, was not re-created after its expiration in January, 1862, despite a report from a special Senate committee in favor of its continuance. Harcourt and Mitchell dissented from the majority report of that committee, saying that "there exists no sound reason for its continuance" and that the "door for future relief" should be closed because "the largest number of claims now offered are thought to be bogus." This time a majority of the Senate agreed with Harcourt's position, and a new mandate for the Court of Claims did not become law.

Texas was a frontier state in the Confederacy, exposed to attack from the north, the west, and the south. The problem of providing protection from the Indian raids that had plagued Texas for a century and a half was not solved by the state or by the Confederacy during this period. The minutemen companies created by the Eighth Legislature bore the brunt of Indian warfare during the first year of the war but were unable to defeat or contain the raiding tribes. Early in 1862 these companies were replaced by the Frontier Regiment, a state organization commanded by James M. Norris. This unit was organized under an act signed December 21, 1861, which authorized the mustering of ten companies responsible for the protection of the northern and western frontiers from the Red River to the Rio Grande and from there down to the mouth of the Rio Grande. These companies were divided into detachments of twenty-five men enlisted for a term of twelve months. Along the western frontier, Norris established a chain of sixteen posts from which these men regularly rode on patrols.

Unlike the regiment stationed on the Rio Grande under the command of John S. "Rip" Ford, the new unit for frontier service would remain subordinate to the state authorities of Texas and was not to be removed beyond the boundaries of the state. To make sure that the Confederate administration understood this point, the legislators sent notice of their intent directly to the authorities in Richmond. Unfortunately, only nine companies mustered, so the unit was officially disbanded and its troops were incorporated into a second frontier regiment under the same provisions as the first but with a new commander, James E. McCord; eight hundred thousand dollars were appropriated to pay the regiment's expenses. By this time, the Confederate conscription act had made state military service very popular, since the militiamen would not be drafted into the Confederate Army. Service in the frontier regiments allowed even some lucky Unionists to escape the Confederate conscription officers. Hoping to surprise the Indians, McCord replaced the ineffective patrols with scouting expeditions. In a joint resolution of March 7, 1863, the "spy companies" which had operated along the frontier for years were ordered disbanded because the legislators concluded that the job was being done well by the state troops.

In his address to the legislature on November 7, 1861, Governor Lubbock protested the limitations placed on the militia system for mustering volunteers in an organized and effective manner. Lubbock declared that the statute shepherded through the previous session by Senator Forbes Britton, "as all other laws made for similar purposes in times of peace, is impractical in its character and unwieldy in its operations." Many companies never received their proper equipment, and not a few disbanded before they could be placed in active service. It was not uncommon for Confederate officers to come into Texas, recruit a company, then march it out of the state before anyone in Texas could intervene. A method had to be established for obtaining the names of all eligible males in each region of the state and for ensuring that a good number of them remained available for state service in the event of a crisis or the implementation of conscription.

The legislators responded quickly. On Christmas Day, 1861, Governor Lubbock signed an act to perfect the organization of state troops and place them on a war footing. The militia system that had been established by an act of February 14, 1860, was largely preserved but was expanded by the new act into a much more efficient structure. Every free white male inhabitant between the ages of eighteen and fifty was made subject to militia duty, but there were a number of practical exceptions. These included postal workers, ferrymen on public roads, engineers and conductors on railroads, officers and crews of steamboats, clerks of the Supreme Court and the district courts of the state, chief justices and clerks of the county courts, sheriffs and officers of the state penitentiary, and Confederate officers, as well as the secretary of state, comptroller, and treasurer. The state was divided into thirty-three brigade districts, each commanded by a brigadier general. All officers elected under the previous statute would remain in command until April 1, 1862, or until successors could be elected. Each would be required to take a loyalty oath. The senior justice of the peace in each county would serve as the enrolling officer, or the brigadier general could appoint someone else if no justice of the peace was present. The hiring of substitutes would still be allowed. One important new provision was added to the bill, requiring officers to drill their men at least once every two weeks.

An amendment to the militia act was signed on March 7, 1863, which altered its exemptions to conform more closely to those of the Confederate conscription act adopted in April, 1862. This law originally applied to all men between the ages of eighteen and thirty-five, but these limits were extended again and again until beardless boys and grizzled old men were included. Exemptions from service in the Texas militia would now include all officers of the Confederacy and of the state of Texas and its counties except coroners, justices of the peace, constables, and notaries public. Others exempted were officers and staff of the state penitentiary and supervisors and professors in the deaf and dumb, blind, and lunatic asylums; professors and teachers in academies with twenty or more students; one captain, two pilots, and two engineers on each steamboat actually in the service of the state or the Confederacy; telegraph operators; an apothecary for each apothecary establishment actually open for business; presidents, secretaries, superintendents, engineers, conductors, and roadmasters of railroads; mail contractors and carriers; public ferrymen and millers and engineers of public mills; mechanics who were actually engaged in the manufacture of spinning jennies or cotton cards; licensed ministers of the gospel; and those who hired substitutes. Unlike the Confederate conscription acts, the Texas militia law did not exempt large slaveholders or their overseers. The amendment of March 7, 1863, did provide that the militia could be called into Confederate service for up to one year, a concession to the increasing demands of the Southern war effort.

Another bill defined the act of advocating resistance to the draft as sedition, a crime punishable by a jail sentence of up to five years at hard labor.

For the most part, the Senate supported both the state draft and the Confederate enlistment effort. Senator Shelley became attorney general of Texas early in 1862, a position which allowed him to facilitate the enforcement of conscription. Because party politics had been subordinated to the Confederate war effort following the passage of the secession ordinances in Texas, any protest against the support of the Confederacy easily was equated with Unionism and viewed as tantamount to treason.

In North Texas, those who opposed the state and Confederate conscription acts, together with others who wished to see the South defeated, founded a secret "Peace Party." As evidence of a Unionist conspiracy was uncovered and the fear of local authorities in North Texas escalated, Governor Lubbock twice requested that Confederate troops be posted there. Confederate General Paul O. Hebert denied the requests because his troops were needed to defend the Texas coast. General Hebert did, however, agree to temporarily accept into Confederate service the troops of William R. Hudson, brigadier general for the 21st Militia District, which encompassed Gainesville, the focus of the allegedly dangerous conspiracy. Lubbock additionally gave the support of the administration to actions needed to quell the conspiracy. Hudson called his troops into active service on September 13, 1862, saying they were needed to protect the populace against an imminent federal invasion. When the threat of federal invasion ended, those who had not responded to Hudson's muster were arrested in a sweep through five counties that began in the early morning hours of October 1. The arrests "continued for thirteen days and nights until . . . 150 men had been captured." James Bourland, whom Hudson had chosen as his provost marshal to direct enlistment, supervised the establishment of "citizens' courts" in Cooke and neighboring counties; these courts took part in hanging more than forty prisoners, including prisoners in Gainesville. Former senator James W. Throckmorton, now a Confederate brigadier general, later managed to stop the hangings in nearby Sherman. The Ninth Legislature appropriated forty-five hundred dollars to reimburse Hudson for his expenses during the affair and congratulated him that the "rebellion has been effectively crushed, and harmony is restored in that part of the state."

The "Great Hanging at Gainesville" was just one symptom of a more general paranoia that infected Texans after the outbreak of the Civil War. The primary focus of this unease was the slaves. On December 9, 1861, Shelley introduced two bills dealing with the control of slaves. Amending an 1846 act, the first bill was designed "to establish a more perfect system of patrol." It provided for county courts to lay out patrol districts and for each to appoint from five to twenty men, half of them slave owners or their substitutes, led by a captain. These were to patrol the district "at least once a week, and as much oftener as the peace and quiet of the community may require, by visiting negro quarters and other places in the district where it may be suspected that slaves are improperly or unlawfully assembled." If the patrol found "any slave off the plantation, or other premises of the master, mistress, or employer, strolling about without a pass, or written permission," it was authorized to administer to the slave any number of lashes up to twenty-five. The sole exemption was for a slave in search of medical aid. The act was approved on January 13, 1862.

Shelley's second bill, which was approved on January 11, 1862, forbade a slave owner or employer to place a slave in charge of a farm or stock ranch where "he had slaves not immediately under his own control, and connected with his or her home or residence." A violation of the act could result in a fine of from fifty to one hundred dollars.

Several bills spoke to an insurrection or invasion by people of color. One, approved March 6, 1863, devoted most of its attention, not to the envisioned invasion, but to the classification, imprisonment, and disposal at auction of the captured people of color (now slaves, regardless of their status before) and the distribution of the profits.

Sedition was addressed in a bill that declared it a "high misdemeanor" to "maliciously and advisedly" discourage people from enlisting in the militia or Confederate forces or to persuade the people "to favor the enemy." These acts were punished by from three to five years in the penitentiary—a sentence clearly designed for white subversives. Blacks would have been sentenced to hard labor.

Governor Lubbock called the special session of the legislature in the winter of 1863 in part to "meet the feared consequences of the Emancipation Proclamation." Abraham Lincoln's formal declaration of January 1, 1863, brought the fear of insurrection in Texas to fever pitch, and the subsequent introduction of blacks into the Union Army heightened the hysteria. The Senate passed an act signed March 5, 1863, which began:

> Whereas, in the prosecution of the unholy war now being waged by the United States against the Confederate States and the people thereof, our enemies are seeking to bring upon us a servile war by arming our slaves and placing them in the ranks of their armies, as well as otherwise, through the action of their government and the commissioned officers of their armies, inciting insurrection and insubordination.

From passage of the act and for the duration of the war, it would be an offense and would be considered as "inciting the insurrection or insubordination of slaves" for any officer in the U.S. military service to enter into the territory or waters of Texas with hostile intent. If one did so and were captured and convicted, he would serve five to fifteen years at hard labor. Any blacks who joined the Union Army and were captured in Texas would be sentenced to a term of hard labor until twelve months after the end of the war, when those who had not been claimed as runaways would be sold at auction.

As the Union blockade severely restricted the importation of foodstuffs, agriculture became an increasing concern for the Senate. Unlike the citizens of the rest of the South, Texans did not go hungry during the war. Despite the lack of able-bodied men, crops were good every year, but foodstuffs needed to be supplied to sister states in the Confederacy. To address that need, Senator Jordan introduced a joint resolution in the regular session urgently asking Texas farmers and plantation owners to curtail the production of cotton in favor of food crops, to no avail.

Governor Lubbock, in his address to the called session, pleaded for an act to forcibly restrict cotton growing, and the Senate duly discussed passage of a House bill to restrict the cultivation of cotton in favor of food crops to provide more food for the war-torn and blockaded states east of the Mississippi. After much acrimonious wrangling over the constitutionality of telling a person what he could do with his land, the bill narrowly failed to become law. On

February 21, 1863, on the motion to engross the bill, Lieutenant Governor Crockett had to break the tie, saying, "I cast it for the preservation of the institution of slavery—for the protection of the slaveholders—I cast my vote in favor of *Government*, the only security of property—I vote yea." The bill lost on the final ballot by one vote, cast by Senator Jordan, who was absent when the engrossment vote was taken and who either had accepted the arguments against agricultural controls by the government or had changed his mind since the regular session. The senators realized that the farmers and planters of Texas would not accept the law and feared that they might even revolt.

Despite the focus on the war effort, civil issues were not entirely neglected. The Senate endorsed charters for the Rio Grande Female Institute and the Dallas Male and Female College. But public financial support for education, which had never been strong, dwindled to almost nothing. A bill for the endowment of professorships in the colleges of Texas had been introduced in the Eighth Legislature but had fallen victim to the excitement over secession. Now much the same bill, introduced by Shelley on November 12, 1862, again failed to become law. Interestingly, Boyd, who had voted against the measure at all its appearances, was not an implacable foe of education and later donated eleven hundred acres of land to create Trinity University, a Presbyterian school located in Tehuacana.

In other matters, the Senate on January 3, 1862, passed a House bill defining the boundaries of McMullen County, created in 1858. An act resetting the boundaries of Live Oak County was signed January 3, 1862, and an act creating Kendall County out of Blanco and Kerr counties was signed January 10, 1862. Prior to these actions, on December 17, 1861, Cass and Buchanan counties, presumably because their eponyms were Yankees, underwent a change of name to Davis and Stephens, for Jefferson Davis and Alexander H. Stephens.

The senators proved to be stalwart Confederates intolerant of dissent. A joint resolution signed on January 13, 1862, declared that "the pretensions of patriotism on the part of the North, in waging a war for the Union, is an enormous falsehood. . . . We utterly disclaim all affinity, all brotherhood with them, and . . . we rejoice that we have escaped the contaminating influence of their base fanaticism."

The Senate passed a number of joint resolutions that indicate the depth of attachment to the Confederate cause. In a resolution approved on November 27, 1861, they welcomed to Texas Major General Sterling Price's wife, who had left Missouri after it became unsafe for her, as well as Captain David Bouldin's wife, who also had fled Missouri "for safety from the abolition Hessians of the North." Mrs. Bouldin was a genuine Southern heroine, having warned Price of the approach of the enemy on the eve of a battle at Springfield, Missouri, thereby preventing a Confederate rout. Senator Cook introduced a joint resolution that congratulated Lieutenant Colonel John R. Baylor for his capture of the Arizona Territory. The resolution passed on January 11, 1862, while the Confederacy occupied Arizona and New Mexico; within a few months, Baylor would evacuate the region. The legislators also thanked Louisiana for the return of the "Twin Sisters," the guns used at San Jacinto, which after annexation had been kept at the federal arsenal in Baton Rouge. The Twin Sisters disappeared after November, 1863, and were reputed to have been buried near Harrisburg in August, 1865, by five discharged Confederate soldiers.

The war came home to Texas most directly through the obituary columns of local newspapers. On December 26, 1861, the Senate adopted a resolution of condolence following the death of Colonel Benjamin F. Terry, commander of the famed Terry's Texas Rangers, 8th Texas Cavalry, "who fell, sword in hand, fighting the enemy near Bowling Green, Kentucky, on the 17th instant." Members of the Senate wore badges of mourning for thirty days and draped the Senate chamber in black. Just before adjournment *sine die*, the Senate also adopted a resolution of condolence on the death of John Hemphill, a representative in the Confederate Congress who had polled more votes on the first balloting for Confederate senator in the Texas Legislature than William S. Oldham, who had won election along with Louis T. Wigfall. Although the Texas state senators were more fortunate than their colleagues elsewhere in the South, they would not escape the impact of the war, as the tide turned inexorably against the Confederacy after 1863.

CHAPTER 2

The Senate of the Tenth Legislature, 1863–64

When the Senate of the Tenth Legislature convened on November 2, 1863, the Confederacy had already passed the high noon of its brief existence. The Army of Northern Virginia had been repelled at the bloody battle at Gettysburg, the Confederate siege of Chattanooga had been broken, and the fall of Vicksburg ensured the isolation of the Trans-Mississippi Department from the primary Southern war effort east of the great river. The senators remained basically hopeful about the outcome of the struggle, but the increasing discouragement that accompanied the declining southern fortunes took its toll, resulting in a series of desperate, and sometimes petty, actions.

Defense of the frontier, protection from internal revolt, and stimulation of industrial development, as well as the overwhelming burden of prosecuting the war, were again the issues confronting the Senate. When those adhering to the Democratic party's peace platform during the U.S. presidential campaign of 1864 proposed a negotiated peace on the basis of a reconstituted United States, the Senate angrily joined the House in rejecting the idea, despite the worsening of the South's fortunes. The legislators were adamant in their insistence that any peace include a recognition of Southern independence. Through all three sessions—the regular session, which adjourned on December 16, 1863; the first special session, which convened on May 9, 1864; and the second special session, which convened on October 17—the senators maintained their belligerent stance.

The leadership of the Senate during this trying period came from

Lieutenant Governor Fletcher S. Stockdale, the former senator who during the Eighth Legislature had participated in the walkout from the National Democratic Convention of 1860 and then agitated for the secession of Texas at the Secession Convention of 1861. Stockdale was elected lieutenant governor in 1863 in the same poorly attended election that put Pendleton Murrah in the executive mansion in Austin. Francis R. Lubbock had declined to run for another term; he elected instead to serve the Confederacy, first under General Magruder, then under General Wharton, and finally as aide-de-camp to President Davis. Murrah and Stockdale, both strong states' rights men, took office on November 5, 1863, the same day that Union forces reoccupied Brownsville, an omen of the difficult administration that lay ahead for them.

Thirty-three senators met for the Tenth Legislature. Unlike their predecessors in the Senate of the Ninth Legislature, few of them would earn distinction in the military, although most would serve the Confederacy in some capacity. James W. Throckmorton continued to serve as a brigadier general, including among his assignments the command of the Third Military District and later the Frontier District. Former lieutenant governor David C. Dickson, the Know-Nothing candidate for governor in 1855, served as a captain in the militia. Dr. William George Washington Jowers, a senator in the Fifth Legislature and Dickson's running mate on the Know-Nothing ticket, raised and then became captain of a company from Anderson County. Freshman senator Henry M. Kinsey served as a private in Captain Border's Company A of the 3rd Brigade.

Spearman Holland was made captain of a company of the 4th Brigade, Texas State Troops, from Precinct Eight, Panola County. Born in Virginia and raised in Tennessee, Holland was a farmer who had settled near Marshall, Texas, in 1842. He began his service in state government in 1845 when he was elected Harrison County's delegate to the Annexation Convention. Holland served as a representative in the House during the First, Seventh, and Ninth legislatures before moving to the Senate for the Tenth. His son, James K. Holland, would later represent Panola and Rusk counties in the legislature.

James Wiley Magoffin of El Paso also participated in the Confederate military effort, first by facilitating the occupation of New Mexico and Arizona by Colonel John R. Baylor and Brigadier Gen-

Pendleton Murrah, governor of Texas, 1863–65.
Courtesy Texas State Library and Archives Commission.

eral Henry H. Sibley, and then, following the occupation of El Paso by Union forces, by serving in Virginia before returning to Texas as a captain and assistant commissary. Despite these military activities, Magoffin is best remembered as a trader, merchant, gourmet, and diplomat and as a man whose adventures in trade took him to Salti-

Fletcher S. Stockdale, lieutenant governor, 1863–65, in Tenth Legislature. Reproduced from holdings of Texas State Archives.

llo, Mexico, and led to his appointment in 1825 as the first U.S. consul at Chihuahua. The story is told that, while in his early twenties, Magoffin left his home in Kentucky and headed for New Orleans, where he joined a cargo ship bound for Mexico. In addition to the dry goods and groceries on the ship, its cargo included wax figures of historic men such as Julius Caesar, Admiral Horatio Nelson, Napoleon Bonaparte, and George Washington. The ship wrecked at Matagorda Bay, an area inhabited by the "cannibalistic" Karankawa Indians. The stranded sailors built makeshift forts of bales and boxes to fend off possible Indian attacks but became bored after days of guarding and no sight of the Indians. Magoffin saved the day with a plan to guard against attacks by strategically placing Caesar and Napoleon facing land and Admiral Nelson fronting the sea. The sailors were saved and taken to Matamoros. After this life-threatening beginning, Magoffin, or "Don Santiago," as he was known in the trading business, began a successful mercantile business in an area stretching from Chihuahua, Mexico, to Independence, Missouri. He settled in Mexico during the period of the Texas Revolution; in the late 1840s he worked as a secret agent for the United States in New Mexico and started building a settlement opposite Ciudad Juarez known as Magoffinsville, one of four early settlements from which grew the city of El Paso. A one-term legislator, Magoffin did not attend the regular session but took the oath of state senator on the first day of the first special session, May 9, 1864.

Another adopted Texan who served the Confederacy, Daniel Montague, was born in Massachusetts. Montague immigrated to Louisiana in 1820 and moved to Texas in 1836, where he was a civil engineer and surveyor of North Texas counties. It was within the boundaries of Cooke County that his principal contribution to the Confederate cause was made. Many Cooke County residents, like many other North Texas residents, had been opposed to secession and deeply resented the Confederate conscription law. In defiance of otherwise overwhelming Confederate support, a secret organization of Union sympathizers emerged in Cooke, Grayson, Collin, Denton, and Wise counties in 1861 and 1862. Known as the Peace Party, it was often referred to as the Loyal League. In the fall of 1862, the senator from Cooke County had served as president of the citizens' court that tried and condemned thirty-nine of the forty or so Peace Party members hanged after being charged with disloyalty and treason to the state of Texas in the incident known as the "Great Hanging at Gainesville." Montague was later one of several Confederates, including Governor Pendleton Murrah, who refused to acknowledge the Union's victory in 1865 and emigrated to Mexico immediately after the war.

One senator, A. O. Cooley from Gillespie County, was a Union sympathizer. Cooley, who was born and educated in Tennessee, had come to Fredericksburg, Texas, around 1850 at about the age of twenty-two and settled into a law practice. He was recognized as a scholar, and his library contained the *Iliad* and the *Odyssey* in Greek and a copy of Shakespeare's plays. Cooley never married; it is said that a wedding had been prevented by the Civil War. The hostilities also had other effects on Cooley's life: although he had been a man of considerable means, he was left penniless after the war. Elected on a Republican ticket, Cooley was a member of the constitutional conventions of 1866 and 1875.

In addition to the senators from the Ninth Legislature who returned, the Senate roster included the names of new members Napoleon B. Charlton from District Two; J. A. Haskell from District Twenty-seven; William B. Knox from District Thirty, who succeeded N. A. Mitchell in the second called session; William M. Peck from District Nineteen, who succeeded William C. Wilson during the first called session (Wilson had succeeded Thomas C. Neal, who died before taking office in the regular session); and Gilbert H. Wootten from District Eight. Senator Charlton was a cotton farmer who came to Texas from Tennessee; he served as a delegate from Tyler County to the Texas Secession Convention of 1861 and as a member of the House of Representatives in the First, Third, Fourth, Fifth, Sixth, and Ninth legislatures. Senator Knox, a native of Arkansas, had formerly been sheriff of Bexar County and was an influential politician and merchant in San Antonio.

The seasoned senator Robert H. Guinn was reelected president pro tempore, and the Senate was attended by a full slate of officers, most of them returning from the called session of the Ninth Legislature. Phineas de Cordova returned as secretary, Nathaniel C. Raymond as assistant secretary, R. H. Clements as sergeant-at-arms, Henry Thomas as engrossing clerk, and William M. Gilleland as enrolling clerk. John McCall was elected doorkeeper, while the office of assistant doorkeeper, adopted during the called session of the Ninth Legislature, was discontinued. Reverend Langford served as chaplain. Attention to one last detail remained before the Senate settled down to business: Senator Wootten proposed that the sergeant-at-arms be required to arrange for the display of the Confederate flag from the Capitol dome while the legislature was in session, and the other senators concurred on November 3, 1863.

Retiring governor Lubbock, perhaps the only governor of a Confederate state to realize from the beginning the necessity of total mobilization for the war, addressed the joint assembly of legislators on November 4, 1863. He opened with an optimistic statement of Texas' situation:

> Gentlemen of the Senate & House of Representatives:
>
> In greeting you thus assembled in Regular Session by virtue of the Constitution and Laws[,] I congratulate you and the Country that, under the Providence of God, our State has been blessed with genial seasons, uninterrupted good health and prosperity, that our granaries teem with the superabundance of our harvests, our loved plains still furnish an abundance of forage and meat, and that the unparalleled bravery of her noble sons has saved our beloved State from the hated presence of the foe.

He assured the legislators that there was "no reason to despond or falter" but admitted that the conflict had "assumed gigantic proportions, demanding sacrifices on the part of all." He insisted that Texans were "unalterably fixed in the determination to prosecute [the war] to the bitter end, and never to yield while a man [was] left to strike a blow for freedom." The enemy had indeed won control of the Mississippi River and, having occupied large portions of Arkansas and Louisiana, stood on the very borders of Texas. With the support of the legislators, however, the defenders of the state would make Texas "the grave, not the inheritance, of the invader." Lubbock asked for the reduction of exemptions from the conscription laws and especially for the elimination of the controversial practice of hiring substitutes, saying, "Let every man answer at roll call to his name." Murrah, in his inaugural address the next day, repeated many of the same points and pledged to enact the laws necessary for their realization. Lubbock outlined the problems of the day, and Murrah proposed some solutions, but it fell to the legislators to implement the program.

The primary concern of the senators and others in state government was to secure a solid financial base for the circulating currency of Texas and the Confederacy. This task proved impossible, but in an attempt to resolve the problem, Murrah called the legislature into two special sessions as the available currency continued to depreciate rapidly and the state debt mounted. Taxes of approximately $37 million were paid in Confederate paper to the government at Richmond, and Texas spent more than $3.5 million at home for military purposes. The public debt stood at $8 million in 1865, more than ten times the amount that had alarmed Sam Houston in 1861.

There was a workable solution to some of these financial problems: Texas, thanks to her proximity to Mexico, could sell cotton across the border for as much as a dollar a pound in gold. However, this unique opportunity to thwart the federal naval blockade was not exploited; bureaucratic bumbling by the government in Richmond made even the rare honest trader resort to smuggling, and corruption was pervasive. The efforts of the State Military Board and the new Confederate Cotton Board to sell cotton to fund currency were unsuccessful, and by the summer of 1864, Texas treasury warrants and Confederate notes sold for as little as five cents on the dollar in trade. Other efforts to secure specie failed utterly; when a mob looted the state treasury on June 11, 1865, it found less than five thousand dollars in hard money.

Texas and Confederate authorities had to rely on the impressment of cotton and other agricultural goods because the more conventional bases for public credit—land and taxes—were totally unreliable. The Senate of the Tenth Legislature, in response to the general disorder, once more extended time limits for the return of field notes and payments thereon by settlers who had preempted their land. On December 14, 1863, the survey and sale of public lands were suspended for the duration of the war. The ban did not include those tracts which were reserved for public schools, the university, or railroads, nor did it include tracts undergoing actual settlement. Although the income from these lands was appropriated for defense, the resulting revenue was insufficient and more taxes were levied, including higher excise taxes on all liquor, beer, and wine; greater direct taxes on all personal property and assets; and higher license fees for professions. Strict penalties for noncompliance, which often included jail sentences, were imposed. Taxes were raised again by the second called session in the fall of 1864, but revenue consistently fell short of what was needed.

Two problems attended the efforts of the Military Board and the Confederate Cotton Board to raise funds: widespread speculation and stubborn resistance to impressment. The senators were quite sympathetic to the frustration over the first impediment. They endorsed an amendment to the earlier act to prevent speculation which had been passed by the Ninth Legislature and signed on January 13, 1862. It specified a number of actions that would now be considered felonious: presenting oneself as a commissary or quartermaster, or as an agent of either, or as a representative of a county court, mutual aid society, or the family of a needy soldier. Those found guilty could be sentenced to as much as ten years at hard labor for each offense.

The Senate, however, shared the common outrage over the general policy of impressment. On May 27, 1864, John T. Harcourt and Throckmorton won endorsement of a joint resolution protesting the impressment laws of the Confederate Congress. Later, as the full import of the law became known, especially its import for those who shipped cotton to Mexico, the Senate endorsed a statute to "punish unlawful interference with private property or private rights." Offenders could spend up to two years in jail. During the second called session, the Senate strongly protested the imposition of export duties on cotton by the Confederate Congress, but to no avail. Another joint resolution, passed at the same time, protested the impressment of beef by Confederate authorities in Texas, who then drove the beef to Mexico for sale for specie. This protest likewise failed to change Confederate policy.

The growing resentment of the Texas Senate toward the Confederate government in Richmond also manifested itself in protests against conscription. On May 28, 1864, the last day of the first called session, a joint resolution was adopted declaring that no officer of a sovereign state, namely Texas, could be placed in the military service of the Confederacy without that officer's consent. The measure referred specifically to the more stringent draft laws adopted by the Confederate Congress, declaring that "the claim of a right in congress to conscribe certain classes of officer, is contrary to our system of government." During the special session of the Ninth Legislature, Senator Rice Maxey had proposed a joint resolution requiring the withdrawal of all Texas troops to positions west of the Mississippi River. His resolution failed of adoption, but the idea persisted. On May 28, 1864, the Senate adopted a joint resolution that requested the return of the 1st, 4th, and 5th Texas regiments from service east of the Mississippi, ostensibly for the purpose of recruiting for service within the state.

Murrah, unlike Lubbock, was in constant conflict with Confederate authorities over the conscription law. The threat on the western frontier had increased each year due to the frequent absence of effective regular troops, and Murrah and the legislators finally attempted to defy another request by the Confederate government for transfer of the Frontier Regiment into service outside the state. An act of March 7, 1863, stated that the regiment would serve only in Texas, but this did not meet with the approval of the Confederate government. The Frontier Regiment became the focus of a defiant joint resolution adopted on May 24, 1864. The resolution proposed that, if Lieutenant General Edmund Kirby Smith agreed to leave the Frontier Regiment alone, the state officials of Texas would remand into the custody of conscription officers all those eligible men who had moved into the Frontier District after July, 1863. Also, the governor would forbid further emigration to the unorganized counties of Texas for the duration of the war. Any eligible males who tried to emigrate would be arrested and turned over to the Confederate authorities for conscription. Kirby Smith stood his ground, and four days later the legislators relented and amended the law to allow state troops to be transferred into regular service. In a joint resolution adopted on November 15, 1864, Murrah was asked to discharge all those in the Frontier Regiment who had not been bona fide citizens of the frontier on July 1, 1863, thereby releasing them for conscription into Confederate units.

The enlistment of the Frontier Regiment into Confederate service left the borderlands largely undefended, a vulnerability the state government had struggled to prevent. On December 16, 1863, Governor Murrah signed an act which extended for another six months the enlistments of militiamen then in service. The same act empowered him to place in the field those militiamen who remained at home. New exemptions to the general requirement for militia duty, which were at odds with those specified by the Confederate Congress, included machinists (especially those in public foundries), tanners, blacksmiths, and all persons engaged in the production of salt and gunpowder. One section of the act was directed at large slave owners who had been exempt: substitutes would no longer be allowed. Denial of substitute service was added in the wake of a resolution adopted by both houses on December 3, 1863, instructing the legislature to repeal all laws exempting persons from conscription due to their ownership of any sort of property whatsoever.

Under the act of December 16, 1863, the twenty-three military districts in Texas were consolidated into six. After the transfer of the Frontier Regiment, the eligible age for militia service was lowered to seventeen in an act signed on May 31, 1864. The maximum age remained fifty, although a measure that would have provided for the organization of a home guard of men aged fifty to sixty received serious consideration. The report of the adjutant and inspector general appended to Lubbock's speech of November 4, 1863, requested the enlistment of all males over the age of sixteen as well as those over fifty. The report stated that it had "become absolutely necessary that the very young, the old, and those but partially disabled, be held to service and required to perform such duties as they are capable of, such as . . . keeping up a proper system of police for safety and protection within the several counties." The Senate balked at the desperate character of such an act, but events beyond legislative control already had made official sanction superfluous. Confederate conscription officers were careless about birth certificates, and many young boys and old men were taken to the war.

Ironically, the Tonkawa, an Indian tribe loyal to the Confederacy, provided a small measure of frontier defense. A special law signed on December 16, 1863, provided for the relief of a tiny group of Tonkawa Indians supported by the members of the Frontier Regiment and for the induction of the male members of the tribe into military service with the regiment. These Indians were all that remained of a tribe that had been reduced by half in the Fort Cobb massacre in the Indian Territory in October, 1862, when the fort was attacked by other tribes allied with federal soldiers. Only about 165 Tonkawa, of whom roughly 50 were warriors, had survived. They had come to Texas because the members of the Frontier Regiment and Colonel Baylor, hoping to use them as scouts, had offered them positions with the regiment. Later, in a joint resolution adopted during the first called session, the Senate endorsed a stipend of thirty-five thousand dollars annually for the maintenance of the Tonkawa.

Fear of a slave revolt had been one of antebellum Texas' main preoccupations, but such an uprising did not occur. Even though the slave population had doubled because of slaves being sent from other Southern states and nearly all able-bodied white men were away from home, the slaves remained quiet and worked hard for the duration of the war.

The Senate, through the Military Board, enacted a series of acts to foster industrial development in Texas. The Senate endorsed the appropriation of two hundred thousand dollars for the installation of spinning jennies to make thread at the State Foundry in Austin; profits from the sale of thread would go into the state treasury. Another two million dollars for the program would be raised through the sale of 6 percent bonds, for whose redemption the cotton reserves of the state government were pledged. This fund, approved on December 10, 1863, was to be used only for machinery except in the event of an actual invasion. Six days later, Murrah signed an act authorizing one million dollars to fund a Military Board program for the manufacture of iron.

Senator Spencer Ford introduced an act, signed on December 15, 1863, which offered a bonus of a half-section of land (320 acres) for every investment of one thousand dollars in a foundry, munitions plant, textile mill, or factory for the production of paper or oil. The resulting flood of new charters was almost overwhelming. John W. Moore introduced a successful bill for the Sulphur Fork Iron Works Company, chartered on December 4, 1863, and Parsons won a charter for the Rusk County Iron Company, signed on December 15, 1863. The Paluxy and Brazos Sulphur, Niter, and Powder Manufacturing Company was also chartered on December 15, 1863. The next day, acts of incorporation for the Bastrop Iron Manufacturing Company, introduced by A. W. Moore, and the Washington Iron Manufacturing Company were signed. During the first called session, the Beaver Iron Manufacturing Company, the Cherokee Furnace Company, and the Texas Copper Manufacturing Company received charters. The second called session approved the incorporation of the Houston Paper Mill Manufacturing Company and the

Austin Iron Company. These charters, however, represented little more than wishful thinking for the industry-starved state; both capital and labor were absorbed by the effort to support the voracious war.

Most of the successful petitions were for the incorporation of textile mills. The Waco Manufacturing Company was chartered on December 8, 1863, as a general-purpose mill for the production of both foodstuffs and textiles. Senator George E. Burney served as its president. Representative William H. Hart introduced a successful bill for the incorporation of the East Texas Manufacturing Company, signed on December 15, 1863, and Chauncy B. Shepard introduced the bill for the Hempstead Manufacturing Company, approved the next day, to produce textiles, grind meal, and manufacture machinery and firearms. Also on December 16, the Brazos Manufacturing Company, the Trinity Manufacturing and Flouring Company, and the Chappell Hill Manufacturing Company, which would produce textiles and cottonseed oil, received charters. During the first called session, the Senate endorsed the incorporation of the Dallas Manufacturing Company, Trinity Mills Manufacturing Company, Star State Manufacturing Company, and Falls of Brazos Manufacturing Company. The latter would produce textiles, grind grain, and operate a sawmill. The Cairo Manufacturing Company, Independence Manufacturing Company, San Marcos Cotton and Woolen Manufacturing Company, Comal Springs Manufacturing Company, and Guadalupe Manufacturing Company—all primarily textile factories—were incorporated in May, 1864. At the same time, a charter was issued to the Tyler County Card and Machine Factory to provide the vital cards and other implements for producing cotton and woolen cloth. During the second called session, the Bastrop Cotton and Wool Manufacturing Company, Houston City Mills Manufacturing Company, and Holly Springs Manufacturing Company were chartered to manufacture textiles.

Despite this flurry of legislative activity, it is doubtful that many of these enterprises got under way. They suffered from an almost total lack of capital, labor, and machinery, the latter shortage aggravated by the interference of military authorities with the Mexican trade. The Senate endorsed a number of measures to render some assistance to industry. A joint resolution passed on December 11, 1863, requested the commanding brigadier general of the militia district encompassing Austin to detail men for work in the Texas Iron Works. Another joint resolution, on December 15, 1863, authorized the Military Board to operate the salines at Double Mountain and elsewhere. On May 28, 1864, the legislature authorized the issuance of rations to employees under the age of sixteen in the State Percussion Cap Factory in Austin. A joint resolution of November 3, 1864, introduced by John W. Moore, directed Confederate general E. Kirby Smith to assign men to help inventors G. W. Johnson and Samuel Hayford construct and put into operation their machine for carding cotton rolls.

The most successful industrial enterprise in Texas during the Civil War was the state penitentiary, which, benefiting from a plentiful labor supply, produced a remarkable amount of textiles. On November 27, 1863, county officials were authorized to receive and imprison those offending against military law, and a separate bill, signed on December 11, 1863, required sheriffs to aid in the enforcement of conscription and other military laws. Offenders against military law were often transferred to the state penitentiary, where they were joined by others from Arkansas, Louisiana, and Missouri imprisoned there under an act approved on November 15, 1864. An earlier measure introduced by Senator Ford permitted the officers of the penitentiary to hire additional labor to fulfill the contracts for manufactures.

The cloth produced by the prisoners was used by the state to meet one of its most important obligations, providing for its soldiers' households. The Senate on November 24, 1863, endorsed a joint resolution that expressed gratitude for the job done by Texans in military service and conveyed assurances that the legislature would provide for their families while they were away. Within the next few weeks, Murrah signed a bill for a hospital fund of two hundred thousand dollars, introduced by Rufus K. Hartley, and one for a relief fund of one million dollars to be distributed to the families of needy soldiers, introduced by Senator Jowers. In May, 1864, the legislature authorized the dispatch of special commissioners with funds for the relief of Texans in particularly desperate straits in the Confederate armies stationed in Louisiana and Arkansas, but such actions were suspended for lack of cash. During the second called session, the legislature repealed the appropriation of one million dollars for the relief fund, then requisitioned six hundred thousand yards of cloth from the state penitentiary production for the maintenance of the indigent families of soldiers, despite the opposition of the Senate Committee on Finance, which proposed instead a complicated bond issue.

The requisition of cloth was only part of a program for the aid of soldiers and their families. In the private sector, the Senate endorsed charters for mutual aid associations in Comal and Gonzales counties. All property taxes in Galveston County were remanded by a special act of December 16, 1863, for the support of indigent families in that county. Later, the Military Board was requested to dispense its supplies of quinine, opium, and "Wright's Pills" to the county courts for distribution to the indigent soldiers in each county. Cotton and wool cards imported through Mexico were given to destitute and orphaned families by the Military Board so that they could support themselves. The legislators voted themselves a similar largess—a special distribution of cotton cards and percussion caps from the Military Board.

The war effort was attended by a heightened reliance on spiritual comfort and, consequently, notable legislative attention to conservative propriety. The Senate endorsed a measure, signed on December 16, 1863, which levied a fine of from ten to fifty dollars on any man or woman who compelled his or her slaves, children, or apprentices to work on Sunday. Exceptions to the Sunday work law included housework, work done on sugar plantations during sugar-making season (an amendment proposed by Senator Harcourt, from the coastal sugar counties), and any work necessary to keep a crop from failing (an amendment introduced by Senator Hartley). Specific prohibitions included the operation of a horse race, a saloon, or a gaming parlor, pursuant to an amendment offered by John W. Durant.

The propriety of the consumption of liquor remained a concern of many Texans. In his opening address Lubbock had spoken against the increase in the number of distilleries "diffusing their blighting influence over the state and demoralizing our people and soldiery" and had asked the legislature to take action to reduce the number of these "pest-houses." In his final address on November 5, 1863, he again referred to distilleries as "one of the greatest curses now in the State." Liquor had been the topic of several petitions to the Ninth and Tenth legislatures and was the subject of much heated debate. In addition to the higher taxes imposed on distilled spirits, the Senate also authorized county courts to declare distilleries to be "prejudicial to public subsistence." While a victory for the temperance advocates, it also was a victory for sound judgment—the grain which was being distilled could be better used for food. The *Tri-Weekly State Gazette* welcomed the act as a sound measure to reduce the sale of liquor, "unless some means can be found to whip the devil around the stump, which we think not at all improbable." The editor, however, predicted the establishment of joint-stock companies for the purchase of the now costly luxury "in every neighborhood."

Along with the concern for propriety came a concern for duty. Both Lubbock and Murrah urged the passage of stringent laws against desertion, disloyalty, and treason, and the sections of the Penal Code dealing with such acts were amended. Up to this time, treason against the state of Texas consisted "only in levying war against it, or adhering to its enemies, giving them aid and comfort." Now, however, it would no longer be "necessary to prove any actual communication between the public enemy and any person charged with treason to establish the offense of treason." Any action whose "tendency" was to give aid and comfort to the "public enemy," to aid his operations, or to hinder those of the Confederacy or Texas would be considered treason. Anyone who knew of another's treasonous acts and failed to report the acts would also be subject to a jail sentence of up to ten years. Similarly, the penalty for the charge of conspiracy to commit a felony, which included treason, would now be a jail sentence of from two to ten years. The penalty for sedition, defined as advocating resistance to the draft, was increased to three to five years. A. N. Jordan introduced a successful bill that defined disloyalty as aiding someone to desert or aiding the public enemy. Encouraging desertion brought a penalty of from two to five years (though the act excluded the wife or mother of anyone in the service who aided a husband or son to desert), and assisting the enemy meant a penalty of from three to five years. The Senate did not authorize the expulsion of anyone convicted of desertion or treason, although some certainly were exiled to Mexico.

The Senate's efforts in the realm of civil affairs, apart from those connected with the prosecution of the war, were primarily concerned with education. The Senate endorsed charters for Parsons

Female Seminary; for Port Sullivan Male and Female College, sponsored by Durant; for Gathings Male and Female College, introduced by Burney; for Henderson Masonic Female Institute; for Osage Academy; for the Southern Minerva Institute; and for the San Saba Masonic College, which also was the beneficiary of an act to prohibit the sale of liquor within five miles of its campus. Such private institutions, however, did not compensate for the lack of public schools or the misappropriation of the school fund.

Despite the sometimes discontented and occasionally desperate tone of the acts passed by the Senate of the Tenth Legislature, the senators maintained a united front against the North. A defiant resolution adopted on December 16, 1863, declared: "Now that our presumptuous enemy treads our soil in heavy number and menacing attitude, we bid him a proud and scornful defiance" and "we here record our full confidence in the patriotism and ability of President Davis." The legislators insisted that they "would not exchange him for any citizen of the Confederacy, as the pilot to carry us through the present stormy struggle for liberty as a people, and for independence as a nation." The declarations of the legislature occasionally took on a vindictive tone. Walker County had been named for Robert J. Walker, a prominent Mississippian who had advocated the annexation of Texas but who had "deserted" the Confederate cause and declared himself a Unionist. The legislature therefore insisted that the county name would honor Captain Samuel H. Walker, a Texas Ranger killed in the Mexican War.

The bitterest invective came in response to a proposal by proponents of the U.S. Democratic party's peace platform. The Democratic party had selected General George B. McClellan as its candidate against Abraham Lincoln in the 1864 election, and the peace party leaders had stated that, if the Democrats were victorious, they would open negotiations for reunion with provisions in the constitution to protect slavery. Many Texans were encouraged by the overture, but the legislators declared in a resolution that negotiation must be through the Confederate government and proclaimed that they recognized in the idea "no good faith, but merely an insidious policy to divide and conquer" by detaching some of the states from the Confederacy. They waxed eloquent, accusing the North of using poisoned weapons and of conducting an "indiscriminate onslaught . . . upon tottering age and tender youth." The "chaste and defenseless women" of the South had suffered many outrages "worse than death." Finally, the North had "deluded and dragged these negroes from their comfortable homes to use them as screens from our weapons in the day of battle."

The legislators included a list of declarations in their joint resolution of defiance. The sixth summed up their argument in a burst of patriotic hyperbole:

> By the just pride of the manhood and the virtue which we claim as individuals and as a people; by the divine command which warns us not to walk in the way with the wicked; by the memory of our murdered dead; by the sight of the bereaved mothers, widows, sisters, daughters, and orphans in our land; by the heart-brokenness of trampled virtue, and by our desolated hearths, we are forbidden to admit a thought of further association with the people of the North. Our heroic soldiers, the living, and the martyred dead, forbid it; and our trust in God forbids it.

Members of the Senate did not entirely lose their sense of humor in the dark days of the war. Senator Kinsey, chairman of the Committee on State Affairs, used the occasion of the report on a petition from Fayette County protesting the overgrazing of sheep to entertain his colleagues. Having duly considered the "evils growing out of the unrestrained sheepherding" within the county, Kinsey declared that "the legislature has no constitutional power to restrain the sheep of Fayette County from biting the grass too short for the horses and cattle to feed on" and that the members of the committee had "no disposition to punish the sheep . . . for a fault not theirs." The committee sympathized with the citizens for the loss of milk but recommended that perhaps a remedy could be found in milking she-goats. In conclusion, they admitted that while the Bible did voice concern for cattle, it also said, "Thou shalt feed the sheep," or something "as near that as the Committee can now recollect."

On the last day of the regular session, December 15, 1863, a bill was introduced by Maxey to incorporate the Order of the Sons of the South. It passed the Senate but failed to become law. The Sons of the South were pledged to uphold the Confederate Constitution on the battlefield and on the home front. They would ensure that the military would remain subordinate to the civil authority and that "the Negro" would remain subordinate to the white man. The group did provide for the indigent families of Confederate soldiers and even took over control of market prices in large towns such as Austin, regulating them downward for the benefit of the poor. The organization "obtained a dissemination quite general throughout Texas, and in portions of the Confederate forces outside the State," according to one of its founders, John S. Ford. Unfortunately, most of the organization's records were burned when federal forces occupied Texas.

The Sons of the South, although not endorsed by the legislature, symbolizes the concern for the welfare of Texas on the part of most of the senators and other government officials. The last two years of the war were bleak and hard, as the days of clear-cut Southern victories passed and the toll of the dead and wounded increased. A resolution introduced by Senator S. Addison White declared that the use of the Capitol for "balls or other amusements" while the country was "draped in mourning" was a "desecration" and should not be allowed.

The Tenth Legislature met in extraordinary session on October 17, 1864, during the second called session. Brigadier General H. E. McCulloch had just reported that Union forces were planning an invasion of North Texas, somewhere on the Red River, from where they would "stir up and combine the disloyal element" while controlling that part of Texas and using it as a base from which to move into other parts of the South. Such reports, in addition to rumors which by this time were "flying thick and fast," stimulated discussion about restoring the Union. The senators firmly opposed such talk and declared in vehement terms that Texas was determined to fight to the "last ditch" and would never participate in a restoration of the Union. The Senate, united with the House, would accept nothing less than southern independence or total defeat.

The report of Lee's surrender was slow to reach Texas, a fact that accounts for Colonel "Rip" Ford's surprising defeat of federal forces at Palmito Ranch near Brownsville a month after the war was over. When Texas did get the news, soldiers deserted to their homes in droves despite desperate last-ditch attempts by Governor Murrah and General Kirby Smith to rally the troops. On May 27, 1865, Governor Murrah issued a call for a special session in July and for the election of a general convention. Neither event occurred. Indeed, by July Governor Murrah had already fled to Mexico. No effective civil or military authority existed in Texas until General

Gordon Granger of the U.S. Army arrived at Galveston on June 19, 1865. Meanwhile, outlaws, Indians, and hundreds of thousands of newly freed slaves roamed the state at will. Violence prevailed.

Texans fought hard and brilliantly to defend their state from hostile military forces during the war, and they succeeded. But that victory, together with most of what was left of Texas' social and economic structure, was lost during the peace.

Lieutenant Governor Stockdale assumed the titular governorship when Governor Murrah left the state, but all government was paralyzed until President Andrew Johnson appointed Andrew J. (A. J.) Hamilton provisional governor of Texas. There was no legislature and no lieutenant governor during this period, and the Eleventh Legislature would not meet until a year later, on August 6, 1866.

PRESIDENTIAL RECONSTRUCTION

CHAPTER 3

The Senate of the Eleventh Legislature, 1866

Texas had defended itself from invasion by federal forces during the Civil War, but it had not emerged from the conflict unscathed. The Eleventh Legislature was confronted with a monumental task of social, political, and economic reconstruction. Many of the state government's special accounts, such as the university and public school funds, were empty, and the state was responsible for a public debt of eight million dollars. In the private sector, capital, labor, and optimism had all disappeared into the maw of war. The most devastating economic blow came with the emancipation of some four hundred thousand slaves, more than two hundred thousand of whom had been sent into Texas during the war by owners in other states. The slave population represented an investment of many millions of dollars.

Even those who did not hold slaves failed to escape the impact of total war, as many Texas sons and fathers never came home to till the fields. According to Governor Lubbock, by February, 1863, Texas had responded to the Confederate call for troops with

> thirty-three regiments, thirteen battalions, two squadrons, six detached companies, and one legion of twelve companies of cavalry . . . making 62,000 men, which with the state troops in actual service, 6,500 men, form an aggregate of 68,500 Texans in military service . . . an excess of 4,773 more than her highest popular vote, which was 63,727. From the best information within reach . . . of the men now remaining in the state between the ages of sixteen and sixty years . . . the number will not exceed 27,000.

Thousands of the 68,500 did not return; at least a quarter of the white male population had been shot away by the end of the war.

The end of the war also brought a period of almost total anarchy to Texas. A horde of refugees, many of them penniless and some of them violent, had poured into the state to escape the advancing battlefront. Ben C. Truman, a reporter for the *New York Times*, wrote in a letter to the president of the United States that an estimated five thousand of these outsiders were still in Texas early in 1866, "depending entirely upon robbery and murder for a precarious existence." State government had collapsed following the flight of Governor Pendleton Murrah and other officers to Mexico; Lieutenant Governor Fletcher S. Stockdale tried valiantly but was unable to restore order. Furthermore, after the assassination of President Abraham Lincoln, strong political leadership was not forthcoming from Washington. As a result, the Eleventh Legislature acted independently to reconstruct legal government in the state and to deal with the resolution of important social questions such as the status of both the newly freed blacks and the former Confederates.

Scholars have divided the Reconstruction era in Texas into three periods: Presidential Reconstruction, June, 1865, to March, 1867; Congressional Reconstruction, March 2, 1867, to April 16, 1870; and Radical Rule, ended de facto in 1873 and formally in 1874. Presidential Reconstruction in Texas began on June 19, 1865, when General Gordon Granger reoccupied Galveston with eighteen hundred troops, declared emancipation to be in effect, nullified all acts of the Texas government after secession, and offered a parole to all officers and men of the Confederate Army. This period ended on March 2, 1867, when President Andrew Johnson relinquished administrative control of the South to Congress. It was during the period of Presidential Reconstruction that the Eleventh Legislature met, convening on August 6, 1866, and adjourning on November 13.

President Johnson's program for political reconstruction, like Lincoln's, was much more lenient than that proposed by Congress, which in 1866 had come under the control of a Republican faction known as the "Radicals" for their vengeful plans to restructure the South. The conflict between the president and the Radicals led to Johnson's downfall and the imposition of military rule on Texas, but for the time being Texans enjoyed a period of relative independence in their efforts to rebuild a state government. On June 17, 1865, Johnson issued an amnesty proclamation for Texas that excluded only fourteen classes of ex-Confederates, most of whom were pardoned after filing individual petitions. A. J. Hamilton, a Unionist who had represented Texas in the House of Representatives before the war and had fled for his life in 1862, returned as the provisional governor. Texans received him cordially, and the press declared his policies reasonably conciliatory. Fifty thousand troops occupied the state, which was within the Military Division of the Southwest under the command of General Philip H. Sheridan, headquartered at New Orleans. At this time most of these troops were stationed on the Rio Grande, but by 1867 many of these soldiers had been moved to the frontier, where the residents were pleased to have them.

One of the first actions Hamilton took when he reached Texas was to call a constitutional convention, which met in February, 1866. The delegates, a majority of whom had favored disunion, acknowledged the supremacy of the U.S. Constitution and declared the Ordinance of Secession null and void without addressing the legality of its passage directly. This declaration was adopted to evade direct resolution of the hotly debated question of nullity of the ordinance by reason of war versus nullity from its inception, or *ab initio*. The Radical position was that secession was not permitted by the U.S. Constitution and that the ordinance was void from the beginning. The conservatives, who were unwilling to agree that their kinsmen and friends had been traitors all through their tragic struggle, considered the Ordinance of Secession void by reason of conquest.

The conservative inclination of the convention became obvious when it refused to ratify the Thirteenth Amendment and disingenuously argued that, first, such an action was redundant, as emancipation had already taken place and, second, emancipation failed to guarantee the equal rights of blacks before the law. The delegates' repudiation of all state debts incurred during the war became one of the most controversial ordinances, but they believed it was necessary in order to free Texas from its last obligations to the Confederacy. The Texas Constitution of 1845 was reinstated with a few changes that reflected the end of slavery. All acts of the state government that did not directly relate to the war effort of the past five years were reaffirmed.

In the subsequent election, James W. Throckmorton was elected

Andrew Hamilton, governor of Texas, 1865–66.
Reproduced from holdings of Texas State Archives.

governor. A conservative who had served as president of the constitutional convention and as a state senator, Throckmorton had been a Unionist before the war but during the conflict earned the rank of brigadier general in the Confederate service. He opposed black suffrage and was removed from office by General Sheridan's order of July 30, 1867, which branded him an "impediment to Recon-

James W. Throckmorton, governor of Texas, 1866–67.
Reproduced from holdings of Texas State Archives.

struction." Lieutenant Governor George W. Jones, a delegate to the constitutional convention who had served as colonel of the Confederate 17th Texas Infantry, was removed from office in part because the senators of the Eleventh Legislature continued their stubborn resistance to political and social change under his leadership.

Thirty-three senators were elected to the Eleventh Legislature, of whom fifteen were attorneys, twelve were farmers, one was a rancher, three were merchants, and one, Abram M. Gentry, was president of the Texas and New Orleans Railroad. Eighteen senators (including Frederick Voight, who represented District Three after the death of James W. Guinn) were new to the legislature: J. M. Blount, James B. Boyd, Samuel N. Braswell, John G. Brown, John K. Bumpass, Richard V. Cook, C. C. Coppedge, John T. Littleton, James M. McDade, Hudson W. Nelson, William M. Neyland, Francis J. Parker, Benton Randolph, J. K. P. Record, William P. Saufley, Henry Warren, John C. Yarbro, and Voight; of these, only Bumpass and Nelson would return to the legislature, both at a later period and both to the House. Six senators returned to the Senate from the Tenth Legislature: George E. Burney, A. O. Cooley, Robert H. Guinn, William G. W. Jowers, William B. Knox, and Benjamin T. Selman. Three others, Gentry, Nathan G. Shelley, and James A. Truit, returned after prior, though not continuous, Senate service. Seven former House members—William C. Dalrymple, Frederick F. Foscue, James W. Guinn, Robert H. Lane, Jacob B. Reid, William R. Shannon, and James W. Stell—joined their colleagues across the rotunda for the Eleventh Legislature. Collectively, the senators were a solidly conservative group.

Several former members of the Confederate military were elected to the Senate. James B. Boyd, a lawyer from North Carolina, was a lieutenant in Company C, 4th Texas Regiment, and was wounded in the Wilderness, at Chickamauga, and before Richmond. As he lay stricken in the field at one of these battles, a comrade approached and said, "Why, Boyd, can this be you?" Boyd replied, "Yes, but I would be over there with those dead if I had done my duty." He lived to perform his duty to his adopted state as the senator from Robertson County in the Eleventh Legislature.

John K. Bumpass, a resident of Collin County and a Unionist before the war, nevertheless served the Confederacy as captain of

George Washington Jones, lieutenant governor, 1866–67, in Eleventh Legislature. Reproduced from holdings of Texas State Archives.

Company F, 5th Texas Partisan Rangers, under Colonel Martin. Originally from North Carolina, Bumpass, a farmer, opposed nearly everything as a legislator. Disapproving of the multiplicity of laws, he advocated the repeal of half the statutes on the books and spoke out against the high cost of government. He was a member of the Constitutional Convention of 1866 before his election to the Senate. Bumpass served only one term in the Senate but would later return as a member of the House for the Twenty-fourth and Twenty-fifth legislatures.

William C. Dalrymple came to Texas in the early 1830s and fought Mexicans and Indians on the frontier; Governor Houston named him commander in chief of the Texas Militia with the rank of colonel of cavalry in 1860. In February, 1861, Houston sent Dalrymple, with four companies of newly organized troops, to protect the frontier from Indians. When he reached Camp Cooper in what is now Throckmorton County, an armed mob of secessionists was preparing to attack the post, and the U.S. Army inside was preparing to defend it. Colonel Dalrymple intervened and persuaded the fort's commander to surrender peacefully. This action prevented Texas from being the state where the first shots of the Civil War were fired and left that notoriety to South Carolina, where the hostilities began at Fort Sumter two months later. Dalrymple joined the fray in 1862, when he began fighting in Arkansas as a private soldier in the Confederate Army. He represented Burnet and Williamson counties in the Texas House in the Sixth and Seventh legislatures and Williamson and Travis counties in the Constitutional Convention of 1866 as well as serving in the Senate of the Eleventh Legislature; in both the legislature and the constitutional convention he strongly opposed Negro suffrage and racial equality.

Abram M. Gentry was an early railroad promoter in Texas and a senator in the Eighth Legislature, where he strongly challenged the claim that a state retained the right to secede from the Union. He established the Texas and New Orleans Railroad in 1859 and had it in operation before the beginning of the Civil War. Despite his opposition to secession, Gentry served with the Supply and Commissary Department of the Confederate Army and after the war returned to politics and railroad development, successfully financing what later became the Texas Western Railroad, based in Houston.

Benton Randolph was an Alabaman by birth who had served in

the Alabama Legislature before coming to Texas. In 1855 he was in the first graduating class of Austin College, where he received a law degree. While Randolph was at college, his landlady once remarked that she had never seen an honest lawyer. He replied, "You're looking at one now." Randolph went on to practice law in Huntsville until he joined Company H, 4th Texas Infantry, Hood's Brigade. Disabled for service by a wound, he was assigned to General Hardee's Corps as judge advocate with the rank of captain of cavalry. After the war, he represented Walker County in the Constitutional Convention of 1866 and later District Seventeen in the Senate of the Eleventh Legislature.

William R. Shannon was born in Kentucky but, after the death of his parents when he was eight, was raised in Ohio by his uncle, Governor Wilson Shannon of that state. At eighteen he went to the Mexican War with a regiment of Missouri volunteers. After his discharge in 1847, he practiced law in Ohio, toured South America, looked for gold in California, and raised cattle and got married in Texas, where he stayed, settling in Johnson County. He liked Texas, and Texans liked him: they elected him to the House of Representatives in the Seventh, Eighth, and Tenth legislatures and to the Senate in the Eleventh, Sixteenth, Seventeenth, Eighteenth, and Nineteenth legislatures. In 1861 he joined Company C, 10th Texas Infantry, in the Confederate Army, and by the end of the war he was a lieutenant colonel. He was instrumental in creating Hood County in honor of his old corps commander, General John B. Hood.

Frederick Voight was born in Prussia and found his way to Nacogdoches by 1848, where he married and settled into the community. He was U.S. postmaster from 1854 to 1861 and was postmaster for the Confederacy in 1861 until he enlisted as captain of Company B, 8th Regiment, Texas Volunteer Infantry. In addition to serving as state senator in the Eleventh Legislature, Voight was three times mayor of Nacogdoches and was state librarian in 1874. He drowned in 1880 while crossing the Angelina River at a point later named Dutchman's Crossing after him.

John T. Littleton of Karnes County was a delegate to the Secession Convention and later a captain on the frontier. He was a recognized member of the Knights of the Golden Circle, a secret pre–Civil War society which proposed to form a slave empire with Havana, Cuba, at its center. Bringing together idealists, adventurers,

Four soldiers in Hood's Brigade. Courtesy Austin History Center, Austin Public Library, # PICA 03674

and seekers of fortune in support of Southern ideas of states' rights, manifest destiny, and slavery, the Knights of the Golden Circle provided its adherents a shelter from the unremitting clamor of the abolitionists. John Littleton was the captain in charge of the Knights of the Golden Circle Castle in Helena in Karnes County. Other Knights active in politics chose to remain anonymous, but several prominent Texans were members of the society.

Due in part to a lack of veterans of the Confederate Army who were willing to serve, some of the men elected to the Senate had not seen service in the Southern military effort. John Blount, a Mississippian, came to Texas in 1856 and assisted in laying out the city of Denton. He served as Denton county judge for several terms and was elected senator in 1866 but was removed from office with the Throckmorton administration as an "impediment to Reconstruction."

Samuel N. Braswell, born in Georgia, came to Texas in 1858. A Jacksonian Democrat, he opposed secession. In the Senate of the Eleventh Legislature, Braswell represented Red River and Titus counties.

From Colorado County, Richard V. Cook, a lawyer from Tennessee, served in both the Constitutional Convention of 1866 and the Senate of the Eleventh Legislature. Cook gave a qualified endorsement of the proposed constitution in the *Star Gazette*, urging its adoption despite its "many obnoxious features . . . and the circumstances under which and the body of men by whom" it was created.

Frederick F. Foscue of Liberty was a native of Alabama who was educated at Washington College in Virginia. He farmed and was in the Alabama Legislature before he came to Texas in 1854, where he continued farming and politicking and served as a representative in the Eighth and Tenth legislatures before his term as a senator in the Eleventh.

Senator James W. Guinn from Angelina, a member of the House in the Tenth Legislature, died in office on August 18, 1866. A memorial resolution was offered by Senator Truit on August 20, 1866, and the Senate adjourned for the day in memory of their late colleague. The senators wore badges of mourning for thirty days. James Guinn was replaced by Frederick Voight.

Robert H. Lane came to Texas from New York, where he had studied and practiced law in Madison County. He entered the army, was elected lieutenant colonel in Rall's regiment of Missouri volunteers, and went to fight in the Mexican War. He fought under Brigadier General Sterling Price at the Battle of Santa Cruz, liked what he saw of Texas, and moved to Bonham in Fannin County after the war. In 1851 he was elected to the House, and in 1866 he was elected to both the constitutional convention and the Senate.

Jacob B. Reid came to Texas from Mississippi in 1844 and settled on a plantation south of Victoria. He represented Calhoun, Jackson, Victoria, and DeWitt counties in the House in the Ninth and Tenth legislatures and those counties plus Lavaca in the Senate in the Eleventh. Reid later returned to Mississippi.

James Alfred Truit began public service in Macon County, North Carolina, where he was sheriff for nearly a decade. He then served as a lieutenant in the Cherokee War of 1838 before moving to Texas. Truit and his family settled in Shelby County in 1840, and he was elected to the House in the Eighth and Ninth congresses and the First and Second legislatures and to the Senate in the Fourth, Sixth, Seventh, and Eleventh legislatures. His son Alfred M. Truit was a senator in the Third Legislature.

Henry Warren came to Texas in 1864 from New York. Although the voters of El Paso elected Warren to the Senate of the Eleventh Legislature, the six-hundred-mile journey from his district to Austin took him so long that the legislature had adjourned before he arrived. His trip was slowed because his fear of an Indian attack led him to travel with mule trains for protection.

The Eleventh Legislature mustered a quorum on August 6, 1866, the first day of the session, and proceeded to elect its officers. For the Senate, these included W. Leigh Chalmers, secretary; Rhodes Fisher, first assistant secretary; J. H. Johnson, second assistant secretary; W. D. C. Nelson, enrolling clerk; J. Pat Henry, engrossing clerk; William A. Pitts, sergeant-at-arms; Joshua H. Truitt, doorkeeper; Rev. John W. Phillips, chaplain; and Joseph Mangum, messenger. Senator Robert H. Guinn was elected president pro tempore by acclamation on August 6, 1866.

The Eleventh Legislature inaugurated Throckmorton and Jones with a notable lack of ceremony. Throckmorton stated in his inaugural address that the two most important tasks of his administration were frontier defense and enactment of the constitutional provisions relating to freedmen. As governor he was committed to a conservative policy of firm opposition to social and political equality for blacks and he also pressed President Johnson for a definite mandate for the restoration of unrestricted civil government, including the withdrawal of all federal troops to the frontier. These plans were frustrated. Texans failed to understand the vengeful mood of the U.S. Congress, which had no intention of seeing the South reinstitute the prewar social order after so much blood had been spilled in conquest.

The choice of the Eleventh Legislature when faced with the task of naming two U.S. senators indicates the illusion of independence entertained by the legislators and their continued defiance of the federal government. By a decisive vote, they chose, instead of the leading Unionist candidates, the elderly David G. Burnet, a moderate Unionist who had loudly denounced the Radicals, and Oran M. Roberts, who had presided over the Secession Convention and then served as a brigadier general for the Confederacy. Because former slaves were now included in the census as full citizens, Texas gained two seats in Congress; Northern congressmen were unhappy with the increased representation of the vanquished and were enraged by the unrepentant election to the Senate of a former brigadier general of the Confederate Army. Following adoption of a new apportionment act, signed on September 8, 1866, Texans elected to the U.S. House of Representatives four men who were just as repugnant to the Radicals as were the senators-elect: former state senators Archer M. Branch and Claiborne C. Herbert, both of whom had served in the Confederate Congress; Benjamin H. Epperson, a Unionist who had served as a Confederate officer; and George W. Chilton, who was accused of kidnapping and hanging without trial one of Governor Hamilton's aides during an abortive invasion of Brownsville in 1863. None of these men could take the iron-clad test oath required of all U.S. officials under an 1862 act, and so all of them were denied their seats.

One of the first acts of the Eleventh Legislature legalized all of the actions of both the officials appointed by Hamilton as provisional governor and those elected in June, 1866. In districts which had not held elections prior to the expiration of the provisional government, the officers appointed by that administration were continued in office. The Senate passed legislation signed on September 26, 1866, which provided fifteen thousand dollars to pay the outstanding debts of the provisional government, including unpaid salaries. The Senate also adopted a resolution proposed by Senator Knox that disavowed the third section of the ordinance, which declared the war debt void. This section had prohibited the legislature from providing funds for the payment of state obligations incurred between January 28, 1861, and August 5, 1865, without exception. The legislators did release those who had not paid the special tax imposed in April, 1861, to fund a loan, thereby nullifying one of the last obligations of the public to the Confederate government of Texas. Overall, though, the Senate refused to allow the state to escape its debts.

By validating and funding the acts of the provisional government and disavowing part of the ordinance of the constitutional convention repudiating the war debt, the Senate accepted a responsibility that was hard to fulfill. The war had left the state with an enormous debt and the economy in a shambles, though in better condition than any other Southern state that had left the Union. Tax revenue heretofore had depended greatly on land, slaves, and commerce; but in 1866 the land was unplanted and unsafe, the slaves were gone, and commerce was destroyed. The Senate adopted several measures for the relief of those who possessed land, most of whom owed taxes and payments to the state because they had settled a portion of the public domain. Chattel slavery, of course, had ceased to exist in 1865. The revival of trade took time—more time than the legislature could afford to wait, pressed as it was to provide for the reconstruction of a defeated and disrupted society. In order to meet the state's obligations, the Eleventh Legislature imposed new income, salary, poll, occupation, and ad valorem taxes that were almost three times higher than the highest ones imposed during the war.

Land continued to be a subject of much legislative controversy in Texas. Relief was accorded to owners of university lands, who were given until January 1, 1869, to pay the interest due on such property. On October 20, 1866, an act suspending the survey and sale of all public lands was repealed, which permitted many squatters to file legal claims for the tracts they had preempted, and on November 1 Throckmorton signed an extension act which allowed all of the settlers who had preempted land until the first day of 1869 to return their field notes and payments to the General Land Office. Those who had filed surveys before January 1, 1861, however, were required to make payment by the first day of 1868 under the terms of an act signed on November 8. Finally, an act signed on November 12 permitted every white person who was the head of a household or over the age of twenty-one to claim 160 acres of unsettled public domain.

Claims against the state concerning matters of the public debt other than land were heard by an Auditorial Board, created by the passage of a bill introduced by Senator Robert H. Guinn. The board consisted of the comptroller and treasurer. Successful petitioners received 6 percent bonds in lieu of currency. The legislators also provided a six-month period during which suits could be filed against former Confederate officials for the loss of any private property or for other grievances. Finally, personal homestead exemptions from forced sale were revised once more to include two hundred acres of land or a town lot of not more than two thousand dollars in value, all tools of a trade, implements of husbandry, and household furniture of no more than five hundred dollars in value, as well as provisions and livestock to sustain a family for a year. Through these acts, the senators tried to provide some relief for impoverished families in Texas even as they raised taxes.

Of immediate importance was the reestablishment of a system of frontier defense against the Indians, who had taken advantage of the wartime weakness of Texas' western defenses to retake some of the lands they had lost to white settlement and who would make major gains in pushing back the frontier between the end of the war and 1871, when frontier defense was weakest. On September 21, 1866, Governor Throckmorton signed a measure introduced by Senator Shannon that provided for the enlistment of three battalions of Texas Rangers. Because a majority of the federal soldiers were posted on the Rio Grande as a warning gesture to Maximilian (who at the instigation of Napoleon III was attempting to establish himself as emperor of Mexico), these newly enlisted Texas troops would be stationed along the northern and western borders of the state. The Rangers were to serve a term of twelve months under elected officers and were expected to furnish their own equipment. Salaries were raised to provide for the expense each Ranger would incur in equipping himself, ranging from thirty dollars for a private to two hundred dollars for a colonel. A later act appropriated only five thousand dollars to defray the expenses of organizing the Rangers, while an additional act, approved on November 9, 1866, allowed the governor to authorize up to five hundred thousand dollars in bonds when they were called to active duty. Like the frontier defense units mustered before the war and for Confederate service, these battalions were subject to the rules and regulations of the regular army but could not be removed from the state for detached service. The acts providing for the reorganization of the Frontier Regiment, first passed in February and December of 1861, were specifically repealed. An act signed on November 13, 1866, reestablished a state militia system. Despite this swift action on the part of the governor and the legislature, these battalions of Rangers were never recruited because General Sheridan would not allow state troops to organize. By September, 1866, however, federal troops began to reoccupy the frontier forts.

Not all of the provisions concerning the Indians were military in nature. The Senate passed an act appropriating twenty-five hundred dollars to ransom hostages held by the Indians. This measure facilitated the return of more than a score of such prisoners but did little to alleviate the general resentment toward the tribes responsible for their abduction, as evidenced by Throckmorton's admonition that efforts to exterminate those groups should continue. Another law prohibited the sale of firearms, ammunition, or liquor to any member of a hostile tribe. An interesting departure from previous policy came in legislation that exempted from prosecution Indians who committed acts normally considered criminal against Indians in the uninhabited portions of the state. On November 1, 1866, Throckmorton signed a measure which set aside one league of land as a reservation for the Tonkawas, under the management of an agent appointed by the state government. The act which provided an agent to attend to the affairs of the Alabama and Coushatta Indians in East Texas, first approved on December 30, 1861, was extended to include the Muscogee who lived in the same region. The latter group also received a half-section of land as a tiny reservation.

Following the suggestion of Governor Throckmorton, who opposed black suffrage in any form, the Eleventh Legislature refused to take any action on the Thirteenth Amendment and rejected the Fourteenth. Because the constitutional convention had acknowledged the supremacy of the Constitution of which the Thirteenth Amendment was a part, the resolution endorsed by the Senate declared any further action as "surplusage if not intrusive." The Fourteenth Amendment was opposed as both unconstitutional and impractical; some insisted that its adoption "would force wholesale negro suffrage and white disenfranchisement upon the southern people and require them to be the instruments of their own degradation." Senator Cook, chairman of the Committee on Federal Relations, reported that "we do not see fit to clothe the freedman with the elective franchise, for the reason that his moral and intellectual status is not of a growth sufficient to render it either a wise or safe step." He hastened to note, however, that the state constitution "guarantees to the negro every other right of citizenship."

These other rights of citizenship were, however, greatly curtailed. All of the acts passed during the Civil War for the control of blacks were repealed, but many acts that limited their civil rights were subsequently approved. Blacks were not allowed to vote, hold public office, serve on juries, intermarry with whites, or even testify in court cases in which blacks were not involved. Under the provisions of an act passed on November 6, 1866, freedmen were required to ride in separate railroad cars. Senator Cook chaired a special committee to inspect the state insane asylum during the Eleventh Legislature, and his report led to the signing of an act on November 12 that set aside ten thousand dollars for the purchase of a separate building to house black patients who were thrown upon the resources of the state after the "withdrawal from them of a master's home, care, and protection."

The Eleventh Legislature ignored the warnings of more politically prescient leaders such as John H. Reagan, the former postmaster general of the Confederacy, who wrote from his prison cell in Fort Warren, in Boston, that the Radicals would win control of Congress if the South continued to resist the loud demands from the North for black equality. The Senate passed measures which provided for apprenticeships, strong vagrancy laws, and a repressive system of labor contracts, all "calculated to keep at least some of the freed slaves in a state of peonage." The apprentice act, described by Governor Throckmorton as being copied from a Massachusetts statute, and the vagrancy act made no mention of race or color and encountered little opposition from Radicals while at the same time reassuring Texans that the familiar social order would be preserved.

But the contract labor law, also colorblind, was applied to both white and black workers and required them to sign a contract for every work period longer than a month for any one employer and to surrender one-half of the crops produced by each family to that employer. The contract labor law drew the ire of important conservatives as well as Radicals. The *Southern Intelligencer* called the bill in its original form a "legislative monster" and opined that "as a law, its practical effect will be to make labor synonymous with crime, and to degrade the free laborer to the condition of a slave." The statute remained in force for only a short time; three months after its passage, the head of the Freedmen's Bureau in Texas, J. B. Kiddo, "announced that contracts made in accordance with its provisions would not be approved." Of more lasting impact was an act signed on October 27, 1866, which required the registration of crop liens and provided that such debts had preference over all others except land rents. This was the first step in the establishment of the tenant farming system that replaced the old master-slave relationship.

Recognizing the urgency of reinstating law and order in Texas, the senators passed a number of laws to provide the missing stability. They passed an act that reorganized Texas into fourteen judicial districts and another act that established the time and place for each session. Another measure required the Supreme Court to hold three sessions annually at separate sites: Austin in the fall, Galveston in the winter, and Tyler in the spring. After passing acts permitting Burleson, Collin, Comal, Denton, Grayson, Marion, and Walker counties to levy taxes for the construction of jails and courthouses, the Senate endorsed two statutes that allowed police courts in the state to collect an ad valorem tax on all property, to issue bonds to pay for the construction and maintenance of public edifices, and to use convicts for labor. These bodies were also allowed to divide the counties into voting precincts to increase efficiency. County courts were given greater jurisdiction over civil and petty criminal cases. The records of the Confederate district courts were preserved under an act signed November 13, 1866, which also permitted such transcripts to be admitted as evidence in a state court.

The Senate passed a series of conservative measures intended to establish a moral society. Included in these measures was an amendment to the act originally approved on June 5, 1837, which provided for marriage in Texas. Under the amended statute, men under the age of sixteen and women under the age of fourteen were forbidden to marry. An act of December 16, 1863, was amended to stipulate that anyone who labored or compelled his children or employees to labor on a Sunday was guilty of a misdemeanor. Exceptions included work on sugar plantations during the sugar-making season, mail service, public transportation and lodging, foundry workers, and stock drivers who already had gathered their herds. Those convicted were fined from ten to fifty dollars, except that those who violated the Sabbath by hunting were fined half of the regular schedule, and those who played games of chance, raced horses, sold liquor, or gambled were fined one and one-half times the usual amount. An act signed on November 6, 1866, prohibited anyone except a military or civil officer from carrying a firearm on a plantation without the proprietor's permission. Many tragic incidents involving young men of both races had occurred, and the Senate felt bound to act to prevent their recurrence.

In order to halt the influx of impoverished and possibly criminal aliens, the Eleventh Legislature passed an act, signed on October 15, 1866, which required the registration of all aliens entering the state for the first time by ship. All those who were sick, physically or mentally incompetent, or destitute could be refused entrance. Any commissioner of immigration or mayor of a port could waive these requirements if evidence existed that such people would not become a public burden, but if the commissioner was mistaken, he would be held liable for the expenses of the aliens' care for two years. Any shipmaster who defied this statute was fined five hundred dollars for each illegal alien landed.

The task of physical reconstruction required special attention. The legislators appropriated two thousand dollars to clear Sabine Pass of obstructions placed there by the Confederates to forestall an invasion. Funds were provided for refurbishing the Governor's Mansion and furnishing the office of the attorney general. For the first time, a state librarian was appointed to maintain and develop the state holdings and to care for the furnishings in the legislative chambers and the Supreme Court room. In other legislation, the legislature allowed the use of convict labor on public works projects, including the building of railroads, mining, dredging waterways, the smelting of iron, and irrigating of land. The employment of convicts was supervised by the Board of Public Labor, which consisted of the governor, secretary of state, comptroller, attorney general, and treasurer. Only those who were convicted of minor offenses were sent to work in the gangs, and those who completed their terms were entitled to one-third of the net proceeds of their wages. All construction of internal improvements in Texas came under the supervision of the Office of State Engineer and Superintendent of Public Works, created by an act of November 13, 1866.

The senators, despite their politically conservative views, realized the tremendous economic change the Civil War had wrought in Texas and the rest of the South. On October 22, 1866, they adopted a joint resolution asserting that the conflict had "changed the whole domestic economy of the South." Admitting that the single-minded devotion to the "purchase of negroes and the culture of cotton" had retarded more substantial development, they invited "skilled labor and capital from the world," especially the United States, to relocate in Texas. The Texas Land, Labor, and Immigration Company was chartered to facilitate new immigration by desirable alien workers, while the Western Texas Colonial Land Immigration Company was to concentrate on recruitment efforts in the United States and Europe.

New businesses incorporated by the Eleventh Legislature included many textile and multipurpose mills: Colorado Cotton and Woolen Manufacturing Company, Caddo Lake Manufacturing Company, Planters and Mechanics Manufacturing Company, Fredericksburg Action Mill Company, Texas Producing Company, and Barnhart Mills, to name only a few. Many new corporations hoped to recover oil in commercial quantities, among them the North Texas and Red River Oil, Salt, and Coal Company; the Texas Oil, Iron, Mining, and Manufacturing Company; and the East Texas Petroleum and Mining Company. Specialized corporations included the San Antonio Ice Company, the Texas Iron and Marble Manufacturing Company, and the Burnet Iron Company. Few of these operations, which were dependent primarily on local capital, lasted more than a year or two.

The Reconstruction years also brought some economic innovations to Texas. A number of business associations were incorporated, including the Young Men's Real Estate and Building Association, the Houston Savings Investment Company, the Real and Personal Estate and Building Company of Galveston, the Contractors' Association, and the American Industrial Agency. Labor also organized. One of the early associations to receive a charter was the San Antonio Mechanics and Laborers Association. The Agricultural, Mechanical and Blood Stock Association of Texas was chartered to promote more scientific animal husbandry and crop cultivation through the use of modern machinery. Companies founded to provide for the latter included the Guadalupe Water Company for the Purposes of Irrigation and Navigation; the San Marcos Irrigation, Manufacturing, and Navigation Company; and the El Paso Irrigation and Manufacturing Company. A final innovation was the appearance of insurance mutual companies; Planters Mutual Insurance Company, Brownsville Mutual Insurance Company, Texas Insurance Company, Jefferson Insurance Company, and Merchants

Mutual Insurance Company all received charters from the Eleventh Legislature.

Charters were also issued to many enterprises that proposed to construct internal improvements in Texas. Those of a purely local nature included Houston and Harrisburg Turnpike Company, Waco Bridge Company, Powderhorn Bayou Dredging Company, Richland Turnpike and Toll Bridge Company, Brazos Internal Improvement and Navigation Company, Corpus Christi Canal Company, Brownsville Levee Company, and Houston Direct Navigation Company.

Companies primarily concerned with coastal and inland water transport included the Trinity River Slack Water Navigation Company; the Houston and Galveston Wharf and Press Company; and the Lake, Lock, and Dam Company, which proposed to establish water travel between Jefferson, Texas, and Shreveport, Louisiana. Land transport was the focus of the Texas Overland Transportation Company and the Corpus Christi Steamship and Overland Transport Company. Several individuals were authorized to construct and operate private ferries and toll bridges across minor waterways in the state.

Charters were received by numerous railroad companies such as the Rio Grande Railroad Company; the Henderson, Marshall, and Jefferson Railroad Company; and the Galveston Wharf Junction Railroad Company. The charter of the Indianola Railroad Company, first issued in January, 1858, was renewed. The Galveston City Railroad Company proposed to operate horse-drawn streetcars in that city, and the Houston and Harrisburg Horse Railroad was chartered for local travel. On November 13, the Eleventh Legislature overrode Throckmorton's veto of an act providing sixteen sections of land for each mile of railroad constructed in the state, but the governor signed separate acts giving sixteen sections for each mile completed by the Washington County Rail Road Company, the Houston and Texas Central Railway Company, and the Eastern Texas Railroad Company.

These measures for economic development facilitated the growth of civil government in Texas. The Senate endorsed the organization of Kinney and Maverick counties and overrode Throckmorton's veto to create a third, Hood County. The governor objected because the latter contained less than nine hundred square miles, but that failed to dissuade the legislature. Many cities received charters or revived old ones, including Brenham, Galveston, Jefferson, and Navasota. Towns incorporated by the Eleventh Legislature included Athens, Cameron, Carthage, Denton, Georgetown, Hillsboro, Kaufman, Lampasas, Linden, Pilot Point, and Wharton. These cities were served by a growing number of utility companies such as Austin City Water Works, the La Grange Fire Company, the Houston Gas Light Company, and the Texas and California Telegraph Company.

Perhaps the most bizarre and bitterly opposed proposal for the reorganization of civil government was the effort to divide Texas into two states. Originally debated in the constitutional convention and then introduced in the Senate by William M. Neyland of Jasper, the measure understandably generated much controversy both in the legislative chambers and the public arena. Senator Stell of Gonzales, chairman of the Senate Committee on State Affairs, spoke against the bill, saying the members had instructed him to declare that such action was "impolitic, unwise, and even dangerous in some respects." A minority of the committee, led by Neyland, dissented from Stell's report and insisted that the matter should be the subject of a referendum. The proposed state encompassed the region from the Sabine River and the Louisiana and Arkansas borders to the Brazos River and the western boundaries of Jack and Clay counties, a territory containing less than one-fourth of the land mass of Texas but half its wealth and population. The reason advanced for such a drastic action was the lack of concern for local interests shown by the state government in the past. Following lengthy and heated debate, the Senate refused to endorse a referendum, and the matter was allowed to drop, only to reappear during the Constitutional Convention of 1868–69.

Public education was the focus of many actions by the Senate. The police court in each county was authorized to serve as a board of school commissioners for the development of a public education system. They were given a free hand in establishing school districts and in distributing public funds to the elected trustees of each institution. In a separate act the police courts were also charged with holding elections on the sale of public school lands; after approval by the electorate, these tracts would be sold to benefit the "perpetual public school fund of the State" and interest on the proceeds would be apportioned to pay the tuition of "all the white scholastic population in those counties." A third act permitted the police courts to levy a tax for the education of indigent white children. No provisions were made for prospective black students, whose education was left up to the struggling Freedmen's Bureau. During its three years of operation in Texas, the Freedmen's Bureau enrolled more than sixty-four hundred black students of all ages and made some progress in teaching them to read and write, as well as explaining the rights and responsibilities of citizenship. Two bills introduced by Senator Foscue failed to become law; one, which was supposed to be racially impartial, was for the creation of the office of superintendent of public instruction, and another provided for the education of "persons of African descent, as teachers for this race."

The Senate passed two acts, signed on November 12, 1866, that repeated its intention to establish the University of Texas in due time. The measures required that $109,472.26 which had been removed from the university fund and used for frontier defense be repaid in the form of a state bond, bearing 5 percent per annum, secured by the sale of the lands set aside earlier for that purpose. The bill also stated that a second university, known as East Texas University, would be built in the state; a resolution adopted on November 13 appointed a board of fourteen men to serve for four years as administrators of this second institution. Twelve days earlier both houses adopted a joint resolution accepting the provisions of the federal Morrill Act of 1862, which provided land for the endowment of agricultural and mechanical colleges, thereby initiating a chain of events culminating in the establishment of the Agricultural and Mechanical College of Texas.

The Senate of the Eleventh Legislature endorsed charters for many private educational institutions, including the Georgetown Male and Female Academy, Galveston Female Institute, Woodland College, Greenville Male and Female Academy, Oakland College, Mount Pleasant Male and Female Institute, Bellview Academy, Sister Grove Male and Female High School, Burnet Male and Female Academy, and Stovall Academy. Like most schools offering secondary education in Texas during the nineteenth century, none of these were authorized to confer degrees. In reply to Stovall Academy's request for authorization to grant diplomas, Foscue, chairman of the Senate Committee on Education, declared that "the Committee are of the opinion that an academy ought not to be clothed with a power so rare and valuable in the scientific world, much less should a board of trustees be empowered to exercise it." The only apparent exception was the Baylor Female College, organized by the Baptist State Convention of Texas and the trustees of Baylor University.

The Senate approved laws forbidding the sale of "vinous or spirituous liquors" in the vicinity of many universities and public schools in Texas, "except for medical or sacramental purposes." These acts apparently were intended to foster proper education rather than to establish a more temperate society, because, at the same time, the Senate repealed the act of December 21, 1861, which had prohibited the sale of liquor within four and one-half miles of the courthouse in Fort Worth. Similarly, Senator Cook's proposed bill to define and punish the offense of drunkenness failed to become law.

Senator William P. Saufley introduced a resolution on August 19, 1866, calling for the establishment of a state cemetery to inter the "sons of Texas" who "laid down their lives upon distant battle fields in defence [*sic*] of what they sincerely believed a sacred and inalienable right." Incensed because the "rites of sepulture have not been properly bestowed upon the *manes* of many of those noble martyrs because of their country," the senator expressed his concern that the spirits of the dead were not at peace until they were properly buried in their native soil. He drew a somber picture of their "sacred forms" lying "undraped and uninterred, exposed to the bleak storms of Northern winters and sultry suns of Southern summers." Senator Stell received public approbation when, as chairman of the Committee on State Affairs, he reported against such creation of a new state cemetery and reburial of identifiable Texas soldiers who had fought for the Confederacy. He argued that the cost was prohibitive and, furthermore, that "many of our martyred dead fell in the front rank of battle on many sanguinary fields, and lie now commingled with those they fought." Stell prevailed in this matter, then later endorsed a successful joint resolution calling for the removal of the body of Albert Sidney Johnston from New Orleans and his reinterment in the state cemetery at Austin.

Governor Throckmorton insisted that President Johnson's manifesto of August 20, 1866, declaring the insurrection in Texas at an end, reestablished the supremacy of civil over military authority.

The Senate agreed with him. As early as August 16 the Senate adopted a joint resolution introduced by Stell calling for the president to transfer those federal troops "uselessly quartered" in the interior of the state to the frontier, where they would be quite welcome and would not hinder "the advancement of the much needed work of restoring civil government." Incidents such as the burning of Brenham by occupation forces on September 7, 1866, added to the senators' desire for the removal of troops from the densely populated areas of the state. Senator George E. Burney of Waco was particularly active in investigating the conflagration and in obtaining redress for the victims.

President Johnson's declining political fortunes, however, led to a precipitous decrease in his powers and frustrated the Texans' efforts. Army officers continued to wield a great deal of power throughout Reconstruction. With the Radical-Moderate coalition and the consequent Radical triumph in Washington, the military removed Throckmorton and Jones from office and prevented the legislature from convening until 1870. Despite the presence of these military officers, the Senate in 1866 voted with the House in stubbornly upholding traditional conservative constitutional principles, which infuriated both the Radicals and Moderates in Congress. By the day of adjournment, November 13, 1866, this conservatism had deepened the conflict between Throckmorton and the federal government and sown the seeds of an enduring and destructive political division in Texas.

CHAPTER 4

Interregnum, 1867–70

Texas Reconstruction politics were intertwined with national partisan events. Following the war, President Andrew Johnson, a War Democrat from Tennessee, had tried to carry out Abraham Lincoln's conciliatory approach for bringing the Confederate states back into the Union fold, but Johnson was not the skilled politician Lincoln had been, and there was little mediation between the federal and state governments. A dismayed and increasingly hostile Congress saw that, under Johnson, former Confederates and slaveholders were regaining control of southern governments and would have a solid bloc of Southern Democratic representation in Congress. This Southern coalition would be larger than it had been before the war, because a freedman was being counted as a whole person for the apportionment of congressional representation, not merely as three-fifths of a person as he had been as a slave. It was not for this that the North had fought the war.

It seemed obvious to the Republicans that the solution to the dilemma posed by an impending Democratic majority in Washington was to organize and ensure the voting rights of a solid black and loyal white Republican vote in the South. Having won a congressional majority in 1866, Radical Republicans used public disaffection in the North to wrest control of Reconstruction from President Johnson, imposing martial law throughout the South in 1867. After Ulysses S. Grant became president in 1869, Republicans were able to gain temporary control of state governments, with the larger design of building durable power.

The Republican party in the South needed to enlist a considerable number of white voters to carry out its program. This white bloc would consist largely of Whigs, who had worked with the Democrats but were not comfortable with their financial policies. The Whigs wanted public investment in internal improvements and were not particularly anxious about the suffrage of freedmen. In some counties, Unionists were perforce enrolled among the Republicans because the Democrats in those counties proscribed their participation. On the other hand, the Democratic party was in fair disgrace among Confederates, who felt they had been betrayed by the party and would have preferred another party, had one existed. Some previously dedicated Democrats wrote off the party and joined the Republicans. In Texas, the German and Mexican communities had never been sympathetic to slavery and were important to the Republican effort. Out of these general influences the Republicans of Texas were able to cobble together a somewhat uneasy alliance.

A complicating factor in postwar Texas was the fact that Texans had neither lost major battles on their own territory nor suffered the devastation of war. Confederate Texans had no sense that Texas had lost its part in the conflict. They did not feel defeated, they felt angry. Unionists and neutrals had been persecuted during the war, and they, too, were angry. A visitor from Washington observed that nowhere in the South had he seen so much continuing conflict between Union and Confederate factions as in Texas.

Under Congressional Reconstruction in 1867, General Philip H. Sheridan, a graduate of the U.S. Military Academy at West Point and an outstanding soldier who had fought against the Indians in the Northwest, assumed command of the Fifth Military District, made up of Louisiana and Texas. Under him General Charles Griffin became commander of the subdistrict of Texas. Sheridan's peacetime skills were not strong, and civil problems multiplied. The general came to detest Texas.

In early 1867, Congress had declined to seat the Texas congressional delegation, and on July 30 of that year, Sheridan and Griffin removed Governor James W. Throckmorton and his administration as "impediments to Reconstruction." Elisha M. Pease, a former governor who had been quite popular until he spoke against secession, was appointed by Sheridan to replace Throckmorton. More officials were dismissed when Sheridan and Griffin strictly enforced voting restrictions that disenfranchised men who had served the Confederacy in any public office, even if only that of school trustee or cemetery sexton. Under "Circular no. 13," white jurors were barred from service if they had ever voluntarily served or supported the Confederacy, and they were subject to the "iron-clad oath" of loyalty to the United States. As state laws prevented most blacks from qualifying for jury duty, so few prospective jurors remained on the rolls during the five months when Circular no. 13 was in force that the civil courts were unable to function and the widespread lawlessness grew worse. In September, 1867, Griffin died in the statewide yellow fever epidemic and was succeeded by General J. J. Reynolds.

On August 17 President Johnson had ordered Sheridan to the upper Mississippi to subdue the Plains Indians. Griffin had assumed temporary command of the Fifth Military District, and after his death an interim administrator, General Mower, took Sheridan's place and quickly lifted the jury order in September, 1867, making all registered voters eligible for jury duty. General Winfield S. Hancock, a Democrat and anti-Radical who permanently replaced Sheridan in November, permitted the registration of about five thousand additional voters and notified civil officials to return to their normal functions. Ironically, General Hancock and Governor Pease would find themselves on poor terms because Pease wanted more military backup than Hancock thought suitable.

Following the failure of the Eleventh Legislature to achieve readmittance to the Union, another effort had to be made, and an election was called for another constitutional convention. By 1868, Arkansas, North Carolina, South Carolina, Louisiana, Alabama, and Florida had complied with the process of restoration outlined in the Reconstruction Acts and had been readmitted to the Union. Still delaying were Mississippi, Virginia, Georgia, and Texas. By 1870, in order to be readmitted, these states had to ratify an additional constitutional amendment, the Fifteenth, which prohibited the states and the federal government from denying suffrage to any citizen on account of "race, color, or previous condition of servitude." A number of Northern states refused to ratify the amendment, and its adoption finally was successful only because the four laggard Southern states had to ratify it.

Since a majority of registered voters had to vote in order to make the election of delegates to a constitutional convention valid, some

Democratic leaders advised boycotting the election and avoiding a convention entirely. At the last minute, however, a sufficient number of Democrats voted, thus validating the election. As a result, of the ninety-four delegates elected to the Texas Reconstruction constitutional convention which met in Austin on June 1, 1868, seventy-eight were Republicans and no more than twelve were conservatives, among them perhaps eight Democrats; ten delegates were black; and only eight delegates were considered as carpetbaggers—a much smaller number than in the other Southern assemblies.

The Republicans in the constitutional convention were hopelessly divided into two clear-cut factions, a liberal-moderate bloc and the Radicals. Thus the final product of the convention was a document reflecting the Radicals' failure to carry any of their three main objectives: a confirmation of the *ab initio* doctrine, division of the state, and a broadening of disenfranchisement. The president of the convention was Edmund J. Davis, one of the Radical leaders. Davis, originally from Florida, was a lean, white-bearded federal judge from Brownsville whose jurisdiction had been the Lower Rio Grande Valley. He was defeated for election to the Secession Convention, but apparently he changed sympathies, because he fought on the Union side in the war and rose to the rank of brigadier general. After the war, Davis declined General Sheridan's offer of appointment as Chief Justice of the Texas Supreme Court and sought a regular U.S. Army commission, which President Johnson denied because he could not get along with Davis. Davis then returned to Texas.

Although Governor Pease's message had warned against a decision by the convention to split Texas into separate states, arguing that the difficulties of reentering the Union were sufficient problems for just one state of Texas to undertake, the Radicals went on to tackle this issue, which had already arisen in previous legislatures. The Radical leaders proposed to split Texas into three states and at that moment had an agreement to this effect from a slight majority of all delegates. Radical leaders in Congress had assured them that at least one of these states would be admitted to the Union under their control, leaving the others in political limbo under military rule. E. J. Davis and six other delegates went so far as to prepare a "Constitution for the State of West Texas," which was to include the region west of the Colorado River and have San Antonio as its capital. San Antonio immediately declared itself against division and certainly against inclusion in a state the press had dubbed "Coyote." In committee, the issue of division stretched on and on, with at times an almost festive air, so enthusiastic and ingenious were the delegates in framing their proposals. At the convention, however, the surfeit of plans created a deadlock. Though the idea of separate states would resurface on later occasions, its rejection by the constitutional convention effectively destroyed the chances of any plan's being adopted.

The Radicals also failed in their attempt to broaden disenfranchisement. After a bitter contest, disenfranchisement was limited to those disqualified by the federal Constitution: the iron-clad oath was no longer required for simple reenfranchisement, though it would be taken by several senators in the Twelfth Legislature along with the oath of office.

All males over the age of twenty-one were guaranteed suffrage, and the constitution included a provision that the freedmen should be protected in their property and person, that all prosecutions against them should be conducted under the same rules of evidence as applied to whites, and that the legislature was empowered to authorize them to serve as witnesses "as to facts hereafter occurring" if their testimony was deemed necessary. These points were construed as a liberal compromise, for conservatives said they went too far in equalizing the races and Radicals said they did not go far enough in guaranteeing and protecting civil rights. Radicals were highly displeased with the document.

The delegates approved the new constitution for engrossment on February 3, 1869, but Davis, as president of the convention, used his position to support the dissatisfied Radicals and contrived a breakup on February 5 and 6, before a final vote on the proposed constitution had been taken. Morgan Hamilton protested that "the majority of the convention have deliberately removed from the constitution every safeguard for the loyal voter, white and black." Two black members, George Ruby and B. F. Williams, resigned from the convention to prevent a quorum, and E. J. Davis and Morgan Hamilton were regarded as having left the party. A. J. Hamilton poured down a torrent of white-hot invective on E. J. Davis, who had used the power of the chair to adjourn the convention until the next morning and had stepped down from the chair but was prevented from leaving the hall. The two wings of the Republican party had come to hate each other more than they did their Democratic opponents. A committee under the direction of General Edward R. S. Canby recovered the documentation, and the convention officially adjourned on February 8, 1869. The final draft of the constitution was prepared by the secretary assisted by a member from each faction plus one of General Canby's officers, all responsible to General Canby. The document was signed by forty-five of the ninety-four delegates, including only seven Radicals, and the president of the convention, Davis, signed under orders from the general.

The Constitution of 1869 was a compromise which reflected the tense mood of the assembly that produced it. It disenfranchised only those disqualified from voting by the Fourteenth Amendment and authorized male black suffrage. Equality of all persons before the law was recognized. The constitution established the permanent public school fund on a sound financial basis by providing that all proceeds from the sale of public lands as well as the revenue generated by an annual poll tax of one dollar would be set aside for educating all young people from six to eighteen years of age. In addition, one-fourth of state taxes each year would be appropriated for the same purpose. The office of superintendent of public instruction was continued. Dueling was prohibited. State government was centralized: the governor would serve four years and appoint the secretary of state, the attorney general, and all state and county judges. County courts were abolished (although they were quickly reestablished when civil government resumed). The governor was empowered to call out the militia to enforce the laws of the state and put down invasions or insurrections. This article set the stage for Davis's most controversial actions. Elections were to be held at the county seat and had to continue through four consecutive days. Despite the high passions of the participants at the end of the convention, the document which finally emerged was forward-looking, not vindictive, and indicated the general intention of getting on with improvements and institutions to restore Texas' health and prosperity.

Meanwhile, General Reynolds was looking for allies who could help him realize his aspiration of becoming a U.S. senator, and he made his first approach to the liberal Republicans. When A. J.

Hamilton curtly informed Reynolds that the liberals would not support his senatorial dream, the general made a bargain with Davis to favor the Radicals in the upcoming elections in return for Davis's pledge to support Reynolds's objective. Reynolds's personal ambition dovetailed neatly with the objectives of the Radical faction. The military commander began to purge Hamilton's known supporters from state offices and voter rolls.

In their 1869 statewide election campaign, the Radicals made a sharp about-face and presented themselves as supporters of the proposed constitution. The moderate "A. J. Hamilton" Republicans supported it, too, and so did the Democrats, who had timidly put forward a pro forma gubernatorial candidate, Hamilton Stuart. The Democrats did not campaign very hard, fearing that a Democratic victory might provoke the imposition of full martial law and hoping to gain enough of the moderate Republican vote to defeat A. J. Hamilton, elect the Radicals, and ensure the destruction of the Republican party in Texas in the future.

In the 1869 elections, the voters ratified the constitution, and the Radical ticket of E. J. Davis for governor and Major James W. Flanagan for lieutenant governor won by a slight edge over the liberal Republican ticket headed by A. J. Hamilton. Several counties were hotly disputed, and the election has been regarded by some as fraudulent due to the control of the polls exercised by the army, the exclusion of many whites from the polls, and the alleged voting of blacks in large groups brought to the polls by political bosses; but the reputedly "lost" election results were finally found in the National Archives. In any event, General Reynolds certified Davis as having beaten Hamilton by 809 ballots in a voter turnout of about 80,000.

CHAPTER 5

The Senate of the Twelfth Legislature, 1870–71

From the removal of Governor Throckmorton and his administration at the end of July, 1867, until April 16, 1870, Texans chafed under the yoke of U.S. military rule, and the Twelfth Legislature convened in provisional session under the military authority of the U.S. government. Dominated by the Radical Republicans, this legislature became infamous for the actions it took to reshape Texas society and establish a durable Republican hegemony. There were four sessions of the Twelfth Legislature: the provisional session, which met from February 8 to February 24, 1870; a called session, from April 26 to August 15, 1870; a regular session, from January 10 to May 31, 1871; and an adjourned session, from September 12 to December 2, 1871.

Governor Edmund J. Davis and Lieutenant Governor James W. Flanagan were confirmed in office by General Reynolds on January 8, 1870, four months after Governor Pease resigned. Davis appointed James Newcomb as his secretary of state and called the provisional session of the Twelfth Legislature to enact the measures necessary for Texas' readmittance into the Union.

Thirty senators were elected to the Twelfth Legislature under the 1869 constitution. Twenty-six members were present when the legislature convened in provisional session on February 8, 1870, but three of these—James P. Douglas, Samuel Evans, and Mijamin Priest—refused to take the iron-clad oath necessary to qualify for their seats. Douglas and Evans would take the oath on February 10, but Priest was declared ineligible by the military government on

Edmund J. Davis, governor of Texas, 1870–74. Reproduced from holdings of Texas State Archives.

February 17. He would, however, qualify and be sworn in the called session.

The four senators who were absent on opening day were Amos Clark, Andrew J. Evans, Edward Bradford Pickett, and Elisha Pettit. Of these, all except Pettit would arrive within two weeks and take the oath to qualify for their seats. Pettit, like Priest, would not qualify and be sworn until the called session.

Lieutenant Governor James Flanagan presided in the Senate during the provisional session, and a full slate of Radical officers was easily elected on February 10: C. C. Allen, secretary; Camillus Jones, first assistant secretary; James M. Hart, second assistant secretary; J. M. Kaumheimer, postmaster; J. M. Page, engrossing clerk; G. R. Spaulding, enrolling clerk; Jeff M. Gibbs, sergeant-at-arms; Thomas J. Powell, assistant sergeant-at-arms; J. P. McKnight, doorkeeper; and Eli Green, assistant doorkeeper. S. G. Wilson was elected to the unique position of phonographic reporter. The calendar clerk, Henry Mordecai, and the journal clerk, Frank Stanley, were appointees.

Of the thirty-five senators who served during any part of the Twelfth Legislature, only four—Marmion H. Bowers, both Evanses, and Pickett—had previous experience in the Texas Legislature and none had experience in the Senate. Several new Republican senators had served the Confederacy in some capacity, and two of those had been in the Confederate Army: Webster Flanagan, son of the lieutenant governor, and General William H. Parsons. The Radical Republican faction included two black senators, Matthew Gaines and George T. Ruby.

Five elections were contested. The Radical John H. Lippard protested the seating of William H. Pyle, R. Peterson tried to stop the admission of Ebenezer Lafayette Dohoney, and Robert K. Smith contested the seat of John G. Bell, accusing him of intimidating the black voters in his district, but all three challenged senators were seated. A conflict between Mijamin Priest, the Republican senator from Cherokee County, and conservative Democrat James E. Dillard resulted in Priest's not being seated during the thirty-day provisional session. From the Nineteenth District, Andrew J. Evans, a liberal Republican, took the oath but was declared ineligible in an election contest and was replaced by Radical Republican S. W. Ford on February 16, 1870. These public controversies, especially the ongoing duel which developed between Priest and Dillard in Cherokee County, contributed to a growing public hostility toward the Radicals.

The Radicals' dominance was threatened by disagreement within the Republican ranks on several important issues that would come before the legislature. Some Republican senators sided with the Democrats in opposing the governor's nominee for superintendent of schools because he supported an integrated free public school system. The issue of state support for railroads also divided the Republicans. The Radical-controlled Senate favored legislation to promote the construction of railroads in the state, but Governor Davis opposed such public support and vetoed most of the railroad bills. Also sparking controversy was the bill to create a state militia. The extensive powers granted to the governor under the bill, including the power to impose martial law, were opposed by many otherwise loyal Davis supporters, and attempts to defeat the bill would further divide the membership and cause some to bolt from the deliberations.

During the provisional session, discord among some members notwithstanding, the Senate promptly passed House joint resolutions ratifying the Fourteenth (citizenship and electoral representation for freedmen), the Thirteenth (emancipation), and the Fifteenth (right to vote for all citizens) amendments on February 18, 1870, thereby returning Texas to the Union and ending military rule. Douglas, Samuel Evans, and George Ross Shannon voted against ratification of the Fourteenth Amendment, but only the latter two voted against the Fifteenth. Absent during the vote on the Fifteenth Amendment were Clark, Pettit, Pickett, and Rawson, while Priest was not on the roll call.

Texas would no longer be an occupied country, but the road to anything approaching normalcy was going to be rough. Before any civil order (or civility) would be achieved, in the course of the Twelfth and the next two legislatures much of the Senate would be arrested, martial law would be imposed, the governor and governor-elect would occupy two different floors of the Capitol with two different groups of armed supporters, and officials would be shot, beaten, and impeached. Although the chronicle of the Twelfth Legislature is complicated, individual histories of the senators provide a context for understanding the dynamics of the sessions.

Senator E. L. Alford was one of four Republicans who voted with the Democrats in the Senate to oppose Governor Davis's nomination of Joseph W. Talbot as school superintendent because they believed Talbot supported integrated schools. After Alford voted against Davis's militia bill, the Republican party expelled him. This left Alford without any organized support, and though his subsequent expulsion from the Senate became the subject of one of the bitterest debates in an extremely bitter session, he lost his seat and was replaced by Reinhard Hillebrand. Alford took his seat anyway at the regular session which began in January, 1871. Later in the month, however, the issue came to a head and Alford was removed from the roll call.

Senator Thomas H. Baker of Lockhart, who represented District Twenty-seven, began as a Radical, then shifted to liberal Republican. He was a partisan of the Texas Central Railroad and was chairman of the Committee on Agricultural Affairs and the Committee on Privileges and Elections. He had served the Confederacy, and his name was listed by the Committee on Political Disabilities among those who had to take the oath and be vouched for to redeem their franchise. Baker drew a six-year term and returned for the Thirteenth Legislature. He served as a district judge and was married twice, first to Margaret S. Baker, a local landowner, and then to Adelaide Porter Baker, who outlived him. He and Adelaide resided in Lockhart from December, 1867, to February, 1877, in Eagle Springs from 1877 to 1881, and in McGregor from 1881 until his death on March 1, 1883.

John G. Bell was a hotelkeeper in Bellville who had been born in Florida in 1820. He served in the U.S. Army in the Seminole War and came to Texas in 1855, when he took over his father's property at Bellville. In the antebellum years he was associated with the Whig and Know-Nothing parties and was characterized as a sturdy farmer of good constitution. He opposed secession and was involved with the Texas Unionist movement, although he served the Confederacy in some capacity and had to take the oath and be vouched for in 1868. He was a member of the Committee on Resolutions of Austin County in 1865 and became the delegate from Austin County to the Constitutional Convention of 1868–69.

Bell came to the Senate from the Thirteenth District in 1870. He voted for the militia bill but was one of the four Republicans who broke ranks to vote against the nomination of Talbot as state superintendent of education. He was chairman of the Committee on Roads, Bridges and Ferries and the Committee on Counties and County Boundaries. In 1871 Bell was named to the Republican state executive committee and was still active in the Republican party in 1876.

Born in Moore's Hill, Dearborn County, Indiana, on April 29, 1823, Marmion H. Bowers received his liberal arts education at Hamilton College, Kentucky, and then graduated from the law department of the State University at Bloomington, Indiana. The young lawyer set up a practice in Aurora, Indiana, and also edited the *Aurora Standard.* He moved to Texas and settled in Burnet in 1852, and within a short time his law practice flourished. The future senator was said to be above average in his pleadings before the bar and very effective with juries. Sometime during this period he married and fathered four daughters.

Bowers entered the war as a Confederate and served as commander of an infantry company recruited mainly from Blanco County. Toward the close of the war, he was elected in absentia as a member of the House of Representatives of the Tenth Legislature. This new office necessitated his return to Austin, where he served as editor of the *Southern Intelligencer* for a short time. He lost a bid for a Senate seat in 1866, before his successful run to represent Travis County and the dozen other counties composing District Twenty-eight. His lack of any clear party identification was well illustrated by an amusing comment in the November 13, 1869, *Austin Republican:* "in 1866 when ex-Confederate Captain Bowers was a candidate for the State Senate, against General Shelley, he declared that during the war he was a Union man, fighting for the Confederacy. Now he is before the people as a Confederate, fighting for the Union. Bowers is a very convenient man." Well liked by his fellow legislators, Bowers played a considerable role in the militia bill fracas. Bowers consistently voted with the moderates and the Democrats. The senator died at home of consumption on March 3, 1872.

E. Thomas Broughton, another attorney, came to Texas from Alabama with his parents in 1847. He studied law and was admitted to the bar in 1858 at Athens and later moved to Grayson County, where he was serving as district attorney when war broke out. He volunteered and was elected captain, C Company, 7th Texas Infantry. He later became a lieutenant colonel and saw plenty of action. After the battle at Fort Donelson, Kentucky, he was taken prisoner, but he reappeared in Mississippi in 1863 with General Bragg, defending Jackson against the army under General McPherson. Taken prisoner again, he was sent to Johnson's Island in Lake Erie for a year, during which time he learned French—and contracted smallpox, which left him partially blind but not helpless. His Rebel zeal was undiminished by this setback, and on his exchange in May, 1864, he joined Hood's Texas Brigade in time to participate in some of the most disastrous struggles of the war. Broughton was among the intrepid soldiers in the Army of Tennessee who were all but annihilated in their last, poorly led battles at Spring Hill and Franklin, Tennessee. At last he resigned his command due to impaired eyesight and an unhealed thigh wound. Broughton returned to Sherman in Grayson County and served as senator from District Twenty-two during the Twelfth and Thirteenth legislatures. Like Captain Samuel Evans of neighboring District Twenty-one, he was unwilling to ally himself with any of the political coteries. He ran for the Senate against both a Democrat and a Republican and was elected.

Senator Donald Campbell came to Texas from Alabama in the late 1850s, settling in Jefferson. He was a devoted Union man who opposed secession, but managed to survive the anti-Union sentiment prevalent in the state until the Federals regained control. Under the Federals, he served as postmaster and chief justice in Marion County. He attended the Constitutional Convention of 1868–69, prior to his election to the Senate of the Twelfth Legislature. After the Senate chose Lieutenant Governor James W. Flanagan to represent Texas as a senator in Washington, Campbell was elected president pro tempore of the Senate on April 27, 1870, and so became ex officio lieutenant governor of Texas. Some senators had expressed reservations about Don Campbell because of his close friendship with James Flanagan's son Webster, but there was no serious opposition to his election. As for his relationship with Flanagan, Campbell proved willing to have the powerful and well-to-do senator arrested along with the other bolters when they broke a quorum in the Senate. Campbell died in office on November 6, 1871, and was succeeded as president pro tempore on November 13 by none other than Webster Flanagan.

Senator Amos Clark of Nacogdoches was born in 1796 in Massachusetts and died in office on February 18, 1871. He was much older than the average senator of the day and was courteously deferred to. Senator Clark was among the men who bolted the Senate chamber in opposition to the militia bill and was subsequently arrested. After Clark's death, William Henry Swift, also of Nacogdoches, was elected to fill his seat.

Lamar and Hopkins counties chose one of their first settlers, David Washington Cole of Black Jack Grove, to represent them in the Constitutional Convention of 1868–69. The former Virginian was one of only twelve conservatives present. Convention records report that Cole was arrested for refusing to vote during the bitter struggle over the division of the state. He was later released and voted to maintain the integrity of Texas. Cole served in the Senate during the Twelfth and Thirteenth legislatures.

James E. Dillard of Rusk ultimately succeeded Priest as senator from District Three (Cherokee and Houston counties). Born in Houston County, Georgia, in 1830, Dillard arrived in Liberty County, Texas, in 1848. There he farmed and ranched until 1853, when he moved to Cherokee County to study law. His law studies were interrupted by the outbreak of the Civil War, and he enlisted in Company C, 3rd Texas Cavalry. He was transferred to the 40th Texas Cavalry in 1862 and saw action at Oak Hill, where he suffered a shot through his leg, but the injury did not deter him from serving in several more battles, including Elkhorn (Pea Ridge), Pleasant Hill, and Yellow Bayou. Dillard was admitted to the bar in 1866. He began his law practice in Rusk and that same year was elected county judge of Cherokee County. A sizable number of Cherokee County voters also attempted to send him to the Texas Senate in 1870, which attempt set in motion one of the longest and hardest fought political struggles of the session. Following Priest's resignation and two special elections, Dillard finally took his seat for good on October 31, 1871, during the adjourned session. He served in the Senate through the Fourteenth Legislature.

Dillard's public service also included three terms as county judge of Kaufman County, where he moved in 1878, and a term in the House during the Twenty-first Legislature. Later he would be appointed district judge by Governor Hogg and be reelected three times before retiring from the bench.

While he lived in Rusk, Dillard owned and edited the *Rusk Observer* for seven years, during which time James S. Hogg, the later governor, and Horace Chilton, a future U.S. senator, were printer's devils in his office, occasioning their nickname, "Old Dillard's Devils." Dillard was a Mason. He was married to Rosa Lee Fallis, and the couple had five children.

Ebenezer Lafayette Dohoney was the most prominent moderate-conservative Democrat in the Twelfth Legislature. The historian Clarence Wharton listed him as one of the fifty men who had most greatly influenced the development of Texas. Born in Adair County, Kentucky, in 1832, Dohoney arrived in Paris, Texas, in 1859 as a law graduate from Kentucky hoping to improve his health. As the Civil War approached, Dohoney believed Texas should stay with the Union and keep her recently achieved statehood. His first political notoriety arose when he successfully canvassed the residents of Lamar County to oppose secession. Like many other Unionists, he served in the Confederate Army, which he joined in July, 1861. The twenty-nine-year-old lawyer served as a first lieutenant, then as a captain, in Company H, 9th Texas Cavalry, Ben McCulloch's Brigade, Van Dorn's Division, Beauregard's Corps, Army of the West. He saw battle at Corinth, Mississippi, and at Elkhorn Tavern, Arkansas, but his health declined, and after a year he left the army. After the war he married Mary S. Johnson and raised a large family.

Dohoney was appointed district attorney of the Eighth Judicial District for 1865–66 by Governor A. J. Hamilton. He performed his duties courageously in those chaotic years, indicting the leaders of a mob which had hanged Union men during the war and prosecuting a U.S. revenue officer at Jefferson who stole cotton.

When he was sent to the Senate in 1870, Dohoney made an indelible imprint on the laws of Texas. He is credited with being the father of the Homestead Law of 1871, which is the basis for the homestead exemption today, and he played a leading role in the Tax-Payers' Convention of 1871. He also declared himself in favor of women's suffrage, a cause he defended all his life. During the Thirteenth Legislature, as chairman of the Committee on Education, he authored the free school bill, which provided for a system of schools with state and county superintendents and districts with trustees, but before this law was made operative, it was repealed and the community system substituted.

Texas Rangers served under General Ben McCulloch in the Confederate Army of the West. Reproduced from holdings of Texas State Archives.

A singular man, Dohoney espoused other views not commonly held in his time: he supported gun control through the "Six-shooter Act," which outlawed the carrying of guns in public places; and he became the father of prohibition in Texas, delivering the first speech favoring local option recorded in the state. He was a popular

General Ben McCulloch, 1811–62. Reproduced from holdings of Texas State Archives.

speaker, and his opinions also were publicized in his newspaper editorials for the *North Texan.* He used his positions as an editor and a legislator to oppose and eventually help repeal the "obnoxious acts" of the Davis administration.

Dohoney was a Democrat until 1877, when he became convinced that the Panic of 1873 had been caused by the financial policy of the

United States and consequently became a Greenbacker. His campaign for Congress on the Greenback ticket in 1882 was unsuccessful, as was his campaign as the Prohibitionist candidate for governor in 1886. In 1892 and 1894 he ran for chief justice of the Texas Court of Criminal Appeals.

After 1894 Dohoney no longer ran for office. At home in Paris, Texas, he continued his work as lawyer, editor, and real estate man until he was stricken by paralysis in 1917. He saw his lifelong support for women's suffrage rewarded in April, 1918, when Texas extended the franchise to women in primary races. He died, however, in March, 1919, only months before the ratification of the Nineteenth Amendment to the U.S. Constitution.

The senator from Smith County, James P. Douglas, was a South Carolinian who came to Tyler with his parents in 1848. His father died six years later, when James was seventeen. The young man capably took over the direction of the family's hotel and livery stable as well as the supervision of the mail contracts placed with such facilities. Having studied with a tutor, he began teaching at the local academy; he read law and was admitted to the bar; and he became part owner and editor of the *Tyler Reporter*. Except for the war years, Douglas kept his newspaper position until he entered the Senate in 1870.

Chosen first lieutenant of the Confederacy's Douglas-Good battery of artillery, he became captain a year later and in 1863 was promoted to major. The young officer survived fourteen battles, including Chickamauga and Missionary Ridge.

After the war Douglas energetically fostered the industrialization that Texas needed so badly. He commenced the Tyler Tap Railway as well as the Kansas and Gulf Short Line Railway; diversifying, he developed the fruit and trucking industry in Smith County and built the first canning factory in Tyler. In the mid-1870s, he engaged in the location, acquisition, and sale of underdeveloped lands in the West; he located about two million acres for the International and Great Northern Railroad alone. Douglas was an originator of the Texas and Saint Louis Railroad and managed to push it through to completion. He returned to the Senate for the Fifteenth Legislature. Twice married, Douglas had six children. He died in 1901.

The senator from District Twenty-one, Captain Samuel Evans, was a hardworking Kentuckian who had come to Texas and Tarrant

County in 1853 at the age of twenty-two. Evans purchased and farmed land in Tarrant County, traded ponies from Mexico, drove sheep to New Orleans, fought and scalped Indians, and otherwise engaged in such sundry occupations as were appropriate for a young frontiersman. When the Civil War broke out, he raised a company of cavalry, and two years later he became the only man to raise a company of infantry in Tarrant County, serving in the 21st Texas Regiment in the Trans-Mississippi Department. The war's end found him in Galveston, and from there he brought his command to Robertson County, where it disbanded. Evans resumed his former numerous activities and even added to them by becoming a cotton trader and by making the first cattle drive from Tarrant County to Kansas, which became a major distribution point for cattle being shipped to Saint Louis, Chicago, and Philadelphia. In 1866 he served in the Texas House. During the Twelfth and Thirteenth legislatures he served in the Senate, where he was instrumental in bringing seven railroads to Fort Worth and fought to reduce the high wharfage fees at Galveston. After these terms he was convinced of the corruption of both the Democratic and Republican parties and, like Dohoney, became a Greenbacker. He declined to accept the Greenback nomination for vice-president and became a member of the Populist party. Evans abstained from tobacco, alcohol, and dancing but refused to join a church. He fathered ten children in two marriages.

In the election following the ratification of the Constitution of 1869 and its acceptance by the federal government, Webster Flanagan easily won the Senate race in District Five, composed of Rusk and Panola counties. In the same election, his father, Major James Winwright Flanagan, was elected lieutenant governor, but the elder Flanagan was later selected by the legislature, along with Morgan Hamilton, to serve in the U.S. Senate. Webster Flanagan frequently served as president pro tempore during Don Campbell's illness and on Campbell's death was finally elected president pro tempore for the remainder of the Twelfth Legislature, serving ex officio in the office to which his father had been elected.

Before moving to Texas, the Flanagan family lived in Virginia and Kentucky. After Texas won her independence, Major James Flanagan made a commitment to the new republic. He sold out his ventures in the South and took his family to Henderson, Texas, when

Webster was eleven years old. There Major Flanagan prospered as a farmer, merchant, and lawyer, acquiring several thousand acres in the newly organized county. Webster grew up in Henderson and, under special act of the legislature, was admitted to the bar at the age of nineteen. He practiced law until the Civil War.

Elected to the House of the Fourth Legislature and then to the Senate of the Sixth, James W. Flanagan became close friends with Sam Houston, and by Houston's order on April 14, 1860, Webster Flanagan was appointed brigadier general in the 5th Brigade District of the Texas state troops. The Flanagans stood with Houston in opposing secession, and when the governor was forced to resign, the elder Flanagan temporarily retired from public life.

Because of their pro-Union views, the Flanagans were thought to be Yankee sympathizers. Yet, Major Flanagan set up a tannery which supplied the Confederacy for the duration of the war, and Webster Flanagan served in the Confederate cavalry until he was discharged with tuberculosis; he then served as chief justice of Panola County. After the war Webster Flanagan was frank about his ambitions. He told A. J. Hamilton, the first Reconstruction governor of Texas, "I want an office, and a good one. . . . I was one of the few who braved the storm of secession in my country." The Flanagans were popular in their district despite their Union and Republican allegiances, and they prevented the stationing of federal troops among their constituents by giving their word that the district was in good order.

James W. and Webster Flanagan were both delegates to the 1868–69 Constitutional Convention. They were dissatisfied with the resulting document and, along with many of the state's most prominent Radicals, signed a memorial to Congress urging the division of Texas into three states because of the existing civil disorder and the incompatibility of interests between the various regions.

His position in the memorial opposing violence did not, however, lead Webster Flanagan to support Davis's militia bill. Within the Senate and without, he fought against the far-reaching executive powers the bill provided. A railroad enthusiast, Flanagan also opposed Davis's resistance to state support of railroads, which achieved a high profile during the battle over the militia bill. As chairman of the Committee on Internal Improvements, Webster reported out of committee the most railroad legislation ever to come from that committee. He was reelected to the Senate of the Thirteenth and

Webster Flanagan, senator in Twelfth, Thirteenth, and Fourteenth legislatures, delegate to Constitutional Convention of 1868 and 1875. Reproduced from holdings of Texas State Archives.

Fourteenth legislatures and also served in the Constitutional Convention of 1875, the second time he helped to write a Texas constitution.

On completion of his second Senate term, Flanagan retired to go into business. He was noted for introducing blood stock to his stable and Island of Jersey cows to his dairy. He was a Mason and a Baptist, twice married, with numerous children born to both marriages. Described as a genial, deeply religious, and courtly man who never lost his zest for life, Webster Flanagan died on May 5, 1924, at the age of ninety-two.

S. W. Ford of Waco, a Radical Republican, was qualified from the Nineteenth District, composed of Falls, Limestone, and McLennan counties, after liberal Republican Andrew J. Evans was unseated in an election contest. Ford was chairman of the Committee on the Land Office. He served in the Confederacy, and his name, like those of Baker and Bell, was listed by the Committee on Political Disabilities. His profession was given as mechanic. Ford also served in the Senate of the Thirteenth Legislature.

Senator Abner K. Foster was born in Missouri in 1835. He was a staunch Unionist and a respected resident of Hallettsville who emerged during Reconstruction as one of the few "honest men" who could both gain widespread support and at the same time be eligible to take the oath of office in the immediate postwar years. During the military occupation he served variously as sheriff, county judge, and postmaster and was called upon to advise provisional governor A. J. Hamilton on appointments in the district. He was elected to the Senate from Lavaca and Colorado counties, District Twenty-five, and it was generally predicted that he would become a significant state leader. Fate, however, intervened. Just after the provisional session ended, Foster contracted pneumonia, and the young senator died abruptly at Hallettsville on March 9, 1870. The seat remained vacant during the called session and was then filled by Robert P. Tendick, a German merchant and Radical Republican from Columbus, who also served in the Senate of the Thirteenth Legislature. Tendick previously had served as county clerk for Colorado County.

The mysterious and controversial Albert Jennings Fountain rode into Texas after the Civil War. Originally from New York, he attended Columbia College, visited China, and covered the William

Walker expedition in Nicaragua as a newspaperman. He was admitted to the bar in California and served in the Union's California Column, which became an occupation force in New Mexico.

Married and with a family, Fountain at age twenty-seven served as a captain in Texas' Volunteer Cavalry and attained the rank of colonel in the territorial militia. He was wounded while fighting the Apaches and was sent to El Paso to recover. Settling his family in this border city, he began a law practice and helped organize the local Republican party. He served as county surveyor and collector of customs for the inland port of entry and prospered financially.

Not the typical carpetbagger, Fountain played an important role in the acculturation of the frontier. He is pictured by his contemporaries as a soldier, amateur actor, singer, playwright, U.S. district attorney, Indian scout and guide, militia officer, prospector, and newspaper editor and publisher, as well as a politician. While Colonel Fountain endorsed the Radical program of Reconstruction and was one of Governor Davis's most stalwart supporters, the issues which so affected Texans farther east were virtually irrelevant in his El Paso district because of the predominant Mexican population and the district's lack of historical or cultural ties to Texans with Southern interests.

Fountain's constituents sent him to the Senate in 1870, not because the majority of voters agreed with his political ideology, but because he promised to secure the local salt supply for El Paso County. Thus Fountain became a player in one of the violent little episodes that make Texas history so interesting—the Salt War. The salt deposits formed by the saline lakes at the foot of the Guadalupe Mountains had traditionally been used in common, but later arrivals laid individual claims to the salines and various factions emerged. The opening move by Fountain's opponents was a petition to the state Senate charging election fraud and requesting his removal. The attempt failed. Next, the same adversaries brought criminal charges of felony fraud allegedly committed when Fountain was collector of customs for El Paso. The senator was indicted on eighteen counts brought before the U.S. district court. For months, newspapers across the state printed vitriolic editorials to Fountain's detriment. Fountain, however, was acquitted, and *Flake's Bulletin*, one of Texas' popular publications, printed an apology and called for other editors to halt the "persecution."

Another conflict in which Fountain was involved resulted in violence. On December 7, 1870, Fountain was shot and wounded by Frank Williams, a local attorney and former political ally of the senator who had failed to receive a judicial appointment that Fountain controlled. The senator was hit three times, but items in his shirt pocket helped him survive a life-threatening shot to the chest. Shortly thereafter, Williams went on to murder Judge Gaylord Judd Clarke, the judge who had received the appointment he had sought, and was then shot to death himself. Fountain was still recovering from his wounds when he returned to Austin in January, 1871, for the regular session of the Twelfth Legislature.

During his four years in the Senate, Fountain chaired the committees on printing and on Indian affairs and frontier protection. He served as president pro tempore for a time during the spring of 1871 while acting president Campbell was ill. Serving as the floor leader for Governor Davis on several important legislative measures, notably the militia bill, Fountain played an important part in the Radicals' effort to shape the future of Texas.

In 1874 Fountain moved his family to Mesilla, New Mexico. He served in the New Mexico House of Representatives, edited the *Mesilla Independent*, and served as an assistant U.S. attorney. In 1896, while acting as counsel for the Cattlemen's Association, Fountain and his eight-year-old son made a trip from Las Cruces to Lincoln to collect some grand jury indictments against cattle thieves. On the way back to their remote home, Fountain and his young son drove their wagon into the White Sands of New Mexico and disappeared without a trace.

One of the most interesting figures in the Senate of the Twelfth and Thirteenth legislatures was Matthew Washington Gaines, a former slave born on the Despallier estate in Louisiana around 1840 and sold in 1859 to Christopher C. Hearne, a wealthy Texas planter on the Brazos River. At the time of his election to the Senate, Gaines was about thirty years old and was an ordained minister in Brenham. Self-educated, he said that a white child on the Louisiana plantation had smuggled books to him, which allowed him to begin his education. He was a gifted orator and engaged in frequent and telling debate on the Senate floor. He was a small man, standing a bit over five feet in height.

Gaines was a passionate defender of education for blacks and in-

Matthew Washington Gaines, senator in Twelfth Legislature, 1870, senator in Thirteenth Legislature, 1873. Courtesy State Preservation Board, Austin, Texas.

tegrated classrooms. According to the *State Journal* of March 30, 1871, during the debate on the school bill "Senator Gaines went through Senators [Webster] Flanagan and Dillard like a dose of salts." The two conservative colleagues had been warning about the problems of "mixed schools." Gaines replied that if they disapproved of the two races sitting side by side, they should resign from the Senate and leave the chamber at once—he added that he was not fond of their company either.

Gaines became such a firebrand as a speaker that Governor Davis had him expelled from the Republican party in October, 1871, after the press of both parties had condemned his contentious oratory. The loss of his party's sanction hastened Gaines's political end.

In December, 1871, Gaines was indicted for bigamy. His first marriage was to Fanny Sutton and had been performed by a lay minister; a visiting bishop of the church later told the members of that district that all marriages and baptisms which had been performed before that lay minister's subsequent ordination were invalid. The couple had separated, and Gaines and the people of his church believed he was a single man. The next year Gaines took out a second license and married Elizabeth Harrison without having divorced Fanny Sutton. While Gaines was awaiting trial, his repeated petitions to have his case heard in a federal court were denied. The case finally came to trial on July 15, 1873, in a state court, where Gaines was found guilty and sentenced to a year at hard labor. But on November 24, 1873, the Supreme Court of Texas reversed the finding, reprimanding the lower court, and Gaines was released. He was reelected to the Senate of the Fourteenth Legislature in a special election following T. G. Davidson's refusal to qualify. Gaines's opponent in the special election, Seth Shepard, challenged the election on the grounds that Gaines was a convicted felon. Senator Dillard, the object of Gaines's scorn in the school bill debate, was chairman of the Committee on Privileges and Elections. Gaines was not represented by counsel and was not given an opportunity to testify before the committee. On March 25, 1874, Dillard reported that Gaines was ineligible and recommended that Shepard be seated. Gaines no longer had the political connections to fight the decision. It was the end of his legislative career, and he retired to the life of a rural black minister. Gaines died on June 11, 1900.

Two children by his first marriage and six sons and two daughters from his second marriage survived him.

Elected from Robertson County in District Eighteen, Senator Phidello W. Hall drew a six-year term and returned for the Thirteenth Legislature. Hall had formerly been the postmaster at Calvert. With the help of Silas Cotton, the black representative from the district, Senator Hall successfully sponsored a resolution to move the county seat from Owensville to Calvert. The legislature designated Calvert as Robertson County's new seat on July 12, 1870. Hall also served on the Republican state executive committee for District Eighteen.

The senator from District Twenty-nine was Dr. Theodore Hertzberg of Menard. German colonists in Texas had built a solid economic base but had not exercised political power as an ethnic group; Dr. Hertzberg, however, was among those who were politically active. Hertzberg, who had settled in San Antonio in 1853, was a prominent Republican, and during the Twelfth Legislature he proved a reliable Radical. He served as chairman of the Committee on the Militia and was one of the four senators who independently voted against the Southern Pacific railroad bill. Senator Hertzberg drew a four-year term but resigned before the Thirteenth Legislature began. Hertzberg was listed among prominent Americans recommended to President Harrison for consular appointment in 1889. He was married to Emilie Grothaus, and they had three children.

Reinhard Hillebrand of Fayette County was chosen in a special election to succeed E. L. Alford after the dispute that got Alford permanently banished from the Senate and the Republican party. Hillebrand, who had been imprisoned by Confederates during the war, emerged as a bedrock social Radical who opposed business subsidies. He scandalized many when he was seen associating openly with black voters in a German beer hall. Hillebrand had some experience as a county judge in 1869 before his election to the Senate.

In 1834, when he was seventeen, Henry Russell Latimer came to Texas from Carroll County, Tennessee. Latimer fought in the Texas Revolution, went off to college, and returned to Texas to open a law office in Clarksville, Red River County. He married and moved to Lamar County, whose citizens elected him chief justice. A signer of the Texas Declaration of Independence in 1836, he went to the

Annexation Convention in 1845 as a member from Lamar and helped draft a constitution for the new state of Texas, which, he declaimed with true Texan hyperbole, was "then about to yield up its existence as a republic, the proudest and most undaunted in the world's history after Athens and Rome." Latimer moved back to Red River County a few years later and represented the Ninth District in the Senate during the Twelfth and Thirteenth legislatures. Latimer lived to be seventy and left thirteen children to mourn him.

John S. Mills of Grimes County, who was born in 1840, listed his occupation in 1870 as a farmer in Navasota. Senator Mills was an active member of the Republican party and had served as vice-president of the state Republican convention on June 9, 1869. Despite his prominence within the party, Mills in protest left the 1870 Republican caucus meeting that saw Senators Alford and Pridgen expelled in the fight over the militia bill. Contemporary newspapers intimated that Mills was brought back into line when his father, a doctor, was offered the position of superintendent of the blind asylum. Mills served as chairman of the Committee on Contingent Expenses. He drew a short Senate term and did not return to the Senate but was elected to the House in 1872. He was also a delegate to the Loyal Union League of America from Grimes County.

William Henry Parsons of Montgomery County was an attorney and former Confederate officer who by 1870 was affiliated with the Radicals. The son of a grocer, the future senator was born in 1826 in New Jersey, and the family moved to Montgomery, Alabama, in 1829. In his teens he entered Emory College at Oxford, Georgia, but in 1845 he left school and enlisted in the U.S. Army at Natchitoches, Louisiana. Parsons served in General Zachary Taylor's army in Mexico as a member of the 2nd U.S. Dragoons. In 1851 he married Louisa Dennard, and in 1852 the couple settled in Tyler, where Parsons became an owner and editor of the *Tyler Telegraph.* He was an ardent advocate of the state's commercial development and the building of a transcontinental railroad through Texas.

Parsons also became a fervent defender of states' rights, and he hastened to Austin during the Secession Convention. He was commissioned a colonel and was authorized to raise a cavalry regiment, ultimately the 12th Texas Cavalry, which became famous as Parsons' Brigade. His command came to include the 19th Texas Cavalry, the 21st Texas Cavalry, and the 10th Texas Field Battery. Several times during the war, Parsons was nominated to the rank of general, and though a dispute over precedence stopped the promotion, his men referred to him as "General Parsons" and so did many Texans.

Parsons was elected to the Senate of the Twelfth Legislature from District Fourteen as a Radical Republican. In the provisional session of the legislature he spoke in favor of immediate passage of the Fifteenth Amendment, saying that it was essential for the senators to speed the relief of their state and concluding, "It is more honorable for us as a man, to now affiliate, as we do, with the party which conquered us, than again affiliate with the party [i.e., the Democratic party] that betrayed us."

Parsons was a leader in the Senate, heading the Republican caucus together with Senator Fountain. Parsons maintained good relations with all factions: Governor Davis trusted him enough to name him for the position of major general of the state militia, and during the militia debate the bolters saw him as the man to communicate with the Radicals on their behalf. He served as chairman of the committees on immigration, state affairs, and gubernatorial nominations.

In 1871 Parsons was appointed U.S. centennial commissioner by President Ulysses S. Grant and moved to New York. He held numerous appointed positions in the federal government and lived in Virginia and Washington, D.C. Parsons died on October 3, 1907, in Chicago.

Elisha Pettit held the title of professor of ancient languages at Marshall University and served as president of that institution from 1852 to 1858. Elected from the largely agricultural District Four, the Republican senator opposed railroad subsidies and other costly measures, although he supported law and order and chaired the Committee on Education. He backed Davis's controversial militia and state police bills, and his speech in favor of the state militia bill provides some insight into the educator's view of the Republican party and his role in Austin. He proclaimed the Republican senators to be present "by the will of Providence to fulfill the high behests of . . . an age of reform." Pettit was among the four senators who independently voted against the Southern Pacific bill.

Colonel Edward Bradford Pickett had passed through Liberty on his way to the Mexican War, liked what he saw of Texas, and after the war brought his wife from Tennessee and settled in Liberty.

Pickett quickly became one of the town's leading lawyers and later served in the House in the Ninth Legislature. He was the owner of a small telegraph set, which he kept in his law office. During the Battle of Sabine Pass, the whole state awaited news of the attack. When a messenger on a handcar brought the news of Dick Dowling's amazing defeat of an entire federal fleet from a mud fort with fewer than thirty men, Pickett was able to relay the news to Houston on his telegraph. Shortly afterward, he organized a volunteer company in Liberty which fought for the Confederacy. After the war, Pickett served as a member of the Senate during the Twelfth and Thirteenth legislatures from District One, which consisted of Chambers, Hardin, Jasper, Jefferson, Liberty, Newton, Orange, Polk, and Tyler counties, and was elected president pro tempore of the Senate for the Thirteenth Legislature.

Pickett also voted "nay" on the Southern Pacific railway bill. When the Constitutional Convention of 1875 was called, Pickett was elected convention president on the first ballot. He served as president of the board of directors of the Agricultural and Mechanical College of Texas when it opened in 1876.

Bolivar Jackson Pridgen, a North Carolinian by birth, came to Texas with his family when he was ten years old. The Pridgens first settled in Harrison County but later moved to DeWitt County, which Bolivar represented in the Senate of the Twelfth Legislature as senator from District Twenty-four. Pridgen was a veteran of the Mexican War. His legislative efforts were directed toward the passage of a free public school bill and legislation for construction of the Gulf, Western Texas, and Pacific Railroad in DeWitt County. During his Senate term, he usually voted with the Radicals and he served as chairman of the Committee on Private Land Claims.

Pridgen was a party in the Sutton-Taylor feud, the longest and most lethal feud in the state's history. He became a Taylor partisan after his brother and nephew were killed by the Suttons, according to an account by Jack Hays Day, himself a Taylorite feudist. Pridgen moved across the state and became postmaster at Eagle Pass in 1889. He later returned to DeWitt County, where he died in 1903.

Historians of Cherokee County report that the election of 1869 was tumultuous. Amid charges that "the ballot boxes were stolen" and that Judge James E. Dillard had rightfully won, Mijamin (also Myaman) Priest was the senator that Cherokee and Houston counties actually sent to Austin. Like Dillard, Priest was a member of the Cherokee County bar. He had served as the delegate from Cherokee and Angelina counties to the Constitutional Convention of 1868–69.

Priest was born in Alabama on December 23, 1808, and was orphaned at an early age. He was elected to three terms in the Alabama Legislature in 1836, 1837, and 1838, after which he studied law. He had earlier served as justice of the peace in Lawrence County, where he and Mary Ann Hicks were married in 1832. The couple's marriage produced eleven children. In addition to his law practice, Priest held a Cumberland Presbyterian pastorate in Woodville, Texas, during the 1840s, moving to Rusk in 1850. Priest was the first pastor to serve the congregation of the Rusk Presbyterian Church. His service to the Confederacy is suggested by the fact that he had to take the amnesty oath and request that the franchise be restored to him. Two sons who fought for the Gray, Henry and William, died in an Illinois prisoner-of-war camp.

During his relatively brief career in the legislature, Senator Priest, who served as chairman of the Judiciary Committee, supported the administration. He led the floor battle for the militia bill, which the administration forced through on June 22, 1870. Shortly afterwards, Priest resigned his Senate seat to accept an appointment as judge of the Fourth Judicial District and was eventually succeeded by Dillard. Interestingly, it was Senator Dillard who later ramrodded removal proceedings against Priest through the Fourteenth Legislature. Priest was removed from the bench, and the elderly barrister retired to Rusk. M. Priest, as he always signed himself, died March 15, 1884, at the age of seventy-six.

Dr. William H. Pyle, the senator from Kaufman, Ellis, Hill, and Navarro counties, had served the Confederacy in General Walker's Division in the Trans-Mississippi Department as a field surgeon. The physician had migrated to Texas from Ohio, where his father, also a physician, was a close friend of the Union's secretary of war Stanton. In fact, the father, at the age of sixty, volunteered to serve as a Union surgeon, and Senator Pyle's two brothers served in the Union Army, one as brigadier surgeon of Carter's Cavalry. This division of families by political loyalties was one of the sad circumstances of the war. Senator Pyle served in the Twelfth and Thirteenth legislatures, where he was a proponent of railroad development and other industrial ventures which many felt were desperately needed in postwar Texas.

Senator Henry Rawson was elected to the Senate to represent Harrison County in the Twelfth and the Thirteenth legislatures. A native of England, he had lived in Marshall before the war but had held no office. Rawson chaired the Senate Committee on Claims and Accounts. Along with the two representatives from his district, he supported the Radicals.

George Thompson Ruby, a New Yorker by birth, had aspirations for black people which led him to Haiti, where he served as correspondent for *The Pine and Palm*, a Boston newspaper edited by James Redpath, a white man who advocated black separatism. By 1864, however, young Ruby's hope for his people in the United States had been rekindled by the course of the Civil War. He embarked for New Orleans, where he was appointed principal of a grade school in the city and soon became school agent for the state of Louisiana. After being severely beaten by a white mob in September, 1866, he obtained an educational appointment in Galveston through the Freedmen's Bureau and promptly left Louisiana.

In addition to his educational work, Ruby plunged into politics. He organized the harbor's dock laborers, joined the Republican party, cultivated a close relationship with future governor E. J. Davis, and joined the Loyal Union League, a political organization whose aims were to ensure that black men registered and voted and attained some understanding of their political rights. By 1868 Ruby had been appointed deputy collector of customs for Galveston, had risen to the presidency of the Loyal Union League, had been selected as the only black in the Texas delegation to the Republican National Convention, and had been elected a delegate to the Texas Constitutional Convention of 1868–69. In 1869 he established the Colored National Labor Convention to speak for nonfarm blacks.

Within four years of his arrival in Galveston, Ruby figured among the most important Republicans in Texas, and he became one of the administration's chief spokesmen in the Twelfth Legislature. On occasion, Ruby presided over the Senate when Don Campbell was absent, and under his direction the Judiciary Committee reported out bills that established a statewide school system and a board of education with both elected and appointed members. This militant legislator placated his white constituents by introducing bills which provided for the incorporation of the Texas Harbor Improvement and Dock Company and the appropriation of state funds for the improvement of the bar and harbor of Galveston.

Ruby and Matthew Gaines, the other black senator, differed in significant ways. Gaines was an agrarian and his constituency was basically agrarian. There were black workers in urban areas for whom he could not speak. It was George T. Ruby who spoke for them.

Ruby's Galveston County was cosmopolitan, bustling, tolerant, and amenable to biracial politics, so long as blacks did not become too demanding. Galveston businessmen wanted a series of Texas canals which reached inland to regions possessing raw materials, and they wanted stretches of railway to transport finished goods and connect Galveston with major rail routes. Questions of race or party politics were of less interest to them, and Ruby saw that if he used his considerable abilities in responsible advancement of white business interests, his goals for blacks would be acceptable to his district. He was quite judicious in his Galveston patronage, giving offices to so many whites that some people of color who aspired to position complained of him, but there was no issue affecting the improvement of blacks which the senator did not vigorously and effectively pursue.

The Radical Republican coalition accomplished little of permanence, other than Texas' readmittance to the Union, before it unraveled, and no other alliance could be molded which was capable of pursuing Ruby's social agenda. After the Thirteenth Legislature and the end of Radical control, Ruby saw no point in standing for reelection. He returned to New Orleans and later died there of malaria.

William A. Saylor, born in 1843, lived in Bryan. He was a member of the Radical faction of the Texas Republican party and was among the few who attended the rump state convention of Republicans sponsored by Morgan C. Hamilton in May, 1869. Saylor was elected to the Senate of the Twelfth Legislature from District Seventeen. In the Senate he occasionally opposed Governor Davis, including voting against the confirmation of Talbot as school superintendent and voting to override Davis on the repeal of the police bill in the Thirteenth Legislature. He chaired the Committee on Retrenchment and Reform.

Saylor was named to the Republican state executive committee in 1871 and the following year attended the Republican National Convention. In 1873, after redistricting, he was a Republican nominee for the state Senate in District Eighteen but was defeated. He continued to play an active role in Republican politics and as late as October 1, 1878, was permanent chairman of the state Republican convention.

George Ross Shannon, his brother, William R., and a sister, Sophie, were among the earliest settlers of Johnson County, Texas, arriving from Ohio in the early 1850s. The brothers signed the original petition to organize Johnson County. The Shannons were deeply involved in their developing Texas community and were engaged in farming, ranching, cotton ginning, milling, and, in Sophie's case, teaching. In the late 1850s, George was the third chief justice of Johnson County. He entered the Senate in 1870. Shannon voted against the militia bill and was arrested with the other senators who walked out of the chamber. He was one of four senators released the day after the walkout so that the Senate could obtain a quorum. In opposing the militia bill, Senators Shannon and Clark entered an expressive minority report on constitutional concerns into the *Senate Journal.* Shannon was generally counted among the Democrats. His brother, William, served five terms in the Senate.

William Henry Swift was born in Abbeville District, South Carolina, on March 12, 1816. His mother died, and the family began to move west when the boy was twelve, settling first in Alabama and then in Mississippi. By October, 1839, William and his brother Willis had settled in Nacogdoches County. In 1844 William married Nancy M. Walker, and prior to his war service they were reportedly farmers of meager means. When the Civil War began, Swift was among the first Confederate volunteers, serving with the 3rd Brigade of the Texas state troops. After the war he was elected sheriff of Nacogdoches County and served for several years. In a special election held October 3–6, 1871, Swift was elected to the Senate to fill the seat of the deceased Amos Clark. Senator Swift served in the Twelfth, Thirteenth, and Fourteenth legislatures. The length of his service indicates that he managed to satisfy the qualifying requirements of the Republicans and still appeal to the Democratic resurgence.

One Senate officer from 1871, Albert Richard Parsons, occupies a peculiar place in American history. Parsons, who had served as chief deputy of internal revenue collections in Austin, was elected second assistant secretary of the Senate during the regular session of 1871 and succeeded W. L. Chalmers in the position of first assistant secretary in the adjourned session. Nepotism was apparently not an issue during this time, as Albert Parsons was the younger brother of Senator William H. Parsons. Albert Parsons had served his brother's cavalry unit as a scout, and the youth actually participated in several skirmishes when he was only thirteen years old. Having served in the Texas Senate, he later moved to Chicago and became involved in the politics which led to the famous Haymarket Riot of 1886. As one of the speakers at the labor meeting that erupted into the riot, Parsons was convicted, along with six others, of inciting the riot. Most scholars believe that if he had appealed to the governor of Illinois for clemency, it would have been granted, but he refused to abandon his associates and was hanged in November, 1887.

Given the cast of characters, it is not difficult to understand why, at the provisional session which began in February, 1870, the Senate's discharge of its responsibility to elect U.S. senators did not proceed as smoothly as had its ratification of the Thirteenth, Fourteenth, and Fifteenth amendments. General Reynolds's fondest hope was to go to Congress as a senator from Texas, although he was not from Texas and lived in the state only as a member of the occupying forces; his opposition to the Hamilton Republicans and his embrace of the Davis Radicals sprang from A. J. Hamilton's brusque dismissal of that senatorial dream. Following the election of a majority of Radicals, Reynolds had considered himself a shoo-in because he had, to the extent possible, handpicked the legislature and certainly the governor. However, with the approaching readmission of Texas into the United States as a civil government on equal footing with her sister states, the military commander was losing much of his leverage. His candidacy was not taken seriously, and James W. Flanagan and Morgan Hamilton went to Washington as the first Texas senators to be seated in Congress since 1861.

On March 30, 1870, President Grant signed the act readmitting Texas to the Union. The iron-clad oath was repealed, though several senators who had served the Confederacy had to take the oath along with the oath of office when they were sworn in for the provisional session. General Reynolds, on April 16, 1870, formally brought military rule and Congressional Reconstruction to an end in Texas by returning authority to Governor Davis. The end of Reconstruction was in plain sight, almost from the day of Davis's inauguration.

The Republicans in the Senate of the Twelfth Legislature were by no means united in their support of Governor Davis. Although the governor-elect entered office with a conciliatory speech, the fractious situation rapidly led Davis to display a characteristic stubbornness. At one point, in order to push through Davis's controversial militia bill, Don Campbell, the president pro tempore of the Senate, was required to place nearly half the senators under temporary arrest.

The Radicals used such tactics to force the passage of several bills that inflamed popular opinion against all Republicans and intensified a conservative Democratic backlash after Governor Davis had served only one term. Termed "obnoxious acts," these measures gave broad powers to the governor for reimposing martial law; created a state police force under Davis's command; permitted Davis to appoint men to fill vacant elective offices, a powerful tool for patronage; postponed the general elections until 1872, thereby ensuring another year for the Davis administration; and created a subsidized press for the Radicals through the election of J. G. Tracy as state printer. Tracy founded the *State Journal* in Austin in February, 1870, and appointed Texas' secretary of state, the Radical journalist James Newcomb, as editor.

Ironically, Davis, who had entered office with a plea for responsible partisan politics, would later be defeated by a coalition of embittered liberal Republicans and conservative Democrats. John Henry Brown, a legislator and Texas historian who lived during the period, said that Governor Davis "was never believed to be guilty of personal dishonesty, and that he was a man of good private character, and gentlemanly deportment as a citizen has never been denied by those who knew him. But most of his advisors were men wholly unworthy of being such in such a crisis. He forfeited the friendship of some of the most able and honest men of his party" and became, with the possible exception of Santa Anna, the most detested man in Texas history.

The third phase of Reconstruction in Texas, the period of Radical rule, began with Governor Davis's summoning of the called session of the Twelfth Legislature to meet on April 26, 1870. Secretary of State Newcomb gaveled the Senate to order and read the section of the newly adopted state constitution requiring the senators to elect a president of the Senate to become the lieutenant governor ex officio to replace James W. Flanagan, who had gone to Washington as a senator from Texas. The next day, Senator Campbell was elected as president pro tempore, with only two dissenting votes. W. H. Baker was elected the new enrolling clerk, and several days later J. W. Tays was elected chaplain.

As the senators had been elected all at once and under the new constitution, it was necessary for them to draw lots for their terms so that future terms would be staggered. On May 2, Senator Campbell, the president of the Senate, ordered the sergeant-at-arms to bring him thirty white marbles, numbered two, four, and six. A blindfolded page drew a marble for each senator, and in that manner each received a two-year, four-year, or six-year term. The drawing was at high noon the same day. Receiving six-year terms were Baker, Broughton, Campbell, Evans, Gaines, Hall, Latimer, Rawson, Ruby, and Saylor; receiving four-year terms were Clark, Cole, Dohoney, Flanagan, Ford, Fountain, Hertzberg, Pickett, Pyle, and District Twenty-five, which was vacant; and drawing two-year terms were Alford, Bell, Bowers, Douglas, Mills, Parsons, Pettit, Pridgen, Priest, and Shannon.

As part of the inaugural festivities on April 28, Governor Davis's old unit, the 1st Texas Cavalry, held a reunion barbecue in his honor, and practically everyone of note in Austin turned out. Davis's inaugural address included a plea that Texans lay aside old distinctions such as "loyal and disloyal" and called for "a fresh departure in political affairs." Of course, the governor conceded, differences would continue, but he urged that issues be debated in an atmosphere of "mutual toleration." He also expressed his opinion of military occupation as an "unpleasant necessity" and expressed the hope that "the same has passed away, never again in our history to return." Ironically, it was to be his own push for the power to suspend habeas corpus that would resurrect the threat of military rule and eliminate the possibility of "mutual toleration" between Democrats, Republicans, and independents in Texas.

In a second message, on April 29, 1870, Governor Davis explained his objectives to the Senate, declaring the state's finances sound but requesting reorganization of the taxation and collection system in order to provide for future improvements. He called for the establishment of civil order as the matter of greatest importance. The scheme Davis proposed included a provision for an elite organization, which he called a "National Guard," within a re-created militia. He also requested statutory authorization to impose martial law in two types of districts: those areas where outlaws congregated and counties where violent "mobs of lawless men" were "assembling and operating in disguise" (an obvious reference to the Ku Klux Klan and similar organizations). Livestock thieves were another target, as Davis requested the creation of a system to prevent such theft. Along with the refurbishment of the state asylum and hospital system, Davis proposed the return of all convicts to the state prison at Huntsville, there to be put to work. He also asked for a state police force and the imposition of special taxes to build more county jails. Schools, too, would aid in reducing the incidence of crime. Finally, he said there was "no good reason why deadly weapons should be permitted to be carried on the person," except in some frontier counties, and called for restrictive laws. More than a century later the issues of importance to Texas remain the same.

Also of great importance to Governor Davis was the establishment of a public school system, as "no better civilizer has been found than a liberal system of education." The public school fund needed to be replenished and augmented; only two railroad companies had made even a token payment on their loans against the school fund since the Civil War. In the meantime, nothing had been accomplished in education. Legislation was needed to enact the provisions of the new constitution for the support of public education.

At the same time, Davis urged the legislature to provide for internal improvements, including railroads, through supportive legislation, but he asked the members not to encumber the state by extending financial aid. Davis believed that, beyond the issuance of a liberal charter and the granting of rights-of-way, state aid to railroads was not necessary. The single exception he entertained would be a trunk road extending from the Red River to the Rio Grande in order to further communication with other states.

The passage of legislation addressing civil order, education, and internal improvements, as requested by the governor, was delayed by the Senate's preoccupation with organizing electoral government within the framework dictated by the new state constitution and the

Republican party. Meanwhile, the initial spirit of cooperation among the members began to dissipate. Senator Latimer, a Democrat, was accused of having served in the Confederate government of Texas. He denied it on his "honor as a Senator," so the Committee on Privileges and Elections, which consisted of Baker, Clark, Cole, Gaines, and Hertzberg, postponed its decision indefinitely and allowed him to remain in the Senate. Shortly afterward, however, new documentation was found in the governor's office indicating clearly that Latimer had accepted a Confederate commission, and the case was reopened on a motion by Republican senator Fountain in June, 1870, despite Democratic senator Douglas's attempts to block him. Latimer countered with a resolution calling for an investigation of Republican senator Rawson's credentials. In the majority report delivered on June 28, 1870, Republican senator Baker, chairman of the Committee on Privileges and Elections, declared that Rawson was a registered voter and entitled to his seat and rejected the accusation from his defeated opponent, John M. Waskom, that Rawson was ineligible because of the residency requirement. The Senate adopted the committee's recommendation on Rawson and allowed the investigation of Latimer to lapse.

The challenges over credentials and vote fraud spurred the governor to propose to the Senate that it endorse several measures to protect and, not incidentally, control the ballot box. The Senate responded with an act for the registration of voters authorizing Governor Davis to appoint district registrars to supervise the proceedings and administer a loyalty oath to each applicant. Furthermore, the law specified that "if, from his own knowledge, or from evidence brought before him, the registrar shall feel satisfied that a person is disqualified from registering, though he may have taken the oath of loyalty and citizenship, he shall strike the name of such person from his list of qualified voters." Those that he disqualified could be heard by a board of appeals and revision, which would meet before the election was held. The appellate board, like the registrars, was appointed by the governor. This was one of the "obnoxious acts" passed by the Radicals.

The centralization of control over the polls was further extended by a House bill for the conduct of elections and the "protection and purity of the ballot box." It barely passed the Senate by a vote of twelve to eleven, with four senators absent and Campbell and Ford refusing to vote; Davis signed it on August 15, 1870. The House bill provided that general elections would be held every two years, the first to be held in November, 1872, rather than in the fall of 1870 as originally scheduled. Ballots were to be handed, in person, to one of the appointed judges of election, who was to ensure that no unqualified voter cast a ballot and that no person took a ballot from a voter and handed it to a judge. The judges were authorized to close all saloons within two miles of the polls and to arrest those who carried weapons within a half mile of the ballot box. Those who caused a disturbance near a poll were guilty of a felony, a category of crime which was expanded to include vote fraud and deliberate intimidation of voters.

This election law, because of its postponement of general elections until 1872, became the second of the obnoxious acts of the Twelfth Legislature so bitterly condemned by the Democrats. Certainly the cancellation of elections in the fall of 1870 and 1871, which had as its only and obvious goal the extension of Davis's Radical administration, was of dubious constitutionality. Democratic outrage was compounded by a third obnoxious act of June 28, 1870, which empowered the governor to appoint a district attorney for each judicial district until the next election and to appoint in each county a treasurer, a surveyor, hide and cattle inspectors, public weighers of cotton, a sheriff, and a district clerk. Davis could also appoint a mayor and a board of aldermen for each city or town, and in the case of Houston and Galveston a city recorder as well. Only vacancies in the offices of state senator or representative would be filled by special election.

Besides establishing civil order, other areas of immediate concern were finance, infrastructure, and taxation. The state held some county taxes, and on June 15, 1870, Governor Davis signed an act requiring their return to the counties to which they were due. On August 4, 1870, legislation was approved authorizing counties to levy a road tax for building and maintaining roads and bridges, and additional legislation extended to the police court of each county the power to levy ad valorem taxes for the construction and maintenance of public buildings. Also, the police courts were authorized to levy a special annual tax for the retirement of county debts. The final act concerning state finances passed by the called session of the Twelfth Legislature, signed on August 15, permitted police courts to levy up to one-half the amount of the state occupation, ad valorem, and poll taxes.

The state government would reap benefits from a variety of new taxes. A bill signed on August 15, 1870, provided a comprehensive tax program that included an ad valorem tax, a poll tax, a tax on the gross profits of railroad, insurance, and telegraph companies, an occupation tax, and personal property taxes. During the regular session of the Twelfth Legislature, on April 22, 1871, this act was repealed in favor of a more detailed measure that included a provision for "an annual poll tax of one dollar" on all men between twenty-one and sixty years of age for the benefit of the public school fund.

The new taxes were intended to support the development of the state without being a burden on the populace or on important institutions. Exemptions from taxation included all property belonging to institutions for education or religious worship, fire companies, and cemeteries. Every head of household was entitled to an exemption of $250 in personal property and could retain two hundred acres of farmland or town lots worth $5,000, as well as books, household and kitchen furniture, tools for a trade, implements of husbandry, one gun, and the livestock, saddlery, and provisions necessary for a family or an individual to survive.

Such considerations limited the initial impact of tax reforms and necessitated new bond issues, despite Governor Davis's desire to reduce debts. The regular session of the Twelfth Legislature authorized the printing of four hundred thousand dollars in bonds bearing 10 percent interest. Another law passed during that session created a temporary Auditorial Board, composed of the attorney general, comptroller, and treasurer, to review claims against the state, with all valid suits to be paid in twenty-year coupon bonds yielding 6 percent interest. On the final day of the adjourned session, Governor Davis signed another bill that permitted him to issue up to two million dollars in additional bonds bearing 7 percent annual interest. These issues to pay for public services, together with a panoply of bond issues that legislators (against Governor Davis's advice) granted to railroad companies, contributed to a mounting debt that became a powerful propaganda tool for the Democrats in the upcoming elections.

During the war, the railroads' repayments on their loans from the school fund had been in Confederate money, which was worthless, and after the war, only two companies had made any interest payments on their loans. The railroads' nonpayment increased Davis's suspicion that the companies' agenda was to fleece the state. Davis pointed out that generous charters and terms had been issued to a number of railroad companies before the war but that only about five hundred miles of track had been laid although a great deal of money had been transferred in the market.

In May, 1870, Senator Flanagan introduced a bill into the Senate to encourage internal improvements, especially railroad construction. Because of the vexation of Davis and other Radicals with industry, however, it was not until after the legislature met on April 12, 1871, that counties and municipalities were authorized to encourage such development by issuing 10 percent bonds, for which an annual tax on all real and personal property of not less than 2 percent would be levied to pay the interest. By that time, a coalition of liberals and Democrats had "fused" and obtained a majority in the Senate and even some Radical Republicans perceived railroads to be necessary.

Rebuilding frontier defense, another high-cost project that added to the state debt, was of great importance to settlers in West Texas, who were perched precariously on a retreating frontier. In 1860, due to the "greatest aggregation of fighting men that ever represented the U.S. Army in the Old West—The Second Cavalry," the frontier had been virtually pacified; as Sam Houston had warned, however, during the Civil War and the following years several warlike tribes—the largest of which were the Comanches—had resumed hostilities and in places pushed the frontier eastward some one hundred miles. The Comanches, located mainly toward the west and northwest, were ruthless in raiding and kidnapping, and groups of Kiowa and Cheyenne were almost as fierce. At least one hundred Texans were believed to have been murdered or kidnapped by Indians in a five-year period shortly after the war. Although that figure seems paltry when compared with the homicide rate, it outraged white settlers, as did reports of torture, rape, and disfigurement and the pitiful condition of returned captives. The senators whose districts were hardest hit by Indian marauders and cattle thieves were Bowers, Broughton, Fountain, Hertzberg, Pridgen, and Shannon.

The repacification of the frontier would require ten to fifteen years. One of the first acts approved by the Senate of the Twelfth Legislature authorized the muster of twenty companies of Texas Rangers, each containing sixty-two men enlisted for twelve months. Although a few companies formed, real organization never materialized because of a lack of funds. In November, 1870, Davis resorted to forming companies of twenty "minute men" in each of the frontier counties from the Red River to the Rio Grande, but these units proved insufficient.

A joint resolution on the subject of Indian depredations, which had originated in the Texas House, was sent to the U.S. Congress on May 24, 1870. The Texans demanded that Congress compel the Republic of Mexico to stop harboring bands of Lipan and Kickapoo Indians who raided along the border with impunity. Three days later, another resolution was sent to the members of the Texas congressional delegation, urging them to secure the passage of legislation for frontier defense by the federal government. Nine months later, Senate Joint Resolution No. 27, passed March 15, 1871, invited a delegation from Congress to visit the Texas frontier and see for itself the results of the "hellish work of murder, outrage, and plunder" conducted by the Lipan and Kickapoo.

At that time, Congress and the military in Texas under General Sherman distrusted Texans and thought that Westerners' accounts of Indian raids were exaggerated. In April, 1871, however, Sherman decided to go on a tour of inspection to see what the outcry was about. While the general was at Fort Richardson in Jack County, a teamster who had escaped from a massacre of a wagon train was brought in wounded. Indians on the warpath had killed the wagon master and five teamsters and had scalped and roasted to death a sixth, in what came to be known as the Salt Creek Massacre. From then on Sherman supported Texas' requests for military assistance, but later memorials to Congress pleading for help with the Indian problem were ignored like the earlier ones.

At the time of its first resolution on the Indian problem, the Twelfth Legislature was already addressing issues concerning law and order in general through its efforts to establish the kind of militia that Governor Davis felt was essential. On May 6, 1870, Senator Hertzberg had introduced a bill to reorganize the state militia that included provisions for a unique "state guard" and for executive imposition of martial law, but it was laid on the table in favor of a more coherent House bill.

This militia bill passed the following month, but only after causing a divisive struggle in the Senate as well as within the Radical faction of the Republican party. For the Radical governor Davis, passing this bill was imperative in order to reduce the high crime rate. Webster Flanagan, who had for years been a solid Radical, nevertheless led the opposition to the militia bill because of its clauses allowing Davis to impose martial law. Cost was part of the reason some Republicans opposed the reorganized militia and state police, but the outspoken black senator Matthew Gaines believed that racism was at the heart of the opposition, since many of the militiamen would be black. All of the Senate, and indeed all the interested parties in Austin and throughout the state, realized that passing the bill would be difficult.

At a Republican caucus held on May 17, Senators Pridgen and Alford announced their opposition to the militia bill and were ousted from the meeting. Alford was soon expelled from the Republican party. Senator Mills left after the dismissal of Pridgen and Alford, and Senator Priest, who supported the bill, was absent from that caucus. On June 14, when Senator Pyle received word that his wife was ill, he was granted permission to pair his vote with that of Senator Priest. The vote remained uncertain and the administration faced possible defeat on the bill.

To make his resolve clear, Davis announced that he would veto any private bills appearing on his desk before his militia legislation. The House, which was more organized than the Senate in its support of the administration, ceased to act on pending legislation and instead went on to debate the printing bill. Two pieces of railroad legislation consequently came to a standstill. Webster Flanagan then offered to support the militia bill in return for passage of his Southern Pacific bill, but this offer was not acceptable to Davis. Some of Davis's men in the House and Senate, however, did work behind the scenes and promised support for the railroads in return for support on the militia bill.

On June 16, 1870, Webster Flanagan proposed a substitute militia bill without the offending sections, but it failed to pass. Priest then spoke in favor of the militia bill as passed by the House, which included the provision for suspending the writ of habeas corpus.

Priest in a debate on June 17 said that Texas existed in a state of war with bandits and Indians and insisted that "a desperate disease requires a desperate remedy." Civil disobedience was widespread, and some counties had turned into havens for outlaws who ranged over a wide area. A report from Secretary of State Newcomb, requested by the Senate, revealed that reported killings in Texas had increased sevenfold over a few years.

Both Flanagan and Priest—and their respective followers—agreed that Texas suffered from an appalling frequency of violent crime, but they differed in their solutions to the problem. Flanagan continued to argue for strengthening the civil courts, while Priest was willing to cast aside civil liberties in order to impose order through military measures. Priest's lack of faith in the civil courts may have been attributable to some cases in which local lawmen were afraid to arrest or prosecute offenders and some trials in which juries returned blatantly biased verdicts. If gubernatorial authorization to suspend the writ of habeas corpus had not been included in the militia bill, the Senate might have voted for it, even though public feeling clearly favored entrusting law enforcement to local authorities in every situation.

The debate on the militia bill continued on June 21, when Flanagan introduced his previously defeated bill as a substitute to the House measure. When he lost his motion to substitute, Flanagan tried for an adjournment. According to a sworn statement by Senator Parsons, Fountain then moved for a vote on the House bill, ending the debate. When the vote was called by roll, Alford, Baker, and Bell voted, but when Senator Bowers's name was reached he rose from his chair without replying to his name and walked rapidly to the main exit, motioning to other senators to follow. Flanagan and Alford responded at once, followed by Broughton, Clark, Cole, Dohoney, Douglas, Evans, Latimer, Pickett, Pyle, and Shannon. As the lobbies were crowded with the public and the press, the dissidents convened privately in a nearby committee room to discuss strategy.

Within the Senate chamber, Ruby moved a call of the Senate, as making a quorum was impossible without some further action. Campbell ordered the sergeant-at-arms, Captain A. Faulkner, to summon the absent senators. The Senate rule on the point stated, as the current rule states, that the sergeant-at-arms could be sent to arrest absent senators to secure a quorum. Faulkner went through the halls to the committee room door, but the bolters had locked it from the inside and he could not get in. Faulkner, having been instructed by Campbell to retrieve at least four senators, crept up to a window in the room and flung himself through it, despite the efforts of the runaways to close the shutters on him. He eventually persuaded them to return to the Senate chamber.

To their surprise, nine of them were placed under continued arrest. The other four (Evans, Shannon, Dohoney, and Alford) were allowed to remain—enough to complete the quorum—and these four, along with Pridgen, proved to be the only senators to vote against passage of the militia bill to a third reading. The next day, June 22, 1870, Alford pled illness, so Pyle was released from arrest, and he joined Evans, Shannon, Dohoney, and Pridgen in making a futile attempt to prevent final passage of the measure, which was passed within minutes.

During the confinement of the arrested members, the remainder of the Senate took full advantage of their absence to pass as many of Davis's bills as could be rushed through the legislature. The House bill to establish a state police force was passed on June 28, 1870, and the appointment as adjutant general of James Davidson, who unfortunately would later abscond with thirty thousand dollars in state money, was confirmed.

On June 22, 1870, after the militia bill was passed and the state police bill was read for the first time, Fountain introduced a motion establishing a committee to investigate the allegation that the bolters had conspired to defeat "reconstruction and the organization of the State government." Latimer and Pickett were soon cleared, but several senators remained under arrest for three weeks. Fountain, Parsons, Saylor, Baker, and Hall, who sat as the committee, also reviewed accusations that senators had sold their votes, and considerable testimony about conspiracy and vote buying was taken, including a carefully phrased statement from former governor Throckmorton that at one point he had the "impression" that John Hancock was offering money for votes against the militia bill. Other testimony put the rumored figure at three thousand dollars for a "nay" vote. A detective hired by Governor Davis to conduct a sting operation testified that Judge Hancock had promised to provide him with a considerable sum of money for the bribes if he could buy votes or prevent any senators from being present at the vote. The detective added that before the vote on the bill, however, he had only gotten as far as offering Saylor a bribe, which the senator turned down. The testimony of William M. Walton, chairman of the Democratic executive committee, indicated that the bribe money was supposed to be provided by "the railroad interest." On the matter of conspiracy, two friends of Bowers testified that, some days before the vote, they had run into the senator on an afternoon walk and he had spoken of mass resignations if the bill were put through, but, they said, they took the remark to be "bravado."

On June 24 a letter of protest signed by Dohoney, Evans, Pridgen, and Shannon argued that the Senate had never been empowered to hold senators under punitive arrest, and on June 25 Dohoney, Evans, Parsons, Pyle, and Saylor failed to appear. Because the *Senate Rules* for the Twelfth Legislature provided that an absent senator could be arrested to complete a quorum, Dohoney's arrest was ordered; he was in the Senate chamber on Monday, June 27, explaining to an amused Senate that he had thought it imperative to go shopping for a horse. Parsons did not appear until brought to the chamber under arrest. He was released on a motion by Fountain in order to make a quorum, as Dohoney had been ordered to remain under arrest.

On July 14, in compliance with a resolution on the subject of the bolt, Senators Bowers, Broughton, Clark, Dohoney, Douglas, Evans, Flanagan, Latimer, Pyle, and Shannon filed a disclaimer to "all premeditated design to break a quorum, and prevent the enactment of laws and the organization of the State, or intentional contempt of the Senate" and successfully requested to "be permitted to resume their seats and their functions as Senators."

All of the accused senators were eventually exonerated except Alford. Webster Flanagan, who had performed the lion's share of work in stirring up the affair but was too powerful to be penalized, recorded a written protest of Alford's expulsion. However, the select investigating committee found that "Senator Alford did, in contempt of the Senate, violently resist said arrest, and did forcibly close the shutters, and did refuse to submit to said arrest by the Sergeant-at-Arms," and this finding provided a material basis for the fifteen-to-five vote which expelled the senator on June 29, 1870, two weeks before most of the other rebels were readmitted to the Senate. Even had the arrested senators been present and voting, however, the outcome would have been the same because fifteen was a majority.

On their release, the bolters—along with Parsons, who had decided to change his earlier vote, and Pridgen—reinstated Alford by a vote of fifteen to twelve on July 30 through a resolution introduced by Cole. The matter was then referred to the attorney general. On August 1, eleven Radicals who opposed the reinstatement of Alford signed a protest which contended that the expulsion of a senator was irrevocable, offering as proof the fact that there was no procedure for reestablishment. Alford himself continued to appear for roll calls and participated in each day's business. Davis, however, agreed with the dissenters and ordered an election to fill the vacancy. No faction even nominated Alford in the special election, as he was truly a man without a party. Reinhard Hillebrand, a Radical, was the victor. Nevertheless, when the regular session convened in January, 1871, Alford continued to take his seat, while Hillebrand waited in the wings. Alford's presence in the Senate became a rallying point for liberal Republicans and Democrats alike.

Some historians have provided a different interpretation of the events surrounding the arrest of the thirteen senators, but a clear understanding of tactics used in the legislative process and the purpose and intent of the rule providing for a "call of the Senate" is missing in that interpretation. Attempts to describe the walkout as an "illegal" act exaggerate a practice that has often been used by the minority when faced with legislation they were unable to defeat. Related to the filibuster in purpose, breaking a quorum to prevent passage of controversial legislation is not as common today as it was in earlier times, though there is the well-known "Killer Bee" incident during the Sixty-sixth Legislature in 1979.

The rule authorizing a call of the Senate goes back to the days of the Republic and remains virtually unchanged today. The purpose of the rule was and is "to secure or maintain a quorum" and was never intended to be used as a punitive measure or to detain a senator for any purpose other than to secure a quorum. The arrest of the thirteen absent senators was certainly within the rules, but the detention and denial of attendance and participation in Senate deliberations of some for up to three weeks was contrary to the intent of the rule and to the democratic process. Historically, this is the only incident where senators were arrested under a call of the Senate but were, instead of being taken to the chamber to obtain a quorum, prohibited from rejoining their fellow senators and from participating in Senate votes. While there may be more to the opposition to the militia bill and to accusations of attempted bribery by railroad lobbyists than previously recognized, the abuse of the rule and the continued detention of the bolters was an oppressive act by the Radical majority.

Under the new militia and state police acts, all males from eighteen through forty-five years of age were required to register for militia duty, with some specific exceptions: judges and justices of the peace, clergy, teachers, regular military personnel, veterans of five years or more of active service in the militia or state guard of Texas, or those serving in the state police. A supplemental act added telegraph operators to the list of those exempted. A nonexempt individual could avoid service only by paying fifteen dollars, but this was lowered to five dollars in an act signed April 12, 1871. The militia was divided into two classes: the state guard of Texas and the reserve militia. The state guard consisted only of volunteers; the reserve militia included all those eligible for duty who did not enlist in the state guard. In practice, the state guard enlisted mainly blacks and Republicans. Both the state guard and the reserve militia served only at the command of Governor Davis. The governor could call these units into active service not only in the case of war, rebellion, insurrection, and invasion, but also whenever there was any resistance to a "civil process" or a "breach of the peace or imminent danger thereof." Davis could also declare any and all counties under martial law in order to suppress "disorder."

The state police force was intended to deal with disorder in settled areas. The force was authorized to enlist 258 officers and men, and an amendment signed May 2, 1871, permitted the governor to muster as many as 20 "special policemen" in each county. The regular state police were under the nominal command of Adjutant General Davidson but could be dispatched by order of the governor. Local law officers, such as sheriffs, deputies, constables, marshals, and town policemen, were considered auxiliaries of the state police and therefore were under the command of Governor Davis and the adjutant general.

Resentment toward the state police became epidemic despite the service of exceptional officers such as L. H. McNelly and his special force of Rangers. Much of the friction was racial: about 40 percent of the force was black. Adding to the problem was the fact that some of the state police troops were of poor quality and that such men could be arbitrary in their actions. During its existence, the state police did weed out many less competent lawmen and worked to upgrade the corps's professionalism. Overall, their efforts helped tone down Texas' pandemic violence and even earned occasional praise from conservative newspapers.

But most Texans felt only resentment on the three occasions when Davis used his power to declare martial law. On January 11, 1871, the governor imposed martial law in Hill County, where a mob had prevented local authorities from pursuing two murderers and had even pressured county officials into arresting state police troopers who had tried to intervene. Martial law was next imposed in Walker County, where a mob had helped convicted murderers escape from authorities. The declaration was made on February 20 by Adjutant General Davidson; the governor had sent Davidson to Walker County to evaluate the situation because the imposition of martial law in Hill County had caused a hostile reaction.

On another occasion, during the congressional elections held October 3–6, 1871, which were won by the Democrats, serious intimidation of voters occurred in several counties, and in several others charges of vote fraud were made by both sides. The board of state canvassers threw out the votes of several counties, but the results changed only in District Three, where the Democrat, William T. Clark, contested the seat and eventually got it. Civil unrest in the district erupted into a crisis, and on October 10, 1871, Governor Davis transmitted to the Senate copies of a proclamation in which he declared martial law in Limestone and Freestone counties. Davis also fined Limestone County fifty thousand dollars.

On October 10, Senator Douglas introduced a resolution "to inquire into the authority of the Governor proclaiming martial law in Limestone County during the sitting of the Legislature," and the Senate referred the matter to a committee for investigation. The governor's proclamation was withdrawn on November 11 without notice to the legislature. Although the lengthy testimony given before the Senate during its investigation supported the governor's description of the profound crisis that came to grip these counties, many senators felt that martial law was unacceptable under any circumstances, and a generally outraged public agreed.

The activities of the Ku Klux Klan, the Knights of the Golden Circle, the Knights of the White Camellia, and various paramilitary organizations especially worried the governor and the senators. In April, 1871, Congress passed the Ku Klux Klan Act, which permitted the president of the United States to suspend the writ of habeas corpus and declare martial law if it was deemed necessary to combat secret societies. In Austin a special act, signed on November 6, 1871, targeted Klan-like activities by providing that those who assembled in disguise for the purpose of coercing any citizen could be fined up to one thousand dollars. The fine would be doubled if the meeting took place at night or if the conspirators were armed.

Additional acts prohibited civilians from carrying deadly weapons—specifically, concealed pistols, knives, slingshots, brass knuckles, or spears—unless they could demonstrate that they were in "immediate and pressing" danger of an assault; the threat had to be unprovoked, and the burden of proof lay with the defendant. Repeated offenses could bring a jail term of up to sixty days. Regardless of any present danger, a person who took weapons into a public assembly, such as a church service, exposition, ball, or election, could be fined up to five hundred dollars. With such broad laws for reducing violent crime in Texas, the state police remained busy; by September 17, 1871, they had reported 3,475 arrests.

If convicted, these offenders had to be jailed somewhere or put to work. A committee of investigation from the Senate reported conditions at the state penitentiary to be good and treatment of the prisoners to be humane. What was needed was a system to make the state prison self-supporting. On March 22, 1871, Davis signed a House bill authorizing the governor to lease the state penitentiary for a term of not less than ten nor more than fifteen years. The lessee would have the sole authority to direct the labor of the convicts according to the laws of the state. The governor would appoint an "inspector of the penitentiary" who would supervise the management of the state prison and the treatment and discipline of the inmates and file a report every month.

Convicts had produced nearly all of the scanty supply of cloth during the war, and convict labor had built most of the five hundred miles of railroad track constructed in Texas thus far. Davis, however, suggested that the practice had too many drawbacks, given the record of successful escapes. In May, 1870, Senator Latimer had introduced a resolution that provided for the construction of two branch penitentiaries, one east of the Trinity and north of the thirty-second parallel, the other near San Marcos. His proposal was endorsed by the Senate Committee on Penitentiaries, chaired by Hall, and a number of petitions were received offering land for another prison, but the idea came to naught.

As for the railroads, Governor Davis vetoed Webster Flanagan's Southern Pacific railroad bill when it arrived on his desk, an act which wounded Flanagan so much that the longtime Radical proclaimed that if he had known Davis would reject his railroad bill, he would never have supported him in the first place. Although the railroad companies' failure to repay their loans had provoked Davis, his main objection to this bill was that, at a time when so many citizens lacked the bare necessities, there was no need for the state to capitalize a private corporation capable of getting all the money necessary from Wall Street. The Senate overrode Davis's veto, with only Fountain, Gaines, Hall, Hertzberg, Latimer, Pettit, Pickett, Priest, and Saylor in opposition. The House, however, sustained the veto.

Another bill for the relief of the Southern Pacific was introduced by Parsons; this was combined with a bill for the relief of the Southern Transcontinental Railway Company by Senator Saylor, the new chairman of the Committee on Internal Improvements. Davis vetoed this measure as well on May 24, 1871, but he was overridden by both houses. In his veto message the governor emphasized that for thirty years Texas would be saddled with a debt load that was larger than all the expenses required to run the state. The reduced version of the original bill, entitled "an act to encourage the speedy construction of a railway through the State of Texas to the Pacific Ocean," offered three million dollars in bonds to each of the corporations for a line from each western terminus in Texas to a junction in Shackelford County. The bonds for the Southern Pacific and the Southern Transcontinental were later traded for land grants. In the next session another law was passed which amended the Southern Pacific and Southern Transcontinental Railroad Company legislation; although Governor Davis still did not approve of the original act, the amendments were more to his liking and he let them pass into law without his signature.

It seems certain that, early on, Davis did not realize that his fellow Radicals had so much enthusiasm for railroads or that they had made so many promises of support to them. The governor's compromises left him more committed to railroads than he had ever wanted to be; on the other hand, his stance against giveaways to railroads moderated a considerable number of bills. On November 28, 1871, for example, Governor Davis returned his veto of a taxation act which would have taxed ordinary businessmen eighty thousand dollars on property valued at four million dollars while providing that railroads would pay only ten thousand dollars in taxes on property worth the same amount. In addition, Davis denied a land grant for the Waco Tap Railroad Company and vetoed the revival of the charter of the Eastern Texas Railroad because it contained a land grant. The Senate, however, was able to override most of the governor's railroad vetoes virtually without discussion.

In all, more than fifty acts for the incorporation or relief of railroads were introduced and supported by senators of every political stripe. It was rumored that improper influence propelled some questionable railroad bills. On the other side of the scale, the vision of shining steel rails and mighty, cloud-belching locomotives that raced the sun from coast to coast had captivated the American imagination, and, more practically, industrial growth in Texas was desperately dependent on a railroad network for reliable transportation.

Six months after adjournment of the called session, the Senate returned for a regular session. The Senate elected a new slate of officers for most of the traditional offices, with only two holdovers from the previous session. Charles M. Campbell was elected secretary; W. Leigh Chalmers, first assistant secretary; Albert R. Parsons, second assistant secretary; Doc Durham, assistant sergeant-at-arms; Abner H. Cook, engrossing clerk; B. W. Pearce, doorkeeper; Tom Hancock, a black, assistant doorkeeper; Sam Houston, Jr., postmaster; and Robert H. Taliaferro, chaplain. Henry Mordecai was returned as calendar clerk, and A. Faulkner, the veteran of the revolt in June, 1870, was unanimously retained as sergeant-at-arms. The elections were hotly contested, with the election of Hancock as assistant doorkeeper taking five ballots. The election of an enrolling clerk was postponed after three unsuccessful ballots.

After the election of officers, the Hillebrand-Alford question remained unsettled. Senator Ruby moved that Hillebrand be admitted instead of Alford, who was present and answering the roll. The acrimonious debate concerning Alford's status stretched over several weeks. On January 17 the secretary of the Senate, under orders from Davis, deliberately omitted Alford's name from the roll call and substituted Hillebrand's. In the ensuing uproar the entire slate of Radical officers was cast out on a technicality. The Radicals, with their hopes for a Republican hegemony fading, then compromised with the liberals.

The next day, Baker successfully moved for yet another election of officers: Albert Parsons became first assistant secretary and E. L. James second assistant secretary; Hancock was replaced by Scipio Thompson as first assistant doorkeeper; Wesley B. Johnston replaced Faulkner as sergeant-at-arms; D. M. Porter took Cook's place as engrossing clerk; Thomas J. Powell replaced Doc Durham as assistant sergeant-at-arms; and C. C. Allen became the general clerk. An enrolling clerk, John G. Collier, was finally elected on the fourth ballot; a journal clerk, James E. Slater, appeared on the roster; and William M. Easton was elected second assistant doorkeeper.

Captain Faulkner had earned considerable popularity as sergeant-at-arms, and his dismissal sparked a controversy, becoming the subject of several reports issued by the Committee on Privileges and Elections. Faulkner's supporters in the Senate lost their last appeal on February 13, 1871, in a tie vote on the question of holding another election of officers, with Hillebrand, who had been left off the roll on the ballot, casting the deciding ballot in the negative when he was allowed to vote.

Meanwhile, there were other sources of controversy. Irate over Davis's militia and police bills and the postponement of general elections, Morgan Hamilton, who was acting without party approval in Austin, Washington, and New York in his self-appointed role as Texas' most scathing political critic and gadfly, censured what he said was a violation of the party's pledges of representative government. But at that time no political faction would support Hamilton, and Davis might have succeeded in getting him out of Washington had the governor not committed a dazzling blunder: he attempted to give Hamilton's U.S. Senate seat to the ever-hopeful General Reynolds. Davis mustered the votes in the legislature needed to declare Hamilton's election invalid and called for another election on January 24, 1871. Despite speeches on the floor of the Texas Senate which accurately pointed out that General Reynolds was not a Texas resident, that body elected him to the U.S. Senate. But even the Radicals in Congress could not stomach this: they refused to seat Reynolds and insisted that Hamilton was legally entitled to continue his term.

In another long-running political clash, the Texas Senate investigated the election of James E. Dillard. He was a popular Democratic judge in Cherokee County who had run second to Priest in the disorderly senatorial contest for the provisional session. When Priest was declared ineligible by General Reynolds on February 17, 1870, Dillard, as runner-up, was to succeed him. The resolution to seat Dillard, however, was tabled February 22 and the seat was vacant for the last two days of the session. Priest qualified for the Senate in the called session but resigned in August to become a district judge, and a special election for the Senate seat was called for November 28. Dillard defeated George W. Lane, a Republican, in a particularly rowdy election whose irregularities gave cause for the Radical-controlled Committee on Privileges and Elections to review Dillard's claim to this Senate seat once again. Dillard, along with Tendick, the other senator-elect, presented himself on the opening day of the regular session, January 10, 1871. Although Dillard managed to "lose" some key evidence which the Committee on Privileges and Elections had allowed him to inspect, on March 25, 1871, a majority led by Chairman Baker reported out a recommendation that Dillard's seat in the Senate be declared vacant. The senators denounced the Democrats in Cherokee County for "violence, intimidation, and fraud," but there was substantial evidence of vote fraud and intimidation by both factions. Meanwhile, Dillard, who had been sworn as senator on January 10, cheerfully participated in the session, including voting on motions relative to his own eligibility. The investigation of the election continued until April 10, 1871, when Dillard was declared ineligible by the Committee on Privileges and Elections. The committee's decision was sustained by a vote of seventeen to ten, and the seat was vacated. Dillard was popular and powerful, and the political cost of denying him the seat was high. In the special election held October 3–6, Dillard won and was again sworn, on October 31, 1871, to take his seat during the adjourned session.

In the spring of 1871, another Senate controversy erupted as impeachment proceedings were brought against William H. Russell, the judge of the Fifteenth Judicial District, who later served as senator in the Fourteenth Legislature. Newspapers all over Texas zealously voiced their opinions about the judge's opposition to Governor Davis's patronage concerning the state printing contract in Brownsville.

Judge Russell had confiscated a letter issued by the governor to a Brownsville attorney, Henry Haupt, who owned one of the local newspapers, the *Ranchero.* The letter authorized awarding the state contract to whatever newspaper was named therein—a blank space having been left for the designee. Disagreement with Haupt over which paper should be favored prompted the judge to seize the letter through his judicial power. Haupt retaliated by publishing in his newspaper a diatribe that began by comparing the Fifteenth District Court to the Star Chamber, the archaic British court notorious for its cruel and arbitrary judgments. These inflammatory words earned the lawyer a three-day confinement in jail for contempt of court.

The House adopted articles of impeachment against Judge Russell on April 10, 1871, charging him with "high crimes and misdemeanors in office and incompetence." The Senate resolved itself into a high court of impeachment to conduct the trial on the charges. After the usual postponements and maneuvering, the court delivered its decision that "respondent William H. Russell go hence without day," on May 4, 1871, thus exonerating the judge.

The vote on Russell's impeachment shows the waning influence of the Radicals, who could no longer count on the support of liberal Republicans. On this issue, the liberals voted with the Democrats in favor of dismissing the charges ("yea"), while most Radicals voted "nay." In political terms, a vote to dismiss charges was at the same time a vote against the Radical governor, Davis.

Developments later in 1871 further weakened the Radical faction. The special elections in October added two Democratic senators—Swift, who filled Amos Clark's seat, and Dillard, who replaced

Mijamin Priest. The death of President Pro Tempore Don Campbell in November further diminished the Republican ranks.

The Senate of the Twelfth Legislature did not spend all its time in pitched battles against itself. Land development was a key concern, and a state geological survey was created, through a bill introduced by Senator Bowers, to explore the resources of Texas. Furthermore, Davis on August 12, 1870, signed a "Welcome Resolution" which granted to every head of household who lacked a homestead a quarter section of land, or 160 acres, as provided by the constitution. Single men twenty-one years of age or older were entitled to 80 acres. An amendment passed during the regular session on May 17, 1871, allowed anyone else to settle on the public domain and purchase up to 160 acres from the state.

A state Bureau of Immigration was established through an act of May 23, 1871, to encourage immigration by procuring transportation from the coast into the interior, providing temporary lodging, protecting new immigrants from "fraud, chicanery, and peculation," and "making all such regulations and provisions as may be in any manner necessary and conducive to their welfare." The bureau would also be responsible for collecting information on Texas and disseminating it to attract more immigrants. Two agents would be dispatched to the other states (north and south) and two to Europe (Britain and the Continent) to conduct recruiting campaigns. The state granted charters to a number of private immigration societies, many of which focused on attracting Europeans.

Individuals and transport companies alike needed an improved infrastructure—not only railroads but also roads, waterways, and ports. Many groups received charters for building bridges and turnpikes, dredging canals, rivers, creeks, and bayous, and operating ferries. A joint resolution was sent from the Twelfth Legislature to Congress in May, 1870, requesting funds for channels to be dug through the bars at Galveston, Pass Cavallo, Aransas Pass, Sabine Pass, and Brazos Santiago. Federal assistance was not forthcoming, however, so private companies were chartered for this work as well as for dredging at Cedar Bayou, Corpus Christi, Texana, and Indianola. Improvements to Texas Gulf ports came none too soon: the Texas and Europe Steamship Company was founded to offer monthly steamer service between Texas and Europe.

The Twelfth Legislature provided for education as well. Although Mexico had established the first public school in Texas in San Antonio in 1828, there was a general resistance to public schools, and the problems entailed in producing a workable blueprint for a school system would resurface many times in the future. The Constitution of 1869 had recommended a free public school system for all Texas children, but to implement such a system, it was necessary to overcome public hostility toward both compulsory education and education for blacks. The free school bill passed in 1870 during the called session was only a watered-down measure. The Senate endorsed the compromise bill on education, produced by a joint legislative committee during the called session, through which the police courts served ex officio as school boards for their respective counties. The same act created the office of state superintendent of public instruction on August 13, 1870. The superintendent would be elected to serve four years and would report to each session of the legislature on the condition of the free schools in the state suggesting legislation for their benefit. He would also disburse the school fund to the police courts on the basis of scholastic population. Each court would appoint a board of trustees and divide the county into subdistricts, each with its own school to be built with the proceeds from the school fund designated for the county. The schools would be open for at least four months each year, and children between the ages of six and sixteen were required to attend a public or private school for at least four months every year.

The free school bill was amended by a measure introduced by Senator Rawson and signed on April 24, 1871, which authorized the superintendent of public instruction to appoint a supervisor of public education in each judicial district. This district supervisor, rather than the police courts, was charged with subdividing the counties into school districts and appointing five school directors in each district. The superintendent, together with the governor and attorney general, constituted a board of education for the state. For the superintendent's position, Davis nominated Joseph W. Talbot, a well-known and respected educator who was reputed to have considered founding a racially integrated school system largely as a cost-conscious measure for the debt-ridden state. A majority of the Senate, including some Republicans, refused to confirm Talbot, and

J. C. DeGress was confirmed as superintendent of public instruction instead.

Financial arrangements for public education were complex. The school fund was made up of all the interest that had accrued since March 30, 1870, plus all funds that would accrue in the future from railroads, from one-fourth of all ad valorem taxes, from occupation taxes, and from any other taxes ever provided for the support of public schools. The comptroller was required by an act of August 12, 1870, to invest the state school funds in U.S. bonds. A separate act signed the next day provided relief for railroad companies which were indebted to the state for loans from the school fund. In order to prevent forced sale, these companies could pay into the state treasury an amount equal to six months' interest plus 1 percent of their total indebtedness under the loan as of May, 1870.

The Agricultural and Mechanical College of Texas, established through a bill introduced by Senator Saylor and signed on April 17, 1871, relied for financial support on federal funds under the Morrill Act, and that act's time limit required action within that year. Three commissioners were appointed by the governor to select a suitable site, but only seventy-five thousand dollars in state money could be set aside for construction.

Economic development was one of the primary concerns of the Twelfth Legislature. At the time, most of Texas was uninhabited or was settled by subsistence farmers with little cash who depended greatly on credit and who, whenever possible, traded and bartered. Though Texans came out of the war in better condition and with more gold in hand than other citizens of the Confederacy, the state was nevertheless cash poor. The Twelfth Legislature spent a great deal of time chartering businesses which would provide for both the physical improvement of Texas and the reorganization of the basic financial framework of the state. These incorporations marked the debut of a market economy which would gradually shift power from the planter class to businessmen, while the subsistence farmer would come to participate in the marketplace by raising a cash crop, usually cotton. Charters were issued for new insurance firms, banks, savings and loan operations, and mutual fund associations.

The Twelfth Legislature not only incorporated banking, insurance, and real estate companies, but also provided for manufacturing. During the adjourned session, on November 25, 1871, Governor Davis signed a bill to encourage textile industries that exempted all capital and property held by such enterprises from taxation by the state or a county or municipal government for five years and excused the operators from occupation taxes for the same period.

Agriculture did not escape the mania for incorporation. Societies for exchanging information and sharing the responsibilities of farming and stockraising developed rapidly; the Twelfth Legislature issued twenty-one charters in as many counties. The "C" Sugar and Tobacco Planting Association was chartered to purchase real property to be cultivated, and the Texas Stockraising Corporation was established to facilitate the business of buying and selling livestock. The San Antonio River Valley Irrigation Association formed at Goliad, and the Pecos Irrigating, Manufacturing, and Live Stock Company began building dams and aqueducts for water power for textile mills as well as irrigation. The Texas Live Stock Insurance Company offered to insure losses of horses, mules, and milk cows.

The legislators also acted to help protect agriculturalists from theft. State inspectors of hides and animals were appointed in districts across Texas through a House bill passed on May 22, 1871. An inspector and his deputies would be responsible for checking all livestock and hides in transit for the proper brand or mark and would seize all unbranded or improperly branded stock or hides.

Pecans had been a commercial export before 1860, and the thousands of bushels going to other states and to Europe increased cash flow into Texas. Many did not recognize the value of the pecan and cut the trees to clear land for growing cotton or to use the wood for wagon parts or farm implements. Although the pecan was not designated the state tree until 1919, the senators endorsed an act that provided a fine for anyone who cut down or otherwise destroyed a pecan tree on land not his own.

The members of the Senate of the Twelfth Legislature can be accused of being blind to the faults of their compatriots, of occasionally issuing charters in bad faith, and of being too generous in supporting railroads, but they did lay the groundwork for a new era of corporate expansion in Texas. As the end of the Twelfth Legislature neared, the legislators released the reins with which the state government traditionally had controlled business development. Although bills on the topic were introduced in the Senate during the provisional session, a general act of private incorporation, which covered all businesses as well as social organizations, was not signed until the final day of the adjourned session, December 2, 1871. After that date the office of the secretary of state was expected to issue charters.

The actions of the Twelfth Legislature to promote the social welfare, which included the building of a public road system, the homestead law, frontier defense, and a public school system that was "fifty years ahead of its time," did not change the balance of public opinion, which had swung irrevocably against the Republicans. The Democrats in Texas gleefully fanned the flames of popular outrage, at first through local associations and then through a new statewide organization founded in January, 1871. They established the *Democratic Statesman* as a party organ to counterbalance J. G. Tracy's *State Journal* and coordinated a statewide Tax-Payers' Convention, with former governor Pease serving as president, in Austin in September, 1871. Delegates at the bipartisan convention, also attended by Morgan and A. J. Hamilton, expressed their anger at the extravagance of the Davis administration and the excessive taxation and spending of the Twelfth Legislature, which was meeting nearby in the adjourned session. Senator Dohoney added color to this truce between enemies, energetically dashing back and forth between the Senate, where he voted for enormous railroad subsidies, and the Tax-Payers' Convention, where he helped Pease and the Hamiltons lead the fiscal protest.

The question of when elections should be held generated constant debate. The newly adopted constitution specified the length of terms and the requirement for elections at certain times. There was, however, strong disagreement concerning when the Texas election requirements took effect. Some based their opinions on the date the election to the provisional government was held, others to the date that the provisional government was called to order or the date the constitution was adopted in Texas, and others figured from the date the regular civilian government was inaugurated. Davis himself figured the period as dating from March 30, 1870, the date that Texas reentered the Union.

Some Radicals were uncomfortable with the plan to delay elections and there was a struggle in the caucus, but the Radicals who wanted a delay prevailed. Ultimately, however, Davis's hand was forced by a combination of state and federal influences. During the special elections for four congressional seats which Davis was constrained to call in October, 1871, many Republicans, including the Hamilton brothers and Pease, allied with Democrats to elect anti-Radical candidates, paving the way for a Democratic resurgence. The results at the polls sent a chill through the ranks of the Radicals. Late in a session devoted largely to incorporations, an act prohibiting discrimination against blacks in public transportation was put through, but even Radical legislators had begun to back away from Davis.

The Senate of the Twelfth Legislature adjourned *sine die* on December 2, 1871. Senator Hertzberg resigned that month despite having drawn a four-year term, and Don Campbell's death had left a vacancy in a seat with a six-year term. The loss of these two Republican seats, along with the fact that Davis never appointed a new lieutenant governor after James Flanagan went to Washington, would contribute to the demise of the Radical cause when the Senate of the Thirteenth Legislature met.

CHAPTER 6

The Senate of the Thirteenth Legislature, 1873

Texas in the early 1870s was a hotbed of violent partisanship as Democrats and liberal Republicans rallied against the Radicals. Chosen as the leader to bring Texas back into the Union, E. J. Davis succeeded in that reunion, but his leadership was otherwise ineffectual, as his key policy initiatives proved ill-fated. Outraged taxpayers charged the Davis administration with extravagance, tyranny, and corruption and demanded a change of leadership. The Radicals did not find enough men of ability to serve in the Davis administration, and the governor's unbending, reserved demeanor did little to unify the splintered Republicans. In addition, the fragile Texas economy and the people's hostility weighed heavily against Davis. Even the weather seemed to conspire against the Radicals: two out of three winters brought disastrous blizzards down on the cattle industry, and wet weather in 1873 delayed the cotton harvest by three weeks during an economic crisis when being early to market was crucial.

Although Texas had fared better economically than the rest of the Confederacy, still only a meager amount of hard currency remained in circulation. In order to restart the civil government, provide for frontier defense, fashion a school system, and build the infrastructure of a growing state, taxes had to go up, but most Texans expected tax rates to remain near their prewar levels. In the years 1871 through 1874, the aggregate total of state taxes amounted to a low estimate of $4 million and a high estimate of $6 million, as taxes rose to $2.175 on $100 valuation, a shocking contrast to the prewar rate of $0.125 on $100 valuation. The average state spending for the years 1870 through 1874 ranged from a low estimate of $1 million per year to a high estimate of $2 million per year, with the biggest expense being the cost of printing. Taxpayers, already angry about Davis's policies, were outraged.

The governor, who was not wholly indifferent to public feeling, in the previous legislature had tried to portray himself as a foe of higher taxes and government waste. In a message on May 24, 1871, for example, he had admonished the upper house for its "very large" appropriation for senators' expenses. In a second message, on November 14, 1871, this time to both houses, Davis pointed out that empowering county courts and police courts to issue bonds and to pass and collect a host of taxes allowed local jurisdictions to tax Texans more heavily than state government did. In districts utilizing all of the sources of revenue available to them, the combined state and county tax burden came to more than twice the amount cited for state taxes alone—during an era when Texans were markedly strapped for cash. Davis blamed Democrats and Republicans alike for this system. In his opening message to the Senate of the Thirteenth Legislature, Davis reiterated this theme, pointing out that the police courts and county courts were not even required to account for their expenditures. In spite of Davis's budgetary admonitions and resistance to excessive awards to railroads, the blame for every woe was laid at the governor's doorstep. Radicals began to distance themselves from their leader. The governor was becoming isolated.

In the search for political alternatives to the Radicals, many Southerners turned to the moderate Republican and Democratic fusionists. In Texas, these middle-of-the-roaders were men who achieved a loose accord through a willingness to compromise and a shared optimism. They accepted monetary policies they believed would aid Texans in the emerging economy and were willing to spend substantial sums on internal improvements and on education. Fusion was seen as the new mainstream in Texas politics by such widely read publications as the Democratic *Houston Telegraph* and the Republican *Flake's Bulletin*, the latter having announced the merger of Republican and Democratic middle-of-the-roaders as an established fact that lacked only a party name. But these town-based pundits were out of touch with farmers and failed to gauge correctly the rising level of public rage that propelled conservative Democrats to victories in the elections of late 1871, 1872, and 1873.

Conservative Democrats wanted government spending pared to a minimum and, unlike the Whig faction, believed that private enterprise should not be subsidized. A general amnesty for any former Confederates who were still disenfranchised and the reform of revenue-raising measures and of the civil service system featured prominently in Democratic party discussions. Conservatives campaigned successfully by addressing the voters' alarm over a depressed agricultural economy, bedrock hostility to the social agenda of Radical rule, and fury over high taxes, while at the same time supporting generous funding for schools and frontier defense. The conservative platform which emerged opposed aid to private corporations, partly because farmers in the eastern, northeastern, and western districts felt their taxes had been used mainly to benefit powerful businessmen.

The congressional special election of October, 1871, had been the first Texas election conducted with the voting rights of disenfranchised Confederates fully restored, and the large number of voters recently arrived from the Deep South had increased the voter rolls another 10 percent in favor of the Democrats. The Republican party responded to its electoral losses of 1871 with a bid, carried out largely by party chairman J. G. Tracy and party secretary James Newcomb, who was also president of the Loyal Union League of America, to attract more white voters. In their attempt to broaden the party's appeal to those voters, Tracy and Newcomb tried to break up the Republicans' one source of concentrated voting power, the all-black units of the staunchly Republican Loyal Union League, in order to switch that membership's allegiance to less controversial organizations such as the Republican county clubs. This policy proved disastrous, alienating both blacks and whites.

The Republican loss of all four congressional districts in 1871 had indicated to Texans that the Davis administration could be ousted, and in anticipation of tax relief from a new administration, citizens began to withhold taxes, which created a crisis in state government. In a message to the Senate, Davis stated his belief that it was largely the wealthy who withheld payment, leaving the burden to fall on the less well-to-do. If the governor was correct, farmers were being ruined while big business and wealthy individuals escaped taxation and even received aid. To keep state operations going, the governor again resorted to the sale of bonds, but the Democrats threatened to repudiate them when they regained power, and the bond sale was poor. The state began to pay part of salaries and operating expenses in warrants which, according to Elisha M. Pease, were "hawked about the streets of Austin at six bits on the dollar, and sold with difficulty." There was talk of impeaching the governor.

The Republicans ran a good campaign for the state and national elections of 1872 despite a shoestring budget. Davis stumped along the Texas Central Railroad line, talking about free speech and an end to violence and telling small farmers that the Republican party stood for the common man and the disaffected individual, unlike the big Democratic planters, who he said had ignored them in the past and presumably would continue to do so; blacks were reminded of the loyalty they owed the party.

At the state Republican convention in 1872, the obvious need to reduce state expenses led all factions tacitly to drop support for the state police and militia, and the Republican budget battle settled into two camps: those led by Tracy, who favored railroads and internal improvements, and those led by Newcomb, who favored schools. Working with Newcomb, Superintendent DeGress had utilized the school administration throughout the state to lobby for the party, particularly in support of Grant as United States president.

The Democrats, meanwhile, concentrated on the issues of taxation and corruption, and they had several good campaigners to speak for them. As the historian Paul Casdorph noted, "Typical of this group was John H. Reagan, ex–Postmaster General of the Confederacy, who made an extended speaking tour through Texas in support of the Greeley-Brown ticket." By smaller margins than in 1871, but still comfortably, the Democrats won all six seats in Congress and regained control of the statehouse for the Thirteenth Legislature.

Republican lawmakers widened their distance from Davis, but talk of impeachment died down. The *Galveston News* editorialized, "Davis is harmless with a Democratic legislature. An effort to unseat him would only invite the intervention of General Grant. Such a situation would produce uneasiness not only with our citizens, but with the capitalists of the North, who are now investing their means in the construction of railroads and other internal improvements and would certainly stop the flow of immigration that is coming in from every quarter of the Union as well as Europe."

When the Senate of the Thirteenth Legislature met in Austin from January 14 to June 4, 1873, it would work in tandem with the House to repeal the basic laws embodying the Radicals' programs. Seventeen of the thirty senators were conservatives, and thus the Radical majority no longer existed. The conservative Democratic faction, however, fell short of a two-thirds majority. Fifteen members were conservative Democrats: the freshman senators Hamilton J. Avinger, Andrew J. Ball, George P. Finlay, John L. Henry, Henry C. King, Joseph D. Sayers, Nathan G. Shelley, and Thomas J. Word; and the returning David W. Cole, James E. Dillard, Ebenezer L. Dohoney, Henry R. Latimer, Edward B. Pickett, Dr. William H. Pyle, and William H. Swift. These fifteen conservative Democrats were joined by E. Thomas Broughton and Captain Samuel Evans, both returning conservative independents.

The Republicans could muster only thirteen senators. New to the Senate were Francis G. Franks, Edward T. Randle, and James G. Tracy. Returning Radicals were Thomas H. Baker, Webster Flanagan, S. W. Ford, Albert J. Fountain, Matthew Gaines, Phidello W. Hall, Henry Rawson, George T. Ruby, William A. Saylor, and Robert P. Tendick.

The newly elected senators came from varied backgrounds. Hamilton Jacob Avinger, descended from a Gottlieb Avinger who arrived in America around 1740, was born in Orangeburg County, South Carolina, in 1833. He attended medical school in Charleston and then at Jefferson Medical College in Philadelphia, where he graduated in March, 1853, at the age of nineteen. At twenty-two, Dr. Avinger traveled to a tiny Texas hamlet called Young's Chapel, returned to South Carolina to marry, and fetched his bride back to Young's Chapel. The new couple settled down to farm and raise a large family, and Dr. Avinger treated patients when his skills were needed. In 1872 Avinger ran for the Senate seat left vacant when the popular Republican member Don Campbell died during the Twelfth Legislature. The senator returned to private life after his term in the Senate of the Thirteenth Legislature, where he introduced a bill to establish drawer and endorser liability for promissory notes and bills of exchange as well as a bill to amend the Penal Code.

The Avingers prospered in the sparsely settled region of Young's Chapel, and when the first railroad came through, Dr. Avinger with his own lumber built a depot and donated it to the railroad; it was the first building in what would become the town of Avinger. On June 27, 1881, Dr. Avinger was murdered in a mysterious case in which a black tenant farmer named Ross was convicted; but Avinger, who took almost three days to die, begged for lenient treatment of him. Recent investigation has led some to suspect that Ross "took the fall" for a white man.

Andrew J. Ball of Weatherford was born in Mason County, Kentucky, in 1832 or 1833. At age eighteen, he taught school and began to read law. He first arrived in Guadalupe County, Texas, in 1854 and was admitted to the Texas bar at Birdville under an old preceptor of his, Judge Reagan, in November of that year. During the war he was commissioned a captain and fought in the Red River campaign and the battles of Mansfield, Pleasant Hill, and Jenkins Ferry. He was a member of the Constitutional Convention of 1866 and the state Democratic convention in 1871 and was elected to serve in the Thirteenth and Fourteenth legislatures, where he was a strong supporter of the Texas and Pacific Railway and frontier defense. In 1875 Governor Coke appointed him to travel to Saint Louis as a delegate to the National Railway Convention. Ball served a two-year term as county attorney of Parker County and in 1877 was inaugurated for one term as mayor of Weatherford. He moved his law practice to Dallas in 1892 and was a professional colleague of former Tyler senator James P. Douglas. A speech by Ball supporting frontier defense delivered to the Senate of the Thirteenth Legislature was much admired by Texans.

Returning to the Senate after a decade-long interval was George P. Finlay. Originally from Mississippi, he moved to Texas in 1853 and settled in Lavaca, where he was active in local affairs, editing the *Lavaca Register* and practicing law in partnership with the prominent lawyer J. J. Holt. Finlay moved to Galveston in 1873. He had served as the state senator from Victoria County in 1861 and later served as city attorney of Galveston from 1878 to 1889 and as state representative in the Sixteenth, Seventeenth, and Twenty-third legislatures. He was a member of the board of trustees of the public schools of Galveston from 1881 to 1887, organizing the system and becoming known as the father of the public schools of Galveston. He had served in the Seminole and Mexican wars, and in 1862, as soon as the Senate had adjourned, he volunteered to serve the Confederate cause and was commissioned a captain in the 6th Texas Infantry. The regiment was captured in January, 1863, and Finlay was a prisoner of war in Ohio until he was exchanged at Richmond, Virginia, in May, 1863. He then served in Georgia, and during the last year of the war he received an appointment as judge advocate of Texas from General Magruder under General Kirby Smith. Despite a murder charge brought against him—but dropped—during the Thirteenth Legislature, Finlay was one of the most popular and best respected men in the legislature.

Senator John L. Henry was born in Culpepper County, Virginia, in 1831, reared in Murfreesboro, Tennessee, and graduated from Union University. The senator first moved to Huntsville, Texas, in 1852 and was admitted to the bar there in 1855. The following year he moved to Livingston, where he served as district attorney for the Thirteenth Judicial District but did not run for reelection, choosing instead to join the Confederate ranks. He served in the Texas coastal defense during the war. In 1869 Henry moved to Tyler, where he was elected to represent Smith and Upshur counties in the Senate of the Thirteenth Legislature and was elected a delegate to the Constitutional Convention of 1875. During his Senate term, he introduced bills to regulate contested elections and to provide for payment of the public debt, as well as an amendment to the Penal Code. Henry moved to Dallas in 1879 and served as an associate justice of the Texas Supreme Court from 1886 until his resignation in 1893. He was president of the Dallas Bar Association at the time of his death in 1907.

Henry C. King of Boerne was born in Wayne County, Georgia, in 1830; was educated at the University of Georgia at Athens and Oglethorpe University; and studied law at Charleston, South Carolina. King grew rice in Georgia but switched to cattle raising when he moved to San Antonio in 1860. A successful attorney, he began his career in state politics with his election to the Thirteenth Legislature, where he chaired the Senate Committee on Indian Affairs. King went on to serve as an authority on problems of immigration

George P. Finlay served with distinction in the Ninth and Thirteenth senates. Courtesy Texas State Library and Archives Commission.

in the Constitutional Convention of 1875 and as commissioner on canals and ditches for navigation and irrigation under Governors Coke and Hubbard. He was an active candidate for the governorship in 1880 but withdrew in favor of Hubbard. During his Senate term, King introduced bills for the protection of the wool-producing interests, the defense of the frontier, and the relief of old soldiers of the Texas Revolution. From 1877 to 1879 King was editor of the *San Antonio Express.* He was appointed by President Benjamin Harrison as Democratic commissioner from Texas to the World's Fair Columbian Exposition in 1893. The senator was a Presbyterian and a Mason. He and his wife, Jean Adams Parland, had seven children. King died in San Antonio in 1911.

A promising legislative neophyte, Joseph D. Sayers had served in the Confederate Army, where he rose to the rank of major in the 5th Regiment, Mounted Volunteers. Sayers was born in Mississippi in 1841, and his physician father moved the family to Bastrop County in 1850. As a boy Sayers was educated at Bastrop Military Institute. After being admitted to the bar in 1866, he practiced law in Bastrop until his election to the Senate. Sayers would go on to become chairman of the Democratic state executive committee from 1875 to 1878. Described as "a man of mark," Sayers would be elected lieutenant governor of Texas in 1878 on a ticket headed by the former archsecessionist and jurist Oran Roberts; from 1885 to 1898 he would serve in the U.S. House of Representatives. He would be elected the twenty-first governor of Texas in 1898 and would win reelection in 1900. Several memorable events marked his term as governor, including the burning of the penitentiary at Huntsville in 1899, the Brazos River flood of 1899, and the Galveston hurricane of 1900. In 1916, as a regent of the University of Texas, he would support the university in its struggle with Governor James E. Ferguson. Sayers would serve Texas in a variety of capacities until two years before his death in 1929.

Nathan G. Shelley was not a newcomer when he won a seat in the Senate of the Thirteenth Legislature, having served in the Senate during the Ninth and Eleventh legislatures. He married Sarah F. Shelley in 1853, and the couple had two daughters and four sons. Senator Shelley died in Austin in 1898.

The remaining conservative senators were men of sound legislative ability who earned the approbation of even such staunchly Republican newspapers as the *State Journal*, but their service during the Thirteenth Legislature proved to be the apex of their political careers. Francis G. Franks, a lawyer, was born in Mississippi in 1838, married a Louisianan named Mattie, and came to Texas, where he was admitted to the bar in April, 1868, at Wharton; Franks served in the House during the Twelfth Legislature. Thomas J. Word, a Democrat, came to Texas from North Carolina and was the sponsor of the bill to consolidate the International and Great Northern railroad companies. The Republican Edward T. Randle from Huntsville succeeded J. S. Mills, who ran for the House instead of seeking a second term in the Senate.

The shrinking list of Republicans contained some Radicals who had fought for the Confederacy. Webster Flanagan, who had served in the Senate of the Twelfth Legislature, and newcomer James G. Tracy were notable among Republicans who had worn the Gray. Tracy's political principles were fluid. In 1865 his name was listed among the printers who joined the newly formed Mechanics Association, one of whose purposes was "to prevent freemen negro mechanics from being encouraged to settle in our city and compete with worthy white mechanics." By 1868, however, Tracy had become a Radical, courting the black voters of Houston. His success after joining the Republican party was notable. He became editor of the Republican *Houston Union* by 1868, the same year he was appointed the city's recorder. The next year he was appointed justice of the peace, postmaster of Houston, and voter registrar of Harris County; by 1870 he was chairman of the state Republican executive committee. Tracy profited so handsomely from his change of party that even in the scramble of Reconstruction politics he was seen as a "thorough spoilsman." After Republican domination waned, Tracy again switched parties, sometime in the late 1870s. During that period of economic crisis and depression he would support the Workingmen's party and urge a coalition with the Greenbackers. Though Tracy was at the center of much controversy, his unflagging interest in building Houston's business community and his promotion of the ship channel were of critical importance to his constituents' prosperity. The records of incorporations during the period list Tracy, along with others, as a founder of several of Texas' most lucrative operations, and he sat on important boards.

The Senate's two black members were among the returning Radicals: the diminutive, fiery-tongued minister from Brenham, Matthew Washington Gaines, a former slave; and the northern-born George T. Ruby, a young journalist and educator from Galveston. Both men focused much of their effort on increasing educational opportunities for blacks.

The colorful Colonel Albert J. Fountain from El Paso, another Radical, returned to the Senate from the Twelfth Legislature having survived several political plots and at least one murder attempt by his enemies.

The opening day of the Thirteenth Legislature was awaited with some trepidation, because of questions about the validity of Webster Flanagan's holding the office of president pro tempore of the Senate on a permanent basis. No one wanted to provoke intervention by federal troops, but no one wanted an irregular Senate president either. On Wednesday, January 15, 1873, Flanagan himself solved the problem: immediately after roll call he delivered a short resignation speech. He noted that he had taken on the office of president pro tempore when Don Campbell died, and he thanked the Senate for the "courteous and liberal support which I received in my efforts to promote the harmonious dispatch of the public business." He continued, "I find now that a difference of opinion exists, even amongst men learned in the law, upon the question whether or not I am now the President of the Senate. I propose to solve this question by a voluntary relinquishment of any claims I may have to that position." He challenged the Senate of the Thirteenth Legislature to work for reconciliation, with the words: "Gentlemen, we will meet you half way. Are you in earnest? We shall see."

The election of officers and the abolition of the two positions of messenger took place for the most part on January 15. John Burleson was elected doorkeeper; J. H. Murray, who died in office in May, 1873, assistant doorkeeper; W. L. Chalmers, secretary; John W. Lane, first assistant secretary; R. C. Hunt, second assistant secretary; J. R. Cole, enrolling clerk; and Rhodes Fisher, engrossing clerk. After five ballots among a field of five candidates, Ed Creary, Flanagan's nominee, won the position of assistant sergeant-at-arms. Cole resigned due to ill health on April 1, 1873, and was replaced by William N. Ramey. The Reverend Taliaferro was reelected chaplain. The Twelfth Legislature's popular Senate sergeant-at-arms, Captain A. Faulkner of Robertson County, who had played such a telling role in the dramatic incident of the conservative walkout on the militia bill, was nominated by Senator Cole and handily won the position of sergeant-at-arms by a vote of nineteen to nine, with a "scattering" of one.

Senator Pickett, who had proven to be both congenial and able and was one of the few to oppose Webster Flanagan's railroad bill in the Twelfth Legislature, was elected president pro tempore by an overwhelming vote of twenty-five yeas and a "scattering" of three. The Senate then moved to adopt new rules. The word *arrest* was removed from the powers of the president of the Senate and the sergeant-at-arms, who were now empowered only to send for a senator. Under the new rules, adopted on January 16, 1873, Senator Pickett also became lieutenant governor ex officio, a position he would hold during the disputed election between Davis and Richard Coke later in 1873. On the motion of Senator Broughton, the thanks of the Senate were tendered to Flanagan, the retiring president of the Senate.

In lieu of a personal address, the Senate received a twenty-five-page message from the governor. Davis wrote in favor of reconciliation; recognizing the opposition to his party's program, he stated his willingness to compromise on parts of it. He hoped, however, that earlier legislation would not be undone. He agreed to changes in portions of the militia and police laws but stated his hope that those laws would remain in effect in some form in order to secure the public peace. The governor believed that if the legislature took steps to spread the tax burden more equitably, many Democratic complaints could be ended.

Davis quoted Governor Pendleton Murrah on the shocking state of crime during the former governor's tenure and noted that Texas society was now more peaceful. Davis went on to emphasize several points concerning taxation and revenue. He insisted that the state system for the imposition and collection of taxes placed an unfair burden upon small landholders, while the large property owners—including many corporations—continued to avoid paying their fair share. He reported that as of September 11, 1872, the sum of $441,402.50 (more than one-third) of the state taxes assessed for the previous year remained unpaid. He attributed most of this shortage to corporations and went on to address undervaluation, or "fraud in assessment" of the assets of large corporations, mentioning in par-

E. B. Pickett, president pro tempore of the Senate and lieutenant governor of Texas in the Thirteenth Legislature, 1873. Reproduced from holdings of Texas State Archives.

ticular the telegraph company and the railroads. He proceeded to criticize county tax officers, such as sheriffs, who he said were delaying tax payments into the treasury and speculating with the float. Texas had a public debt of less than $1.7 million, which could be retired by a year's tax on all real and personal property of less than one-half of 1 percent; the tax was necessary because only a fraction of the state bonds authorized by the Twelfth Legislature had been sold. Davis attributed this problem to "opposition from home" and slander in Texas newspapers. The governor asked the Thirteenth Legislature to squelch the rumors of repudiation that were undermining the state's credit.

In his message the governor stated that Treasurer Beriah Graham, who had been appointed following the removal of George W. Honey, had found the records of his office in great confusion, the cash short, and the treasury practically "turned into a broker's office for the shaving of the state's warrants with her money." At that time, about seventy-seven thousand dollars could not be accounted for, and Honey was under suspicion. The missing money was soon found in an Austin bank, but the outside auditors who were brought in to ensure the integrity and order of the treasury commented bluntly on Honey's conspicuous lack of organization: "We find that the books are kept in an inaccurate and confused manner, and in reckless disregard of any system whatever." Honey was prosecuted for improper conduct but was later ordered reinstated by the Texas Supreme Court.

The governor called for more meticulous bookkeeping and more frequent reports of revenues and expenditures. He pointed out that the general incorporation act, which moved most of the business of incorporations away from the legislature, had not included railroads and other industries which were consuming enormous amounts of legislative time and effort. He suggested that comprehensive general incorporation legislation would relieve both houses of such distractions. Finally, the governor condemned impediments to the developing public school system and asked the legislators to aid in establishing a more permanent one. Although the governor previously had appointed the school boards, in his message he recommended the creation of local, elected boards to give the people more control over how their money was spent.

Additional matters of interest were addressed in the governor's message. Regarding elections, Davis said, "The term of office of the present Executive should expire on the twenty-eighth day of April, 1874. The election law should therefore be changed so as to authorize a general election, at some day before that date, for State officers, members of the Legislature, and such county officers as may be then elective." He went on, "I further recommend that the election law be amended to permit the opening of election polls within each of the justice's precincts, and to reduce the number of days of election from four to one."

The governor concluded his message with an issue of concern to all Texans: "I will close this communication by inviting a close scrutiny of the accounts and disbursements of all State officers. This is due to the people as well as to honest officers, who, being so, are entitled to relief from the scandalous imputations which in this day blacken the good and bad alike."

Two of the most significant elements mentioned in the governor's message—the expiration date of the governor's term and the number of days during which the polls were constitutionally required to remain open—would become the focal points of legal maneuvers in which Davis, in the fall of 1873, contested both Coke's election to the governor's office and the date his term would begin. The dispute would lead to the famous 1874 occupation of a portion of the Capitol by Davis, backed by armed men, while equally well-armed Democrats, using ladders to crawl through second-story windows, held the other portion.

Despite the governor's plea to leave Radical measures intact, the five "obnoxious acts" passed by the Twelfth Legislature quickly came under attack in both houses of the legislature and were repealed. These unpopular edicts gave the governor broad discretion for reimposing martial law; created a state police force under Davis's command; passed an enabling act that empowered Davis to appoint men to fill vacant elective offices, a powerful tool for patronage; postponed the general elections until 1872, thereby ensuring another year for the Davis administration; and endorsed bills that created a subsidized press for the Radicals.

The assault on the obnoxious acts of the Radicals continued. Senator Swift introduced a bill to repeal the act regulating public printing approved on August 13, 1870; Senator Dillard introduced one to repeal the act which established a state police, approved on July 1,

1870; and Senator Saylor introduced corrective legislation to amend the act providing for the conduct of elections which had been approved on August 15, 1870.

On January 16, the election of officers was completed and the standing committees were set. There were twenty-eight of them:

- Committee on the Judiciary
- Committee on Internal Improvements
- Committee on Penitentiary
- Committee on Private Land Claims
- Committee on Education
- Committee on Immigration
- Committee on Finance
- Committee on the Militia
- Committee on Public Lands
- Committee on State Affairs
- Committee on Amendments to the Constitution (at least five members)
- Committee on Privileges and Elections
- Committee on Roads, Bridges and Ferries
- Committee on Counties and County Boundaries
- Committee on Claims and Accounts
- Committee on Contingent Expenses
- Committee on Printing (at least three members)
- Committee on Federal Relations
- Committee on Public Buildings
- Committee on Public Debt
- Committee on Land Office
- Committee on Indian Affairs and Frontier Protection
- Committee on Stock and Stock Raising
- Committee on Retrenchment and Reform
- Committee on Agricultural Affairs
- Committee on Engrossed Bills
- Committee on Enrolled Bills (at least three members)
- Committee to Examine Comptroller's and Treasurer's Accounts (no more than nine members)

By Saturday, January 18, the Senate had completed routine matters and was ready to address the pressing concerns of the day. Senator Dohoney hastened to introduce three measures: a joint resolution to urge Congress to open up the Indian country north of Texas to settlement, a bill to organize courts of common pleas in several counties, and a key antiadministration bill repealing the power of the governor to appoint certain officers to fill vacancies. Senator Henry introduced another key antiadministration bill to repeal "an act to provide for the enrollment of the militia, the organization and discipline of the State guards, and for the public defense, approved June 24, 1870."

Also on January 18, Senator Flanagan addressed the immediate physical needs of the Senate by offering a resolution instructing the sergeant-at-arms "to hunt up and recover the furniture taken from the room of the President of the Senate, and fit up said room in good order for the use of the President of the Senate, and that said officer be fully authorized to hunt up and recover all the furniture belonging to the Senate Chamber, together with the rugs, etc." The Senate took action to authorize the secretary of the Senate to furnish thirty copies of *Paschal's Digest* to be used during the session.

Still trying to get physically organized, the Senate adopted a resolution by Senator Shelley directing the sergeant-at-arms to "provide suitable rooms for the committees within the Capitol building, if the same can be had, and if the same in the basement of the building be occupied, . . . report to the Senate in writing how and by whom they are so occupied, and . . . report as soon as practicable."

The ever-present search for more space and equipment is evident in the continuing actions of the respective houses. Immediately upon adoption of his resolution, Senator Shelley read a report from the sergeant-at-arms to the president of the Senate stating that "the sergeant-at-arms of the House has possession of the room known as the President's room, and has been instructed by the Speaker of the House to hold it." This bit of inter-house struggle was still in evidence on May 30, when Senator Shelley offered yet another resolution, directing the sergeant-at-arms "to make report to the Senate what he has done under the resolution aforesaid [to search for and recover the furniture from the Twelfth Legislature for the use of the president of the Senate], and what portion of the furniture he has recovered and the disposition he has made of the same, and also all the information he has obtained as to the whereabouts of any portion of said furniture he has not recovered possession of." The requirement that the sergeant-at-arms give an accounting at the end of each session of all Senate furniture continues in force at the time of this writing.

On Monday, January 20, the session continued, with notification by the governor that the U.S. secretary of the treasury was prepared to pay out to the state the balance remaining in the fund for payment of the creditors of the Republic of Texas. The federal government still held some $101,113.27 that was earmarked for claims against the Republic of Texas, and the money was received on behalf of the state by the comptroller of public accounts through legislation passed on January 30, 1873, with the tacit understanding that if future claims against the former republic were presented, responsibility would be assumed by the state.

During the Thirteenth Legislature, the Senate endorsed a number of measures for refilling the public coffers. Most importantly, an annual tax of one-half of 1 percent on real and personal property was signed into law on June 3. One-quarter of the proceeds would go into the public school fund and three-quarters into the general revenue fund. In addition, every male between twenty-one and sixty years of age had to pay an annual poll tax of one dollar. An extensive schedule of taxes on occupations was also included in the measure. Gaming tables were allowed once more but were taxed heavily.

Additional temporary taxes were authorized for the amortization of outstanding bonds to fund frontier defense and other measures. The Thirteenth Legislature permitted Governor Davis to sell nine hundred thousand dollars in state bonds authorized by the previous legislature for maintaining ranging companies on the frontier and meeting deficiencies in the state revenue. Under an act signed on May 30, 1873, holders of warrants against the state treasury were allowed to exchange them for new state bonds bearing 10 percent annual interest, to come due ten years from the date of issue.

Legislation in the previous session authorizing county courts to levy a tax for the construction and maintenance of public roads was repealed, but county courts were given permission to levy a licensing tax on occupations at one-half of the state level, as well as a tax of five cents on every one hundred dollars of valuation on all real and personal property, in order to construct and maintain roads and bridges. Thirty-seven counties were permitted to levy a special tax or issue bonds to finance courthouse and jail construction. Justices of the peace kept the accounts and assessed the taxes, while sheriffs collected all taxes except the occupation tax, which was collected by the county treasurer.

Convinced of widespread corruption at the county level, Davis refused to sign most of the bills authorizing county courts to receive funds and levy taxes, but those he did not sign became law anyway. The Thirteenth Legislature did provide, however, for stricter supervision of county funds. In an act approved on March 8, 1873, the Senate acquiesced in requiring all county courts to submit a quarterly record of their expenditures, assets, and indebtedness and to post these statements every six months on the courthouse door as well as in the county newspaper having the largest circulation. If there was no such publication, posting the report in four additional public places could be substituted.

In a separate act, the Thirteenth Legislature made it unlawful for any law officer or public official to receive money or property when settling a criminal or penal charge. County and city law officers were required to take a monthly oath and present an accounting of public funds they had handled. Under another act, every three months each sheriff was to forward to the comptroller a statement of all taxes collected for the state and for the county on property held in counties other than his own. Whenever a sheriff failed to submit the statement, the comptroller or the county treasurer could file suit on that sheriff's bond, which was made mandatory. Finally, a House bill signed on March 28, 1873, required sheriffs and constables to execute all subpoenas and other processes issued by the speaker of the House, the president of the Senate, or the chairman of a committee in either house.

Keenly aware of their mandate to repeal the obnoxious acts, both houses promptly voted to repeal the existing militia bill. To provide for some type of militia, the Senate on January 24, 1873, passed an earlier, alternative bill "to provide for the enrollment of the militia, and organization and discipline of State guards, and for the public defense." The House did not concur and, moving quickly, on January 30 confirmed its passage of a Senate bill which repealed the existing militia bill and left the state with no militia at all. Davis vetoed this bill on the grounds that the Texas and federal constitutions required the state to have some sort of militia. The Senate turned the issue over to the Militia Committee, which began to wrestle with various amendments to the original bill.

A more limited measure, which the governor did not sign, repealed some sections of the act enrolling the militia and the state guard. This second bill eliminated only the more objectionable features of the existing statutes. Davis had anticipated such action in his annual address but admitted that "it would not be within the province of the Executive to object," provided that the militia system was left essentially intact. As he had imposed martial law on only three occasions, he expressed no regret at the loss of that power.

The reorganized militia more closely resembled the antebellum system. Exemptions from compulsory service were extended to include the judges and clerks of the supreme and district courts, secretary of state, auditor, treasurer, comptroller, justices of the peace, post riders, public ferrymen and millers, postmasters, teachers, managers, and telegraph operators. The maximum penalties that could be imposed by the militia in its own courts-martial were reduced to imprisonment of one month or a fine of one hundred dollars. All sections of the previous acts that provided for the organization of the state guard were repealed, and those who had already enlisted in such units were considered to be members of the ordinary militia. The Galveston Artillery, a paramilitary organization whose members were exempt from militia duty, was reorganized and given a new charter. The Galveston Artillery bill, like the new militia act, became law without the governor's signature.

Another assault on the obnoxious acts was Dillard's bill repealing the one establishing the state police. The Senate engrossed the bill by January 24; however, a House substitute was adopted. In his April 19 veto message, Governor Davis discussed at length the problem of lawlessness, but—with the help of three Senate Republican votes cast by Flanagan, Franks, and Saylor—his veto of the repeal was nevertheless overridden. The *Democratic Statesman* exulted over the end of the state police and declared that the "three Senators, who had the manhood to throw off party allegiance in this matter, will receive the grateful acknowledgment of the intelligent public of Texas." The extent of exultation and the depth of relief most Texans felt about the repeal of this particular act was expressed by House member and historian John Henry Brown, who authored its repeal. Ecstatic over the vote in its favor, he wired his hometown newspaper: "The police law is abolished over the Governor's veto. Glory to God in the highest; on earth peace, good will towards men." The Thirteenth Legislature later appropriated fifty thousand dollars to pay the salaries of the state police up to April 21, 1873, the date of their official termination.

Also on January 24, the Senate passed its bill to repeal prior legislation authorizing the governor to appoint certain officers to fill vacancies and a Senate joint resolution requiring the treasurer to pay all warrants presented, without regard to number or date. A House substitute for the Senate bill repealing the act regulating public printing was taken up and, on motion of Senator Fountain, referred, along with the original bill, to the Committee on Printing. Of the five obnoxious acts the legislature particularly wanted to repeal, it was the issue of a state printer that would become the source of considerable disharmony between the House and Senate.

Instead of electing a state printer, the Senate early on had decided that that body's Committee on Printing should contract "with some competent party for the proper printing of the journals of the Senate daily until otherwise provided." On January 21 the Committee on Printing had reported awarding the contract to J. D. Elliot of the *State Gazette.* The House wanted a different printer, and the issue remained unresolved for a good portion of the session. Irregular printings had become a bottleneck which considerably slowed the legislature's work on its agenda. A House motion for a joint meeting on January 21 to elect a state printer was defeated in the Senate by a coalition of both parties. A House resolution on January 24 inviting the Senate to meet in joint session at noon on Saturday, January 25, to decide the printing issue was laid on the table in the Senate by a vote that again saw some conservatives and Radicals siding together. The yeas included Avinger, Broughton, Dillard, and Word, as well as all the Republicans, for a total of seventeen, while the thirteen nays consisted entirely of the remaining conservatives.

After numerous disagreements and haggling, the House and Sen ate finally agreed on a printing bill, signed by Davis on February 17, 1873, which was remarkably similar to the one they had just repealed. In his message on the bill, Davis pointed out that in 1866 the old printing system of choosing the low bidder was dropped and the new one adopted, and the governor had some blunt words to say on the result: "The public printing has come to be considered one of the spoils to be enjoyed without dispute by the political party that may, for the time being, control the Legislature."

Both the Senate and the House finally agreed to engage John Cardwell, founder of the *Austin Democratic Statesman*, as the state printer. The editor of the *Houston Telegraph* was shocked by the allegation of both parties that the Democrat-controlled legislature had authorized even larger printing expenditures than had the Radicals. Shortly after the patronage was switched to Cardwell, Governor Davis chided the senators on the large foreign-language printings they were ordering of trivial bills that concerned small doings in counties far from any German or Spanish readers. An invoice from the stationer who supplied the Senate revealed an attempt to cheat the state. He had been paid in government warrants that had depreciated in value and came to the Senate complaining that extra money or additional warrants were needed to fully pay the Senate's debt. On examining the charges, however, the senators concluded the invoice was so padded that the stationer had already received a fair amount.

On January 27 Senator Sayers introduced a bill conferring the right of suffrage on foreign-born residents who declared before the clerks of the district courts their intention to become citizens. It passed both houses, but on March 6 Davis vetoed it on the grounds that it offered a possible loophole for misrepresentation. He illustrated the need for cautious procedures by citing a recent election in the Rio Grande Valley in which about two hundred Mexican citizens who actually lived in Mexico crossed over the border, registered, and voted fraudulently.

In addition to such contentious matters, both houses dealt routinely with "special bills" such as the incorporation of cities or the granting of city charters, the incorporation of businesses, or acts for the relief of individuals or corporations.

By January 31 it was clear that the Democrats felt keenly their lack of a two-thirds majority, and eventually the election of three Radical senators—Randle, Tracy, and Tendick—would be challenged in cases of questionable merit. First, the Committee on Privileges and Elections, chaired by Dillard, made its report on the election challenge of Wells Thompson to the seat held by Robert P. Tendick on the grounds of election irregularities. Tendick, who had won by 134 votes in a turnout of 3,390, protested that Thompson had no standing to protest the election after Tendick had already been seated during the Twelfth Legislature, but the committee overruled him. At that point the Radical committee member, Rawson, quit attending the meetings. The other committee members—Dillard, Word, and King—recommended hearing testimony on the protest, and it became a long-drawn-out case followed by a curious public.

In February the Republican editor of the *State Journal* had asserted that the investigation of the credentials of the three senators was simply a bold attempt by the Democrats in the Senate to elect three additional Democratic members in order to obtain a two-thirds majority. In Tracy's case, Senator Word differed with both the majority and the minority reports and held that the election in Harris and Montgomery counties should simply be invalidated, that neither man should get the seat, and that another election should be held. Some Democrats criticized Word as disloyal, but others defended his position as truly impartial. Broughton, a conservative independent who had defeated both a Democratic and a Republican candidate in his district, had been much criticized by conservatives for his vote to sustain the sitting members. On April 25, 1873, Broughton offered a resolution asserting that the Senate, in its decision not to expel either Tendick or Tracy, "was not controlled in its action by political or partisan motives" and that, furthermore, "the vote of no Senator should subject him to the imputation of infidelity to his party; nor should his integrity as a man, or member of this body, be impugned." In the end, the Senate refused to expel any of the three senators.

Newspapers of the time record that Senator Broughton was angry about a reporter's having accused him, soon after his vote to sustain Tendick, of taking a bribe from a lobbyist. Broughton requested a Senate investigation of the accusation, but the Senate did not act on his request. Broughton's refusal to vote to unseat Tendick, however, had earned him considerable hostility from the Democrats and resulted in a petition from some members of his district asking him "respectfully" to resign. The Republican *State Gazette*, however, vigorously defended both Broughton's good faith and the propriety of his decision in the Tendick case.

The challenge to Randle's election was of little import, and the dismissal of the case came almost as an anticlimax to the farcical proceedings that had engaged the Committee on Privileges and Elections for much of the Thirteenth Legislature. Randle's seat had been contested by the venerable George M. Patrick, a veteran of the Texas Revolution. Democratic senator Dillard, as committee chairman, submitted the majority report, signed by all the members of the committee, which stated that there was no basis for contesting the seat. The report was adopted with little debate. Randle went on to serve in the Senate of the Fourteenth Legislature.

A House-Senate conference committee chaired by Senator Thomas H. Baker, a Republican more moderate than radical at that point, investigated the background of Democratic senator Finlay. The committee alleged that Finlay had deserted the Confederate Army and had been indicted for murder, with eyewitness testimony against him. The Democrats, however, would not support an effort to expel one of their own, no matter how controversial he was.

The Senate investigations of Republicans Randle, Tracy, and Tendick for electoral fraud revealed a need for voting-reform legislation. Most of the evidence consisted of eyewitness testimonies on the alleged Republican practice of excluding white Democratic voters and encouraging black Republican voters to vote more than once. Voting irregularities were rife in both parties, and interfactional struggle had intensified during Reconstruction.

The Senate, however, cooperated in endorsing a series of acts for election reform. All elections were to be publicized for twenty days in advance, and election managers were to be chosen from within each precinct, preferably one from each of the parties. Managers had to take an oath and were immune from arrest while at the election except in cases of treason, another felony, or a breach of the peace. They were given the power of a district judge to preserve order and keep the peace during an election, including the authority to enlist the local constabulary and to confine unruly persons during the election as soon as they had voted. All sales of liquor were banned during elections, and any place that sold alcohol could not open for business until the polls closed. All ballots were to be cast in secret; detailed procedures were established for keeping records of those who had voted, for marking official ballots, for counting votes, and for transporting the ballots to the district clerk. District judges were authorized to appoint a district clerk until the next general election in the event of a vacancy. The district courts were to decide contested elections for any district or county office, and the legislature would investigate all others. Tie votes no longer would be resolved in the legislature, but rather by another election.

Strict penalties were provided for interfering with the election process. One could be imprisoned up to five years for casting or attempting to cast more than one ballot. Persons who caused a disturbance, aided by one not legally qualified to cast a ballot; who obstructed a legally qualified voter from voting; or who carried a dangerous weapon within one-half mile of a poll could be fined as much as five hundred dollars and jailed for one month. In an act signed on April 29, 1873, district clerks were appointed to act as voter registrars. A board of revision, composed of three justices of the peace, would review the registration lists and hear complaints. A redistricting act for the state legislature became law without the governor's signature, and the previous legislature's voting act, passed on July 11, 1870, was repealed.

A shocking event occurred on February 19, when a House member, Louis Frankee of Fayette County, was murdered on the Capitol steps. In an article dated February 20, 1873, the *Houston Telegraph* reported the following:

> Yesterday evening Mr. Rhodes, Sergeant-at-Arms to the House, drew for the members and officers of the House twenty-eight thousand dollars in currency. In the early afternoon he, assisted by his assistant, Mr. Reeves, and the Chief Clerk, Mr. Walsh, began paying it out, and was thus occupied most of the evening, all of the members not being present. About six P. M. he and the first assistant clerk counted the money still on hand and ascertained the amount still unpaid to members. He had then a little over four thousand dollars. About an hour and a half later Mr. Rhodes paid Mr. Francke [*sic*] two hundred and sixty dollars, and the latter left the Hall. The former almost immediately after walked into the passage between the Representative Hall and Senate Chamber, intending to go below, but went instead into the Senate Chamber. Returning in two or three minutes he was told of the attack on Mr. Francke [*sic*]. The latter most probably went down the steps inside the building, and near the steps fronting south, was knocked down and robbed of two hundred and sixty dollars and his watch. Mr. Web Flanagan seems to have been the first man who discovered him. He had recovered enough to sit up, but was not rational, as he replied to the questions of Capt. Sayers as to who struck him, that it was a member of the committee. Messrs. Nelson and Robb bore him to his room, where he died about half past four A.M. He received his consciousness sufficiently before his death to state

> that he had been attacked by two men, neither of whom he knew. He was struck above the right eye with such force as to break the skull and drive it inwards upon the brain, and his leg was also broken.

On the same day as the *Telegraph* article, the House agreed on new safety measures requiring the sergeant-at-arms "to place two lamps at the foot of the steps on the south side of the capitol, and two in the centre of the lower hall of the capitol, and one on the south gate of the capitol enclosure, and to light the same from dark until eleven o'clock each night during the remainder of the present session of the Legislature."

In early February, the Democrats initiated the first in a number of removal proceedings aimed at Republican district judges. On February 3, 1873, an address removal procedure was instituted against Judge T. C. Barden, a member of the Republican state executive committee, when the House resolved that "the joint resolution asking the Governor to remove T. C. Barden, Judge of the Sixteenth Judicial District, be referred to a special committee of five, to act in conjunction with a like committee of the Senate." An address procedure, less punitive than impeachment, involves a trial before a joint session rather than the presentment of articles of impeachment and a trial before the Senate. Both types of removal procedures would be used in a series of attempts to remove judges, continuing into the next legislature.

In March, the election contest between Wells Thompson and Tendick continued, as did Tracy's contest, and the investigation of Judge Barden had hardly moved forward at all. In April articles of impeachment were presented against another Radical Republican, Judge John G. Scott of the Tenth District, and his trial before the Senate was begun. By May, the attempted impeachment of Scott, which had become a serious procedural problem in the House as more charges were prepared, began to create problems in the Senate, and entire days were spent on motion after motion and vote after vote on procedural issues, with Democratic senators sometimes refusing to vote at all. Ultimately, it was decided that only the Senate could penalize a senator for not voting, and none of the senators made a proposal to that effect. The melodrama and questionable legislative procedures stretched taut the already frayed nerves of the Republican legislators, prompting several outbursts in the Senate. Some of the angry Republicans threatened a "revolution" in the Senate, and all of them—along with Democrat Pyle—signed a formal protest penned by Fountain. But when the senators reconvened after a restful trip to the fair in Houston, the storm clouds had dissipated.

The problems entailed in the ongoing impeachment proceedings against Scott and the investigation of Barden did not prevent an additional attempt to impeach Judge William Chambers of the First District. None of these judges were removed from office. Chambers's impeachment trial occurred during the next legislature, and he was acquitted.

The Senate's inquiry into the improprieties of Comptroller Albert A. Bledsoe and Treasurer George M. Honey contributed indirectly to the passage of a measure which prohibited the treasurer from using public funds for his own purposes, making loans, or keeping in the treasury building any money other than state funds. The attorney general, together with the comptroller, was charged with reviewing the bond of the treasurer on a semiannual basis and reporting on his conduct. Governor Davis refused to sign this bill, but it became law without his signature on May 3, 1873.

Four senators—Democrats Sayers, Avinger, and Ball and Republican Hall—met briefly with delegates from the House in a conference committee to conduct an investigation into the actions of Superintendent of Public Schools Jacob C. DeGress. A Union veteran of Prussian birth and education, DeGress had come to Texas in 1866 as an assistant commissioner for the Freedmen's Bureau for the eastern district of the state. His background, combined with the fact that he had been appointed by Davis, made DeGress suspect in the eyes of the Democrats.

The senators on the committee were more scrupulous in their review process than their House counterparts; they conducted their review separately from that of the House members after the latter insisted on closing their meetings to the public and refused to allow DeGress to testify in his own behalf. The result, however, was just as partisan, as only Republican senator Hall refused to sign the report condemning DeGress. (Hall was also the only committee member to dissent from the indictment.) The report's most damning charges included the superintendent's decision to pay "six teachers of colored schools, who were ladies from the North," more than other teachers of the same grade were paid. It also alleged that De-

Gress had appointed to positions on school review boards George W. Smith, a federal officer reviled in Texas for his role in the military's stonewalling on the events that led to the great fire of Brenham, and W. B. Bonner, suspected of election fraud in his home district. DeGress was not removed, but he was not reelected under the new statute providing for election of the superintendent.

In several bills, the Senate acted on Governor Davis's mandate to provide for public education, but the overall results disappointed him. One measure of which he did approve, a House bill passed by the Senate and signed by the governor on March 18, 1873, set aside one-half of the public domain for the support of the public school system. All previous and subsequent land grants to railroads and other corporations for internal improvements would be surveyed in alternate sections (640 acres), and every even-numbered section would be set aside for public schools. On April 30 the act providing for the election of a superintendent of public instruction every four years, which had been introduced by Senator Dohoney, was passed over the governor's veto. The superintendent was in charge of the disbursal of all school funds through the county supervisors and retained nominal control over all other aspects of the operation of the public schools; elected boards of directors in each county were responsible for establishing curricula and selecting textbooks. The superintendent of public instruction was required to report to the governor by the first of December preceding each regular session of the legislature on the status and condition of the public school system. Schools were required to be open four consecutive months of every year, and funding was apportioned according to the school-age population of each county. In his veto message the governor argued that the four-month school year to be established under the measure would prevent professional teachers from teaching because they would not be able to live on a four-month salary. Davis also objected strongly to local control over the selection of textbooks and the employment of teachers because of the lack of uniformity local control would create. He did not wish to entrust the future of public education to the county governments, which he believed had already been proven to be hopelessly corrupt.

Proponents of the new school bill pointed out that the sections dealing with the number of months schools must remain open—four annually, with the option of continuing for a longer term—

were virtually the same in both the Radical and Democratic measures. Both bills left the issue of longer school terms up to the county trustees and left the question of how to use the budget up to them as well; if they wanted long terms, they could always finance extra months from taxpayers within the county. In the eyes of conservatives the most praiseworthy new feature was the equity ensured by the new bill: all the school-fund money would be divided among the counties by scholastic population and among the school districts on a per-pupil basis.

The governor's veto was also overridden on another bill, one providing four hundred thousand dollars for the salaries of a number of public school teachers who had not been paid during the previous year. Davis objected that the bill did not provide enough money to compensate all the petitioners and that the manner of distribution was unfair. The veto nevertheless brought accusations of callousness and favoritism against the governor from the conference committee and the press and increased public opposition to him.

The Senate also continued to provide for private education. The charter of Nacogdoches University, first granted in 1845, was renewed through the end of the century. Two charters that had lapsed were revived: DeKalb College, first granted in 1839, and Concrete College, first incorporated by the Tenth Legislature. The Synod of the Presbyterian Church of Texas was granted permission to move Austin College from Huntsville to any place of the synod's choosing. New private schools that received charters included Burleson Male and Female Academy and Excelsior College in Bastrop County, Little River Academy in Bell County, Rusk Masonic Institute in Cherokee County, Marvin College in Ellis County, Hallville Masonic Institute in Harrison County, Centreville Academic School in Leon County, Jefferson Institute in Marion County, Davilla Institute in Milam County, Owensville High School in Robertson County, Garden Valley Seminary in Smith County, and the Odd Fellows' Male and Female College in Upshur County.

Senator Dohoney continued his efforts to restrict liquor sales in the areas surrounding schools but failed to secure passage of his bill to make any saloon keeper or liquor retailer liable for civil prosecution for "whatever evils may result from the use of intoxicating liquors sold by him." The senator maintained that his bill was not intended to bring about prohibition, but a majority of his peers thought otherwise and the measure failed to pass the Senate. The Thirteenth Legislature did, however, prohibit liquor sales in several towns. Four townships prohibiting the sale of liquor in response to petitions for reasons other than education were Mountain Home in Bell County, Oak Grove in Coryell County, Center Point in Kerr County, and Pattonville in Lamar County.

On the subject of land policy, the Thirteenth Legislature acted to standardize procedures and remove the element of politics. The Senate endorsed legislation allowing any settler who had preempted and cultivated a portion of the public domain for three years to file for a homestead. Each tract would be laid out by surveyors operating for the first time with a high degree of standardization. Under other legislation, the district or county surveyors were required to establish a "substantial monument" at the true meridian of their county, to calibrate all of their instruments to it, and to keep a chain measuring a true ten *varas* (333.3 inches) for the measurement of all other chains.

Fencing became an issue almost as important as accurate surveys. On April 23, 1873, Governor Davis signed an act making it unlawful for anyone to pull down or cut a fence, to leave a gate open, or to pasture livestock on another's land without the permission of the property owner. The possible jail sentence was stiff—twelve months in the county jail—but the cash fines were small: from ten to one hundred dollars. A separate act, signed on June 2, 1873, provided that anyone who pastured a herd of more than twenty-five horses or cattle on land that was not his, including public land, within one-half mile of a residence without the permission of the resident could be fined up to one hundred dollars for each hour that he failed to remove the herd after having been given due notice.

The legislature devoted considerable attention to public health matters. An act for the registration of all births was signed on May 3, 1873: district court clerks were made responsible for keeping the records for their counties, and a fine of five dollars was to be levied for every month a parent neglected to report a birth after the first six months of the child's life. A statute regulating the practice of medicine in Texas became law without the governor's signature on May 16, 1873. The act required every person practicing medicine to have studied at "some regularly established and well accredited medical college" and to have been certified by the new state board of medical examiners. The board was to be composed of "not less than three practicing physicians of known ability, and graduates of some medical college, recognized by the American Medical Association." Finally, incorporated towns of fifteen hundred inhabitants or more situated along the coast or on a railway line were authorized by the Thirteenth Legislature to levy a tax not exceeding one-fifth of 1 percent for three years to finance the construction of hospitals charged with the duty of admitting indigent patients from the surrounding county, whose care was to be paid for by the aldermen or county court.

Because harbors and waterways were crucial to Texas' development, the Senate endorsed the cession of a right-of-way along the coast from the eastern border of the state to the Rio Grande for the construction of a canal by the federal government. In a joint resolution introduced by Senator Ruby, the legislature urged the state's delegation in Congress to press for a canal across the Florida peninsula to expedite Texas' trade with the East Coast and Europe. Ruby also proposed a joint resolution, endorsed by Davis on May 3, asking the Texas congressional delegation to secure federal aid for improvements to Galveston harbor, and five days later Ruby offered a second resolution which called for dredging the channel into Matagorda Bay over Pass Cavallo Bar. The city of Galveston was permitted to issue five hundred thousand dollars' worth of 10 percent bonds for harbor improvement and to levy a tax of one-fourth of 1 percent for a sinking fund for amortizing the bonds. The city of Corpus Christi was granted sixteen sections of land for each canal mile between Aransas Bay and Corpus Christi Bay. The canal was to be eight feet deep and at least one hundred feet across at its bottom.

The Thirteenth Legislature also encouraged intrastate transportation, as a number of turnpike and bridge companies and numerous individuals received charters for the operation of pay ferries and toll bridges. Free public bridges were authorized for the city of Jefferson and for Gonzales County. In an act that Davis did not sign, the governor was empowered to appoint a commission from among the shippers of Liberty, San Jacinto, Trinity, Galveston, and Polk counties to organize efforts to make the Trinity River navigable from White Rock Shoals in Trinity County south to Moss Bluff in Liberty County. For every mile of river cleared of obstructions, the commission would receive four sections of land, to be located anywhere in the unappropriated portion of the public domain, for the payment of contractors and such. Land was also granted to the previously incorporated Texas and Mississippi River Canal and Navigation Company, which proposed to dredge a canal along the coast from Galveston Bay to Sabine Lake. Lake City Navigation Company was chartered to improve navigation along Big Cypress Bayou near Jefferson.

The legislature advocated internal improvements for other areas. For example, a joint resolution on April 9, 1873, requested Texas' congressmen to secure funding for telegraphic communications between the frontier posts along the state's western and southern borders.

Many railroad companies successfully petitioned the legislature for financial incentives or relief. Some of the smaller firms merged in order to achieve their goals. (For example, the Waco and Northwestern Railway Company was merged into the Houston and Texas Central Railway Company, which connected with the Missouri, Kansas and Texas at Denison to give the state its first through line to Saint Louis.) At the same time, however, there was a proliferation of new rail companies fostered by the largesse of the Thirteenth Legislature, which granted sixteen sections of land for every mile of track laid. The legislature was bombarded by requests from new firms seeking to take advantage of this revived land policy. Many of these corporations never existed other than on paper, but some grew quickly and were later integrated into larger networks. (Streetcar companies such as the Paris Street Railway Company began developing, too, although they did not receive land grants.)

The Senate took further action on the railroad bill passed during the Twelfth Legislature, variously referred to in the *House Journal* and the *Senate Journal* as the Southern Pacific, Texas Pacific, or International railroad bill. According to an account in the *Houston Telegraph*, the charter approved by that legislature had not been fulfilled, and a charter was requested for a new company which combined two proposed roads. The new company asked for a year's relief, continuation of the land grants and bonds given to the original road, and, in addition, new land grants for the new entity. The amount of land potentially to be acquired was staggering, comprising much of the remaining public domain. The legislature could have abrogated the earlier charter and contract entirely and negotiated far less generous terms, but instead it gave the new company everything it had requested. The public was scandalized and the legislature was vehemently denounced, especially by Democrats but also by Whigs and Republicans who believed in aid to railroads but not in what amounted, in their view, to robbery of the state.

On July 25 the *Telegraph*, which had sharply criticized the charter, published an addition to the story, describing the International's amazingly generous charter from the Mexican government to build a line all the way to Mexico City and the Pacific. The whole package was in accord with the interests of the Great Northern, the Missouri, Kansas and Texas, the Saint Louis and Iron Mountain, and the Cairo and Fulton companies. The survey was to be done at the company's expense within two years and be approved by the Department of Public Works, with work from Mexico City to commence within nine months from May 24, 1873; the completion of a substantial, specified number of miles per year was to be guaranteed. Mexico obligated itself to pay $9,000 for each kilometer and $1.6 million on completion of the railroad and a branch line across the Rio Grande through twelve Mexican states to a terminus on the Pacific Ocean. The company would receive, among other things, absolute mineral rights; 213 feet of right-of-way; and land for stations, warehouses, and water tanks, with no taxes for fifteen years on materials used; exemptions from military service for its officers and employees; government guards for the roads, if necessary; and no excise duty on through passengers or through goods for fifty years. The benefits of the charter filled almost two newspaper columns. The prospects were simply dazzling.

Several days later the *Telegraph* tried to straddle the issue and came out in favor of the venture, softening its tone toward the Texas portion of the deal while nonetheless cautioning against public subsidies to private enterprise and expressing the hope that the company would yet effect a compromise on the bonds, as a "bitter feeling [exists] among the masses against a subsidy which they believe was obtained by fraud and bribery."

On June 2, two days before the session ended, Wesley B. Johnston—who had replaced Captain Faulkner as the Senate sergeant-at-arms in the Twelfth Legislature when the entire slate of officers was removed in a power struggle—appeared before the House. Johnston presented an impressively polished memorial, leavened with considerable sardonic wit, in which he attested that in his capacity as Senate sergeant-at-arms of the Twelfth Legislature he had been present on several occasions when the railroad's agent, James H. Bell, bribed several senators and representatives. Unfortunately for the curiosity of later generations, Johnston did not provide any other names or evidence, though he said that each case would be described in detail in papers to be "almost simultaneously" presented to the House. Since adjournment was only two days away and the Senate rejected a resolution to keep a committee on after the session to pursue the issue, Johnston's memorial simply stood as read, much to the frustration of newspapermen all over the state.

On March 14 and April 22, 1872, Comptroller Bledsoe had refused to countersign and register the bonds for the International, charging that the International had agreed to pay certain legislators for their votes for the 1870 legislation. The whole state was in an uproar, with some defending Bledsoe and others saying he should issue the bonds so that the matter could be fought out in court. Davis had no choice but to replace Bledsoe with an acting comptroller; the bonds were then issued, and the whole matter went to the courts. The case reached the Supreme Court, but the controversy was settled by a compromise law in the Fourteenth Legislature which traded land for the bonds at the minimum amount of land required to fulfill the contract rather than the maximum.

In May, Senator Fountain focused on the most important issue affecting the western and border districts—raids into Texas by Mexicans and Indians "who murder our citizens and plunder their property." Concerned that "thousands of cattle are killed by these marauders for the sake of their hides, which are taken across the Rio Grande into Mexico," Fountain offered petitions and affidavits to "establish the fact that a predatory warfare is being waged upon our State." Numerous affidavits detailing the huge number of cattle carcasses found skinned and naming Texans who had been murdered by the bandits were introduced into the *Senate Journal*, signed in equal numbers by men with Hispanic and Anglo surnames. In a joint resolution, the legislators urged Washington to press Mexico for redress of this problem but received little attention; frontier protection became a bone of contention between the state and federal governments. In a bill endorsed by the Senate that became law without the governor's signature, the Thirteenth Legislature relieved all of the counties on the southern and western borders of Texas from the collection of the state ad valorem and poll taxes on the grounds that, since the United States refused to assign any regular troops to those regions, the residents had suffered a great loss of property to hostile Indians and might soon abandon the area if relief were not forthcoming. A special note of fear was sounded in this and other measures over the presence of Indians armed with repeating rifles. In a joint resolution, the Thirteenth Legislature urged the adjutant general to secure a quantity of improved Winchester rifles for use by some valiant citizens who had defeated a party of thirty-eight Indians in Blanco County who were armed with the improved breech-loading rifles.

In the closing days of the session, Davis returned a number of vetoes. Among the most notable was his veto of a bill for the Agricultural and Mechanical College of Texas, with which he set an important precedent for higher education in Texas by stating that the control of lands directly owned by the university must be given to the administrators and not to the legislature. Davis further noted that the legislature had appropriated about three and one-half times more money than he believed necessary to construct the buildings, which in his view "invites looseness of expenditure on the part of the commissioners." However, Davis's instructions to Secretary of State Newcomb to proceed on the Morrill Act and the governor's personal supervision in the acquisition of the scrip for land grant colleges which the federal government was providing were crucial to the foundation of the college. Within three years the Agricultural and Mechanical College of Texas would open its doors near Bryan with a new charter.

Despite its achievements in civil organization and internal improvements, the Thirteenth Legislature is remembered chiefly for the initial pledge of its Democratic members to undo the radical reforms of the Davis administration—a pledge which they fulfilled. Virtually all of these repeals met with general approval, though the inclusion of the educational system among the programs which were dismantled occasioned much debate. And although they failed to convene a constitutional convention, legislators such as Dohoney would keep that issue alive in an effort to repeal the compromise Republican constitution adopted in 1869, and a convention would be called in 1875.

The Senate accomplished its agenda with remarkably little rancor, despite occasional heated exchanges on the floor. The *Democratic Statesman*, at the close of the session, predicted that the "verdict of the people of Texas, after they fully understand what has been effected by their representatives, will be, 'Well done, good and faithful servants.'" The Republican *State Journal* retained to the end its bitter tone toward the House but grudgingly admitted that the Senate presented a strong contrast to the lower chamber in its moderation and careful deliberation.

On April 12, the Senate had adopted a House concurrent resolution calling for a joint committee to consider "the propriety of a general election during the present year, and report by bill or otherwise at as early a day as practicable." This action would lead to the famous contested election in the fall and end with a showdown between Davis and Coke.

On June 4, 1873, Finlay offered a resolution thanking the Honorable E. B. Pickett, president of the Senate, for his service to that body. The chaplain offered up a prayer for the Senate, after which the president rose and gave a brief farewell message commending the senators for hard work well done and wishing them prosperity and happiness as they returned to their respective parts of the state. Thus the Senate of the Thirteenth Legislature came to a successful conclusion during an immensely difficult era. Of particular note was the goodwill with which all the senators agreed to step down for the new elections. The *Telegraph* said of the election law, "The passage of the law alone covers the present Legislature with glory. . . . The Senators, who drew the four and six year terms, and yet supported the bill, deserve great credit, and its effect is to put them out of office, and to require them again to submit their claims to the people, if they wish to come back here."

RESURGENCE OF THE DEMOCRATS

CHAPTER 7

The Senate of the Fourteenth Legislature, 1874–75

The end of Republican rule coincided with the spectacular installation of the Fourteenth Legislature, when Governor Davis barricaded himself in the first floor of the Capitol and the legislators used ladders to climb into the House and Senate chambers. This far-from-comical comic opera had its roots in the preceding elections, in which the Democrats had emerged victorious and Davis had lost the governorship to Richard Coke. Governor Davis, following a decision by the Texas Supreme Court, had declared the election unconstitutional and the Thirteenth Legislature the only legal representative assembly for Texas. The Democrats had dominated the election, which was characterized by fraud and intimidation on both sides, and were eager to assume control of the government. During a weeklong siege, they succeeded in inaugurating Richard Coke as governor and Richard B. Hubbard as lieutenant governor despite the occupation of the Capitol by hostile black and white militiamen. Once they had secured power, the Democrats in the Fourteenth Legislature, whatever their moderate sentiments upon arriving in the capital, carried out a vindictive program to eradicate the last vestiges of Republican authority. At the same time, they did not neglect the ordinary affairs of state.

The constitutional crisis of 1874 unfolded in the following manner. On January 5, prior to the assembling of the Fourteenth Legislature, the Texas Supreme Court handed down its decision in *Ex Parte Rodriguez*, declaring the 1873 elections to be unconstitutional. The constitutional challenge to the election law was that the constitution provided that "all elections . . . shall be held at the county seats of the several counties until otherwise provided by law; *and the polls shall be open for four days*" (emphasis added). Despite this provision, the Thirteenth Legislature had, in its election reform legislation, allowed polling at precinct boxes and also limited the election to one day. The election challenge asserted that the semicolon made the two clauses independent, that the phrase "until otherwise provided by law" applied only to the first clause, and that the legislature, consequently, was not authorized to change the length of time for the election. The court's decision, the last by a Radical Republican Supreme Court in Texas, was denounced as merely a partisan attempt by Davis and his supporters to retain control of the state government, and the justices were derisively termed the "Semicolon Court."

Governor Davis adhered to the Texas Supreme Court's decision invalidating the Thirteenth Legislature's election law reform, and the Republican minority appeared ready to continue its rule, by force if necessary. The staunchly Republican *Austin State Journal* reminded its readers that former Democratic senator Pickett had taken note of that same semicolon and had voiced his concern that the election reform legislation would require a constitutional amendment. The *State Journal* asked: "What has become of Pickett? Did he not warn them that four days were more than one day, by about three days? Aye, that did he! And must he now yield the chair to the mighty haunches of Royal Dick? Shall *de jure* yield to *de facto?*" From the Texas electorate, the answer to the last question seemed to be a resounding affirmation of the Democrats' resolve to expel the Republicans, and Pickett prudently lay low as his party laid plans for a final conquest.

The Democrats, enjoying overwhelming support from the electorate, wanted Davis to resign in January, 1874, so that they could proceed with the organization of the government, but Davis refused to step down. Davis's refusal led to a caucus of the Democratic leaders. Rejecting several proposals, the Democrats finally decided to convene the legislature, inaugurate Coke, and gain control of the government or be overthrown by federal troops.

Tension mounted alarmingly when Coke arrived in Austin on January 8, 1874. In a message to the Senate dated January 13, Davis warned the assembling Democrats not to press the issue and called on federal authorities to support him in his claim. President Grant

The Political Contest at Austin, 1874. Gathering of the Democrats to oust the Radicals. Reproduced from holdings of Texas State Archives.

refused to send troops, suggesting to Davis that he "yield to the verdict of the people."

After Grant's refusal and in response to the progression of Democratic control, Davis occupied and barricaded the Capitol with the assistance of thirty armed freedmen under the command of his brother-in-law, Adjutant General Frank L. Britton.

The Democrats, seeing that the governor's troops occupied only the basement and first floor, obtained a pass key and quietly took possession of the legislative chambers on the second floor. Early on the morning of Tuesday, January 13, the Democrats of the Fourteenth Legislature climbed a ladder to the second floor of the Capitol and readied themselves for business.

After the Senate had completed its organization on January 13, President Pro Tempore John Ireland addressed the members:

> Senators—We meet under peculiar circumstances. For ten long years we, a disarmed people, have been struggling to establish a government of our choice. We have yielded everything except honor, for the sake of peace, and to-day, though we have been chosen as representatives of the people, by a majority of near fifty thousand, we find ourselves menaced and embarrassed in the discharge of our duties.

Militia assembled on Capitol grounds following the 1873 election that ended Reconstruction and put Democrat Richard Coke in the governor's chair. Reproduced from holdings of Texas State Archives.

Ireland called for the exercise of "cool, calm, deliberate judgement," insisting that "if we act from passion, we do wrong."

Governor Davis, when the customary delegation informed him that the Fourteenth Legislature was organized and ready to open the session, replied with a letter in which he refused to recognize the members present as the constitutionally elected Fourteenth Legislature. He held fast to the decision of the Texas Supreme Court and insisted that the *Thirteenth* Legislature was the only assembly which he could legally recognize. As for his own term in office, Davis added that he considered the election returns for governor "conclusive" and that he would "in no event continue to exercise the functions of the office . . . beyond [his] constitutional term of four years." These words rang ominously in the ears of the members of the new Senate because Davis's "constitutional term," as he and the Texas Supreme Court defined it, would not expire until

April, 1874. Downstairs, three Republican senators from the Thirteenth Legislature—Thomas H. Baker, Phidello W. Hall, and Henry Rawson—vainly tried to assemble a quorum in defiance of the legislators above.

On January 15 a committee recommended that the Fourteenth Legislature assemble to count the votes for governor and lieutenant governor and inaugurate the victors as soon as possible. The members of the committee unanimously declared that Davis's term would end as soon as his successor qualified. Secretary of State James P. Newcomb refused to surrender the election returns, but they were forcibly wrested from him. A joint session held in the House chamber counted the ballots and declared Coke the victor over Davis for governor and Hubbard the winner for lieutenant governor over Republican Robert H. Taylor, who had been a member of the House during the Eighth Legislature. Coke and Hubbard, as staunch Democrats and former Confederates, were both anathema to Davis and his supporters. Coke had risen to the rank of captain in the Confederate Army and then, after the war, had served on the Texas Supreme Court until he was dismissed in 1867 as an "impediment to Reconstruction." Hubbard had commanded the 22nd Texas Cavalry Regiment and had remained active in politics after 1865, becoming a noted opponent of Radical policies.

After the certification of their victories by the joint session, Coke and Hubbard were conducted to the speaker's rostrum, where Coke delivered a lengthy inaugural address and pledged to defend "local self-government" by the people of Texas. The senators then returned to their chamber and adopted a resolution by Dillard that the "sergeant-at-arms be instructed to employ sufficient force to prevent the Senate chamber from any intrusion to-night." They authorized the mustering of additional assistant sergeants-at-arms to aid in this task. Outside, the capital had become an armed camp as Texas militia and former soldiers streamed in to ally themselves with one side or the other. Before adjourning for the day, Hubbard addressed the Senate, invoking memories of Texas' pantheon of heroes from the period of the Republic and urging the senators to stand fast.

Within the Capitol building, relations between the two factions soon deteriorated. Davis's troops, reinforced by bands of whites and blacks armed from the state arsenal by Adjutant General Britton,

Richard Coke, governor of Texas, 1874–76.
Courtesy Texas State Library and Archives.

threatened any of Coke's supporters who used the stairs to the second floor. Rumors circulated that the Davis forces had discovered that they could shoot through the floors of the legislative chambers from below. Both groups maneuvered for possession of the few cannon on the grounds, and Coke's men gained control of the arsenal.

The Texas Contest—Radicals arresting the Mayor of Austin—1874. Thomas Benton Wheeler. Reproduced from holdings of Texas State Archives.

On Saturday, January 17, Davis telegraphed once more to Grant requesting federal troops. The president again refused to intervene, and Davis left the Capitol about the middle of the day on January 19. Also at noon on January 19, a "mob" led by Coke took official possession of the offices on the lower floor of the Capitol. The doors had been barred by the Davis faction, but Dillard, whom the *State Journal* characterized as a "Ku Klux Senator from East Texas," ordered them broken down with an ax and placed Secretary of State Newcomb, who remained inside, under arrest.

On January 20 the Senate dismissed the six additional sergeants-at-arms and unanimously adopted a joint resolution introduced by Senator William H. Westfall to raise the U.S. flag over the Capitol, signaling the opening of the session. Radical Republican rule in Texas had come to an end.

Although there had been a Democratic majority in the Thirteenth Legislature, it was Coke's win over Davis and the seating of the Fourteenth Legislature which officially marked the end of political Reconstruction in Texas. On February 14 the Fourteenth Legislature, by a joint resolution introduced by Senator William D. Wood, conveyed its gratitude to President Grant for "declining to furnish troops to Edmund J. Davis, late Governor of Texas, to enable him to set at defiance the popular will, and to destroy popular government in our State." Davis remained in Austin and continued to play an active role in politics, but he never held another elective office.

The Democrats formed an overwhelming majority in the Senate of the Fourteenth Legislature. Only three Democratic members of the Senate of the Thirteenth Legislature—Ball, Dillard, and Swift—were reelected, but they were joined by twenty-three additional Democrats in the first session: Robert D. Allison; William R. Baker; L. D. Bradley; Amzi Bradshaw; John L. Camp, Sr.; David B. Culberson; Jewett H. Davenport; Joseph E. Dwyer; Olinthus Ellis; George B. Erath (who had served in the Senates of the Seventh, Eighth, and Ninth legislatures); William R. Friend; Edwin E. Hobby; John Ireland; Thomas M. Joseph; William E. Moore; Joseph Morris; Cader A. Parker; William H. Russell; Seth Shepard; Reverend Winfield B. Stirman; William H. Trolinger; William H. Westfall; and William D. Wood. (Bradley, Culberson, Ireland, Joseph, Stirman, Trolinger, Westfall, and Wood had previously served in the House.) N. S. Craven later replaced Trolinger, who resigned, and Culberson and Camp resigned without successors. William H. Ledbetter, although he now labeled himself an independent, had been a Democrat in the past and would wear that label again in the Fifteenth and Sixteenth legislatures.

Though united in their conservatism and their opposition to Republicans, the Democratic senators reflected a variety of interests and backgrounds.

Robert D. Allison of McKinney, born in North Carolina on September 10, 1810, was sixty-three years old when first elected to the Texas Legislature as a member of the Senate. Although a farmer by occupation, he had been a colonel in both the Mexican War and the Civil War, a soldier of renown wounded in battle six times. Allison would serve only one term as a senator but would return to the legislature as a member of the House of Representatives in the Fifteenth, Eighteenth, and Twenty-first legislatures.

One of the rare old Texians still serving in a political office, William Robinson Baker of Houston was the son of a veteran of the War of 1812, Asa Baker, and of Hannah Robinson, daughter of a prominent Philadelphia merchant. Asa and Hannah resided in Cheshire County, New Hampshire, through the War of 1812. Following the war, the Bakers moved to Onondaga County, New York, where William was born on May 21, 1820. The family could not afford a private education for the children, and except for a four-month stint in school, William and his siblings were tutored by their father. From age ten, the lad lived out in the community with kinfolk and friends, performing manual labor. In 1837, at age seventeen, he decided to go to Texas and settled in Houston for life. For about two years he was bookkeeper of the Houston Town Company, and from 1839 to 1841 he "carried on a kind of general store." In February, 1841, he was elected for the first time as county clerk, a position he would hold for the next sixteen years. From 1856 to 1877 he served in various positions with the Houston and Texas Central Railroad. When he sold out his interest he had served as president, vice-president, and manager of the road.

"Five feet ten inches in height, and weighing one hundred and seventy pounds, of dark complexion, brown eyes, and a high, intellectual forehead." He entered the Senate in 1874, retired from business in 1878, and was elected mayor of Houston in 1880. His wife, whom he married in 1845, was Hester E. Runnels, niece and adopted daughter of the governor of Mississippi. Baker was a longtime Mason, and he believed in the principles of morality but not in the Bible as interpreted by denominations. Baker died April 30, 1890, of "cerebral effusion."

Born in Dallas County, Alabama, on April 13, 1831, L. D. Bradley was a graduate of Transylvania University at Lexington, Kentucky, and practiced law at Selma and Cahawba, Alabama, before moving to Texas, where he practiced law at Fairfield in Freestone County from 1855 to 1861. At the beginning of the war he raised two companies for the Confederate service and was elected captain of the second. Bradley "entered Wall's Legion, served through the entire war, and was promoted for gallantry and faithful duty to the Coloneley [*sic*] of the regiment." At the close of the war he resumed his law practice and was elected to the House of the Eleventh Legislature and the Senate of the Fourteenth. While serving in the Senate, he was elected judge of his judicial district, composed of Freestone, Limestone, and Navarro counties. He was reelected and served on the bench until his death on October 6, 1886. Bradley was tall for his day, about six feet, and weighed about 250 pounds. His size, black eyes, black hair, and swarthy complexion made him notable even in a large crowd. His wife, Mary Grayson, and he produced nine children.

Amzi Bradshaw of Waxahachie was born in Hickman County, Tennessee, on January 13, 1824. His grandfather was from Scotland and his father, Elias Bradshaw, was born in North Carolina. The senator was a young boy when his father died; his mother then married Elias Hicks, and the family moved to Hardeman County, Tennessee. Since they were poor, Amzi was not sent to school but was presumably given some education at home. At age twenty-one, he attended school for eight months and subsequently taught school for nearly two years. In 1849, he moved to Rusk County, Texas; he taught school at Enterprise and then engaged in various pursuits for a couple of years. He began the study of law in 1852 and was admitted to the bar the same year by Judge L. D. Evans. The new attorney moved to Waxahachie, which became his permanent residence. He arrived there with virtually nothing but a spirit of determination and over the next three decades became a man of considerable substance.

Elected district attorney in 1860, Bradshaw resigned when the Civil War broke out the next year. He represented Ellis, Tarrant, Parker, and Johnson counties at the Secession Convention and at the Reconstruction Convention in 1866. In the war he served in regiments commanded by Colonel Nat Buford, General Henry McCulloch, and a Colonel Shoalwater. Bradshaw served only one term in the Senate. The *Encyclopedia of the New West* described him as being

> opposed to class legislation, whether for whites or negroes; he holds to the Jeffersonian platform that regards special legislation as one of the greatest enemies of republican government. He holds that in politics, as in religion, there is one eternal truth, and that Democracy is the exponent of that truth; Democracy cannot, in his estimation, be progressive—its object being always the same, to-wit: To protect

> life, liberty and property. There can be no advance in this object, any more than in a square or circle, without breaking its unity and destroying its essential characteristics. He is a Democrat by nature, sympathizing with the masses and firmly relying for the preservation of constitutional liberty upon the virtue and intelligence of the people.
>
> As an orator, he is impressive and emphatic, rather than brilliant; augmentative [*sic*] rather than persuasive. Self-reliant and accustomed to form his own judgment, he is rather tenacious of his opinions, and rather inclined to think that any other view than the one he holds on a given subject is violation of sound reason. Energetic and laborious, he pushes his point with great pertinacity.

Another single-term senator was John Lafayette Camp, Sr., who was born February 20, 1828, in Elyton, Alabama. Camp graduated from the University of Tennessee at Knoxville in 1848 at age twenty. That same year he left for Texas, settling at Gilmer in Upshur County, where he taught school, practiced law, and, in 1851, married Mary Ann Ward. Camp joined the Confederate Army in 1861 and was elected captain of an Upshur County company. He was later elected colonel of the 14th Texas Regiment, was severely wounded at Murfreesboro, Tennessee, and at Altoona Heights, Georgia, and was imprisoned twice. A member of the Constitutional Convention in 1866, he was elected to the Senate of the Fourteenth Legislature in 1873 and elected district judge in 1878. He declined an appointment to the board of regents of the University of Texas due to ill health. In 1884 Camp was appointed land commissioner of Arizona, at the end of the term returning to Texas and settling in San Antonio, where he died in 1891. Camp's son John Lafayette Camp, Jr., served two terms in the Texas Senate.

David B. Culberson of Jefferson, the son of a minister, was born in Troup County, Georgia, September 29, 1830. Culberson was educated at Brownwood Institute, La Grange, Georgia. He read law at Tuskegee, Alabama, in the law school of William P. Chilton (then chief justice of Alabama) and was admitted to the bar in 1850 by Judge W. B. Dougherty of the circuit court at Tuskegee. He moved to Texas in 1856, first settling in Upshur County but moving to Jefferson in 1861.

Culberson earned a considerable reputation as a successful—and controversial—criminal defense attorney and served as a judge of the Sixth District Court. He was elected to the House of the Eighth

Legislature but resigned because he opposed secession. He strongly debated advocates of the Confederacy such as William Ochiltree. When war came, however, he helped raise the 18th Texas Infantry, of which Ochiltree was elected colonel and Culberson lieutenant colonel. After the regiment was merged with General Hawes's brigade under General J. G. Walker, Colonel Ochiltree resigned and Culberson was promoted to colonel. The regiment took part in engagements in the Lower Mississippi Valley, largely in the Vicksburg area.

In the winter of 1863, after his health had broken, Culberson was assigned to duty in Austin, being appointed on November 17, 1863, as adjutant general of the state. In the winter of 1864, he was elected to the House of the Tenth Legislature from Marion County and resigned his military commission in order to serve. His health was still poor—he had weighed over 200 pounds when he entered the army but mustered out weighing 125.

Colonel Culberson was "born in the old line Whig faith, but went over to the Democracy after the disbandment of the Whig party." He was a presidential elector for Greeley in 1871 and a member of the state Democratic convention that nominated Coke for governor in 1873. In 1874 he was elected to the state Senate. As a senator, he was an enthusiastic supporter of land grants to railroads. In 1875, while still a senator, Culberson was elected to the Forty-fourth Congress of the United States from the Second District and resigned his Senate seat. He served in Congress for twenty-two consecutive years, until 1897. In that year he was appointed by President William McKinley as one of the commissioners responsible for revising the U.S. Criminal Code and served in that capacity until he died at his home in Jefferson on May 7, 1900.

Culberson was a Master Mason and an Odd Fellow. He and his wife, Eugenia Kimball, raised two boys. One of them, Charles Allen Culberson, served as governor two decades after his father had been elected to the Senate of the Fourteenth Legislature.

Jewett Harbert Davenport was born in Clarke County, Georgia, on November 1, 1828, and moved to Texas in 1854, locating in Coryell County. He entered the Confederate service in 1862 as a major in the 30th Texas Cavalry under Colonel Gurley, serving for three years in the Trans-Mississippi Department. After the war he moved to Bell County, from which he was elected to the Senate of the Fourteenth Legislature. Davenport returned to Senate service in the Sixteenth and Seventeenth legislatures as the senator from Eastland County and later Hamilton County.

Joseph E. Dwyer was born in San Antonio in 1841. He finished his education in Paris, France, and at age twenty entered the Confederate Army, serving with distinction as a captain and aide-de-camp on the staff of General Sibley. Dwyer rose to the rank of major. He married Annette Magoffin, a daughter of Captain James Magoffin, another aide-de-camp on General Sibley's staff during the war. The couple had seven children.

A one-term senator, Dwyer served for ten years as alderman in San Antonio and was chairman of the Bexar County Democratic Executive Committee for twenty years. He was a delegate from Texas to the National Democratic Convention in 1876, as well as the next three conventions, and received the honor of membership on the notification committee. He rose to committee chairman and in that capacity informed Grover Cleveland of his nomination for the presidency. Dwyer was a prominent member of the city council of San Antonio, serving as mayor pro tempore and as a member of the finance committee. He was only forty-three years old when he died from malaria and heart problems on September 14, 1884.

Olinthus Ellis was born in Henry County, Kentucky, on May 5, 1840. He was a bookkeeper in Louisville when the South seceded. When federal troops came to Louisville, Ellis returned to his old home at Newcastle and remained there for a year. Finally, in the fall of 1862, he enlisted for the South with General Humphrey Marshall and later went to join his brother in Texas, where he mustered into the regiment of Colonel Joseph Bates. In Texas he was appointed sergeant major of the 8th Regiment, Texas Infantry, of General John G. Walker's Texas Division, with which he served until the end of the war.

Ellis was admitted to the bar at Hallettsville in 1865 and married Mattie Dibrell, niece of General George Dibrell, in 1867. He practiced law in Hallettsville until he was elected to the state Senate in 1873. He moved to Uvalde in 1881 and, after the death of his first wife, married Grace Oglesby of Louisiana.

William R. Friend was born at Petersburg, Virginia, on April 27, 1832. He studied law at Princeton and was admitted to the bar at Tuscaloosa, Alabama, in 1852. He visited Texas in 1854, returning in 1857 to settle in Clinton, DeWitt County. He was married to Ella Lightfoot of Iuka, Alabama. During the war Friend became captain of the DeWitt County Rifles on April 22, 1861; in September that same year, he joined Terry's Texas Rangers and was elected a first lieutenant in Company E. Wounded and captured at Macon, Georgia, on November 26, 1864, he was paroled from Demopolis, Alabama, on June 6, 1865.

Friend was elected to the Senate in 1873. When his Senate term expired, he returned to Clinton, but after the Southern Pacific Railroad reached Cuero, he and his family joined the exodus from Clinton to Cuero in 1877. Friend was a Mason, and when he died in 1889, he was buried at Cuero with Masonic honors.

Edwin E. Hobby of Woodville, Tyler County, was born in 1844 to Martin and Anna Hobby of Tallahassee, Florida. In the 1850s, his mother was widowed and moved with Edwin and her other son, A. M., to Galveston. A. M. established a store in the newly founded town of Saint Mary's of Aransas, Refugio County, about 1857. Edwin was still a lad, but A. M., who was twenty-two, quickly became a political leader in the county. With the boldness of a romantic youth, he also joined the Knights of the Golden Circle. When the war broke out, the nineteen-year-old Edwin enlisted in his brother's well-known regiment, Hobby's 8th Texas Infantry Regiment, and was elected captain. His unit was instrumental in preventing a federal invasion at Corpus Christi in August, 1862, and in September captured J. W. Kittridge, commander of the federal fleet. The regiment was engaged in crucial battles and skirmishes in Texas' defense.

Following the war, Edwin divided his residence between Polk and Tyler counties and studied law, being admitted to the bar at Woodville in 1867 and licensed to practice in federal court in 1868 and before the Supreme Court in 1870. He was elected to the Senate for the Fourteenth, Fifteenth, and Sixteenth legislatures. As judge of the Ninth Judicial District, he presided for ten years over the commission of appeals until the court of civil appeals was organized. A learned jurist and gifted conversationalist, he authored many articles and opinions and a book, *Texas Land Law.*

Edwin married Dora Pettus in 1866. One of their five children, William Pettus Hobby, married Oveta Culp; he owned two Beaumont papers and became editor and eventually owner of the *Houston*

Post. The first native-born lieutenant governor of Texas, W. P. later served as governor of Texas. William and Oveta's son, Edwin's grandson, also named William Pettus Hobby, later served as lieutenant governor for eighteen years—the longest tenure of any lieutenant governor in Texas history—until he retired, undefeated at the polls, to teach at Rice University and at the Lyndon B. Johnson School of Public Affairs. In 1995, he was appointed chancellor of the University of Houston System.

A newcomer to the Senate but not to the legislature, John Ireland of Seguin was born in Hart County, Kentucky, on January 1, 1827. Raised on a farm, he obtained an "old-field" school education; that is to say, he had some attendance at the common schools in his area but mostly learned from his family. At the request of the businessmen of the town of Mumford, the state legislature removed his disabilities of minority when he was eighteen so that he could qualify as county constable. He went on to serve for several years as deputy sheriff.

Ireland then studied law under Robert Murray and Henry Woods and was licensed in Kentucky before he moved to Texas. Arriving in San Antonio in January, 1853, he soon moved to Seguin, opening his practice there in April of that year. His practice kept him busy until the Civil War broke out. Elected a delegate to the Secession Convention, he voted to secede and, after the Constitutional Convention of 1861, volunteered as a private. He rose rapidly to captain of his company, major of his regiment, and ultimately lieutenant colonel. He saw some action in the Trans-Mississippi Department but was stationed mainly on coastal duty among the "Horse Marines." After the war he was elected to the Constitutional Convention of 1866. Ireland began his service as a district judge that same year but was dismissed from the bench by General Sheridan in 1867 as an "obstruction to Reconstruction." During the Democratic resurgence, Ireland was elected to the House of the Thirteenth Legislature and to the Senate of the Fourteenth, where he was elected president pro tempore. His opposition to grants for the International Railroad earned him the nickname "Oxcart John." Later, as governor, Ireland was one of a number of Texas chief executives who worried about "railway combinations and oppressions." In 1875 he was appointed associate justice on the Supreme Court and served until the new Constitution of 1876 reduced the number of justices from five to three. In 1876 he lost the U.S. Senate race to Richard Coke and in 1878 was unsuccessful in his bid for the U.S. House of Representatives. He was chosen in April, 1880, along with Governor Hubbard, Governor Throckmorton, and Colonel Jack, as a delegate to the Democratic National Convention that met at Cincinnati and nominated General Winfield Scott Hancock for president.

Described as a compelling speaker who disdained verbiage, Ireland was successful in his race for governor of Texas in 1882 and again in 1884, having been nominated by acclamation and without opposition on both occasions. In 1887 he campaigned for a U.S. Senate seat but lost to John H. Reagan. After his retirement from the governorship, Ireland practiced law in Seguin. He was a Knight Templar and a Presbyterian and was married twice. His first marriage, in 1854, was to Mrs. Matilda Faircloth née Wicks and ended with her death in 1856. A daughter, Matilda, was born to that marriage, and a stepdaughter continued to live with Judge Ireland after her mother's death. In 1857 he married Anna Maria Penn, the niece of Thomas Rives, who died at Goliad. They had four children. The quiet and reserved John Ireland died on March 15, 1896.

Thomas M. Joseph of Galveston was descended from an immigrant from Lisbon, Portugal, Antonio Joseph, who married Annis Rogers of Hartford, Connecticut. Thomas was born at Hartford on February 11, 1823. He was educated in classical schools in Connecticut and Vermont. He arrived in Galveston in 1841 at the age of eighteen and taught school there for two years while reading law under the Honorable Benjamin C. Franklin. Admitted to the bar in 1845, he was elected judge of the county court in 1851 and was reelected four times. Like Ireland, Joseph was a Presbyterian. He married Mary Minor Truhart, the daughter of a Galveston lawyer and surveyor, in 1851, when he was twenty-eight. After serving in the House of the Seventh Legislature, he became mayor of Galveston in 1858 and was reelected five times, serving until 1863. Joseph returned to the House for the Thirteenth Legislature in 1873 and the following year was elected to the Senate of the Fourteenth, filling the seat left vacant by the death of member-elect Benjamin C. Franklin, his former law tutor. Franklin had been elected to the Senate twice but never served as a member of that body: his first election was to the Senate of the Tenth Congress, which never convened and was never sworn, due to Texas' joining the Union; his second election to the Senate was for the Fourteenth Legislature, but his death on December 25, 1873, prevented him from taking the oath of office.

William Hamilton Ledbetter was a prominent attorney from Fayette County. He was born in 1834 to Hamilton and Jane Peacock Ledbetter, a Tennessee couple who in 1838 or 1839 moved to the Lone Star State and in 1840 settled with their slaves on the land where the city of Victoria now stands. Ledbetter was educated in the schools of Fayette County and finished his schooling at Independence, Washington County. At the age of twenty-one he began studying law under General Webb of La Grange and was admitted to the bar in 1857, setting up his practice in La Grange. Ledbetter and his father were among the small group of Texans who owned a hundred or more slaves, and both were nearly bankrupted by the Civil War. According to his biographers, William enlisted in Flournoy's 16th Texas Infantry in 1861 or 1862 and participated in several battles in Louisiana. His account of his experiences during the Civil War, which is found in *Reminiscences of the Boys in Gray*, compiled by Mamie Yeary, paints a vivid picture of those events.

Following his service in the war, Ledbetter resumed his law practice, took an interest in politics, and was elected to the House of the Tenth Legislature and to the Senate of the Fourteenth, Fifteenth, and Sixteenth. He was mayor of La Grange for several terms. His first marriage, to Bettie Pope, produced two children. Their son, William, graduated from the U.S. Naval Academy at Annapolis and later moved to Panama. In 1868 Ledbetter married his second wife, Tennie Hill of Virginia, with whom he had at least two children. Although he is listed in legislative records as an independent, a local biographer stated amusingly, "Mrs. Ledbetter is a member of the Episcopal Church, and Mr. Ledbetter is a Democrat." The exact date of Ledbetter's death is uncertain. His wife returned from a visit to Virginia and found him dead at home on April 24, 1896.

Little is known of William E. Moore save for his Civil War account in *Reminiscences of the Boys in Gray*. Moore was born January 9, 1836, in Leon County, Florida. He enlisted in the Confederate Army at Shreveport, Louisiana, as a member of the Confederate Grays. The Grays were armed by the state and were well drilled. Their services were offered to the governor of Louisiana, who ordered them to proceed to New Orleans, where they were mustered into the Confederate service for one year. Moore was elected captain at Williamsburg, Virginia, the same evening that his unit skirmished with General McClellan's cavalry. Moore was at Seven Pines, Malvern Hill, and Second Manassas, where he was promoted to lieutenant colonel in the field. His next two battles were Harpers Ferry and Sharpsburg, and he was promoted to colonel of the 1st Louisiana Regiment and was temporarily in command while the permanent commander was in the hospital. He was transferred to service under General McCulloch at Bonham, Texas, where he remained until the surrender of the Trans-Mississippi Department. After the war Moore remained in Texas, and when he was elected to the Senate of the Fourteenth Legislature, he listed his home as Blossom in Lamar County.

Joseph Morris of Greenville listed his occupation as farmer and his state of birth as Georgia. Morris moved to Texas in 1843. He was married and fifty years old at the time of his service in the Senate.

Cader Atkins Parker of Lone Star in Titus County had earned considerable experience in public service in Georgia and Alabama before joining the Texas Senate. He was born in Cumberland County, North Carolina, on May 16, 1810, to Ica and Nancy Parker; the family moved to Randolph County, Georgia, in 1828, and Cader married Louiza Beard in Stewart County on November 7, 1830. The young husband was licensed to preach in the Primitive Baptist Church, and the couple moved to what is now Cusetta, Georgia, where conflict still existed between whites and Indians. He was commissioned a captain of the Stewart County Guards of the Georgia militia and engaged in some fighting between the settlers and the Creek Indians. In 1834 he was a justice of the peace. The family moved to Bullock County, Alabama, in 1852, and Cader served in the Alabama House of Representatives from 1861 to 1865. Four of his sons served in the Confederate Army; one, Cader Atkins Parker, Jr., was killed at Gettysburg. Unhappy with postwar conditions in Alabama, Parker and his family decided to relocate to Texas in 1867. He and his wife and six of their eight remaining adult children and their families settled about three miles east of Mount Vernon. Parker was elected to the Senate in 1873. He was pastor of the Glade Springs Church for many years. Parker died in 1886, his wife in 1889. Both are buried in Providence Cemetery near Mount Vernon.

William H. Russell of Brownsville was identified in the *Directory of the Members and Officers of the Fourteenth Legislature, 1874*, as a lawyer, thirty-five years old, married, and born in Texas. Little is known of Russell other than that he had been the subject of scrutiny by the legislature for his judicial conduct prior to his election to the Senate. In 1871, when he was serving as judge of the Fifteenth Judicial District in Brownsville, Russell had confiscated from Henry Haupt, a Brownsville attorney and owner of the newspaper *Ranchero*, a letter from Governor Davis which empowered Haupt to appoint himself or someone else as state printer in Brownsville. Accounts of the event do not reveal what Judge Russell's intentions were in confiscating the letter, but his actions enraged Haupt, who then vilified the judge and spent three days in jail for contempt of court. Judge Russell's actions put him on the wrong side of either Davis or the local Republicans of Brownsville, and the Radical faction in the Twelfth Legislature attempted to impeach him. The House brought charges of "high crimes and misdemeanors in office and incompetence." The effort failed in the Senate, however, indicating that even during the Twelfth Legislature, the Radicals had rapidly lost assured control of the Senate and thus of the legislature.

One of the more notable senators in the Fourteenth Legislature was Seth Shepard, a Democratic lawyer who set up practice at Brenham in Washington County in 1869. Shepard had to battle Senator Matthew Gaines for a seat in the Fourteenth Legislature. The Senate found Gaines ineligible due to his indictment in a bigamy case and awarded the seat to Shepard, who took the oath on March 26, 1874. Shepard was a native Texan, having been born to Chauncey Berkeley and Mary Hester Shepard on their plantation eight miles from Brenham on April 23, 1847. At the age of seventeen he enlisted in the Confederate Army in the closing months of the war. He was educated under Rudolph Krug, headmaster of a private school at Greenvine, and went on to receive law degrees from Washington College (now Washington and Lee University) in 1868 and Georgetown University in Washington, D.C. in 1895.

Shepard's service in the Fourteenth Legislature was the beginning of a very interesting career. Shepard and Ireland became leaders in the fight against the International Railroad bonds and helped force the substitution of land grants in lieu of money. In 1874, 1876, and 1878, Shepard repeated his frustrating experience with primaries when he failed by narrow margins to win the Democratic nomination for Congress from his district. In 1880 he was nominated unanimously by the convention but was defeated in a close race by the Greenback candidate, George Washington Jones.

Shepard served on the board of regents of the University of Texas from 1883 to 1891 and wrote the introduction and the chapter "The Alamo" for *Comprehensive History of Texas*, edited by D. G. Wooten. Shepard moved to Galveston and worked as the attorney for the Gulf, Colorado, and Santa Fe Railroad. He moved his practice to Dallas in 1886 and was a leader in the fight against state prohibition the following year. He opposed the establishment of the Railroad Commission and supported the change from an appointive to an elective commission in 1892. A delegate to the Democratic National Convention in 1892, he helped to write the party platform. When James Hogg's faction, which was advocating the free coinage of silver, split from the platform at the 1892 state convention, Shepard joined the George Clark faction, which supported Grover Cleveland and the gold standard.

In 1893 President Cleveland appointed Shepard to a position as an associate justice of the Court of Appeals in the District of Columbia, and in 1905 Theodore Roosevelt made him chief justice of that court. He had been considered for a seat on the Supreme Court in 1893 and 1895. He taught law at Georgetown University for twenty-one years.

Justice Shepard found the original manuscript of the Texas Declaration of Independence, which had been lost for sixty years, in the National Archives. On June 11, 1895, it was returned to the Lone Star State. The famous document bears the endorsement: "Left at the Department of State, May 28, 1836, by Mr. Wharton. Original."

Shepard was married three times: to Caroline Nelson Goree, who died in 1889; to Etta K. Jarvis, who died in 1909; and to Mrs. Julia B. Towsley, who, along with four children, survived him. He retired from the Court of Appeals in the spring of 1917 and died on December 3 of that year. Shepard was among the few senators to serve in the Civil War and also live to see World War I.

Winfield Brown Stirman of Athens came to Henderson County from Kentucky in 1847. His political career began with his service as county constable. He was the first state representative from Henderson County and ended his political career as a senator in the

Fourteenth Legislature. He was also a pioneer preacher in the area. Stirman was married to Sara Elizabeth Newbern for seventy years, and they raised four children.

William Henry Trolinger of Whitesboro in Grayson County was born August 11, 1827, in Pulaski County, Virginia. The oldest of four children, he moved with his parents, Henry and Attila Cecil Trolinger, to Henry County, Missouri, in 1832, where William received his medical training. He married a widow, Mary Jane Thompson Montgomery, in January, 1850, and they had six children. After the start of the Civil War, Dr. and Mrs. Trolinger moved to the log cabin village of Whitesboro with their slaves, and in 1861 Dr. Trolinger helped survey the original townsite, which was also called Whites Colony.

Dr. Trolinger was elected to the House of the Thirteenth Legislature and to the Senate of the Fourteenth. After resigning from the Senate, he returned to Whitesboro and energetically promoted its growth. He and Mrs. Trolinger belonged to the First Baptist Church, where he was a deacon and she a Sunday school teacher. Dr. Trolinger died at his home on October 28, 1895. His three surviving children all graduated from Baylor University, where Dr. Trolinger had served as a trustee. Mrs. Trolinger wrote a number of articles about her family during this period of Texas history.

The other physician in the Senate of the Fourteenth Legislature, William Harrison Westfall of Burnet, was from Virginia stock of Prussian extraction. Westfall was born in Upshur County (now in West Virginia) on December 16, 1822. He grew up there and was educated in local schools. He obtained his medical education during five years at the medical department and teaching hospitals of the University of New York. He delayed going into practice, however, as he was struck with gold fever and by the spring of 1850 was on his way to California, where he spent several months in the gold fields. The next year he returned to "the States," stopping in Missouri. There he got together the means to make a speculative cattle drive back to California. The men and the cattle covered two thousand miles of desert and wild Indian territory without serious mishap, and the venture turned out profitably. In the fall of 1853 Westfall returned to Missouri, where he formed a partnership with Dr. G. Y. Salmon, a well-known physician, at Clinton in Henry County. In November of that year, he married Mary A. Bates of Clinton.

Four years later, the couple moved to Austin, where Dr. Westfall set up his practice. They also acquired a ranch in Williamson County, where they lived during the war. They were living in Williamson County when Westfall was elected to the Texas House in 1872. While in the House he actively supported the public school system, the security of public funds, laws regulating taxes, and the protection of agricultural interests, and these remained his main interests during his term as a senator.

Westfall moved back to Austin in 1876 and then to Burnet in 1879. Together with his son-in-law, he opened the Westfall & Company Bank. Dr. Westfall also had mercantile and real estate interests and opened the quarry at Granite Mountain which provided the stone for the new Capitol. This stone also went into the jetties at Galveston and the dam at Austin. Dr. Westfall was associated with the Austin & Northwestern Railroad and was a Mason.

William D. Wood of Centerville was born in Edgecome County, North Carolina, on March 11, 1828. While he was still young, his parents moved to Randolph County, Indiana, where he grew up and qualified for the bar. In 1850 the family moved south to Choctaw County, Alabama, where Wood taught school for a while before he and his brother walked from Alabama to Texas in 1851. At age twenty-two or twenty-three, he took up the practice of law in Leon County. In fact, he and his brother made their living principally by printing a small newspaper. The first issue of the *Leon Pioneer* appeared in the spring of 1852. They kept the paper for three and a half years, then sold it to John Gregg and Morris Reagan, who was a brother of Judge Reagan. In 1857 Wood was elected to the legislature. He enlisted when the war started and was posted to Tyler, to Walnut Hills, Louisiana, and to Little Rock, Arkansas; but there he had to muster out due to physical problems. He eventually served the Confederacy during the remainder of the war as assessor and collector of taxes in Leon County and as a member of the home guards. At the end of the war he resumed his law practice. Wood entered the House in 1873 and the Senate in 1874. In 1876 he was elected district judge and held the office for four and a half years. In 1883 he moved to San Marcos and, in addition to practicing law, served as president of the Glover National Bank.

Walter M. Burton of Fort Bend County was one of only three Republicans to serve in the Senate of the Fourteenth Legislature—

Flanagan and Randle, both of whom had been in the Thirteenth Legislature, were the other two. Burton was a black newcomer whose admittance was delayed by a protest from Senator Wood on behalf of Z. Hunt, who contested the election. The Committee on Privileges and Elections split in its verdict on the legality of Burton's election. For the benefit of voters who could not write, ballots in different colors, with the candidates' names already printed on them, had been provided. Voters who chose to write in a candidate's name were provided with a blank ballot. At least two typesetters assumed that W. M. Burton, who was actually Walter Moses Burton, was Wm. (William) Burton. At several polls, the name printed on the correctly colored ballot was "Wm." or "William." Some voters who wrote in the name also wrote in "Wm." or "William." Dillard and Parker were willing to accept the ballots reading W. M. or Wm. but wanted to invalidate the ballots for "William Burton"—which would have thrown the election to the Democratic contender. Hobby and Davenport, however, spoke in favor of seating Burton. Wood's resolution that the seat be declared vacant, neither candidate having qualified, was refused by the Senate. Burton finally gained his seat late in the first session by a vote of fourteen to eleven.

Walter Moses Burton thus began the first of his four consecutive terms in the Senate. Burton was active in introducing legislation designed specifically to assist freedmen. For example, during the Sixteenth Legislature he introduced an act to place on a sounder footing the Agricultural and Mechanical College of Texas for the benefit of colored youths. He also introduced a bill to establish a normal school to train colored teachers, and another resolution proposed the establishment of a manual school in connection with the Agricultural and Mechanical College for colored youths, so that young African Americans could do farm work in return for all or part of their tuition.

Senator Burton's career in public office had begun with his election to the office of sheriff and tax collector in 1869, an office he held until his election to the Senate in 1873. Local history has it that Burton was pretty well pushed aside for the sheriff's office—and consequently into the Senate race—by an up-and-coming young black competitor, Henry C. Ferguson, who went on to control politics in Fort Bend County for the next thirty years. It is more likely, however, that Ferguson began his career as Burton's protégé.

Born in North Carolina on August 9, 1840, Burton had been a slave on the Burton plantation in the Isaaks League before the war. In 1858 his master, Thomas Burke Burton, brought him into Texas. The youth had been taught to read and write. During the legislative session, he was reported to be a married and well-respected farmer.

A Republican also won in the Sixteenth District but never served. T. G. Davidson ran as a Republican and officially won but declined to qualify, in a letter submitted by Senator William H. Ledbetter, an independent who was a Confederate veteran and an experienced politician. A new election was ordered on January 20, and another Republican, former senator Matthew Gaines, produced a certificate from the presiding justice of Washington County declaring Gaines the winner. However, the Democratic contender, Seth Shepard, contested the election and was seated.

The Senate elected a full slate of officers, all Democrats: J. F. Beall, secretary; John W. Lane, first assistant secretary; Nat Q. Henderson, second assistant secretary; W. Leigh Chalmers, calendar clerk; E. L. Shropshire, sergeant-at-arms; Fred Voight, assistant sergeant-at-arms; J. P. Farrell, doorkeeper; L. D. Miller, assistant doorkeeper; H. C. Surghnor, enrolling clerk; William B. Davis, engrossing clerk; William Neal Ramey, committee clerk; and Alex Sampson, committee clerk. Robert H. Taliaferro served as chaplain. After the close of the first session on May 4, 1874, Davis was succeeded by C. F. Maillot as engrossing clerk for the second session, which met from January 12 to March 15, 1875.

On January 26, 1874, Governor Coke delivered his message, stating that, because the previous department heads had retired without making reports, there was much information he could not give the legislature at that time. In the meantime, he invited attention to several subjects. In the matter of frontier protection, he noted the responsibility of the federal government but added that, as Washington was remiss in the matter, "Texas must discharge her duty" and protect citizens and their property; he suggested the formation of a commission to document and publicize to the nation the extent of the frontier losses that Texas was suffering. As for immigration, the governor supported it; this was, in effect, a pro-railroad position, as the railroads were giving cut-rate fares to new immigrants. With regard to internal improvements, he noted that "the policy of Texas has been, since 1850, to encourage the construction of railroads by granting land subsidies." Coke believed the results had been good. He acknowledged, however, that in the election campaign just conducted, the Democrats had promised to limit grants to railroads in settled areas and to restrict land grants to railroads to underdeveloped portions of the state. Concluding that such a policy would assure the unity of Texas, he admonished the legislature to issue charters only to companies that proved their solvency.

Discussing education, Coke noted that the current law "brings the machinery of the system home to the people themselves. . . . We should begin to utilize every source of revenue in our reach for this purpose. . . . I cannot see the practical wisdom of keeping the almost entire school fund of the state locked up and lying dormant. . . . These lands are of three classes, to-wit: First, University lands. Second, the alternate sections of the public domain; and third, the school lands, belonging, at least originally, to the several counties." The governor urged the establishment of a normal school for teacher training. Following a discussion of other subjects, he drew the legislators' attention to the practice which had developed in both houses of suspending the rule requiring bills to be read on three separate days and suggested that the constitutional requirement was a wise one and ought to be followed. He concluded with best wishes to the legislators in their endeavors.

Coke's position generally, as well as in his message, was basically pro-railroad; yet, by February, newspapers reported that he was favoring repudiation, a position which helped influence legislators not to assist the International and Great Northern in retaining its bond subsidy. The *State Journal* also observed that Coke had "centered a Waco strength around him . . . that bids fair to estrange the powerful . . . influence of the Democracy of Austin."

The first acts of the Fourteenth Legislature, signed by Coke after his inauguration but before Davis had left the Capitol, circumscribed the powers of government wielded by the Republican administration on the first floor. An act signed by Coke on January 16 prohibited any public official from giving state revenues to Comptroller Albert A. Bledsoe or Treasurer George W. Honey. Another measure signed on the same day forbade Honey and Bledsoe to spend money except in the act of turning the funds over to Comptroller S. H. Darden or Treasurer A. J. Dorn, both Coke appointees. A later resolution, approved on March 7, 1874, prohibited Dorn from paying any warrants drawn on the state treasury by Bledsoe.

The Fourteenth Legislature fulminated along with the public about the irresponsible way in which Treasurer Honey, and to some extent Comptroller Bledsoe as well, had handled the public money. It appears that Honey lent the state's money and shaved the state's warrants, but at that time there were no laws against those practices, and Honey had already been tried and acquitted. Bledsoe possibly had done some minor lending, but that is not certain. The legislature did take action, however, against James Davidson, the former adjutant general. In a resolution introduced by Senator Ireland, the legislature instructed the attorney general to bring suit against Davidson for the recovery of funds embezzled from state police accounts sometime prior to the opening of the Thirteenth Legislature, where Davis first reported Davidson's defalcation to the senators. Davidson, however, had escaped to Belgium. The bill also contained a provision which prevented the sale of Davidson's property in Texas until the money had been repaid.

Another problem for the legislature involving public funds was the state printing contract, usually the most lucrative contract the state had to offer. Following the example of its predecessors, the Fourteenth Legislature would continue to order large printings of its proceedings in three languages, a practice criticized as wasteful. Some newspapers printed verbatim texts of these same activities and included information of great use to historians, such as debates, speeches, and comments, which were edited out of the bound copies of the *Senate Journal.* The state printer nevertheless was paid exceedingly well to print in his own newspaper the official transcript of proceedings as they occurred, as well as to print and bind the final, edited text and perform all other printing authorized by the legislature—such as the printing of bills. Despite this generosity, the state printer, John Cardwell of the *Austin Democratic Statesman*, was not publishing the Senate's proceedings. (Cardwell had been elected state printer by the Thirteenth Legislature and was supposed to continue until replaced.) Several resolutions were introduced during the early weeks of the first session demanding to know why Cardwell was not performing, but each of these was tabled.

One obstacle to the criminal prosecution of public officials was

Congress Avenue looking north toward the Colonial Capitol, circa 1875.
Courtesy Austin History Center, Austin Public Library, # PICA 02442.

the lack of a statutory mandate for punishing misconduct in office. An act of March 30, 1874, made it unlawful for any county official to be a party to a contract requiring the expenditure of public funds until after a full settlement of the revenues collected by the official. Two additional acts provided for more stringent bonding of county officers. During the second session, an amendment to the Penal Code was adopted that mandated a sentence of up to five years for any misappropriation or misuse of state funds, which was defined as any action other than the transport of funds to the seat of government or their payment into the public treasury. Senator Shepard introduced legislation that defined those actions of a justice of the peace or a member of a county court that would be considered "non-feasance, mis-feasance, and mal-feasance in office" and provided stiff penalties. Similar acts followed for mayors, aldermen, tax collectors and assessors, and sheriffs. A final measure stipulated that any county officer who had been removed could not be reelected or reappointed for two years.

The *Senate Journal* of the entire first session would be archived at last in three loose-leaf typescript journals with neither an index nor a bill history. John Elliot of the *State Gazette* finally got the state printing contract, and the *Journal* of the second session was printed as usual.

The Fourteenth Legislature adopted a joint resolution to ratify all of the constitutional amendments proposed by the Thirteenth Legislature and approved in the general election of December, 1873. The resolution passed the Senate by a two-thirds majority on January 18 and by a two-thirds vote in the House six days later. Section 20 of Article I of the 1869 constitution was amended to reserve to the legislature the sole power to suspend laws. Sections 2, 3, and 4 of Article V provided for a Supreme Court consisting of four associate justices and a chief justice, appointed for nine years by the governor with the advice and consent of the Senate. A second joint resolution passed on March 12, 1875, amended the same article to provide for the election, rather than the appointment, of five Supreme Court justices every seven years, with the justice receiving the most votes to be chief justice. Another amendment stipulated that the legislature could adopt no special laws concerning county affairs when a general law would do. This limitation would lead to some very interesting changes in legislation during the Fourteenth Legislature. The same joint resolution on amendments permitted the legislature to regulate the rate of interest, to provide for the construction of roads, and to establish segregated schools, but not to create a peacetime deficit of more than five hundred thousand dollars. Through a law approved on April 2, 1874, the Supreme Court, which had met at Austin and Galveston since the Civil War, received authorization also to meet at Tyler.

Once they had consolidated their grip on power, the Democrats of the Fourteenth Legislature kept expanding the list of judges appointed by Davis whom they wanted to remove. Several of these judges were not qualified to hold their positions, but the charges against some of the others indicate little more than a desire to establish a Democratic hegemony in the judiciary, the third branch of government and the last bastion of Republican patronage in Reconstruction Texas. Presentment of address resolutions began in January and continued into April. In all, nine judges were the subjects of address removal proceedings in which the governor would be requested to remove the judge if he were found guilty before a joint session of the legislature. Special joint committees consisting of five representatives and three senators were appointed to investigate allegations against each judge. The targeted judges were L. W. Cooper, M. Priest, Martin W. Wheeler, J. B. Williamson, Henry Maney, J. J. Thornton, S. B. Newcomb, James R. Burnett, and J. P. Osterhaut.

Some of the requests for removal were clearly justified. Maney had consistently defied the efforts of the Texas Supreme Court to discipline him and had conducted his court in a very irregular manner. For example, he had cited the entire local bar for contempt of his court, then released five murderers because the prosecution did not appear for their trial; Senator Ireland was among those involved in this peculiar affair, and he was determined to have Maney removed. As for Judge Newcomb, he had tried "about one hundred persons" on the spurious charge of "fornication" but in each case collected only the costs and fees of his court. Thornton had been paralyzed for two years and had declined into a pitiable state of "physical debility and mental imbecility"; on at least one occasion, he had fallen into a stupor or deep sleep for several hours while presiding over a case. The senators were even more skeptical about the condition of Wheeler, whose "real or pretended" illness prevented him from holding court, and they demanded his removal on the grounds that in any case he was unqualified. The remainder of the cases seem to have been motivated by partisanship. Cooper was to be removed on the grounds that he was an incompetent who possessed no legal training, and Priest was targeted for "being a tool, ignorant of the laws of our State, [who] proceeded to carry out the dictates of his master, E. J. Davis." It was said of Williamson, unjustly, that he was "not sufficiently learned in the law, and has not the mental capacity to become so learned."

James P. Newcomb, editor of the *State Journal*, wrote on March 9, 1874, that a probable cost of one hundred thousand dollars "stares the people in the face for the sake of addressing out judges whose places are demanded by hungry office seeking Democrats." However, all the judges mentioned were subject to investigation by joint select committees; some had trials before a joint session. Only Priest, Williamson, Maney, and Newcomb were convicted and removed. The accusations against Thornton, Burnett, and Wheeler were dropped by concurrent resolutions. Although Judge Chambers, whose impeachment proceeding was carried over from the previous legislature, was found not guilty, a new law added all but one of the counties in his District One to District Two, which according to the *Senate Journal* "practically beheaded Judge Chambers." Judge Cooper also had his district pared to one county after the address procedure against him failed to remove him. Until the bills concerning misconduct in office were passed during the second session, the Senate had little basis for prosecution. Nevertheless, a joint resolution approved on April 3, 1874, appointed a rotating committee of two senators and three representatives to "investigate all cases of bribery, fraud, or corruption, which may have occurred since the year 1868, in any part of this State, connected with the affairs of legislation, railroads, the judiciary, executive, heads of departments, education, public buildings, and public printing"; a second joint resolution empowered the governor to hire assistant counsel to prosecute persons for fraud against the state. The two justices of the Supreme Court who had returned the decision of *Ex Parte Rodriguez* on the "Semicolon Court," Moses B. Walker and Wesley Ogden, were painlessly removed from office when Governor Coke appointed five new Supreme Court justices as set forth in the new amendments to the Constitution of 1869.

Early in the first session, newspapers zealously reported on the activities of the various candidates and lobbyists who were trying to influence the legislature in its election of a replacement for Republican U.S. senator James Flanagan, whose term expired that year. On January 24 the *State Journal* reported on the public address by the candidates to the legislature and on a "secret meeting of anti-railroad members of the Legislature" who were "bitterly opposed" to the Texas Pacific candidates, namely Throckmorton and Culberson, and to the Great Northern and International Railroad candidates, Reagan and Flournoy. The secret meeting ended with the friends of Samuel Maxey proposing to give up on his candidacy and unite behind Wigfall, as the only way to "defeat the two railroad rings."

In a joint session held on January 28, Samuel B. Maxey, despite all predictions to the contrary, was elected to succeed Flanagan. The votes were tallied as: McGary, 1; Reagan, 1; Senator Edward T. Randle (Republican), 13; Throckmorton, 40; Maxey, 59. Senator Culberson had apparently withdrawn from the contest. On January 31 an article by the *San Antonio Daily Herald*'s correspondent commented, "The election of General Maxey to the Senate took everybody by surprise . . . many who voted for him only intended a complimentary vote." Maxey, who received a majority of the votes from the Senate, was a former Confederate major general. He served with distinction in the U.S. Senate for the next thirteen years.

The controversial issue of government assistance to railroads was raised early in the Fourteenth Legislature and continued throughout both sessions. The *Daily Herald* complained on January 20, "Whether our new Comptroller will sign the International Bonds, or whether they will be left *in status quo* is discussed in the *third* house but not in Legislative circles." The joint resolution of March 7, 1874, forbidding Treasurer Dorn to pay any warrants drawn on the state treasury by former comptroller Bledsoe had put the controversial bonds for the International Railroad into the spotlight once more. Indeed, a huge controversy continued to surround the International's claim, provided under a previous act, to thirty-year, 8 percent bonds, with a 2 percent sinking fund representing ten thousand dollars per completed mile, in addition to grants of sixteen sections of land. The ten thousand dollars per completed mile was just about what construction cost, but payment on the loan would cost Texans more each year for thirty years than it cost to run state government, and the state would receive only about fifteen million dollars. This loan was running during a period in which the interest on money ranged from 30 percent to 100 percent for ninety days; farmers, cattlemen, and businessmen were being ruined by high interest on short-term notes; and almost no long-term credit was available. The International had been granted its most-favored status by a coalition of Democrats, Republicans, and independents in two successive legislatures, and Davis's vetoes had been overridden consistently.

But by 1874, the issue of the International and Great Northern had become far more complex than when the first bill was passed in 1870, and the state was hotly divided over the issue. The International, in fact, had laid an impressive amount of track in East and Central Texas. As they had already acquired service, the eastern and central regions had little hesitation in calling for repudiation of the bonds. West Texas was due to receive service next, and West Texans were enraged that the politicians of the "Trans-Colorado" sector were threatening the railroad company.

Those who supported the railroad complained that the International was getting a raw deal, that it would have to go into receivership, and that Texas would lose a major road that was actually laying track, all because the legislature refused to honor a contractual obligation. The depression had caused railway construction in the nation to drop drastically, and—so the argument went—it would not be all that easy to find another company which was actually performing. Other observers, however, said the outcry over the threat of state actions detrimental to the International came from those along the projected route westward, while the mass of taxpayers remained opposed to the subsidy. Coke, in his opening message to the Senate at the start of the second session, stated that the matter needed to go before the courts and perhaps the International might be granted permission to sue the state. He said that without a court order the state would neither collect nor pay out the taxes necessary to support the bonds.

As the affair dragged on, senator after senator tried his hand at writing a bill to resolve the problem, and bill after bill was killed. The editor of the *San Antonio Daily Herald* grew more and more enraged about the slights to the Trans-Colorado region of Texas by the Texas Legislature and was outspoken in advocating a separate state of Western Texas if the International bill failed passage by the Fourteenth Legislature. In his veto message, however, the governor provided solid reasons for his disapproval. The bill failed to provide a mechanism to ensure that the loan would be repaid in a situation in which all the railroad's land, equipment, track, and buildings already had first and second mortgages. Coke noted that one of the bill's financial provisions simply gave the company three million dollars.

It appears that Coke would have preferred that the legislature continue to waffle on a solution, so that he would not ultimately have had to say either "aye" or "nay." But this was not to be. After the veto, a committee substitute, which was entitled "an act for the relief of the International Railroad company now consolidated with the Houston and Great Northern Railroad Company," emerged from the Senate and passed both houses, with Lieutenant Governor Hubbard saying publicly, "They compelled me to stand up and face the music; and, now, I want to see them make Coke do it." The *Daily Herald* reported that "this struggle has been probably the closest and most hotly contested of any that ever came before the Legislature. In the House, Epperson of Jefferson and the gallant McLeary of the West . . . were the recognized leaders of the friends of the bill." The act was presented to Coke on March 10, 1875, and he signed it. Members of the committee were Camp, Erath, Flanagan, Ireland, Joseph, Westfall, and Wood. The bill, under amended provisions of the constitution, provided the substitution of land grants of twenty sections for each completed mile.

The question of dividing the state continued to haunt Texans. Just as West Texans had threatened to separate from the east and create their own state over the railroad issue, they made the same threat whenever the matter of a constitutional convention came up. Under the proposal for a convention being considered, the western portion of the state, with a population of about two hundred thousand, would receive only fourteen delegates, while the great mass of delegates would come from the northern and central portions and could be expected to dominate the framing of the new constitution. By February 25, 1875, westerners were enraged at being treated like "serfs" and considered calling for a division of the state. The resolution providing for a constitutional convention, which had been introduced fairly early on, languished for much of the Fourteenth Legislature as the issue was debated. Those who wanted a convention accused the administration of merely trying to hold on to office; those who did not want one said that the expenditure of time and money involved was unjustified. Finally, however, the scales were tipped in favor of calling the convention, and the joint resolution providing for a constitutional convention to assemble in Austin on the first Monday in September, 1875, with the election of delegates to be held on the first Monday in August was approved by Coke on March 13, 1875.

The matter of the public debt was a growing concern. In his initial address to the Senate, Governor Coke had said that the public debt was not very large, but as the year proceeded, both the politicians and the public began describing the public debt as "large," then as "very large," and finally as "huge." The Fourteenth Legislature endorsed a state bond issue of one million dollars, payable in thirty years from the date of issue, January 1, 1874, and bearing 7 percent annual interest to be paid semiannually in gold coin. All proceeds were to be applied exclusively to the payment of warrants drawn by the comptroller on the treasury since January 1, 1866. Governor Coke was also directed to dispose of the previous bond issues by sale and to settle the accounts with the agents to whom they had been entrusted. During the second session, the remainder of all previous state bond issues, a total of about $610,000 in scrip, was burned.

After a flood of petitions, the Fourteenth Legislature during the first session passed a general law permitting counties in need of a courthouse or jail to levy a tax of one-third of 1 percent on every one hundred dollars of taxable property in the county, an occupation tax amounting to 10 percent of the state rate, and a poll tax of fifty cents. These funds would be managed by the county courts, and no county officer could have an interest in any contract let under the new statute. A separate act provided that county courts with an indebtedness of five hundred dollars or more could organize a claims court and levy an ad valorem tax of one-fourth of 1 percent on all real and personal property, an occupation tax of one-tenth the state level, and a poll tax of fifty cents for the payment of those who held county scrip, except for previous bond issues. Valid claims would bear an annual interest of 8 percent until paid, with a four-year limit on amortization and taxes. A measure signed on February 26, 1874, authorized incorporated cities in Texas to build and operate free municipal libraries. All of these bills helped to place a portion of the state's financial burden on the counties, for whose benefit most of the previous appropriations had been approved.

Frontier defense was also decentralized to the county level. The governor was authorized to muster a company of no less than 25 nor more than 75 troopers in each county "infested" by "hostile Indians, Mexicans, or other marauding or thieving parties" that were "depredating upon the lives or property of the citizens." The aggregate total of such a force under arms at any one time could not exceed 750 men, and their maximum term of enlistment was twelve months. The state would pay all expenses apart from basic equipment such as a pistol, horse, and bedroll and would provide each minuteman with an "improved breech-loading cavalry gun." The governor could also muster a battalion of 450 mounted men to be dispatched to any emergency. Although "not designed as a standing force," the men would serve at the command of the governor for "as long as in his judgment there may be a necessity for such a force." The act differed subtly from the militia law of the Davis administration. All other frontier units were disbanded. Following a number of requests from the frontier counties for additional aid, the Fourteenth Legislature authorized the adjutant general to request the assignment of another regiment of federal cavalry.

Despite these actions, violence continued to escalate along the southern and western borders of Texas. Senator Friend introduced a bill to authorize a sheriff, deputy sheriff, or constable to muster a posse. Friend acknowledged that the measure revived portions of the "obnoxious police law of Governor Davis' administration" but insisted it was necessary because a "band of desperadoes" had made it almost impossible for peaceable citizens to live in his district. The legislators included some very specific restrictions in this bill. Posses could be enlisted only after prior notice to the governor of "unlawful combinations" or dangerous conditions and could never be enlisted during a general election. Signed on March 13, 1875, the new law provided that a member of a posse would be paid four dollars a day by the police court.

Cattle rustlers began to cut heavily into the livestock trade in Texas. A House bill endorsed by the Senate provided that each county, except for a number of counties in East Texas, would comprise a district for the employment of an elected inspector of hides and animals. These inspectors and their appointed deputies would be bonded, and their duties would include preventing the sale of unbranded or freshly branded cattle or hides. Owners of livestock were required to register a brand and to brand all cattle, and district court clerks were required to keep accurate records. A separate act required auctioneers to demand title or proof of purchase for any horse, mule, or ox being sold. Senator Russell proposed a more severe bill outlawing "bodies of armed strangers and Indians" caught stealing livestock and authorizing state officers to have them "quickly dispatched when caught." Neither this bill nor an amendment to the Penal Code introduced by Senator Bradley permitting whipping as a penalty for theft passed the Senate. Ellis, as chairman of the Committee on the Militia, reported a House bill to offer a bounty of five dollars for "wolf scalps." On behalf of the other members, the chairman asked that the word "Indian" be substituted for "wolf" wherever it occurred and that the bounty be increased to fifty dollars. Once the bill had been amended to reveal its true purpose, he said, he would respectfully request the members to reject it. The "wolf" scalp bounty did not pass.

Other measures for the promotion of agriculture focused on less violent topics. Disease was the primary concern of sheep farmers; an act signed on May 2, 1874, provided stiff fines for any owner of scab-infested sheep who grazed them anywhere other than on his own land. The Office of Public Weigher was created to provide some standardization on commodity measurements. Officers were to be appointed in Austin, Dallas, Galveston, Houston, Sherman, Waco, and any other city the governor might deem necessary. These officers were responsible for registering the true weight of shipments of cotton, wool, sugar, and hides.

The effects of the national depression were reflected in acts passed by the Fourteenth Legislature for the collection of debts. "An act concerning rents and advances" stipulated that a landlord who was renting property had a preference lien on that property for all rent due and, in the case of a tenant farmer, on all equipment, animals, provisions, and seed provided by the landowner to the tenant to enable him to make a crop. This lien prevented the tenant from selling any of the proceeds from his crop for his own profit until the landowner had given his consent. When the rent became due, it was legal for the landowner to call on any law enforcement official to seize the property of the tenant until his demand had been met. A similar act authorized an artisan, mechanic, or craftsman to retain possession of any article he had created or repaired until the amount due for the work was paid. If after ninety days the bill had not been paid, the article could be sold at public auction. Pawnbrokers could also sell property left as security for a loan, but only at public auction and only after five days' public notice following the date for retrieval. Common carriers could sell unclaimed freight at public auction if left unclaimed for ninety days, or less if the items were perishable or alive, such as livestock. Livery stable owners were given a special lien against all animals, carriages, and wagons left in their care, and hotel owners and boardinghouse keepers were given a lien on all baggage and other property deposited with them.

The financial shortage did not prevent the Fourteenth Legislature from providing for public education. On April 2, 1874, Governor Coke signed an appropriation of forty thousand dollars to complete the buildings for the Agricultural and Mechanical College of Texas. During the second session, an additional thirty-two thousand dollars was set aside for the same purpose, and a board of directors was created for the college. The board of directors consisted of the governor, the lieutenant governor, the speaker of the House, and six directors, one from each congressional district, to be elected by a joint ballot of the legislature every two years. Several bills were signed during the first session calling for Governor Coke to expedite the sale of the lands set aside for the endowment of a state university so that construction could begin on that institution; and other acts urged the quick sale of lands appropriated for the public school funds and of the lands designated for the benefit of the Deaf and Dumb, the Lunatic, and the Blind asylums. Another act, signed on March 15, 1875, provided that any incorporated city could create an independent school district.

The Fourteenth Legislature incorporated relatively few private schools, but Southwestern University at Georgetown received a charter on February 6, 1875. Under the aegis of the Methodist Episcopal Church, South, it was authorized to establish separate schools of law, medicine, and theology. Under the terms of the act, the university inherited the right to confer degrees that had previously been granted to Rutersville College and Rutersville Wesleyan College in San Augustine, to Soule University in Chappell Hill, and to McKenzie's College in Clarksville. Southwestern University also inherited the responsibility for the alumni of those institutions, who would be entitled to all of the privileges accorded graduates of the new university. In other special legislation on education, the legislators repealed the prohibition against alcohol in the neighborhood of the Moscow Masonic High School but passed an omnibus bill enacting prohibition in the area surrounding schools and churches in numerous counties, including Baylor University in Washington County.

On March 15, 1875, the governor signed an amendment to the acts for a public school system passed by the Thirteenth Legislature in May, 1873. The amendment mandated the creation of separate schools for white and black students, reflecting an increasingly conservative view of race relations on the part of those within the state government—which in turn was a reaction to the vitriolic prejudice that was developing, in part because of black support for the Radical Republicans. With the return of a Democratic majority to the Senate, racial prejudice frequently was expressed in official debate.

Actual disenfranchisement of blacks, however, would not occur for another decade and would come about then largely because of the black alliance with the Populists. To the contrary, the Fourteenth Legislature protected black voters' rights by providing, in an act signed on April 3, 1874, that any municipal charters that had made the right of suffrage dependent upon the payment of municipal taxes were to be amended by the local aldermen. True, the procedures for voter registration were streamlined in a separate act without direct reference to race, but the legislature went on to make its stance on this issue quite clear: it passed a new amendment of the 1858 act regulating municipal charters, declaring that the right to vote could be exercised "without distinction of race, color, or previous condition." The only stipulations were that the voter must be male, be twenty-one years of age, and have resided within the prescribed limits for sixty days.

The Fourteenth Legislature also proved to be progressive in the laws it enacted for the conservation of wildlife in Texas. The Senate endorsed an act for the protection of fish in inland streams and waters of the state during spawning season. From February 14 to June 14 of each year, it would be unlawful to harvest fish with a net, seine, trotline, or trap in any stream, lake, or pool in Texas above tidewater, although a single hook and line would be permitted. An act approved May 2, 1874, authorized the posting of private lands against trespass by shooting, hunting, fishing, or fowling.

In business matters the Fourteenth Legislature, taking notice of judicial trends in the United States, passed a measure providing that any public or private corporation, excluding municipalities, could be sued. A general law establishing basic guidelines for chartering private corporations was signed on April 23, 1874. It defined the purposes for which three or more persons could incorporate and required only the filing of a charter with the secretary of state. A broad framework for charters was delineated: they were to be twenty years in duration and would allow the chartered corporations to hold property, to establish bylaws and elect officers, and to issue stock and borrow money. Specific details were provided for the incorporation of road-building companies, telegraph corporations, railroads, public utilities, educational institutions, cemetery corporations, religious and charitable institutions, banking institutions, and bridge and ferry operations. A gas works was incorporated in Austin, and the legislature decided to install the fixtures necessary to light the Capitol and Governor's Mansion with gas.

A separate measure provided for the regulation of life and health insurance companies, which were flourishing. No agent was permitted to operate without a license from the comptroller, who required the submission of a complete financial statement from the date the parent firm was incorporated. The license had to be renewed annually. No company could be incorporated with less than one hundred thousand dollars in capital. A similar bill regulating fire and marine insurance companies or those founded for "any other purpose than life insurance" was signed into law during the second session. The same act included points Governor Coke had requested that required foreign-owned insurance companies to deposit funds with the comptroller for security, as well as provide a copy of their charter.

No act provided for the incorporation of municipalities, although aldermen, by an act of April 24, 1874, were authorized to amend civil charters through a general election. Several city charters were subsequently revised, among them the charters of Brenham, Brownsville, Galveston, Houston, and Jefferson. The charter for the town of Ysleta, incorporated by the Twelfth Legislature in 1871, was revoked. A number of counties were organized or created: Camp, Crockett, Franklin, Kinney, Lee, Morris, Presidio, Somerville, Tom Green, and Young.

The constitutional amendment requiring general laws instead of specific enactments led to the passage of two laws for internal improvements. During the second session, a bill introduced by Senator Russell to encourage the construction of canals for navigation and irrigation was signed on March 10, 1875, and provided for the classification of canals, with specific land grants attached to each class. No canal would qualify if it were less than three miles in length. A similar bill for the classification of roads was also passed during the second session. It directed the county courts to classify the roads in their counties from first class to third class and provided that no farmer would be required to cede a right-of-way more than twenty feet in width. All first-class roads had to be free of obstructions, but property owners could construct a gate across second-class and third-class roads as long as they "were hung so that any person on horseback can open them without alighting from his horse, and so arranged that the gate will shut itself." If a gate were left open, the traveler would be liable for any damage that occurred through his neglect. An interesting act approved during the first session made it unlawful for anyone to leave the dead body of a horse, ox, steer, cow, "or other animal, which may die while in the actual possession of such person," on or within fifty yards of a public road, thereby eliminating another hazard.

Public corporations still had to request legislative approval. An ambitious effort was endorsed which required the appointment by the governor of six of the "largest shippers of the counties of Tyler, Jasper, Jefferson, Orange, Newton, Hardin, Angelina, Nacogdoches, Sabine, Shelby, Cherokee, and San Augustine" to a commission for the dredging of the Sabine, Neches, and Angelina rivers, along with Pine Island Bayou. During the second session, the governor was authorized to appoint another six-man commission to provide for the dredging of the Neches from Weiss's Bluff to Bunn's Bluff.

Land became the standard means of compensation for public works. The legislature pledged eight sections of land for every mile of the Guadalupe and San Antonio rivers cleared by a three-man commission from Victoria, Refugio, and Calhoun counties. Land grants were provided as an incentive for any town or individual to construct irrigation ditches in El Paso County. The Houston and Brazos Canal and Navigation Company, incorporated during the first session, also received land in return for its work, as did a contractor who proposed to build a canal from Marble Falls to Austin. During the second session, the Senate endorsed a standing offer of eight sections per mile to anyone who built a macadamized road north from the San Marcos town limits three miles in the direction of Austin. Due to the financial pinch, all public contracts for the completion of internal improvements were extended for one year.

In spite of the heated debate which broke out in the Senate during the second session over the grant to the International and Great

Northern Railroad, other railroads received land grants with much less debate. The San Antonio Street Railway Company was incorporated but not given land, although at the same time the Rusk Transportation Company was chartered to provide a tram or horse-car railway from the town of Rusk to a point on the International and Great Northern Railroad and was to receive eight sections of land per mile.

These and other land grants committed a large portion of Texas' public domain to private corporations, but the Fourteenth Legislature rectified that situation. On January 25, 1875, the governor signed an act of the second session rescinding the grants of February, 1854, and February, 1856, that had ceded a total of seventeen leagues of land in West Texas to the United States for Indian reservations; because the federal government had long since abandoned these tracts as reservations and settlers had preempted sections of them, believing them to be public domain, the Fourteenth Legislature provided that they could now be surveyed and the proper claims filed. In addition, lands previously granted to the German Immigration Company for the Fisher and Miller Colony were declared open to all settlers. These were just stopgap measures, however; in the future, action would have to be taken for more conservative management of public lands.

The legislators also supplied labor for internal improvements. An act for the employment of convicts extended the powers of county courts to employ prisoners in public works and reduced the daily compensation due such laborers to no more than a dollar a day, to be paid upon their release. During the second session, funds were appropriated for the construction of two new state penitentiaries to be situated "with a view to the utilization of the convict labor of the State in mining and manufacturing enterprises." Selection of the two locations, one northeast of the Trinity River to exploit the iron ore in that area and the other west of the Colorado River with an eye to manufacturing textiles, was to be made by a five-man commission appointed by the governor. The senators, at the same time, endorsed an appropriation for a "library of moral and useful books" for the inmates at the state penitentiary.

The Democrats of the Fourteenth Legislature expressed their goals most vehemently through their resolutions. They demanded that the Texas delegation in Congress secure appropriations for the improvement of Soda Lake and Cypress Bayou and for the completion of the controversial Texas and Pacific Railroad. A resolution introduced by Senator Moore asked the governor to negotiate with Arkansas for the cession of part of Lafayette County on the west side of the Red River. A similar request for Caddo and De Soto parishes in Louisiana was vetoed by Coke. The governor did support the movement for a new constitution. The proponents of a convention failed during the first session to agree on a resolution, but a measure calling for an election of delegates to a constitutional convention to be held in September, 1875, easily passed both houses during the second session. Its passage signaled the culmination of efforts to repudiate Radical Republican rule and set the stage for the conservative Democratic backlash that would develop throughout the next decade.

CHAPTER 8

The Senate of the Fifteenth Legislature, 1876

When the Fifteenth Legislature convened in Austin on April 18, 1876, its most pressing task was to complete the reforms initiated by the delegates to the constitutional convention which had met in the fall of 1875. The Democrats, led by Edward B. Pickett, a former state senator and lieutenant governor, had controlled the convention and had produced a conservative constitution that was later endorsed by more than a two-to-one margin in the subsequent election. This Constitution of 1876 was to endure for more than a century and is today the organic law of Texas. Although much amended and containing many obsolete provisions (for example, the governor still has the power to call out the militia to protect the frontier from Indians), the Constitution of 1876 continues to reflect Texans' basic ideas of state government.

The new constitution provided a mandate for retrenchment and for economy—to the point of penury—in the future affairs of the state: the legislature was forbidden to incur an indebtedness greater than two hundred thousand dollars; its powers of taxation were severely limited; and many government salaries were reduced. The Senate of the Fifteenth Legislature adhered to the conservative spirit of the constitutional convention in its deliberations, which ironically extended beyond the ninety-day limit, eliciting a heated protest from ten senators. Most of the legislators, however, declared that supporting the intent of the Constitution of 1876—conservatism in government—was more important than following the letter of the law, and this sentiment would predominate.

The Constitution of 1876 limited the number of state senators to thirty-one, reduced their terms from six years to four, and stipulated that the legislature would meet biennially, not annually as the 1869 constitution had specified. The adoption of the constitution and new elections took place in February, 1876. During the Fifteenth Legislature, senators would draw lots to determine which ones would serve four-year terms and which would serve two-year terms. An ordinance of the constitutional convention provided, however, that state officers elected in the elections held in conjunction with the adoption of the new constitution would hold office as though they were elected in November, 1876. Lots were drawn on April 27. The senators drawing the long terms were Blassingame, Brown, Burton, Edwards, Ford, Grace, Guy, Hobby, Ledbetter, McCormick, McCulloch, Moore, Motley, Ripetoe, and Storey; those drawing the short terms were Ball, Brady, Carroll, Crain, Douglass, Francis, Henry of Limestone, Henry of Cass, Martin, McLeary, Piner, Smith, Stephens, Terrell, Thompson, and Wortham. Future statewide elections would be held simultaneously with the national elections in November of each even-numbered year.

Because of the adoption of the new constitution, any member of the Fourteenth Legislature who wished to continue to serve had to run for reelection. Only three senators from the Fourteenth Legislature (Burton, Hobby, and Ledbetter) served as senators in the Fifteenth, though another ten members of the new Senate had previous House or Senate service. Eighteen legislative newcomers were elected to the Senate of the Fifteenth Legislature: Thomas Ball, William Blassingame, William M. Brown, William H. Crain, Peyton F. Edwards, Christopher C. Francis, Charles D. Grace, Robert S. Guy, Francis M. Henry, John R. Henry, B. D. Martin, Andrew P. McCormick, Thomas J. McCulloch, John W. Motley, Finis E. Piner, Walter Ripetoe, Alexander W. Terrell, and Wells Thompson.

Most of the newcomers were Confederate veterans. Of the eighteen senators who were new to the legislature as well as to the Senate, only three had not fought for the South: William H. Crain, John R. Henry, and Walter Ripetoe, who was black.

Among the Confederate veterans was Thomas Ball, a Virginian who had attended William and Mary College and practiced law in Northumberland County, Virginia, before joining the 47th Virginia Infantry as a lieutenant in 1861. Ball was captured and was a federal prisoner from 1864 to 1865. After the war he came to Texas to find a better life and resumed the practice of law in Weatherford. He moved one more time, to Jacksboro in Jack County, and it was from this town that he was elected to the Senate in February, 1876. He served only one term in the Senate before being appointed assistant attorney general by Governor Oran Roberts in January, 1879.

Senator William Blassingame, a native of Greenville, South Carolina, was one of five medical doctors in this exceptionally Hippocratic group of solons. He had entered the Confederate Army as a private in May, 1861, when he was twenty-five years old, and served as assistant surgeon in General McCulloch's Missouri campaign. After the war, he moved to Texas from Versailles, Missouri, with his wife. The couple settled in Whitesboro, Grayson County, in 1865, where Blassingame established a medical practice and did a little farming. Apparently popular with his new compatriots, he was elected to the Constitutional Convention of 1875 as a Grange delegate and was one of the signers of the Constitution of 1876. In February of that year he ran for the Senate as a Democrat and was elected by a margin of nearly one thousand votes over his Republican opponent, Dr. Alexander Marshall. Dr. Blassingame left the Senate after serving out his term during the Sixteenth Legislature.

William M. Brown was a Virginian who had been educated at Washington College and who served nearly all through the war in the Army of Northern Virginia, until he was captured in 1865 and imprisoned on Johnson's Island in Lake Erie. He had been a first lieutenant of the Rock Bridge Artillery and had fought in the famous battles of the Virginia campaigns and at Gettysburg, where he was wounded in both legs.

Following the surrender at Appomattox, Brown was released from prison; he was twenty-seven years old, lame, and ready for a different life. Now "Colonel" Brown, he settled in Marlin, Texas, and entered into the cotton commission business. Successful in this and other ventures, he accumulated a fortune, which was later lost "through no fault of his own," according to a biographer. Brown began his career in public service to the state following his unopposed election to the Senate in 1876. He served during the Fifteenth and Sixteenth legislatures and in 1880 was elected comptroller of public accounts. During his term as comptroller he was an ex officio member of the Capitol Board that contracted for the building of the present State Capitol. The board was also responsible for the sale of the three million acres of the public domain that the Sixteenth Legislature had set aside to finance the building, and Colonel Brown's business sense stood the state in good stead during all these negotiations. From 1887 to 1891 Brown served in Governor Ross's administration as state oil inspector, and he later accepted a position in the comptroller's office which he held until his death in 1902.

Colonel Brown was instrumental in organizing the John Bell Hood Camp for Confederate Veterans in Austin in 1884; this organization, supported by the Albert Sidney Johnston Chapter of the Daughters of the Confederacy, established the Confederate Home for Men in 1887. After the turn of the century the number of residents in the home, located in Austin, began a gradual decline to only six veterans by 1943, the year when the home began accepting senile patients from other state hospitals. The last Confederate resident, Thomas Riddle, died in 1954 at the age of 108, but the home was not closed until 1964. Another enduring reminder of the efforts of Colonel Brown and the John Bell Hood Camp to provide for Confederate veterans, living or dead, is the Confederate monument on the Capitol grounds.

William Henry Crain, a lawyer, came to the Senate after distinguishing himself as the flamboyant district attorney of the Twenty-third Judicial District for four years. Crain was born in Galveston on November 25, 1848, and was educated in New York at Saint Francis Xavier College, graduating in 1867. He returned to Texas, where he studied law and taught school in Indianola. He was licensed to practice law in 1871 and was recognized early on as one of the most powerful speakers in the state, being described as "bold, patriotic, and fervid." In July, 1873, he married Angelina G. Mitchell, a granddaughter of Colonel James Kerr, who in 1825 had settled west of the Colorado near Gonzales, the first American pioneer to do so. Senator Crain resigned his seat in the Fifteenth Legislature on August 20, 1877, and was replaced by Ellsberry R. Lane of Goliad, who was sworn in during the Sixteenth Legislature. Senator Crain was elected to Congress from the Seventh Congressional District in 1884 and served in the House of Representatives from March 4, 1885, until he died on February 10, 1896, in Washington, D.C.

Senator Peyton Forbes Edwards, whose senatorial sobriquet was "the Red Rooster of Nacogdoches," was a graduate of the University of Virginia law department who was practicing in Nacogdoches and serving there as county treasurer. He was elected to the Senate as a Democrat in February, 1876, and drew a four-year term but resigned in October, 1879. Later that year, he began serving as judge of the Third Judicial District, in which capacity he remained until 1884, when he served as a presidential elector in the national election. In 1886 he moved to El Paso, where he became a prominent member of the bar and practiced with his son Peyton James Edwards in the predictably named firm of Edwards and Edwards. He died in El Paso in 1918.

Peyton Edwards was a Texan born and bred: his grandfather, Haden Edwards, had been one of the founders of the Fredonian Republic; and his father, Haden Harrison Edwards, had fought in the Texas Revolution, achieved the rank of brigadier general under the Republic, served in the House of Texas' First Congress, and been a member of the House in the First and Eighth legislatures. Peyton himself left school at the age of seventeen to fight for Texas and the Confederacy; he enlisted in Company A, 17th Cavalry, and became brigade quartermaster after transferring to Company H, 4th Texas Cavalry, Sibley's Brigade. His first wife, Odelia Arnold, was the daughter of another veteran of the Texas Revolution, and upon her demise he married her sister Minnie. His third wife was Callie Stewart. Some authorities connect Peyton Edwards with an important aspect of Texas' future as well as of her past: he and Emory Starr may have been the first discoverers of oil in Texas. They dug holes in the banks of Oil Spring Branch in Nacogdoches County and skimmed off the crude oil as it collected on the water's surface, later selling it in Nacogdoches for softening leather.

Senator Christopher C. Francis of Rusk was a doctor and a former surgeon in the Confederate Army. Senator Francis appeared before the Penitentiary Locating Commission to argue in favor of placing the state's iron plant in Cherokee County. He contended that the Rusk Tramway, which connected the town with the International and Great Northern Railroad, albeit with wooden rails, provided the industrial base that would justify situating such an endeavor in the Piney Woods. Apparently the argument was persuasive, although the fledgling company collapsed three years later because no one could be found to install iron rails. Senator Francis left the Senate after serving in the Fifteenth Legislature.

The senator from the Ninth District was a Southern gentleman from Georgia, Charles Dougherty Grace. Born in 1842 as the son of a Methodist minister, Grace became interested in public speaking as a youngster. In April, 1861, he enlisted in Company B, 4th Georgia Regiment, Colonel J. M. Mathews Doles's Brigade, as a private. Although he was recommended for the position of major by his officers and General Lee, he never received a commission. He served as a sharpshooter and had a reputation for dashing bravery and for kindness and courtesy as well. After the war he went back to Georgia and returned to the practice of law, which he had abandoned to join the army.

In 1867 Grace joined the flood of Southerners who decided to try their luck in Texas. The captain of the steamboat that "Major" Grace (for so he was called despite the lack of a formal commission) boarded in New Orleans to take him to Texas via Shreveport was Colonel N. C. Bradford from Bonham. A friendship developed between the two, and Grace became Bradford's neighbor in Bonham, where he practiced law. Apparently he also became something of a local legend. An old-timer described him as the only person he ever saw who could strut sitting down; other, kinder folk called him "gentle as a child, brave as a lion and proud as a king." Because of anecdotes about him, Grace became one of Bonham's more colorful mayors. He was fond of recounting his numerous war experiences and told of standing two hundred feet from Stonewall Jackson at Chancellorsville when Jackson was mortally wounded. He could describe at least thirteen battles in which he took part, including Gettysburg. Grace served in the Senate during the Fifteenth and Sixteenth legislatures. He married Mrs. Leonora Bond in 1876 and continued to practice law in Bonham until his death in 1906.

Yet another transplanted Southerner in the Senate of the Fifteenth Legislature was Robert S. Guy of Lancaster in Dallas County. Guy was born at Stanton, Virginia, in 1825. His father moved the family to Callaway County in Missouri, where young Guy was educated. Guy came to Texas in 1852 and settled at Lancaster, where he practiced law after being admitted to the bar in Dallas in 1855. In September, 1861, he went off to the war as a captain in the Confederate Army and stayed in for the duration of the conflict. He was elected to the Senate as a Democrat by a majority of three hundred votes over John Henry Brown and completed his term during the Sixteenth Legislature.

The senator from the Fifth District, Captain Francis M. Henry, was a lawyer from Linden in Cass County. Henry was born in Rhea County, Tennessee, in 1832, the third of eight children. When he was twenty-six, he moved west to Arkansas, where he was admitted to the bar at Hot Springs in 1860. He managed to squeeze in a little lawyering before he enlisted in the Confederate Army in 1862, when he raised a company of which he was appointed captain. The company became Company I of the 19th Arkansas Infantry and participated in the battles at Shiloh, Corinth, and Vicksburg; Henry was then transferred to the Trans-Mississippi Department as captain of a cavalry company in the spring of 1863. He served in that capacity through the final surrender, when he again decided to go west. He settled at Linden, the county seat of Cass County, where he resumed the practice of law. Francis Henry was elected to the Senate in 1876 and moved to Texarkana in Bowie County, still in the Fifth District, in 1877. He continued to practice law after his term in the Senate was over and raised two lawyer sons.

Unlike most of his fellow senators, John R. Henry, from Mexia in Limestone County, was not a professional man and was not a Confederate veteran. Neither doctor nor lawyer, he was a successful merchant who had established the first permanent mercantile business in Springfield. He had come to Texas in 1837 at the age of twenty-one from his birthplace in Blount County, Tennessee. He enlisted for six months in a company of frontier militia, and when his time was up, he settled in Franklin, Robertson County. In addition to trading, he served as mail contractor for a time and then became a land locator, and he even chopped wood in Austin for a while. He had traded with the settlers and Indians in Robertson County for a decade before he decided to have a look at another location; when he got to Springfield in 1847 he liked the place enough to settle there, with all the supplies he had brought on his heavily laden wagon for trading. He picked a lot near the spring and built his store. In this area, trading was carried on mostly by exchange: cows were ten dollar bills, and chickens and hogs were the change. What money there was in circulation was usually held by

Henry, the unofficial banker, who became the richest man in the county. He prospered enough to marry a Miss Perry, daughter of a prominent family. In 1872 he moved to Mexia and continued his merchandising while helping to organize the First National Bank of Mexia. He was a large shareholder and the bank's first president, a position he held until his death in 1889.

Henry engaged in many social and political activities. In addition to serving one term in the Texas Senate, he was president of the board of Southwestern University, treasurer of the State Grange, a delegate to the World's Fair in London, a member of the Constitutional Convention of 1875, a lifelong active Methodist, and a prominent Mason. He died on his farm about three miles south of Mexia in October, 1889, leaving an estate of $125,000. That was an enormous sum in those times and testifies to Henry's business acumen and hard work.

Senator B. D. Martin was fifty-three years old when he came to the Fifteenth Legislature; married and living in Greenville in Hunt County, he was a farmer and merchant and a former magistrate. He was from Virginia and had served as a captain in the Confederate Army from March 10, 1862, until the war's end. He had been the mayor of Greenville for two years before his constituents elected him to the Senate as a Democrat by a majority of seven thousand votes.

One of the diminishing number of Republicans in Texas government, Judge Andrew Phelps McCormick was elected to the Senate of the Fifteenth Legislature by a plurality of seven hundred votes over his Democratic opponent, the Honorable C. L. Cleveland. The judge was an old Texian, having been born in Brazoria County in 1832 while Texas was still part of Mexico. He attended Centre College in Danville, Kentucky, and graduated in 1854. He came back to Texas and in 1855 opened a law office in Brazoria, where he practiced until the outbreak of the Civil War. Like many patriotic Texans, he joined the Confederate Army and served throughout the war, much of the time in Texas. Unlike many others with a similar background, however, he decided after the war that the Republican party would better serve his state and country and thereafter always acted with the Republicans.

McCormick served as chief justice of Brazoria County in 1865, until he was elected to the Constitutional Convention of 1866 and later to the Constitutional Convention of 1868–69. His next office was that of judge of the Eighteenth Judicial District, which he held from 1871 until his election to the Senate in 1876. During the Sixteenth Legislature McCormick was appointed U.S. attorney for the Eastern District of Texas, and President Rutherford B. Hayes nominated him to a federal judgeship in the district of North Texas and McCormick resigned from the Senate on April 12, 1879. In March, 1892, he was elevated to the U.S. Circuit Court for the Fifth District. Judge McCormick died in 1916.

Thomas Jefferson McCulloch, a doctor from Jewett in Leon County, represented the Fifteenth District. Dr. McCulloch was born near Abingdon, Virginia, on August 7, 1835, and educated at Emory and Henry College in his home state. In 1857, he graduated from Jefferson Medical College in Philadelphia and went back to Abingdon to set up his practice, but a year later he went to Jackson, Mississippi. In the election of 1860, Dr. McCulloch served as a presidential elector from Mississippi on the conservative Union ticket of Bell and Everett. When war broke out he became a surgeon in the Confederate Army, and after peace came he left the Old South and moved to Leon County in 1867. He was elected to the Senate as a Democrat on February 15, 1876, over the conservative Republican Captain Faulkner and the Republican Judge John B. Rector. He drew a four-year term but resigned on September 3, 1879, after serving in the Fifteenth and Sixteenth legislatures.

Another former Confederate Army surgeon was John W. Motley, a native of Autauga County, Alabama, who came to Texas in 1846 at the age of ten and settled in Harrison County. Motley went to the University of Louisville in Kentucky to study medicine, graduating in the spring of 1858. By May he was back in Texas and located in Rusk County, but soon the war claimed his services. When the conflict was over and he had returned to his home in Overton, his fellow citizens elected him to the Senate as a Democrat. He won by an overwhelming majority over Dr. A. D. Lindsley, a Republican, on February 15, 1876. Motley served in the Senate during the Fifteenth and Sixteenth legislatures.

Senator Finis E. Piner of Denton was another barrister in the Senate of the Fifteenth Legislature. Piner was born on December 4, 1837, in Obion County, Tennessee—not the last, as his given name would imply, but the third of eleven children. He moved with his family to Panola County, Mississippi, in 1847, where he spent most of his youth and received his education. In 1856, his father, Franklin Piner, moved his family to Texas; Finis went along but returned to Mississippi to enroll in the law department of the University of Mississippi. He graduated and received his license to practice, and for one year he did indeed pursue the profession, in partnership with Colonel D. L. Herron at Coffeeville, Mississippi. However, the South in the early 1860s was no place for the peaceful pursuit of any occupation. Lawyer Piner became soldier Piner in Company H, 15th Mississippi Infantry, acting as color-bearer. He was wounded at Shiloh and never recovered sufficiently to resume active duty. Returning to Texas, where the rest of his family was, Piner taught school at Honey Grove for a year and then resumed the practice of law in 1866. He was appointed county attorney in 1866, but since he could not take the "iron-clad oath," he was removed during Reconstruction. He was elected district attorney in 1873 and discharged that office until 1876, when he was elected to the Senate. He was defeated when he ran for Congress in 1878 but was elected district judge for the Sixteenth Judicial District in 1884; he served in that capacity until 1888. Piner had married Elizabeth H. McCleary on March 1, 1864, and they had eight children.

Among the increasingly beleaguered Republicans in the Senate was Walter Ripetoe, one of the two black senators, who had come to Texas from Montgomery County, Alabama, in 1850 at the age of twelve. He settled in Marshall, Harrison County, and was elected to the Senate on February 15, 1876, by a majority of twenty-six hundred votes. In 1876, he was a family man and a professional mechanic who for some time had been engaged as a schoolteacher. He was a man of extraordinary size, with prominent features. His term in the Senate during the Fifteenth and Sixteenth legislatures appears to have constituted his only service in a political office.

A Senate neophyte in 1876, Alexander Watkins Terrell was destined to be one of Texas' outstanding legislators, serving many years in the Senate and the House of Representatives and authoring several bills of far-reaching importance. His influence was such that, on the occasion of the presentation of his portrait to be hung in the Texas House of Representatives, the chairman of the Judiciary Committee said, "Judge Terrell has been the author of more good laws for Texas than any other man, living or dead."

Terrell was born in Patrick County, Virginia, on November 3, 1827; when he was five, he moved along with his family to Cooper County, Missouri. He graduated from the University of Missouri and studied law and was admitted to the bar in 1849, in which year he was elected city attorney of Saint Joseph, Missouri. In 1852, in search of a better climate for his wife, Ann E. Bouldin, he moved to Austin. Despite the move, Mrs. Terrell died in 1860, leaving five children. Meanwhile, Terrell in 1852 had entered into a law partnership with the Honorable W. S. Oldham and practiced in the firm until he was elected district judge in 1857. He served on the bench of the Austin district until 1863, when he entered the Confederate Army as a major in the 1st Texas Cavalry Regiment, Arizona Brigade. Later he was promoted to lieutenant colonel as commander of Terrell's Texas Cavalry Battalion, and when the battalion expanded into Terrell's Texas Cavalry Regiment, he became a colonel. He commanded the regiment in the battles of Mansfield and Pleasant Hill, Louisiana, in 1864 and was promoted to brigadier general by General Kirby Smith in 1865. When Texas finally accepted defeat, Terrell left for Mexico with Kirby Smith, Magruder, and other intransigent Rebels. In Mexico, Terrell found service in another lost cause: he became commander of a battalion with the French forces under Maximilian.

Having second thoughts about a military career, Terrell returned to Texas and attempted to practice law again, this time in Houston. The unsettled condition of the courts and the laws during Reconstruction, however, inclined him to retire to the country. He farmed in Robertson County, the home county of his second wife, Sarah Mitchell; when she died in 1871, he returned to Austin and the practice of law. In 1876 Terrell began his long and successful public life with his unopposed election to the Senate of the Fifteenth Legislature. He was to serve four consecutive terms in the Senate, ending with the Eighteenth Legislature in 1883, and several terms in the Texas House: in the Twenty-second Legislature in 1891, the Twenty-eighth in 1903, and the Twenty-ninth in 1905. In the 1890 elections he did not campaign or appear as a candidate, but even so he was elected to the Texas House by the largest percentage of votes yet recorded by a candidate in Travis County. He had been appointed reporter for the Supreme Court of Texas in 1874 and filled that position for thirteen years, leaving an indelible mark on Texas law. A Texas lawyer arguing before the U.S. Supreme Court was asked from what authority he was quoting and replied, "From a Texas report by Judge A. W. Terrell, who as a reporter has no superior in the United States."

Judge Terrell more directly affected the laws of Texas by authoring a good many of them. His first act as a senator was to offer a bill to reform the jury system by requiring that jurors in both civil and criminal cases be able to read and write. Later, after ensuring the passage of the various laws necessary for the construction of the State Capitol, Judge Terrell took up the cause of establishing a state university, and the original bill which became the law establishing the University of Texas is in his handwriting. As a member of the House, Terrell perfected legislation establishing the railroad commission. He was the author of the Terrell Election Law, which instituted the direct primary in the place of the convention system of nominating candidates. While chairman of the Education Committee, Senator Terrell framed the school law that established the "community system," which endured until its later replacement by the "district system"; he also was a strong advocate for eleemosynary institutions and originated acts for the enlargement and rebuilding of asylums for the mentally ill and schools for the deaf and the blind. In 1909 Governor Thomas Mitchell Campbell appointed Judge Terrell to the board of regents of the University of Texas, which he had done so much to create; during his two-year term as a regent he worked effectively to secure funds for the library building. In 1893 President Cleveland appointed him minister plenipotentiary to the Ottoman Empire, in which capacity he brought about some improvement in the conditions of the Christian Armenians and in the protection of Christian missionaries in Armenia.

Judge Terrell was married a third time in 1883 to Mrs. Ann Jones, formerly Miss Ann Holliday. The judge was a scholar as well as a "Ciceronian orator," as historian John Henry Brown describes him; he contributed to the *Southwestern Historical Quarterly* and was president of the Texas Historical Society when he died on September 8, 1912.

Senator Wells Thompson of Columbus was born in Marengo County, Alabama, on December 12, 1840. His family, well-to-do planters, moved to Texas in 1839 and settled in Matagorda County, where young Wells grew up. He went back to the South for college, graduating from the University of North Carolina with honors in 1859 and going on to law school at the University of Georgia, where he graduated as valedictorian in 1861. After graduation, he enlisted in the Confederate Army as a private in the University Battery, attached to General Cobb's Legion. He fought all through the war, mainly with the Army of Tennessee, and at the final surrender held the position of captain of Company I, 36th Alabama Regiment of Infantry. He was wounded in the battles of Chickamauga and Lost Mountain.

After the war was over, Wells limped home to Matagorda, where he practiced law and where the First Judicial District (Matagorda) elected him district attorney in 1866. Considering Judge Thompson one of the "impediments to Reconstruction" which infested Texas, General Sheridan had him removed from office. In that same year Thompson participated in the constitutional convention, helping to write a constitution that also was destined to be removed from service. He moved to Columbus in 1868, where he practiced law and married Miss Caroline Tait. He was elected lieutenant governor in 1869 but was again removed by the military, this time by General Reynolds. In 1871 he was elected to the state Senate but was once more unseated by the Republicans. Finally, when he was again elected to the Senate in 1876, he managed to take his seat and serve his term and on the first day of the session was elected president pro tempore. When Governor Coke resigned to become U.S. senator on December 1, 1876, Lieutenant Governor Hubbard succeeded him the same day, leaving Senator Thompson, president pro tempore of the Senate, to function as president of the Senate and as lieutenant governor. He held that position for two years. Thompson was an Episcopalian, an Odd Fellow, and a member of the board of regents of the Agricultural and Mechanical College of Texas. He died at his home in Bay City on January 17, 1914, after a long and exemplary life of public service.

The eighteen neophytes discussed above were joined by thirteen senators who previously had served terms in the legislature: Edwin Hobby, William H. Ledbetter, and Walter M. Burton (one of the two black members) had served in the Senate of the Fourteenth Legislature; James P. Douglas in the Senate of the Twelfth; John W. Moore in the Senate of the Ninth and Tenth; John S. "Rip" Ford in the House of the Ninth Congress of the Republic of Texas and the Senate of the Fourth Legislature, following Edward Burleson's death; William A. Wortham in the House during the Eighth and Ninth; John T. Brady in the House of the Tenth and Eleventh; John W. Carroll in the House of the Thirteenth; and James H. McLeary in the House of the Fourteenth, along with Tillman Smith, John D. Stephens, and Leonidas J. Storey, who served in the House of both the Thirteenth and Fourteenth. James R. Burnett succeeded Smith when Smith resigned on November 19, 1876, and Ellsberry R. Lane replaced Crain when he resigned on August 20, 1877. Burnett and Lane were sworn during the Sixteenth Legislature.

Some of these members were war veterans. McLeary and Smith had been enlisted men in the Confederate Army, while Storey had been a captain, Douglas had risen to the rank of major, and Wortham had been a lieutenant colonel. Ford, of course, was conspicuous in state military service during the war.

Senator John T. Brady of Houston was a well-known public figure even before his election to the Senate. He had already served in the Texas House during the Tenth Legislature, when he was chairman of the Committee on Finance; and during the Eleventh, when he chaired the Committee on Internal Improvements. His parents were farmers in Charles County, Maryland, where Brady was born on October 10, 1830. He was educated at Charlotte Hall Academy and at the age of seventeen became a teacher himself, using his earnings to finance his legal studies. He became a member of the Maryland bar in his early twenties and practiced in his home state for two years. Brady then went west to Westport, Missouri, where he continued to practice law and became a journalist as well. After another two-year stint in Missouri, he left for Houston, where he arrived in 1856 and where he stayed for the rest of his life. He married Caledonia Tinsley, of a wealthy planter family, in 1858, when he had already made something of a name for himself as a lawyer; after her death he married Lennie Sherman, daughter of San Jacinto veteran Sidney Sherman, in 1880.

Brady is described as a man of boundless energy and faith in the bright future of his adopted state, and certainly he was a principal developer of Houston, being one of the first to see the city's future as a major deepwater port and as a great city of the Southwest. His interests included the breeding of fine cattle, and it was that interest which led him to conceive and promote the idea of the Texas State

Fair, of which he was a lifelong supporter. In 1876, his friends and neighbors in Harris County sent him to the Senate, where he chaired the Committee on Public Debt. In 1880 he ran for Congress as a Greenback candidate against Roger Q. Mills but was defeated. Returning to his lucrative and distinguished law practice and his visionary projects for Houston, Brady abandoned politics. It was John Brady who pushed the development of a belt railway connecting all the railroads coming to Houston, the opening of a deepwater port at the junction of Buffalo and Brays bayous, and a public park "suitable to the growing demands of a seat of wealth, culture, and refinement like Houston." While inspecting work on a wharf at Port Houston on June 20, 1890, Brady was stricken with a "cerebral effusion" and died not long afterward, much mourned by the fellow Houstonians who had benefited so much from his enthusiasm for their city.

Another graduate to the Senate from the House was John W. Carroll, of Caldwell in Burleson County, who had emigrated from his native North Carolina nineteen years earlier. He was forty-three years old and a merchant at Caldwell when he came to the Senate as a member of the burgeoning Democratic majority.

The Senate of the Fifteenth Legislature boasted one genuine mythic Texas hero, John Salmon "Rip" Ford, who had fought for Texas through all her vicissitudes since the day he first reached her boundaries in June, 1836. He had also served in all of her political transmutations: he was a member of the House in the Ninth Congress of the Republic; in 1852, he served in the Senate of the Fourth Legislature of the State of Texas; in 1861, he was a delegate to the Secession Convention; he was a delegate to the Constitutional Convention of 1875; and he returned to the legislature as the senator from Brownsville in 1876, serving two sessions. He earned his nickname during the Mexican War when, as surgeon and adjutant of Jack Hays's regiment of Rangers, he would kindly append "Rest in Peace," and later, when things heated up, "R.I.P.," to the death notices he had to send.

Senator Ford was born in Greenville County, South Carolina, in 1815, and later moved along with his family to Bedford County, Tennessee. He finished his education there, completed his medical studies, and married. In 1836 he heard about the war for Texas independence and raised a company of fellow Tennesseans to go to

Texas and help out, but by the time he got to Texas, the war was over; Texas was, however shakily, independent. This did not mean fighting men were unwelcome, however, and Ford joined the Texas Army and fought Indians under Colonel Jack Hays, attaining the rank of lieutenant before he resigned in 1838. He settled in Saint Augustine with his wife and practiced medicine there until 1844, when he was elected to the Texas House of Representatives in the Ninth Congress, where he prepared and introduced the resolution to accept the terms for annexation offered by the United States. He liked Austin and moved there in 1845. Together with Michael Cronican, he purchased the *Texas National Register* newspaper, which later became the *Texas Democrat.* Ford became its editor and also, along with Cronican, was named public printer by the legislature. When General Winfield Scott came through Texas on his way to the Mexican War, Ford joined up with his old leader, Colonel Jack Hays, as part of a nimble Ranger force that operated before, behind, and all around the enemy. The Rangers rendered invaluable service to the regular army, and Ford was quickly promoted to captain and given his own company of scouts. He excelled at this type of warfare and used all the Indian-fighting skills he had acquired in Texas to such good effect that Generals Patterson and Lane both commended him to the War Department and to the commander in chief.

After the close of the Mexican War, Captain Ford returned to his journalism, but in 1849 he was off again to the frontier, where with R. S. Neighbors he explored the country between San Antonio and El Paso with the object of establishing a road west. He published a report and map of the route, which was known as the Ford and Neighbors Trail. Later in that year he was made captain of a force of Texas Rangers which patrolled the lawless area between the Nueces River and the Rio Grande. He returned to Austin as a member of the Senate in 1852 and started another newspaper, the *State Times*, in partnership with Captain Joe Walker; the paper was published until 1857. Ford became an Indian fighter again in 1858, when he was commissioned a captain in the state troops; he led his men in two battles on the Canadian River which were major defeats for the Comanches. In 1859, he was back on the Mexican border with his Texas Rangers, where he was in charge of operations against the bandit-hero Juan Nepomuceno Cortina. Cortina was a hero to many Mexicans on both sides of the Rio Grande, but he was a bandit to the ranchers on whose cattle he preyed, also on both sides of the river. His activities eventually provoked the intervention of the U.S. Army as well as the Texas Rangers. Ford eulogist Charles L. Martin writes that "Colonel Ford outgeneraled and circumvented Cortina at every turn and ably seconded by the government troops under Lieutenant-Colonel Robert E. Lee . . . in a short time succeeded in driving Cortina and his cutthroats from the country."

In 1861 Colonel Ford was elected a member of the Secession Convention, where he was an ardent supporter of withdrawing from the Union. When the ordinance of secession was adopted, the convention commissioned him a colonel of state cavalry and ordered him to raise a regiment and proceed to the Rio Grande and capture the federal forts and troops along the river. He performed this duty at once, capturing the upriver forts and persuading the Union commander of the strong garrison at Fort Brown to leave without a fight. Later he initiated a trade agreement between Mexico and the Confederacy and was elected colonel of the 2nd Texas Cavalry, commanding in the Rio Grande district. In 1863 he was assigned to conscript duty, a job he detested but discharged fairly. At the end of the year he was called to a duty which was much more to his liking: he was to raise a regiment of cavalry to campaign along the Rio Grande and especially to rescue Brownsville from the federals, who had retaken it, and restore the profitable cotton trade through Mexico. Ford at once posted notices for men to come to his standard and bring their horses; he called his outfit the Cavalry of the West, and he and they accomplished more than anyone expected. They retook Brownsville, drove the Union troops out of South Texas, reopened the only conduit of trade still available to the South, and on May 12, 1865, won the last battle of the Civil War, at Palmito Ranch. The war had been over for a month, but word had not reached Texas yet.

After the war, Ford was Confederate parole commissioner. In 1868 he moved to Brownsville, where he edited the *Sentinel*, a local newspaper. In 1872 he went to Baltimore as a delegate to the Democratic National Convention, and in 1873 he was a special sergeant-at-arms at the violent inauguration of Governor Coke, where he prevented a riot between the citizens of Austin and the supporters of ex-governor Davis. In 1876 he was elected to the Senate of the Fifteenth Legislature, where he was a strong advocate for public education and for encouraging immigration. During these postwar years, Ford also served as cattle and hide inspector for Cameron County, which meant that he was still chasing cattle rustlers along the Rio Grande. He served as mayor of Brownsville in 1874 and was superintendent of the Deaf and Dumb School. He became a charter member and contributing writer of the Texas Historical Society and ended his days as a writer of reminiscences and articles about Texas history, the study of which he encouraged. The old warrior died peacefully in 1897, having outfought and outlived his enemies—and most of his friends—during his amazing career as medical doctor, prominent journalist, representative in the Texas House, captain in the U.S. Army, colonel in the Texas forces during the Civil War, senator, mayor, and, most memorably, Ranger captain. In the words of the historian T. R. Fehrenbach, he was "the only man in Texas history who was involved in a major way in every action or controversy of his time. He was one of the fantastic, but forgotten, figures of the old frontier."

The Honorable James Harvey McLeary was a newcomer to the Senate but not to the legislature; he had represented his San Antonio district in the House during the Fourteenth Legislature. McLeary was born on July 27, 1845. Like many of his contemporary Texans, he was a native of Tennessee. His family moved to Texas in the late 1850s and settled in Colorado County, where McLeary attended country schools. He later studied at Soule University at Chappell Hill in Washington County before becoming a Confederate soldier in Company A of the 5th Texas Cavalry in Sibley's Brigade. He was wounded at the battle of Valverde, New Mexico, and survived the painful retreat. He was wounded again at Donaldsonville and yet again at Yellow Bayou, where he was wounded twice and left on the field for dead.

While still on crutches, he returned to his studies at Soule but in 1866 transferred to Washington College in Lexington, Virginia. He received his bachelor of arts degree in June, 1868, and as the student with the highest grades, delivered the "Cincinnati oration." The following year, he received his law degree from the same school, returned to Texas, began to practice law at Columbus, and married Emily Mitchell, his fiancée of several years. In December, 1869, the couple moved to San Antonio, where the young wife died, survived by one child. In 1875, McLeary married Mary King, daughter of Texas scholar V. O. King.

When he moved to San Antonio, McLeary had formed a law partnership with Judge C. L. Wurzbach. This continued until 1873, when McLeary was elected to the Texas House of Representatives, where he served until his election to the Texas Senate for the next session. His legislative service included chairmanship of the House Committee on Education and of the Senate Committee on Privileges and Elections and the Senate Committee on State Affairs. He authored the bill giving control of the schools to towns and cities, and he gave fifty-six new counties in the Panhandle good Texas hero names, including those of men who fell at the Alamo.

After his legislative career, McLeary was elected to a two-year term as attorney general, in which capacity he managed to recover 4,680 square miles of the public domain from the International and Great Northern Railroad Company. He declined to run for office again and returned to his practice in San Antonio. In 1884 he was an elector on the Cleveland ticket and was able to vote for the first Democratic president in twenty-five years. He was appointed an associate justice on the Supreme Court of Montana in 1886 but stayed in Montana for only two years, finding the climate too severe; he came back to San Antonio and resumed his lucrative law practice under sunny Texas skies. He abandoned San Antonio once again to fight in the Spanish-American War as a major and yet again to serve as a U.S. judge in Puerto Rico. Bad health forced him to return to Washington, D.C., where he died on January 6, 1914. He had been a loyal Democrat, a friend of President Cleveland, an ardent Mason, and an orator much in demand at scholarly and political events, as well as a respected legal practitioner.

Tillman Smith of Navasota in Grimes County was elected to the Senate of the Fifteenth Legislature after serving in the House of the Fourteenth. Smith was born in North Carolina in 1844, was educated at the University of North Carolina, and enlisted as a private in the Army of Northern Virginia—all before he was eighteen years old. He was wounded at Sharpsburg and Chancellorsville. At the end of the war, he came west, arriving in Texas on June 28, 1865. Here he studied law and went into practice at Navasota. When Smith was a representative in the Texas House in the Fourteenth

Legislature, he was a member of the Judiciary Committee, and in the Senate he became chairman of the Committee on Constitutional Amendments, a very responsible position so soon after the adoption of the new constitution. His description pictures a man of ordinary height, inclined to rotundity, with an open, generous, and good-natured expression who bid fair to become a man of note. But he resigned his senatorial seat on November 19, 1876, and was replaced by James R. Burnett, who was sworn during the Sixteenth Legislature.

The senator from Comanche, John D. Stephens, had also been a representative in the House of the Fourteenth Legislature. Stephens was born in Tennessee on April 19, 1845. He became a Confederate soldier in 1862, joining the 62nd Tennessee Regiment under Colonel J. A. Rowan. He served until the end of the war, surviving service at Vicksburg, capture at Big Black River, imprisonment and escape at Fort Delaware, and final service in Virginia during the death throes of the Confederacy. He was twenty years old when he surrendered and was paroled at Washington, Georgia, in 1865.

In 1868 Stephens came to Texas, and by 1871 he was studying law under Judge George McCormick at Columbus; in December of that year he moved to Comanche County and began the practice of law with Judge J. R. Fleming. Two years later, his fellow citizens elected him to the Texas House, and in 1876 they sent him to the Senate. Stephens was an energetic legislator: he wrote the land bill providing for the sale of school lands in 160-acre tracts, opposed the subsidy measures for the International and Great Northern Railroad, and advocated the successful frontier battalion bill.

When his legislative service was over, Stephens prospected in California and Mexico but came back to Texas, where 1886 found him occupied as a grass commissioner—a state agent who inspected the school lands in the west and reported on them to the land board. After his wanderings, he was persuaded that Texas was the best place to be and decided to locate permanently "out west."

When Leonidas Jefferson "Jeff" Storey came to the Senate, he was well along in a political career that would lead to his becoming lieutenant governor in 1880 and a railroad commissioner from 1892 until his death in 1909. Senator Storey was born in Chattooga County, Georgia, in 1834; his family moved to Mississippi and then to Texas and reached Gonzales County in 1845. They moved from there to Lockhart in 1847, where Jeff worked and studied until he was able to go to Austin College for a term when he was twenty-one. He came home in bad health but began studying law in the firm of Rogan and Whitis at Lockhart and was admitted to the bar in October, 1858, by Judge A. W. Terrell. He practiced law for twenty-eight years in the firm of Nix and Storey and from 1886 practiced as senior partner in Storey and Storey until his appointment to the railroad commission in 1894.

Meanwhile, there was the Civil War. Storey opposed and canvassed against secession, but he believed in the right of the states to secede and so he followed Texas into the war. He helped raise, and became second lieutenant of, Company B, 26th Texas Cavalry, De Bray's Brigade, the first company raised in Caldwell County. He fought at Galveston, in the Red River campaign, and in the Louisiana battles near the end of the war and returned home very poor but happy to be alive. His inability to take the iron-clad oath prevented his practicing law, but he was able to become a surveyor and took to the woods with his compass to support his family. His life as a family man had begun in 1859 with his marriage to Lucinda Ellison; they eventually had ten children, of whom nine lived to adulthood.

After the war, Storey was a dedicated Democrat and as such was elected to the Texas House of Representatives of the Thirteenth Legislature, was reelected to the House of the Fourteenth, was elected without opposition to the Senate of the Fifteenth, and served again in the Senate of the Sixteenth. He was a member of the Judiciary Committee in the House for both terms and in the Senate for both terms there as well; he chaired the Committee on Finance in the Senate. In his second Senate term, he was unanimously elected president pro tempore. Senator Storey was elected lieutenant governor in 1880 and served with Governor Oran M. Roberts in his second term. In 1894 Governor Hogg appointed him to the new railroad commission, where he continued to serve after the position became elective; he was elected chairman of the commission in 1903 and retained that office until his death in Fort Worth in 1909. Governor Coke had appointed Storey a special judge of the district court of Blanco County, and he was twice appointed special judge for the Court of Civil Appeals in Austin. Thus he often was called "Judge Storey," as well as "Senator Storey."

Leonidas Jefferson Storey, lieutenant governor, 1881–83, in Seventeenth Legislature, senator in Fifteenth and Sixteenth legislatures. Reproduced from holdings of Texas State Archives.

Senator William A. Wortham of Sulphur Springs in Hopkins County came to Texas from Maury County, Tennessee, with his widowed mother in 1842, when he was twelve years old. They settled in Harrison County, where he was educated in Marshall and apprenticed himself to a printing office, emerging three years later as an experienced journeyman printer. Armed with this trade, he married Adeline Ashcroft in 1852 and settled in Sulphur Springs in 1854 to begin his career as newspaper editor and publisher. This career was interrupted by the Civil War: Wortham volunteered for service in the Confederate Army in December, 1861. He was elected first lieutenant of his company and attached to Crump's 1st Texas Battalion, which was later attached to Ector's Brigade. At war's end, after fighting in the battles at Elkhorn, Richmond (Kentucky), Perryville, Murfreesboro, Jackson, Mansfield, Pleasant Hill, and Yellow Bayou, as well as other engagements, he was a lieutenant colonel commanding the 34th Texas Cavalry. Colonel Wortham was a devout member of the Methodist Episcopal Church, South, and was accustomed to leading worship services in his tent during campaigns. An anecdote which illustrates his kindness to anyone in distress tells that in the middle of an August battle he gave the last water in his canteen to a wounded and dying federal soldier.

Wortham was always a fiercely partisan Democrat and thought that a person who was politically "independent" lacked both principle and firm opinions. He fully supported secession until the war settled that issue. During Reconstruction he became one of the most outspoken advocates for civil liberty and honest government. He used his newspaper, the *Sulphur Springs Gazette*, to excoriate the Republicans, earning threats of incarceration by the federal troops in Sulphur Springs. He was one of the ablest and most widely known editorial writers in the state.

Colonel Wortham represented Hopkins County in the House of Representatives of the Eighth, Ninth, Fourteenth, and Eighteenth legislatures and in the Senate of the Fifteenth. He also served as House engrossing clerk during the Thirteenth Legislature and as justice of the peace and district clerk. In 1891 he was appointed superintendent of the State Orphan's Asylum at Corsicana by Governor Hogg and was reappointed by Governor Culberson, serving in that post for a total of eight years. He died on October 1, 1910, in Fort Worth.

The Senate of the Fifteenth Legislature reflected two major changes that had come about in Texas since the war: the collapse of the plantation economy and the decline of the Republican party. The senators were predominantly professional men or merchants—only Burton and Martin farmed, and Martin was also a merchant. Senator Terrell had farmed for a few years after the war and Senator Blassingame had been a Grange sympathizer, but the interests in the chamber were decidedly town-centered. As for the Republicans, each succeeding election reduced their numbers, which would soon shrink to zero, and Texas would become a one-party state for the next century.

For now, however, the Senate, though overwhelmingly Democratic, still included a few Republicans. Ripetoe, serving his first term in public office, and fellow Republican Burton were the only black members of the Senate of the Fifteenth Legislature. The tiny Republican minority often felt besieged. The election of Republican McCormick, a Confederate veteran and a delegate to the constitutional conventions of 1866 and 1868–69, was contested by Charles L. Cleveland, who said that McCormick was not eligible for elective office because he had been a district judge during the election. Furthermore, Cleveland said the election had been accomplished fraudulently through the county courts' abolition of all polling places at which the white voters outnumbered the black voters and the preservation of those at which the opposite was true. Finally, Cleveland alleged that the Republicans in the region had used threats of violence to coerce the voters into rejecting the Democratic candidates. McCormick replied to the allegations by pointing out that being a district judge did not disqualify him from election and that the redistricting of the county had not resulted in a practical disenfranchisement of many voters; in fact, the vote cast was the largest in the history of Brazoria County. McCormick also denied any knowledge of intimidation. The Senate Committee on Privileges and Elections, chaired by McLeary, ruled in favor of McCormick, and the Senate adopted the committee's report on May 2.

The officers of the Senate were elected during the first two days of the session. W. Leigh Chalmers was elected secretary; John W. Swindells, first assistant secretary; William N. Ramey, second assistant secretary; Asa M. Belvin, engrossing clerk; G. N. Beaumont, enrolling clerk; E. J. Chew, calendar clerk; William Fitzhugh, doorkeeper; J. B. Wilkins, sergeant-at-arms; James A. Hardin, assistant sergeant-at-arms; and John L. Lovejoy, chaplain. After Senator Thompson's election as president pro tempore on April 19, the Senate proceeded to have Governor Coke's annual message read, as was customary; but during the reading of the lengthy and ponderous missive, the senators adopted McCulloch's resolution that further reading be dispensed with and ordered five thousand copies to be printed. On April 25 Coke addressed a joint session of the Fifteenth Legislature in person, thereby holding his audience captive, to demand the reforms he thought necessary.

Coke had pushed hard for the ratification of the new constitution, but there had been much opposition to it from the legal profession, which pointed out that the proposed judicial system was more cumbersome than the old one. The article of the 1876 constitution providing for the judiciary was indeed unclear. Governor Coke in his message on April 19 asked the legislators to remedy these shortcomings, and the Senate took the lead in judicial reform. Hobby authored an act, signed on May 6, which organized the Court of Appeals and made clear its subordination to the Texas Supreme Court. Three days later, all cases pending in courts presided over by justices of the peace operating under special laws approved by previous legislatures were transferred to the appropriate courts and, at the same time, all of the proper cases pending in district courts were surrendered to the justice courts. The caseloads of the criminal courts, which had opened under the 1869 constitution but had now been abolished, were transferred to the district courts. County courts, as Governor Coke recommended, were established as probate courts through a bill introduced by Piner, and the duties of clerks, notaries, and justices of the peace were formalized. Terrell introduced a bill that established stricter qualifications for juries; among the provisions was one that permitted either counsel, in both civil and criminal cases, to challenge and remove jurors who could not read or write.

Crain introduced a bill to authorize sheriffs to pursue suspects across county boundaries, to muster posses anywhere, and to call on military units for assistance if necessary. The bill was opposed by many who recalled all too well the abuses of the state police, and it was vetoed by Governor Coke. He objected at some length to the provision that permitted a sheriff to shoot a fleeing suspect who did not respond to an audible command to halt; to him it was obviously a mandate for vigilante justice, a social sickness that was becoming epidemic in Texas. Coke also objected to the power of a sheriff to command military units, an authority he termed a "palpable violation of the Constitution." Instead, he reiterated his confidence in the company being formed for the protection of the frontier. The Fifteenth Legislature authorized Governor Coke to enlist a company of fifty-three privates and officers for at least six months. This force would act much as the state police had: to aid local peace officers by arresting those accused of illegal acts and delivering them to the proper court for trial. The Senate was not quite satisfied with these measures; Edwards introduced a joint resolution, which was adopted, that called on the federal government to send more troops and to reimburse Texas for its expenses in frontier defense.

The protection of settlers in the western portion of the state took on added importance with the formation of fifty-four counties from the territories of Young and Bexar through a bill introduced by Senator Stephens. These new counties included Andrews, Armstrong, Bailey, Borden, Briscoe, Carson, Castro, Childress, Cochran, Collingsworth, Cottle, Crosby, Dallam, Dawson, Deaf Smith, Dickens, Donley, Fisher, Floyd, Gaines, Garza, Gray, Hale, Hall, Hansford, Hartley, Hemphill, Hockley, Howard, Hutchinson, Kent, King, Lamb, Lipscomb, Lubbock, Lynn, Martin, Mitchell, Moore, Motley, Nolan, Ochiltree, Oldham, Parmer, Potter, Randall, Roberts, Scurry, Sherman, Stonewall, Swisher, Terry, Wheeler, and Yoakum. In addition, the boundaries of several central and western counties—Callahan, Eastland, Hardeman, Haskell, Jones, Knox, and Taylor—were redefined, and the statutes creating Wegefarth County were repealed.

Along with the more frequent occurrences of vigilante justice, the mistreatment of state prisoners within the convict lease system had become a subject of much concern. An investigating committee appointed by Governor Coke reported that the conditions in which many prisoners worked were less than satisfactory; in fact, between August 31, 1874, and January 1, 1876, a fifth of all the prisoners held by the state had died or escaped. The newspapers regularly reported atrocities committed by "penitentiary birds," as escapees were known, and demanded reform. On August 19, Coke signed a measure, introduced by Senator Thompson, which allowed the state to resume control of the prison at Huntsville. Henceforth, the management of the prison would be entrusted to a three-man commission appointed by the governor, who would arrange for the subsequent leasing of the institution under fifteen-year contracts, but these contracts would be subject to the approval of the legislature. The state would retain all control over the convicts, with "special regard being had, as far as practicable, to the exaction of the penalty imposed by law on each convict, and to the protection, well being and humane treatment to which each convict is entitled at the hands of the State."

A separate measure also continued the practice of hiring out county convicts to private companies under governmental supervision. The requests of many reformers to provide a system for reducing jail sentences for good behavior, which some counties had initiated, were not heeded, but neither were the demands of some for a return to a more draconian law. Senator Grace led a successful fight to revise the Penal Code, condemning it as one that "sends a poor devil who steals a little old hat not worth twenty-five cents to the penitentiary for two years." There were some who opposed the liberal impulse; for example, Senator Guy responded to Grace that anyone guilty of theft should be sentenced to prison for life. The Fifteenth Legislature could hardly be called liberal, but neither would it bring back the stocks and the whipping post.

The conservatism of the Fifteenth Legislature was reflected in a law signed by Governor Coke on June 24, 1876, providing that the legislature would no longer impose temperance or prohibition, an issue which would now be decided by local plebiscite. A petition by fifty registered voters in a county, or twenty in a justice precinct or town, to the commissioners court would be sufficient to bring about an election in which the matter would be decided by a simple majority vote. An election could not be held more than once every twelve months. A separate act defined drunkenness in public office as an "offense against the laws of this State." It provided that any state or district official would be removed if found guilty, but that county and municipal officers would be removed only on the third offense; they would be fined for the first two convictions. On August 17, 1876, the legislature approved an act which prescribed a fine of up to one hundred dollars for public drunkenness. Habitual drunkards were specifically included in an act signed the next day which provided that the county courts could appoint guardians for them, for minors, and for "persons of unsound mind."

The Senate also endorsed a number of amendments to the civil code. An amendment to the act providing for divorce and alimony, first approved in January, 1841, became law without the governor's signature. It stated that a divorce would be granted in only three events: adultery by either spouse; abandonment for a period of at least three years; or conviction of either party for a felony, but only after the prisoner had served twelve months and not at all if the governor pardoned the offender. A curious law, signed on June 22, 1876, provided that anyone who bought personal property after nightfall which later proved to be stolen would be liable to the owner for three times the value of the property, as well as being subject to criminal prosecution. The legislators also set the maximum annual interest rate for private contracts at 12 percent and provided that in cases where no interest rate was specified, 8 percent would be assumed. An act signed on June 24 prohibited anyone from removing rock, earth, sand, coal, slate, or minerals from the property of another and made offenders of this provision liable upon conviction for a fine of up to ten times the value of the material removed.

The legislators relied on land and new taxes to fund education. The 1876 constitution abolished the office of the superintendent of public education in favor of a board of education, which would consist of the governor, the comptroller, and the secretary of state. The constitution also eliminated compulsory attendance, established segregated schools, and made no provision for local taxes to support public education. Instead, a state public school fund would receive one-fourth of the ad valorem and occupation taxes collected since March 30, 1870, one-fourth of those taxes collected in the future, an annual poll tax of one dollar, and the interest on the bonds and the revenues from the lands set aside for the public schools. Separate acts provided that the ad valorem tax would be one-half of 1 percent on all real and personal property, with certain exceptions listed in a lengthy additional act. The Fifteenth Legislature provided for a two-part bond issue of $875,000 to be applied to the retirement of that portion of the floating debt of the state which would come due in 1876 and 1877. These bonds would bear 6 percent annual interest, payable semiannually in gold coin, and would be redeemed in thirty years. Another act provided that the U.S. bonds then in the public school fund were to be sold and the revenue invested in state bonds.

The legislators, in providing for public education, managed to kill two birds with one stone. Texas suffered from a surplus of dogs during the 1870s, many of them wild. There were many articles on the subject, the *Democratic Statesman* remarking that "the people west of Cuero have quit killing one another, and devote their leisure moments to the annihilation of mad dogs abounding in those parts." An unusual tax of one dollar per dog was imposed on dog owners for the benefit of the public school system. One dog per family was exempt, but all dogs subject to the tax for which the levy had not been paid could be destroyed and their owners fined. To aid those people who had little or no means, the tax could be paid in pelts, whose value for this purpose ranged from two dollars for a panther, bear, catamount, or wolf to twenty-five cents for a raccoon.

The legislators, pursuant to the Constitution of 1876, provided for racially separate schools but, in the spirit of a principle soon to become the law of the land, required that schools for whites and blacks have equal facilities. The act for the appropriation of the public school fund clearly stated that "each race shall receive its just pro rata, as far as practicable, in each county, according to the number of children of each race within scholastic age." All children "without regard to race or color," from eight to fourteen years of age, would be counted in the scholastic census, yet race would be recorded and "all children known to the Assessor to contain an admixture of African blood shall be returned as colored." These children would not attend the same institutions as whites, and no integrated school would receive public funds, according to the provisions of an act that also excluded sectarian academies from receiving state aid. The principle of "separate but equal" was obvious in the theory of the legislation, but the Senate contained virulent racists such as Smith and Terrell who would ensure that the practice remained unequal in favor of an educated white populace and an illiterate, subordinate, primarily black class. The strongest protests would come from champions of the agrarian faction like Senator Blassingame, who realized that measures furthering the subordination of blacks, such as the abolition of compulsory attendance, would also affect poor whites.

Higher education received careful attention from the Fifteenth Legislature. A delegation visited the Agricultural and Mechanical College of Texas, and forty thousand dollars was set aside to put that institution "in immediate and successful operation." On August 14 the legislators endorsed a smaller appropriation for the establishment of a mechanical and agricultural college for blacks, then authorized a three-man commission appointed by the governor to select a site. This institution would be under the aegis of the board of directors for the Agricultural and Mechanical College of Texas. The Constitutional Convention of 1875 had rescinded the 1858 grant of 3.2 million acres, scattered across the state, for the endowment of a university and replaced it with a grant of 1 million acres to be specified later. Senator Stephens introduced bills to survey these tracts as well as 3 million additional acres to be set aside to fund the construction of a new Capitol. The measure for the benefit of the university passed, but the lands were located in arid West Texas. Only the discovery of oil beneath those barren lands almost fifty years later rescued the University of Texas from a legacy of enforced poverty. The bill for funding a new Capitol failed to become law during the Fifteenth Legislature, preoccupied as it was with the mandate for economy. In 1876 the only construction on College Hill in Austin, the site of the university, was the digging of a new reservoir by the City Water Company to supply the government buildings in the area.

Land was also the focus of one of the bitterest controversies concerning railroads ever fought in the Texas Legislature. The Senate of the Fifteenth Legislature, normally unified and decorous in its deliberations, split angrily over the issue of extending more time to the Texas and Pacific Railroad Company. This corporation, which had been the subject of much debate ever since the Twelfth Legislature had issued its charter, had failed to build the required number of miles of track by the specified deadline and stood to lose a tremendous amount of land: twenty million acres of the public domain, one-ninth of the total surface area of Texas. This generous grant, which had been substituted for the original bond issue following a long debate in the Thirteenth Legislature, reflected the great interest of the Texas government in a transcontinental railroad through the state.

The opponents of further extensions of the contract argued that

Tom Scott, the president of the company, could not fulfill his obligations and that the land should be returned to Texas for the benefit of the public school system. They pointed out that Scott had petitioned the federal government for payment on the bonds it had authorized for him but that Congress had not yet decided in favor of an extension of its contract with Scott and might very well refuse his request. Nevertheless, the bill for an extension passed the Texas Senate by a vote of eighteen to twelve, with the active support of Lieutenant Governor Hubbard. Eight senators—Burton, McLeary, McCormick, McCulloch, Stephens, Storey, Terrell, and Thompson—signed a protest to be entered in the *Senate Journal*, while Ford entered a separate, and much briefer, disclaimer in which he stated that he would not vote for a bill in favor of a railroad company that had not acted "in apparent good faith."

Much of the debate on the Texas and Pacific issue divided along sectional lines, east versus west. Senator Ripetoe, taking notice of the animosity evidenced by the legislators of the western counties toward those from the east, introduced a sardonic resolution that would require the governor to call an election to determine "whether the great empire State of Texas, with all of its glorious memories, gallant deeds, and hallowed associations," should be divided, or if the "gallant sons of Texas, forgetting the issues of sectionalism, will swear that Texas, the brightest star that shines in the galaxy of States, shall remain . . . one and indivisible." The resolution was referred to the Senate Committee on State Affairs, where it was tabled on a motion by the chairman, McLeary.

An unsuccessful attempt was made to prevent a vote on the extension act in the House and Senate with a concurrent resolution to adjourn on July 31 as required by the newly ratified constitution. The *Democratic Statesman* deplored the passage of the extension act, attributing it to the active lobbying of Scott and his associates in the antechambers of the Texas Capitol. Seven senators from West Texas who on July 24 had voted no in a vain attempt to prevent passage—Crain, Ford, McLeary, Stephens, Storey, Terrell, and Thompson—were hailed as heroes. The editor predicted that Scott would next engineer a division of Texas into eleven new states, each represented in the Congress of the United States by a Radical Republican.

No such apocalypse occurred, of course, but the doubts of many about the validity of the railroad were confirmed. The Texas and

Pacific Railroad Company completed a line to El Paso, but continued no farther west. The railroad patented a little more than five million acres in Texas, most of it in the arid western portion of the state, which was of little use to either farmers or ranchers. In 1886 the company, crippled in part by poor land sales, went into receivership, and control of the tracts passed to a trust formed by speculators who had purchased mortgage bonds issued with the original land grant as security. Today that trust operates an oil lease business for the benefit of the heirs of the original land bonds.

A number of separate relief acts for railroad companies, as well as a general incorporation act for the organization of a company once ten stockholders had subscribed, were endorsed by Coke. The latter bill was introduced by Senator Douglas and provided for fifty-year renewable charters. A separate measure also introduced by Senator Douglas provided sixteen sections of land per mile for railroad companies that completed at least ten miles of track with a gauge of no less than three feet. This measure repudiated the precedent set by the Thirteenth Legislature, which had given twenty sections per mile to the Texas and Pacific Railroad.

In other measures concerning internal improvements, the act for the construction of public roads passed by the Fourteenth Legislature was amended. Road construction became the responsibility of county commissioners courts. First-class roads would be no less than forty feet wide. Stumps less than six inches in diameter would be cut level with the surface of the ground, but those which were larger would only be cut to within six inches of the surface, then "rounded off." In no instance could a first-class road exceed sixty feet in width. Second-class roads could be no less than thirty feet wide and third-class roads no less than twenty feet wide, with the same rules for clearing obstructions. The commissioners would divide their counties into road precincts, each under an overseer responsible for maintenance and construction. The commissioners were empowered to purchase lands for rights-of-way and, in the event an owner refused to sell, could appoint a five-man commission to arbitrate the dispute. All males between eighteen and forty-five years of age, except ministers and invalids, were required to "work on, repair and clean out" public roads, for which they were subject to the call of the overseer for no more than ten days a year. If drafted, one could send a substitute or pay a dollar a day instead of working. The labor of those hands who showed up could be bartered with nearby property owners for the use of plows, wagons, and teams if necessary. The overseers were also responsible for erecting and repairing mileposts along the roads, marking the distance from "the court-house or some other noted place or town." The schedules for the classification of canals and the compensation of contractors with land grants were continued.

Agriculture remained a vital concern of Texas legislators. Under an act approved August 15, upon a petition by fifty freeholders in a county, or twenty in a justice precinct or town, the voters would be authorized to decide whether certain types of livestock would be permitted to run loose in the county. This measure was intended only for sheep, goats, and swine; no law was passed restricting free grazing by cattle, horses, mules, jacks, or jennets. If a property owner maimed or killed cattle, horses, mules, or jennets which came onto his property, he would be held liable because his fence was obviously insufficient, but he could bring suit for the damages caused by loose hogs, goats, and sheep and even impound the animals until the owner was located and paid the damages. An additional act for the benefit of stockraisers expanded the powers of the inspector of hides and animals to ensure that all cattle were properly branded before sale or export.

The Department of Insurance, Statistics, and History was created through an act introduced by Senator Ford and signed on the last day of the session, August 21. The department was headed by a commissioner, who was principally responsible for the regulation of insurance companies but was also required to gather statistical information on the state and publish it annually; to serve as a liaison between the farmers in the state and the U.S. Department of Agriculture; to gather and record "any reliable information, in the form of narrative or otherwise, respecting the incidents of the early history and settlement of the different portions of the State of Texas, for the future use of the historian"; and to collect and preserve official records, publications, and even "historical relics, mementos, antiquities and works of art connected with and relating to the history of Texas." For this last task, the commissioner was expected to conduct an active correspondence with historical societies within and beyond the state, to obtain from Mexico the original archives or copies of documents relating to Texas colonial history, and to operate the State Library.

The historical responsibilities of the new department expanded when a pension plan for the surviving veterans of the Texas Revolution and their widows was endorsed by Governor Coke. In addition, a new act for the organization of medical boards—one that increased the department's record-keeping workload—replaced the act rendered inoperable by the 1876 constitution; the new law passed the Senate with the support of Blassingame, Ford, Francis, and Motley, four of the five physicians in that body. Two acts for the regulation of the legal profession sponsored by John R. Henry and McLeary failed to become law; and the act for the registration of births that had been enacted in 1873 by the Thirteenth Legislature was repealed, but the statistical burden began to crowd out the activities of the division created to address the liaison responsibilities until the latter was made an independent division.

The Fifteenth Legislature ended on a harmonious note in spite of feuding over the U.S. senatorial election. Governor Coke, the choice of the Texas Senate, was elected U.S. senator on May 5 to replace the retiring Morgan Hamilton. It was a hotly contested race; some of the senators had supported former state senator John Ireland for the position and were not willing to accept Coke. Senator Storey offered a joint resolution on May 10 which would have prevented future Texas governors from holding any other office, practicing another profession, or being elected by the legislature to a different position. Storey's bill went to the Senate Committee on Constitutional Amendments, where it died without reaching the floor again. Coke resigned as governor on December 1, 1876, at which time Hubbard, who had retired from his duties as president of the Senate on August 9, 1876, succeeded him. Wells Thompson, as president pro tempore of the Senate, had presided over the Senate since Hubbard's renunciation of his duties and now became lieutenant governor ex officio. The Democratic senators, having wrested control of the state from the Radical Republicans, were loathe to let personal squabbles endanger their hegemony. However, the conservatives would soon face their greatest challenge from within their own party as agrarian and other populist factions struggled to be heard.

CONSOLIDATING DEMOCRATIC CONTROL

CHAPTER 9

The Senate of the Sixteenth Legislature, 1879

During the Sixteenth Legislature the Democrats, in the wake of the Republican collapse, united to consolidate their dominance in state politics, facing only a weak challenge from the Greenback party. The legislature met for a regular session from January 14 to April 24, 1879, and for a called session from June 10 to July 9, 1879. Strong leadership was provided by Governor Oran M. Roberts, who was inaugurated on January 21, 1879, and by the lieutenant governor, former state senator Joseph D. Sayers, who had served during the revolt against Radical Republican rule in the Thirteenth Legislature. Roberts and Sayers were Confederate veterans and were conservative in political philosophy, and together they would rally the Senate of the Sixteenth Legislature to reduce state expenditures and services through legislation devoted to retrenchment and reform.

Roberts had been an associate justice of the Texas Supreme Court until the Civil War, when he was unanimously elected president of the Secession Convention that met in January, 1861. During the war he served as a colonel in the 11th Texas Infantry until his appointment in 1864 as chief justice of the Texas Supreme Court. He was removed from the bench at the end of the war but attended the Constitutional Convention of 1866. Although the legislature elected him to the U.S. Senate later that year, his Confederate service prevented his being seated. In 1874 Roberts again became chief justice of the Texas Supreme Court, where he remained until his election as governor. Although he was a compromise candidate for the Democratic party and won by only a slim majority, Roberts interpreted his victory as a mandate for conservatism.

As governor, Roberts initiated measures for fiscal conservation that further dismantled the social programs begun by the Radical Republicans during Reconstruction. These actions came initially as a response to both the lingering depression and pressure from the Greenback party in Texas. The Greenback party, which sprang from the Grange movement, had by 1878 become the second-largest political party in the state. Roberts's policy of "pay as you go" embraced Greenbacker goals such as refunding the state debt at a lower interest rate and reducing government expenditures. Roberts repudiated other Greenbacker tenets, however, by reducing funds for education and slashing pensions for veterans of the Texas Revolution. He liberally granted pardons to relieve the crowded penitentiary system, thus contributing to a rising crime rate, but he did not end the convict lease program, another Greenbacker objective, preferring instead to make the prisons self-supporting. Unlike his predecessors, Governor Roberts kept in constant communication with the legislature through executive messages, and the members of the Senate proved to be allies in the retrenchment of state government.

Wells Thompson sat as president pro tempore when the Senate assembled on January 14, 1879. Sixteen members returned from the Fifteenth Legislature: William Blassingame, William M. Brown, Walter M. Burton, Peyton F. Edwards, John S. Ford, Charles D. Grace, Robert S. Guy, Edwin E. Hobby, William H. Ledbetter, Andrew P. McCormick, Thomas J. McCulloch, John W. Moore, John W. Motley, Walter Ripetoe, Leonidas J. Storey, and Alexander W. Terrell. James R. Burnett and Ellsberry Lane had been elected to fill vacancies during the Fifteenth Legislature but were not sworn until the Sixteenth.

Four of the recently elected members had served in the Texas Senate in earlier legislative sessions: Francis Marion Martin during the Eighth; William D. Lair during the Ninth; William R. Shannon during the Eleventh; and Jewett H. Davenport during the Fourteenth.

Francis Marion Martin of Corsicana would go on to become lieutenant governor. Martin's political career began when he was elected to the Senate of the Eighth Legislature as a supporter of Sam Houston. During that term, he canvassed his district for support against the Secession Convention. Despite his opposition to the dissolution of the Union, when the war broke out he enlisted in Bass's Regiment and was commissioned a captain. He was unable to serve because of ill health and was discharged early on, spending the war years at home in Corsicana. Martin had come to Texas in 1853 from Livingston County, Tennessee, where he was born on April 1, 1830. He was orphaned young and made his way on his own, holding various jobs. He served for a time as a slow-boy-boat hand on the Ohio and Mississippi rivers and later worked as a clerk in a store. When he arrived in Texas he bought a small farm, then added to his original holdings until his spread had reached fifteen hundred acres and he had become a farmer of some note. Prior to his return to legislative service during the Sixteenth Legislature, Martin had been a member of the Constitutional Convention of 1875. Following a third session as a senator in the Seventeenth Legislature, Martin was elected lieutenant governor in 1882. He held no further public positions after his service as lieutenant governor but did run for governor as a Populist party candidate in 1888.

William D. Lair of Melissa in Collin County had served in the Ninth Legislature during the special session in 1863, succeeding J. J. Dickson. After his election as a Democrat in 1878, he served a full term during the Sixteenth and Seventeenth legislatures. A native of Kentucky, Lair had served in his home state's legislature before immigrating to Texas. He was a physician as well as a prosperous farmer.

William Russell Shannon was an attorney from Weatherford. Shannon was a Democrat whose previous legislative experience included service in the House of Representatives in the Seventh, Eighth, and Tenth legislatures, in addition to his service in the Senate during the Eleventh. Shannon served in the Senate for three more legislatures following the Sixteenth and was president pro tempore of the Senate during the regular session of the Nineteenth Legislature.

Jewett Harbert Davenport of Eastland, an attorney, returned to the Senate after an absence lasting one legislature. Davenport was a native of Georgia. He had represented Bell, Falls, and Milam counties during the Fourteenth Legislature but represented Eastland and the surrounding counties in the Sixteenth and Seventeenth.

Two of the new senators, Swain and Tilson, had previous state legislative experience in the House of Representatives. William Jesse Swain, a lawyer and newspaper editor from Clarksville, was born in Estill County, Kentucky, on February 19, 1839; he had come to Texas from Mississippi in 1859, settling in Clarksville. Swain attended McKenzie College. In 1862 he entered the Confederate Army as a private in Whitfield's Cavalry Legion and by the end of the war had risen to the rank of captain. After the war he returned to Clarksville, where he practiced law and was editor of the *Clarksville Times*. Swain served as justice of the peace and as county tax collector for Red River County. He was a member of the House of Representatives during the Fourteenth Legislature and was elected to the Senate of the Sixteenth as a Democrat. Swain completed his term in the Senate during the Seventeenth Legislature and was elected state comptroller in 1882. He served in that post for two terms before making an unsuccessful bid for the governorship in 1886.

William H. Tilson of Texarkana had served in the House of Representatives during the Thirteenth Legislature. Like Swain, Tilson was a lawyer and a Confederate veteran. Born in Washington County, Virginia, on March 26, 1837, he moved to DeKalb, Bowie County, Texas, in 1859. Having enlisted in Crump's Battalion in 1862, he participated in the Battle of Corinth and served until he was disabled. Tilson was a teacher and read the law while he was teaching school. He was admitted to the bar in 1866 and began his practice in Boston in Bowie County, and he had served as the county attorney for Bowie County before his election to the House in 1873. He was elected to the Senate in 1878 and went on to serve a second term.

Burnett and Lane were the two senators who had occupied vacant seats during the Fifteenth Legislature but did not take the oath until the Sixteenth. James Russell Burnett of Anderson replaced Tillman Smith as senator of the Sixteenth District after Smith resigned November 19, 1876. Burnett was born on June 20, 1843, in Summerville, Georgia. He was in Arkansas when the Civil War broke out and promptly joined the LaFayette Guards, the first company organized in the local county. He was elected captain of the company on the death of his commanding officer at Shiloh but resigned because of disability later in 1862. He returned to the army as adjutant of the 13th Texas Cavalry, which had been organized by his

Texan brother, Colonel John H. Burnett. After disability again compelled him to resign, he married and moved to Crockett, Texas, in 1864. In Crockett he established the *Crockett Quid Nunc* and published it until after the war. At the same time he was publishing the *Quid Nunc*, he was reading law in Judge William M. Taylor's office. He was admitted to the bar in 1865 and became licensed to practice in the Texas Supreme Court and the federal courts in Tyler in 1866. He was elected and served as a Republican delegate to the Constitutional Convention of 1868–69 and served in the House during the provisional session of the Twelfth Legislature. In 1870 he moved to Huntsville and in August of that year he was appointed judge of the Thirtieth Judicial District by Governor Davis, serving as district judge until the adoption of the Constitution of 1876. In the 1878 elections Burnett ran as an independent and, benefiting from the endorsement of the Republican county convention of the district and the support of the Greenbackers of Waller County, defeated the Democratic candidate, William A. Leigh of Huntsville, to capture the Senate seat for the Sixteenth District. Burnett left the Senate after his service in the Sixteenth Legislature but returned to public office in 1894, when he was elected district judge of Anderson, Houston, and Henderson counties. He later organized the First State Bank at Kerrville. Burnett died in 1907.

Ellsberry R. Lane of Goliad had filled the Twenty-eighth District seat vacated by William H. Crain on August 20, 1877. Lane was born in Indiana in 1839. He came to Texas with his father in 1852 and settled in Goliad. He graduated from Bastrop Military Institute in 1860, just in time to join up and fight in the Confederate Army throughout the war. Like Crain, his predecessor in office, Lane had served as district attorney for the Twenty-third Judicial District before he was elected to the Senate on November 5, 1878, as an unopposed Democratic nominee. He would serve in the Senate of the Seventeenth Legislature until his resignation on February 1, 1882.

There were seven new members with no previous legislative experience: John C. Buchanan, John M. Duncan, John Y. Gooch, William K. Homan, Augustus W. Houston, Samuel C. Patton, and Charles Stewart. All of these new senators were attorneys, and although none of them had served the public at the state level, all except Gooch and Houston had served as city, county, or district attorneys.

William Kercheval Homan of Caldwell had served as the district and county attorney in Burleson County prior to his election to the Senate in 1878, and he had also served as district and county clerk and as special judge in the district court. Homan was born in Fayetteville, Tennessee, on August 14, 1847. He moved to Texas in 1860, locating in Austin. After reading law in Austin with the firm of Chandler and Turner, he was admitted to the bar in 1869. Homan worked as a journalist in Cameron for three years and then, in October, 1873, moved to Caldwell to practice law. He was elected to the Senate as an independent Greenbacker to represent Burleson, Austin, and Washington counties. Following his service in the Senate during the Sixteenth and Seventeenth legislatures, he served as a U.S. attorney for the Eastern District of Texas and later as editor of the *Christian Courier* in Dallas. Homan fathered twelve children. He died in 1908 at the age of sixty.

Samuel Collier Patton of Hallettsville had been the district attorney for the Twelfth Judicial District before his election to the Senate. Patton was born in Troup County, Georgia, on October 4, 1842. As a child he moved with his family to Mississippi and then on to Texas in 1850. He enlisted in the Confederate Army in 1861 and served with Terry's Rangers, and he was captured near Knoxville, Tennessee, in September, 1864. Following the Civil War, Patton attended the University of Mississippi. He graduated in 1868 and that same year began to practice law in Hallettsville. Elected to the Senate in November, 1878, on the Democratic ticket to represent Lavaca, Colorado, and Gonzales counties, he would continue his service in the Senate through the Eighteenth Legislature.

Prior to his election to the Senate, John Creighton Buchanan of Anderson had served as county attorney for Wood County. Buchanan was born in Greenwood, Louisiana, on February 24, 1850; the family moved to East Texas that same year and settled in Rusk County. Buchanan was educated in Gilmer in Upshur County and later taught school in Louisiana while studying law; he was admitted to the bar in 1873 and established a legal practice in Quitman in Wood County. Elected county attorney in 1876, he won his senatorial seat in 1878 as a Democrat representing Grimes, Madison, Trinity, and Walker counties. He would be reelected in 1882. Senator Buchanan died in 1885 at the age of thirty-five. His wife, Rosalie Patten Buchanan, was a teacher who would later be appointed by

Governor James S. Hogg to teach English at Sam Houston Normal College. Mrs. Buchanan went on to become the first woman in Texas to be named a full professor at a state college. Buchanan Hall on the campus of Sam Houston State University was built and named in her honor.

John Martin Duncan of Longview was an attorney who had been elected county attorney for Gregg County in 1876. Duncan was born near Lawrenceburg in Lawrence County, Tennessee, on February 7, 1856. His family located near Jefferson after immigrating to Texas. Although too young to serve in the military during the Civil War, Duncan did serve the government of the Confederacy at the Nash Iron Works in Marion County. He studied law at Jefferson in the office of John C. Stallcup and was admitted to the bar in 1872. He was elected senator from Gregg, Smith, Camp, and Upshur counties as an independent Democrat over the Democratic nominee. After his service in the Senate during the Sixteenth and Seventeenth legislatures, Duncan practiced law in partnership with future governor James S. Hogg in Tyler. He was elected county judge for Smith County in 1884. In 1907 he returned to legislative service when he was elected to the House of Representatives of the Thirtieth Legislature, and he served until his resignation on December 12 of that year.

Joining the group of new senators with public service at the local level was Charles Stewart of Houston, who had been the city attorney in Houston. A freshman senator in 1879, Stewart would be a U.S. congressman by 1883. Stewart was born in Memphis, Tennessee, on May 30, 1836. He moved with his parents to Texas in 1845 and settled in Galveston. He attended the common schools there and later studied law in law offices in Houston and Galveston. Admitted to the bar in 1854, before he had reached the age of eighteen, he practiced law in Marlin in Falls County and was elected district attorney for the Thirteenth Judicial District, serving in that position from 1856 to 1860. He married Rachel Barry of Marlin during his last year as district attorney. Stewart was a delegate to the Secession Convention in 1861. During the war he served in the Confederate Army in Nelson's Regiment of Texas Infantry and in Baylor's Regiment of Cavalry. Following the war, he moved to Houston and resumed his legal career. In 1872 Stewart was elected to the Senate but was counted out or ruled out by a contest with his opponent in the Thirteenth Legislature. He served as the Houston city attorney from 1874 to 1876—a position his son would hold some twenty years later—and in 1878 was elected to the Texas Senate as a Democrat. Subsequent to his service in the Senate during the Sixteenth and Seventeenth legislatures, Stewart was elected to the U.S. Congress, where he served as a member of the House of Representatives from March 4, 1883, to March 3, 1893. While in Congress he pushed for the development of commercial relations between the United States and her neighbors in Central and South America. Stewart was a Mason and served as Grand Master of Texas in 1883. He died on September 21, 1895.

Although their first political office was during the Sixteenth Legislature, freshman senators John Y. Gooch and Augustus W. Houston were both from families with records of public service. John Young Gooch of Palestine was an attorney who was born in Kentucky on November 30, 1848. His father had served in the Kentucky Legislature before moving the family to Texas in 1853, where he established a law practice. The younger Gooch began reading law in 1866; he was admitted to the bar and established a practice in Athens in Henderson County in 1869. Gooch was elected senator in 1878 from Anderson, Cherokee, and Henderson counties as a Democrat. He served as chairman of the Committee on Public Debt during the Sixteenth Legislature and as president pro tempore and chairman of Judiciary Committee Number 2 during the Seventeenth. Gooch returned to the Senate for the Eighteenth Legislature. At one time he was a law partner of John H. Reagan in the firm of Reagan, Greenwood & Gooch. He also served as a district court judge in Palestine.

Augustus Weyman Houston of San Antonio also followed a family tradition of legislative service. Born in Lauderdale County, Alabama, on August 3, 1850, he was the nephew of a former U.S. senator from Alabama, George S. Houston. Augustus's family immigrated to Texas in 1851 and settled in Bexar County, where his father became a planter. A distinguished student at a young age, Houston attended Washington and Lee University in Virginia, where he was intimately acquainted with Robert E. Lee, the university's president at that time. In 1871 Houston was valedictorian of his law school class at Cumberland University in Lebanon, Tennessee. After graduation he returned to Texas and began the practice of law in San Antonio with a firm he organized with his brother.

Houston's campaign as the Democratic candidate for the Thirtieth District Senate seat in 1878 was his first political race, and he was elected by an overwhelming majority from a district that stretched from Comal County in the east to El Paso County in the west. He introduced legislation that allowed the purchase of the Alamo by the state, and he was also instrumental in the passage of an early equal rights bill that allowed women to work in state government offices. Houston met and married Mrs. Sallie Moore Winstead of Austin during his time as a senator. Houston was a member of the Senate through the Nineteenth Legislature and served as president pro tempore during the regular session of the Eighteenth. Following his public service he went on to become a prominent member of the San Antonio bar, serving as general counsel for the San Antonio and Aransas Pass Railroad and playing a part in establishing the street railway system for the City of San Antonio. Senator Houston was a 32nd degree Mason and Knight Templar and in 1913–14 was Grand Master of Texas.

The election of officers was quickly carried out after seating the senators: W. Leigh Chalmers was elected secretary; William A. Fields, first assistant secretary; William N. Ramey, second assistant secretary; Asa M. Belvin, engrossing clerk; Thomas P. Martin, enrolling clerk; John W. Swindells, calendar clerk; William Fitzhugh, doorkeeper; James M. Barton, sergeant-at-arms; Walter P. Fisher, assistant sergeant-at-arms; and the Reverend C. C. Chaplin, chaplain. Hobby was elected president pro tempore on January 24, 1879. Enrolling Clerk Thomas P. Martin resigned in February, 1879, and was replaced by H. C. Surghnor; Secretary of the Senate W. Leigh Chalmers resigned in April, 1879, and J. P. C. Whitehead, serving as reading secretary at the time, was elected in his place. During the called session, Second Assistant Secretary William N. Ramey also served as the journal clerk.

The customary address of the outgoing governor was read to the Senate on January 16, 1879. Hubbard's financial forecast was gloomy: the public debt of Texas, although it had decreased since the adjournment of the last legislature, at $5.1 million still exceeded the funds available in the state treasury, which held less than $3.4

Austin street scene looking east from Colorado Street on 6th Street, circa 1879. Courtesy Austin History Center, Austin Public Library, # PICA 01977.

million. Hubbard estimated that state expenditures for the coming year would exceed revenues by more than $100,000. He recommended, in addition to some measures for economy, refunding that portion of the debt—about $1.1 million—that would come due in July, 1879, through the issuance of new bonds bearing a lesser rate of interest. To pay for these new bonds, revenues would have to increase soon. Hubbard pointed out that the taxable value of property in Texas had shrunk by $15 million between 1877 and 1878. Some of this decline could be attributed to a depreciation in property values of all kinds due to an agricultural depression and a slump in industrial production; but the amount of new land and commercial products being developed each year by immigrants, Hubbard declared, should have offset some of the loss. He proposed a uniform and thorough system of property assessment and tax collection as a long-term remedy for the state's financial ills.

Governor Roberts endorsed Hubbard's call for tax reform and added a demand for more occupation taxes as a means of taxing a transient type of capital that did not produce enough ad valorem tax revenue to support the state. By shipping cotton, wool, wheat, beef, cattle, and other commodities from Texas before the first day of each year, retail and wholesale grocers and commodities brokers avoided payment of state taxes. New taxes on professions and common carriers would reach that itinerant population, whose occupations were fairly lucrative. But the Senate's discussion of occupation taxes spawned public opposition, especially from the Greenbacker faction. Citizens in Kaufman County, for example, sent a petition characterizing the taxation of occupations as "class legislation, a reproach to the State, a blot upon the statute books and a disgrace to civilization." Despite Senator Tilson's introduction of a joint resolution to repeal occupation taxes in favor of a system of license fees, the Senate endorsed a new schedule that was signed by Governor Roberts on April 22, 1879. Roberts's basic position regarding taxes was that tax increases should be accompanied by a retrenchment in state expenditures, in the hope that future generations would be free from the "onerous burden of taxation."

One exception to Governor Roberts's plan for a permanent reduction in taxes was his support of a higher tax on liquor in order to reduce its consumption. Through a measure introduced in the House, a unique occupation tax, commonly known as the "bell-punch law," was levied on retailers of "spirituous, vinous, and malt liquors in quantities less than a quart." Retailers had to pay a tax of $250 per annum, or $25 for the sale of malt liquors only, plus two cents per drink, or one-half cent on malt liquors. The state would provide special cash registers, called bell-punch registers, at a cost of $10 each for retailers to use only for the sale of alcoholic beverages. Separate registers were to be kept for the sale of malt liquors and vinous or spirituous liquors, and they were to be clearly marked as such. A bell and a crank on the side of each register recorded the sales for which tax was to be paid, and the number of turns of the crank indicated the size of the drink. Anyone who either sold or purchased liquor that was not so registered could be fined up to $250. These provisions did not apply to druggists or retailers of patent medicines, who were covered under less restrictive portions of the new occupation tax schedule.

A measure introduced by Senator Shannon and signed by Governor Roberts on March 8, 1879, provided for a standardized system of assessing state property taxes. In addition, the county commissioners courts were empowered to sit as a "board of equalization" during June of each year to review the records of the county tax assessor. The commissioners courts had the authority to raise or lower assessments and to hear appeals. An act passed during the special session allowed tax assessors to seize, levy on, and sell all personal or real property subject to taxation if taxes were not paid.

These measures did not solve the problem of delinquent taxes. Due to the depression, many people in Texas were already in arrears, leaving the state and county governments unable to meet their obligations. On April 21, 1879, Governor Roberts signed a bill introduced by Senator Edwards that authorized the state to issue almost $3.6 million in bonds to retire its outstanding debt. The bonds were to be issued in three denominations or classes: the first and second, with face values of $1,000 and $100, were redeemable in gold in thirty years beginning July 1, 1909, and yielded 5 percent per annum, while the third, with a face value of either $5 or $10, could be redeemed in twenty years and returned 4 percent per annum. As they matured, the coupons on the third class of bonds would be receivable as payment on state taxes. An act introduced by Senator Duncan permitted commissioners courts to levy a tax of 50 cents per $100 in real and personal property for building courthouses and jails. In a separate bill, counties and municipalities were authorized to fund their existing debt with another bond issue.

The Senate of the Sixteenth Legislature did not restrict itself to legislation concerning the financial woes of the state. Several measures were passed that provided private-sector relief by allowing the reclaiming of lands confiscated for state debt or by granting extensions of deadlines for paying taxes and land fees. The Senate gave even greater help to Lamar County, where a "hail storm of such destructive severity as has not been known to have occurred within the recollection of the oldest inhabitant of this state" had devastated a portion of the area on May 21, 1878. Many crops and fences, much livestock, and even homes were lost. A long list of Lamar County homesteaders was exempted from state taxes for the year in an act that had originated in the House and was signed on March 8, 1879, over the opposition of the Senate Committee on Finance, chaired by Senator Storey. Storey declared the bill to be primarily local in nature and uneconomical and argued that other counties had suffered similar calamities without receiving the same relief.

A few tax-relief measures more enduring in nature also passed the Sixteenth Legislature. A constitutional amendment was submitted to the voters of Texas through a House resolution to exempt "farm products in the hands of the producer" as well as "family supplies for home and farm use" from future taxation except by a two-thirds vote of the legislature. This amendment, which was adopted in a special election on September 2, 1879, and became Section 19, Article VIII, was the first amendment to the 1876 constitution—a distinction that some have called a "dubious honor."

The tax on the "privilege" of keeping dogs was repealed by a House bill adopted on February 10, 1879. Senator Homan had introduced a similar bill in the Senate. It had been reported unfavorably from Judiciary Committee Number 2 by Senator Stewart, but Homan, Gooch, and Ledbetter had delivered a dissenting minority report which argued tellingly that the law produced little revenue, with almost all of that coming from the poorer classes. When the House version was considered later by the same committee, the chair reported it favorably. At least on the issues of the farm produce exemption and the dog tax repeal, the Greenbackers had won clear-cut victories.

Financial retrenchment did not include the state judicial system. The courts, overburdened and understaffed, had drawn harsh public censure for their high expenditures and the large number of cases that were remanded or reversed because of hasty or poor decisions. In the face of a rising crime rate, a few newspapers in Texas were even demanding a return to the gallows and the whipping post. Hubbard, in his message to the Senate on January 16, 1879, had called for a reorganization of the state courts to increase efficiency, and his demand was echoed by Roberts in his inaugural address. Once established in office, Roberts sent a special message to the legislature on January 28, 1879, outlining a plan of action. He asked for a constitutional amendment increasing the number of state Supreme Court justices to nine and dividing them into three tribunals, two charged with civil matters and the other with criminal affairs. He advocated this expansion because the Court of Appeals, created to review decisions in criminal cases, had not decreased the burden on the state Supreme Court. At the end of the previous judicial term, both courts were inundated with cases, with over nine hundred cases left pending in the Supreme Court and over two hundred in the Court of Appeals. Roberts pointed out that his proposal would be less expensive than the one before the legislature, which called for two courts and a commission for appeals.

Despite opposition from Roberts and Hubbard, on July 9, 1879, the last day of the called session, a measure introduced by Senator Street became law creating the Commission of Arbitration and Award. The commission, to be appointed by the governor, was to review decisions on civil matters handed down by the Supreme Court and the Court of Appeals. After the submission of written appeals by each of the parties involved in a case, the commission would review the evidence, and its decision would stand in place of the court's. The commission was governed by the same rules as the Supreme Court, but its decisions were not published in the ordinary digests and did not have the weight of precedent. This plan was continued until 1891. It is unclear why Roberts endorsed this system, but after the members of the legislature rejected his request for the creation of a judicial department, he probably realized that the commission was the only viable solution to the overextended judiciary.

The rising crime rate in Texas also required an expanded state prison system. A new East Texas penitentiary at Rusk was directed to be put in order for receiving convicts; it opened in 1883. The legislature paid lip service to the accepted principle that convicts should be employed within prison walls but continued the lease system as a financial necessity. Convict labor from the lessees of the state penitentiary at Huntsville were even contracted to work on the structure at Rusk. A lengthy act introduced by Senator Hobby and signed on March 24, 1879, provided for the administration of the expanding state penitentiary system through a director, who would serve as an administrative officer, at each site. The directors were to meet at least three times each month and report once a month to the governor on the condition of the prisons. A superintendent, who acted as an executive officer, and an assistant superintendent were appointed for each prison as well, along with a physician and a chaplain. The law also included provisions for the treatment of convicts that prohibited whipping, starvation, isolation, and other harsh practices that had been common in the past.

Most of the business of the Sixteenth Legislature during the regular and called sessions concerned the establishment of new judicial districts and provision for their sessions. An act introduced by Senator Gooch provided for replacement justices without a change of venue in the event a judge was absent or disqualified, a situation that was particularly common on the frontier.

Several senators resigned to accept appointments as judges. Andrew P. McCormick was appointed a U.S. district judge for the Northern District of Texas in April, 1879; Peyton Edwards became the judge of the Third Judicial District; and Edwin E. Hobby resigned as president pro tempore in April in anticipation of becoming judge of the Ninth Judicial District. Storey was unanimously elected to replace Hobby as president pro tempore on April 19, 1879. Both Edwards and Hobby served through the special session.

McCormick's successor in the Nineteenth Senatorial District seat was Robert G. Street, an attorney, who was sworn on the first day of the special session. Born in Greensboro, Alabama, on December 12, 1843, Street was a junior at the University of Alabama when the Civil War began and he enlisted in the Confederate Army. He served in the 20th Alabama Infantry and the 51st Alabama Cavalry and rose to the rank of sergeant major before being captured in June, 1863, at Shelbyville, Tennessee. Street was imprisoned for nearly two years before being released in March, 1865. Following the war, he studied law in Alabama under the tutelage of John T. Morgan, who would later serve as a U.S. senator from Alabama. Street was admitted to the Alabama bar in 1866. In 1867 he moved to Galveston, where he became a prominent member of the legal community. He served only one term in the Senate but later was elected judge of the Fifty-sixth Judicial District.

Extensive revisions of the civil statutes, the Penal Code, and the Code of Criminal Procedure were adopted during the Sixteenth Legislature. These revisions had been authorized by the Fifteenth Legislature, and Governor Coke had appointed a law revision committee. On January 1, 1879, the law revision committee made its report and submitted two bills for introduction. Senator Ledbetter introduced the bill revising the civil statutes, and Senator Hobby introduced the bill revising the Penal Code and the Code of Criminal Procedure. A third bill provided for the production and printing of a volume to be titled *The Revised Statutes of the State of Texas*, which was to contain the Revised Civil Statutes, the Penal Code, and the Code of Criminal Procedure. This bill provided for the appointment of a codifier, who was to include in the volume all amendments to the laws contained in Ledbetter's and Hobby's bills enacted during the Sixteenth Legislature. Governor Roberts appointed John N. Lyle as the codifier. Lyle's work was completed and the first *Revised Statutes of the State of Texas* was available by September, 1879.

Whether the appropriations for frontier defense would be continued was an issue from the beginning of the session. Even the election of Senate officers seemed to some observers to reflect sentiment on this issue, as James M. Baron of Rusk County was elected sergeant-at-arms over frontier battalion leader Lee Hall of Grayson County. However, as the *Galveston News* reported in its summary of the first day of the session, "The impression upon some is that the defeat of Capt. Hall for sergeant-at-arms of the senate portends hostility to frontier protection, but Hall says it was owing to the active and energetic work of his competitor, who is also well-fitted for the position." On January 28, Senator Grace of Fannin County introduced a resolution that asked the Committee on Indian Affairs and Frontier Protection to consider the advisability of abolishing the frontier battalion. The same committee had referred to it numerous petitions received from citizens and officers of western and southwestern counties requesting the continuance of frontier protection. The petition from Mason County was summarized in the *Senate Journal* as "giving many reasons for the continuance of frontier protection against both the Indians and desperadoes which abound throughout said border, and among them they state that . . . without such protection the frontier will be driven back at least eighty miles and that many counties will be abandoned." Senators opposing the frontier defense funding cited cases where settlement occurred beyond the areas where protection was available. Senators in favor of the funding maintained that the amount spent on the Rangers and the frontier battalion was a small investment considering the increased tax revenues from newly developed communities.

Senator Davenport, in a speech supporting the continued funding of defense of the frontier, rebuked his colleagues for failing to support the appropriation for frontier defense, which was forty thousand dollars less than had ever been requested, and reminded them that continued protection of the frontier had been a plank in the political platforms of all three parties. Davenport, Houston, and Shannon, along with famed former Ranger captain Ford, were the strongest supporters of continuing the appropriation and felt that frontier defense should not fall victim to the policies of retrenchment and reform. Senator Swain spoke against the appropriation, observing that lawlessness existed in all parts of the state. Governor Roberts generally supported efforts to provide public law enforcement in Texas, especially on the open frontier, but he opposed a permanent police force under the control of the central state government. Before Roberts came to office, the Rangers, out of financial necessity, had been reduced from fifty to twenty-five men, and Hubbard had recommended that they be continued at that strength. Roberts preferred abolishing counties on the frontier that could not defend themselves and annexing them to stronger counties with well-established constabularies, but his ideas found little support in the legislature. The governor ended up signing the bill introduced by Senator Lane to continue the Rangers as an auxiliary police force made necessary by persisting lawlessness in some parts of the state.

At one time during the session it was thought that the controversy over the continued funding of frontier defense might derail the whole appropriations bill. In the end, the appropriation for this purpose was not eliminated but was reduced, under a compromise amendment offered by Senator Burnett, from $150,000 to $100,000, which was to cover the support of the frontier battalions as well as the auxiliary police force.

The maintenance of some level of frontier defense was a victory for representatives of western and southwestern counties, but time and continued settlement would ultimately resolve the matter. The frontier was changing, as the following newspaper description of the situation, published while the Sixteenth Legislature met, indicates:

> Two counties in the Panhandle and several beyond the present line of organized counties are preparing to vote upon organization within the next six weeks. The frontier lines have advanced a hundred miles in two years, and an area of 40,000,000 acres of good lands opened to settlement, reclaimed from savage rule, the cayotes [*sic*], buffalo and Comanches giving place to the farmer and stockraiser. Counties are being organized now in a section which two years ago was 300 miles from any Texas court. It will take little time for the counties to fill up and be able to protect themselves.

Unrest along the border and frontier defense were the subjects of several joint resolutions addressed to the U.S. Congress during the regular session. The first, introduced by Senator Houston and passed on February 14, 1879, proposed that the Texas delegation to Congress press for appropriations for internal improvements that would encourage commerce with Mexico and make "friends of enemies." The second, introduced in the House, asked the federal government to repay all of Texas' expenses for frontier defense between 1855 and 1878, almost $1.8 million, as well as the unexpended balance of the funds entrusted to the U.S. government to settle the debts of the Republic of Texas, about $101,113. Another resolution from the House asked that the Indians raiding into Texas from the Fort Stanton and Fort Sill reserves in the Indian Territory be rounded up and that further incursions be prevented. Finally, a joint resolution introduced by Senator Stewart requested that four batteries of artillery be handed over to the adjutant general of Texas by the federal government for disposition as he saw fit. However, Texas received neither federal money nor federal cannon to defend her frontier.

Perhaps the most heated issue debated by the Senate during the Sixteenth Legislature was the disposition of the public domain in Texas. Governor Roberts advocated an expansion of the land sale program, especially for the railroad companies, as they were "the best immigration agents we ever had." He insisted that selling the public lands to private developers would not slow or halt immigration and would bring revenue into the state coffers immediately. In his inaugural address Lieutenant Governor Sayers seconded this initiative for expediting land sales. The inclusion of public school lands in this sale, however, coupled with memories of a tremendous land fraud just a few years before, generated popular opposition. On January 16—before Roberts and Sayers had taken office—the *Austin Democratic Statesman* labeled land sales a "robbery of posterity."

The Greenbackers led the protest against the disposal of the public domain, and putting an end to land grants to railroads had been a basic plank of their platform. Senator Homan introduced a measure to repeal the law which gave railroad companies sixteen sections of land for each mile of track constructed and put into operation. Homan's bill failed to become law, however, after Senator Shannon, as chairman of the Committee on Internal Improvements, recommended against passage. Homan responded by filing a dissenting report, reiterating his position that lands of the state should go to homesteaders and to the school fund, not to private developers, but he argued in vain. In 1876 Texas' public domain totaled over 61.2 million acres; by 1882 the land committed to railroads exceeded the amount available for that purpose by nearly 8 million acres.

The Senate rejected the Greenbacker-led protest against selling the public domain and endorsed the "fifty-cent law," which permitted the sale of 41,000,000 acres of land. The purpose of the fifty-cent law was twofold: to further endow the public school fund and to provide a means of paying the public debt. Under this law all the state's nondedicated public land, mostly located in West Texas counties, was reserved and placed on sale at fifty cents per acre. Half of the proceeds was to go into the public school fund; the other half was earmarked to pay the state's bonded debt. The law proved to be effective in providing some relief for the revenue-starved state treasury. Except for a time during 1883 when the law was suspended due to pressures from land speculation, land sales under the act approved July 14, 1879, continued until 1898, when the nondedicated public domain was exhausted. In all, 3,201,283.1 acres of land were sold under the act, bringing in $1,600,641.55 of revenue.

A seemingly similar bill introduced by Senator Terrell and passed during the regular session called for augmenting the public school fund by appropriating all the public domain in Greer County for sale at fifty cents per acre, with half to be reserved for the support of the "public free schools for the education of children in Texas, without reference to race or color," and the remainder for payment of the state debt. This legislation had the secondary purpose of pressing the issue of settling a border dispute between Texas and the federal government. The controversy involved the northern boundary of the state at the Prairie Dog Town Fork of the Red River. The Texas government claimed the northern fork as the main channel of the river, while the federal government argued that the south fork, commonly known as Prairie Dog River, was actually the border. In an attempt to end the controversy, the Sixteenth Legislature appropriated the public domain in Greer County, which encompassed nearly all of the disputed territory, for the support of public schools in Texas. This gambit did not work as planned, as the border continued to be in dispute until 1906, when a decision handed down by the U.S. Supreme Court placed Greer County wholly within the Oklahoma Territory.

Through another bill introduced by Senator Terrell, over three million acres of the public domain were set aside in Bailey, Castro, Cochran, Dallam, Deaf Smith, Hartley, Hockley, Lamb, Oldham, and Parmer counties to be sold to fund the construction of a new state Capitol and other necessary public buildings in Austin. Half of the proceeds from the sale of the first fifty thousand acres would go into the public school fund. A separate act provided that once the surveyor had finished his task a superintendent and two building commissioners would be appointed to contract for the construction itself. The only stipulations were that the interior and exterior walls of the building be of the "most durable building rock accessible" and that the Capitol contain fireproof vaults "surrounded and protected by masonry in the most approved manner" for the state archives. The fund would also be spent to refurbish the Governor's Mansion, which was reported to be in poor condition.

As the provisions for education through land sales indicated, the legislators were reluctant to follow Roberts's directive to reduce funding for public education. The governor's plans for retrenchment included a reduction in the appropriation for public free schools from one-fourth to one-fifth of the general revenue of the state. Despite some opposition to the large proportion of state funds dedicated to the schools, notably from Senator Terrell, who delivered a speech against the sizable appropriation, the legislature failed to reduce the proportion of funding in the appropriations act. The governor exercised the line-item veto to eliminate the appropriation for schools. Roberts justified his veto by saying that once the appropriations for public schools and for payment of the interest on the state's debt were deducted from general revenue there was not enough money left in the treasury to fund the ordinary administration of government. The *Galveston News* of April 18, 1879, "bottom-lined" the issue, saying that once the appropriations for deficiencies, for schools, and for interest payments were made, the state's current revenue of $1,650,000 was reduced to $250,000 for all other purposes. The required funding for these other purposes, according to this report, was $920,000—specifically, $260,000 for the judiciary, $100,000 for the asylums, $100,000 for frontier defense, $250,000 for various state offices, $20,000 for quarantines, $40,000 for the penitentiary, and $100,000 for the sinking fund. Businessmen and several prominent newspapers across the state were reported to support the veto, hoping that it signaled a new era of sound financial policy for the state. A veto override was attempted but fell short of the necessary two-thirds vote.

Democrats were widely criticized for a lack of support for public education. Senator Homan, in a speech delivered during the special session in support of the public school system, stated that Senator Blassingame was opposed to the free school system altogether and identified Senator Lane as denouncing free schools as "anti-American" and as an "importation from imperial Germany." Some apparently thought the state was not getting its money's worth from the current system, and this sentiment contributed to the strong support the establishment of state normal schools received.

Despite criticism on the issue, neither Roberts nor the conservative members of the Sixteenth Legislature actually opposed public education. The governor in his inaugural address solemnly pointed out the high illiteracy rate in the state and concluded his remarks on the topic by saying, "Ignorance, when wide spread, is a viper which strikes the poison of its fangs into the vitals of free government, giving food to the mob, destroying, under the leadership of ambitious charlatans[,] the purity of the ballot, and, at last, the life of the state."

Even before the veto of the school appropriation, however, education had become one of the first casualties of the Texas Democrats' drive for fiscal restraint. The Democrats made no provision for local support of schools, even after Roberts signed a measure on April 3, 1879, that provided for the establishment of independent municipal school districts in Texas. An act signed on April 23 provided that all proceeds from renting and leasing school lands which had previously been granted to counties for educational purposes would now go directly into the state public school fund. The emergency clause of this legislation, which was introduced by Senator Burnett, indicated that this measure was necessary because counties were spending these rental proceeds for purposes other than the support of local schools.

Roberts stated that funding for the public free schools was the "subject mainly entered in the occasion of the Legislature being convened in special session." He must have been pleased with the result of the session on this issue. The proportion of general revenue earmarked for the schools was reduced from one-fourth to one-sixth, a cutback greater than he had originally requested. This resulted in the appropriation of $275,000 rather than $410,000 for the 1879–80 school year, a significant reduction in any case and especially significant when compared with the appropriation of $600,000 for the 1878–79 school year which had been made during the regular session. It was believed that profits from newly authorized land sales would increase the public school fund enough to support elementary education and vocational training (the basic curricula with greatest popular support at the time). Funding of the state's educational system would continue to be an important issue in the following legislatures and would be a point of controversy well into the next century.

Higher education received more support from the Sixteenth Legislature. On April 21, 1879, Governor Roberts signed a bill providing for the organization of a normal school for blacks at Prairie View Normal Institute, formerly known as Alta Vista Agricultural College. The normal school would remain under the control of the board of directors of the Agricultural and Mechanical College of Texas. The directors had already initiated unsuccessful efforts to conduct vocational training for black students at the college, but when an investigating committee from the Sixteenth Legislature (including Senators Moore and McCormick) visited the institution, it found no students in attendance. The committee's report recommended that the institution be closed because "the colored race in Texas is not yet sufficiently advanced in the love of learning or in the acquisition of wealth to enable them practically to avail themselves of the state's bounty as offered in the institution" to learn the "mechanical and agricultural arts." The committee endorsed the option of converting the institution into a normal school. Senator Burton introduced the original version of this legislation on the day the report was made, but a committee version ultimately was adopted. The bill, as adopted, allowed one black student, male or female, to be admitted from each state senatorial district and three more from the state at large. All of them would be required to sign an oath pledging to spend a year teaching black children in exchange for each year at Prairie View.

On April 21, 1879, following a pledge of matching funds by the Peabody Foundation and the donation of buildings that had formerly housed Austin College, legislation based on a bill originally introduced by Senator Burnett was passed establishing a state normal school. The school would be called the Sam Houston Normal Institute. Two students—presumably white—would be admitted from each state senatorial district and six from the state at large. Like those at Prairie View College, the students would attend free of charge in return for a pledge to teach one year for each year of education. The establishment of these two institutions of higher education signaled an end to an era of state support for private schools in Texas, as several bills to endow private colleges and preparatory schools with land grants failed to pass.

Land grants were given in exchange for some internal improvements, but these grants often were less generous than those in the past and were sometimes accompanied by mandates or provisos (especially in the case of railroads). The directors of a project at Corpus Christi to dredge a channel eight feet deep and one hundred feet wide across the "Bulkhead" in Corpus Christi Pass received land for their efforts. Apparently no private contractor would dredge the bar at Aransas Pass, where a shift in tides had reduced the depth from ten to five feet, so a joint resolution was sent to Congress requesting funds.

An interesting measure, introduced by Senator Stewart and signed on February 18, 1879, provided that all mechanics, laborers, and operatives who had worked for a railroad had a prior lien before all others upon the railroad and its equipment for unpaid wages. Another act that concerned the "evils" of railroad companies required corporations whose "line of road" terminated at the Texas state line to stop their trains for at least thirty minutes on the Texas side of the boundary. This act also required those companies to build a depot in Texas within three hundred yards of the state line. Although ostensibly general in nature, the act had a very specific target. The Texas and Pacific Railroad Company had sold many lots at its terminus at Texarkana, pledging that depots would be established there, but instead depots were built on the other side of the line in Arkansas. A flood of petitions had brought down the wrath of the legislature on the Texas and Pacific.

The Texas economy in the latter part of the nineteenth century depended primarily on agriculture and related industries for development. These industries generally had been unpoliced by the state government, but the need to regulate them had become apparent and the Sixteenth Legislature took steps in that direction. Through a House bill, sheep inspectors were appointed in counties in which twenty or more sheep owners, or a majority of the sheep owners in a county with fewer than twenty, petitioned for such an officer. The primary responsibility of the inspectors was to look for infectious or contagious disease, and they had the authority to quarantine. Fence laws were strengthened despite protests that barbed-wire fences were deadly to cattle. A compromise bill that originated in the House required those who erected barbed-wire fences to hang boards from the top wire.

A House bill signed on March 8, 1879, designated as public property all oyster beds not privately owned and forbade the culling of oysters from public beds during the months of May, June, July, and August. Those caught illegally taking oysters from public beds could be fined up to fifty dollars. Private oyster beds were defined as those existing or sown in nonnavigable streams, bayous, and lakes that flowed through or lay within or beside private property. One could also create a private oyster bed in public navigable waters by sowing the oysters and placing stakes at the four corners of a claim, which could not be more than two hundred yards square. This right did not extend to staking a claim on a public oyster bed, and one could not place beds within one hundred yards of the low water mark without the permission of the riparian owner, who had the sole right to place beds there. The stakes could not interfere with navigation, and all claims had to be registered with the county clerk. It was also made illegal to purchase oysters for bedding during May, June, July, and August.

The nascent interest in conservation extended into other areas as well. An act introduced by Senator Ford required the construction of fish ladders around all obstructions, such as dams, in the waterways of the state. Senator Shannon introduced a successful resolution to require that the Senate Committee on State Affairs investigate the "propriety of suppressing, if possible, the indiscriminate slaughter of buffalo within the limits of the State." Through a House bill, those engaged in rafting timber or lumber on the waterways of Texas were required to register a brand; this provision was designed primarily to prevent theft, but the law included a requirement that those so engaged submit quarterly reports of the amount of timber cut and transported, which would expedite efforts to keep records and provide for future growth.

The Sixteenth Legislature's tendency to employ economical methods of regulation and reform extended to public health laws. Legislation was passed making it illegal to practice medicine in Texas without having a degree from an accredited school. The quarantine laws to contain yellow fever in the coastal towns, including Houston, were rewritten in a bill initiated by Senator McCormick which provided stiff penalties for noncompliance. The Sixteenth Legislature, however, did not follow Hubbard's directive to create a state board of health, and the House rejected Senator McCulloch's resolution to amend the constitution to that effect after the Senate had passed it. A bill to regulate the practice of pharmacy also passed the Senate but failed in the House. Apparently the lower chamber was even more parsimonious than the Senate, as demonstrated through its refusal to endorse anything more than the most basic measures for public health.

The two chambers did agree with Governor Roberts on at least one economy measure. The act of the Fifteenth Legislature that provided pensions for the surviving soldiers of the Texas Revolution and the signers of the Texas Declaration of Independence, or their widows, was repealed through a House bill because "at least ten times as many names have been presented as was contemplated at the passage of this act." Approximately $20,000 had been set aside originally for pensions; but by 1879 the fund registered a deficit of $150,000, and more claims were being presented every day. Instead of pensions, all indigent veterans who had fought in the Texas Revolution up to and including the Battle of San Jacinto, or their widows, were given land grants of 640 acres in an act introduced by Senator Lane and signed on April 26, 1879.

The Senate of the Sixteenth Legislature, which the *Galveston News* praised for its "large grasp of subjects" and "remarkable facility for the rapid dispatch of business," was also notable for its high degree of unity on most major issues. The members divided bitterly only once, and that was over Senator Terrell's continued attempt to amend the state constitution to require payment of the poll tax before voting. Terrell and his few supporters on this issue insisted the intent of his resolution was only to ensure revenues to the state, but many editors and conservative Democrats undermined the whole effort by prematurely praising the campaign as a way of disenfranchising blacks and "white trash." Terrell's resolution did pass the Senate, where a strong effort enforced a vote along Democratic party lines, but it failed in the House, where Republicans, Greenbackers, and independents wielded a little more influence. Despite its failure to have its way on this issue, the Texas Senate already was becoming noted as a Democratic stronghold, a posture that would make it the focus of many heated campaigns in the future.

CHAPTER 10

The Senate of the Seventeenth Legislature, 1881–82

The Seventeenth Legislature met from January 11 to April 1, 1881, and again in called session from April 6 to May 5, 1882, under the continued domination of Oran M. Roberts, who in his bid for reelection in 1880 easily defeated Greenback candidate W. H. Hamman and Republican E. J. Davis. Former state senator Leonidas J. Storey replaced Joseph D. Sayers as lieutenant governor. Sayers had led a feeble challenge to Roberts in the Democratic convention, running on a platform that included several planks identified with Greenbacker reforms, such as more state support for public education, land donations to settlers instead of corporations, better frontier protection, and measures to encourage immigration. The Democrats, having closed ranks in favor of fiscal conservatism during the 1880 campaign, then undercut the Greenbackers by incorporating a portion of their program in the reforms of the Seventeenth Legislature and thus laid to rest that challenge to Democratic hegemony in Texas for good.

Slightly more than half of the senators from the Sixteenth Legislature also served in the Seventeenth: John C. Buchanan of Wood, Walter M. Burton, Jewett H. Davenport, John M. Duncan, John Y. Gooch, William K. Homan, Augustus W. Houston, William D. Lair, Ellsberry R. Lane, F. Marion Martin, Samuel C. Patton, William R. Shannon, Charles Stewart, William J. Swain, Alexander W. Terrell, and William H. Tilson. Fifteen of the senators at the regular session of the Seventeenth Legislature were newly elected, many of them serving in the Texas Legislature for the first time. There was much public apprehension at the beginning of the regular session that this relatively inexperienced group of legislators might lose its way in the labyrinth of Texas politics. Governor Roberts addressed this concern by proposing a joint resolution to amend the state constitution to provide for six-year terms for senators and four-year terms for representatives, in rotating succession so that there would never be less than two-thirds of the Senate or half of the House returning for a session except immediately after reapportionment. The Senate endorsed the measure, but it failed to pass the House.

The performance of the Senate during the Seventeenth Legislature proved a pleasant surprise for all the naysayers. The Senate contained a remarkable number of legislative rookies—John T. Buchanan of Grimes County, William H. Burges, Samuel B. Cooper, Andrew J. Harris, John N. Henderson, Robert L. Hightower, Henry W. Lightfoot, Anson Rainey, Lawrence Sullivan "Sul" Ross, James B. Stubbs, William W. Weatherred, and Richard M. Wynne. Only three of the newcomers had served previously in the Texas Legislature—J. M. Martin in the House of the Fifteenth Legislature, A. W. Moore in the Senate of the Ninth and Tenth, and Stephen Powers in the House of the Thirteenth. Martin and Powers both died before the called session and were replaced by newcomers William O. Davis and Charles A. McLane. Two other newcomers saw their first service in the Senate in 1882: Lucas H. Brown to take the place of Lane, who had resigned; and James G. McDonald, a veteran of the House of the Ninth and Tenth legislatures, to replace John T. Buchanan, who had died suddenly at the age of twenty-nine. Despite their lack of legislative experience, several neophytes, such as Wynne and Cooper, emerged quickly from the ranks to provide vital leadership and forge a unity that was not achieved in the more fractious House. This working union was based primarily on a common adherence to a conservative Democratic program outlined by party leaders such as Governor Roberts and refined through each senator's contribution.

Though the freshman senators of the Seventeenth Legislature generally were Democrats, they arrived with diverse experiences and beliefs. There was one experience that many of them shared, however, and that was service in the Confederate Army. No fewer than eleven had fought for the Confederacy.

None of the first-time senators had a more distinguished military career than Lawrence Sullivan "Sul" Ross of Waco. Born in Davenport, Iowa, on September 27, 1838, Ross was only a few months old when his parents moved to the Indian village of Waco, Texas. He attended Baylor University and in 1859 graduated with distinction from Wesleyan University in Florence, Alabama. During the summer vacation of 1858, along with 135 friendly Indians and with the help of the U.S. cavalry, he engaged in battle with the Comanches. He was seriously wounded, and 95 of the Comanches were killed. At that battle he encountered an eight-year-old white girl whose parents were unknown, and he raised and educated the girl, whom he named Lizzie Ross. When Sul Ross returned to Texas after graduation in 1859, Governor Sam Houston put the young man of twenty-one in command of the Texas Rangers. In 1860 he captured and destroyed the principal village of the Comanches, killing a great number, and "rescued" Cynthia Ann Parker, who had been a captive for almost twenty-five years and did not want to be rescued and who was the mother of the great Comanche chief Quanah Parker. Peta Nocona, the chief of the Comanches, was killed in a confrontation with Ross.

Sul Ross married Lizzie Tinsley of Waco in May, 1861, and that same year he entered the Confederate Army as a private. He was soon promoted to major, then to lieutenant colonel and later colonel. In 1863, he was made a brigadier general. After the war, he was a planter and was the sheriff of his county and a member of the constitutional convention before becoming a senator. During his one term in the Senate, Ross was chairman of the Committee on Finance. He was elected governor in 1886 and was reelected in 1888; following his second term as chief executive, he became the president of the Agricultural and Mechanical College of Texas and held that office until his death in 1898. Sul Ross State Teachers College (now Sul Ross State University) in Alpine and the community of Ross in McLennan County were named in his honor.

Another former Confederate who achieved high rank was James G. McDonald of Anderson, who was elected in 1882 and sworn at the beginning of the called session to complete the term of John T. Buchanan. McDonald was born in Smith County, Tennessee, on September 20, 1824, and studied law in Lebanon, Tennessee. Having come to Texas in 1851, he first located in Austin, then moved to Anderson. McDonald had married Julia Davis of Nashville on February 13, 1850, and through this union had ten children. He was a district attorney from 1856 to 1860 and then was elected to the Texas House of Representatives. He resigned in 1861 and served as brigadier general of Texas troops for two years, but his impaired physical condition made it impossible for him to engage in active service. He again was a district attorney from 1872 to 1876. Senator McDonald returned to private life after serving in the called session in 1882. He died March 11, 1903.

Andrew J. Harris of Belton also had health problems while in the military. He was promoted to captain in the 27th Mississippi Regiment, but his poor health required him to leave the army in 1864. Harris, who was also a member of the Senate in the Eighteenth Legislature, was born in Talbot County, Georgia, on January 27, 1839. He moved with his family to Mississippi when he was six years old. He graduated with high honors from the University of Mississippi but did not receive a degree until after the Civil War.

Harris first moved to Waco in January, 1865; he taught there for one month and then at Salado College for two years. While at Salado, he was involved with the Euphradian Society, an organization for the study of parliamentary law and practice which afforded opportunities for young men to improve themselves in public speaking and debate. He next moved to Belton, first to practice law and later to teach, then went back to Salado in 1871 to teach for two years. He was elected county superintendent of public schools in 1873. After serving in the Senate of the Eighteenth Legislature, he returned to private life. Harris had married Olivia Sugg of Mississippi on July 31, 1866, and they had six children.

Some of the Confederate veterans had been wounded in the war. Charles A. McLane of Brownsville, who was elected to finish the term of the deceased Stephen Powers after the regular session, entered the army in January, 1864. While a soldier, he was wounded en route from Eagle Pass to Brownsville. At the hospital at Rio Grande City, he avoided amputation of his leg by threatening to kill anyone who tried to perform the operation. Born in San Antonio on December 3, 1846, he was only seventeen when he entered the military. After the war he was for a time a local editor of the *San Antonio Daily Herald.* In 1885 he was appointed city attorney of Laredo and served until 1891, when he was elected mayor.

William H. Burges of Seguin served for four years in Hood's Texas Brigade and was seriously wounded in the battle of Sharpsburg on

September 17, 1862. Burges was born in Madison County, Tennessee, on January 8, 1838. He initially came to Texas at the age of seventeen and was admitted to the bar in 1859. In order to improve his legal education, he obtained a degree from the law department of the University of Louisiana. In 1866 he was the county attorney for Guadalupe County, but he was removed by the federal administration. Senator Burges, who would later serve as a senator in the Twentieth and Twenty-first legislatures and was president pro tempore ad interim during the latter, had a large and successful law practice in Seguin. He was married three times and had five children.

Anson Rainey of Waxahachie was wounded in the left foot in a battle near Mobile and permanently disabled on April 2, 1865. Born March 1, 1848, at Eldorado, Union County, Arkansas, he had enlisted in the Confederate Army at the age of fifteen in August, 1863. Rainey came to Texas in 1867 and stayed until he left for Delhi, Louisiana, in 1869. He studied law in Louisiana and was admitted to the bar there on July 6, 1871; he moved to Waxahachie on February 12, 1873. Rainey's one term in the Senate was followed by a long career in the judiciary. He was appointed judge of the Fourth Judicial District on July 6, 1885. In 1893 he was named associate justice of the Court of Civil Appeals in Dallas, where he served until his death on August 5, 1922. Rainey was married to Fannie Meriwether on February 17, 1874, and had two children.

Richard M. Wynne of Henderson joined the Confederate Army in 1862 at the age of seventeen and was elected a second lieutenant the following year. He was severely wounded twice—the second time he was completely paralyzed for nine weeks and permanently lost the use of his right arm and kept only partial use of his right leg. Left on the battlefield, he ended up a prisoner until late in 1865.

Wynne was born in Haywood County, Tennessee, on June 2, 1844. Soon thereafter his family moved to Rusk County, Texas. He came home from the war in December, 1865, and became sheriff of his county, marrying Laura Bikelly on January 23, 1867. He read law at night and was admitted to the bar in 1870. In the Senate, Wynne was one of five men who were instrumental in pushing through the bill that created the University of Texas. During the called session, he advocated the passage of the "Three-cents-a-mile Bill" limiting the amount that rail passengers could be charged per mile and requiring the free transport of one hundred pounds of baggage. Wynne also called for the creation of a railroad commission; however, this did not occur for another ten years. He supported the Confederate land pension bill and was thought of as a champion of the masses against the corporations. He authored a bill, which was successful, requiring the registration of instruments related to real estate in unorganized counties. Wynne was made permanent president of the state Democratic convention in 1886 and became a candidate for governor in 1898 but lost at the convention. He died on July 15, 1912.

John N. Henderson of Bryan also suffered a serious injury during the war. Born in Abbeville, South Carolina, in the early 1840s, Henderson had moved to Texas with his family when he was a child and entered Baylor University at Independence, Texas, at the age of fourteen. He left in his junior year to go to war, joining the 5th Texas Regiment of Hood's Brigade. At Sharpsburg a minié ball took off his left arm, yet he returned to service until the end of the war as a captain on the staff of General J. B. Robertson. Henderson graduated from the law department of Baylor and began practice in 1867. He moved to Bryan and was district attorney of the Fourteenth Judicial District for eight years before his election to the Senate.

Although Henderson served just one term, he was an active senator. In the regular session, he authored a bill that allowed three students from every senatorial district to attend the Agricultural and Mechanical College of Texas free of charge; also passed was his joint resolution granting certain judges permission to absent themselves from the state. During the special session, he authored a successful bill to provide temporary shelter for lunatics of the asylum, which had recently burned. After his term in the Senate, Henderson served for several years as judge of the Twentieth Judicial District, beginning in 1887.

Another Confederate veteran who had joined up at an early age was Henry W. Lightfoot of Paris, who was born on December 29, 1846, in Lawrence County, Alabama. Lightfoot enlisted in the 11th Alabama Cavalry at the age of sixteen. He graduated with honors from the law school of Cumberland University in Tennessee in 1869. After coming to Texas in 1872, he met Samuel Bell Maxey, with whom he started an enduring partnership.

After serving two years in the Senate, Lightfoot decided to return to the law firm, as his partner, Maxey, was serving in the U.S. Senate.

He was elected president of the Texas Bar Association in 1889 and was named chief justice of the Court of Civil Appeals in Dallas in 1893. He held that post for several years and then returned to private practice. In 1874 Lightfoot married Maxey's adopted daughter, Dora Bell Maxey, who died ten years later; he married Etta Wooten in 1889. There were two children from his first marriage and two from his second. He died while on legal business in Alaska on August 27, 1901.

William W. Weatherred of Hemphill came to Texas before the Civil War and returned to the state after four years in the Confederate Army. He became clerk of the district court of Sabine County and after study was admitted to the bar; he served as county judge from 1875 to 1876 but declined the office of district judge in 1876. Nominated for the Senate without his permission in 1880, he refused to run for reelection in 1882. Weatherred returned to the private practice of law in Sabine County after his term. He was married and (as of 1880) had five children with his wife, Eliza. He died on February 2, 1895, in Hillsboro.

Lucas H. Brown of Helena in Karnes County served as a lieutenant in the 3rd Texas Infantry. While in the military, he was a judge advocate pro tempore of the military commission in session at San Antonio. He, too, had migrated to Texas, having been born in Madison County, Arkansas, on December 17, 1837. Brown was admitted to the bar at Goliad in 1873 and moved to Karnes County in 1877. In the Senate, he succeeded Ellsberry R. Lane, who had resigned February 1, 1882; Brown served only in the special session.

A number of the new senators had no military service. Samuel Bronson Cooper of Woodville was born in Caldwell County, Kentucky, on May 30, 1850; his family moved to Texas in December of that year and settled at Woodville. Cooper commenced clerking in a general store in Woodville at age sixteen. He began the study of law and was admitted to the bar and began to practice in 1872. He joined a law firm that included among its senior partners Edwin E. Hobby. Cooper was elected county attorney of Tyler County in 1876 and was reelected in 1878. He had friendly relations with the Alabama-Coushatta Indians, and the chief of the Alabamas named his newborn son Bronson Cooper Sylestine after him. Cooper's son was born the same day, March 28, 1878, and Cooper made a promise, which he later kept, to make a gift of a new rifle to each of the two young men on their twelfth birthday. On that day, the two youngsters participated in a shooting contest which, to the delight of the tribe, the chief's son won.

As a senator during the Seventeenth Legislature, Cooper was the author of a bill which gave indigent Confederate veterans or the indigent widows of such veterans two sections of land (1,280 acres) each. Also, he advocated that public land be sold only to actual settlers. Cooper was reelected to a second term in the Senate in 1882 and was president pro tempore during the called session of the Eighteenth Legislature. He went on to serve in the U.S. Congress from 1893 to 1905 and from 1907 to 1909. Cooper died on August 21, 1918.

William Owen Davis of Gainesville was born in Heard County, Georgia, on February 26, 1847, and was admitted to the bar at Newnan, Coweta County, Georgia, on March 20, 1870. He moved to Texas in the 1870s and located in Gainesville. Davis was elected to the Senate of the Seventeenth Legislature to fill the vacancy created by the death of J. M. Martin and was reelected in 1882 and 1884. He was chairman of Judiciary Committee Number 2 and a member of Judiciary Committee Number 1, which dealt with finance and penitentiaries, among other matters, during the Nineteenth Legislature.

James B. Stubbs was born August 28, 1850, in Montgomery, Alabama, and moved to Galveston with his family when he was three years old. Stubbs received a degree from Pass Christian College in Mississippi and a bachelor of laws degree from the law department of Washington and Lee University in Lexington, Virginia. He was admitted to the bar at Galveston in 1872.

In the special session in 1882, Stubbs authored a bill, which became law, extending the time for persons whose lands had been sold for taxes to redeem their property. After serving in the Senate, he was city attorney of Galveston from 1882 to 1885 and from 1899 to 1901; in 1902, he was president of the Texas Bar Association. He was married in 1876 and again in 1901 and had two children.

Robert L. Hightower, the senator from Harrison County, was a member of the Citizens party. Born May 24, 1836, in Somerville, Fayette County, Tennessee, Hightower moved to Texas with his family in 1840 after a year in Shreveport, Louisiana. He was married three times, first to Martha Powell, then to Martha Fortson, and finally to Alice Fortson. He was successful as the defense attorney for Abe Rothschild, who was accused of murdering his wife, known as "Diamond Bessie" because of her habit of wearing diamond jewelry.

Before his election to the Senate, Hightower had never held political office, although he had been a candidate for state representative in 1872, running on the Citizens party platform. The Citizens party attempted, with some success, to appeal to the freedmen with its message of reconciliation of the races. The sincerity of the appeal was questionable, however, as a few years earlier Hightower and other Citizens party officials had been arrested and charged with preventing some black citizens from voting; they were released after a determination was made that the black citizens' voting had only been delayed, not prevented. Despite this controversy, according to some estimates as many as two-thirds of the black voters of Harrison County supported the Citizens party, and several of its members were elected to office in 1880. During his one term in the Senate, Hightower secured the passage of a bill he authored that permitted district courts to transfer certain cases to the county courts. He died on April 5, 1890.

Stephen Powers of Brownsville was born in Damariscotta, Maine, on June 1, 1814, and moved to New York with his family in his childhood. By the age of fifteen he was a schoolteacher, and at twenty-one he was admitted to the bar at Buffalo, New York. He later became a U.S. consul in Basel, Switzerland. Powers first came to Texas as a lieutenant in the army of General Zachary Taylor during the Mexican War and in 1849 settled in Brownsville, where he was a county judge in 1852 and later became mayor. He married Pauline V. Butler Impey there in 1855. Powers was a judge of the Twelfth District during the Confederacy and became a state representative in 1873. He died on February 5, 1882, and was succeeded by McLane.

John T. Buchanan of Anderson, who died before the called session, was a county attorney in Grimes County before his election to the Senate. Born in Harris County, Georgia, on April 14, 1852, Buchanan entered the University of Georgia as a youth and graduated with distinction in the class of 1873. Though not sworn until the Seventeenth Legislature, he had been elected in a special election on February 17, 1880, to finish the term of James R. Burnett, who had resigned during the Sixteenth.

J. M. Martin of Gainesville was born in Sumner County, Tennessee, in 1848. He was admitted to the bar at Lebanon, Tennessee, where he had graduated from Cumberland University, and moved to Texas in 1873. Martin was a member of the House in the Fifteenth Legislature and had been a newspaper editor. He died on March 9, 1882, and was replaced for the called session by William Owen Davis.

Despite the prevailing desire for economy in state government, the Senate of the Seventeenth Legislature employed a full slate of officers. John P. C. Whitehead was elected secretary; William Neal Ramey, first assistant secretary; C. M. Boynton, second assistant secretary; John W. Swindells, calendar clerk; Fergus W. Kyle, sergeant-at-arms; Alexander Cromwell, assistant sergeant-at-arms; V. F. Dubose, enrolling clerk; A. M. Belvin, engrossing clerk; William Fitzhugh, doorkeeper; F. C. Wilkes, chaplain; and Robert Josselyn, postmaster. During the called session, William Hunter became first assistant secretary, J. H. Kirby replaced Swindells, J. E. Kaufman succeeded Dubose, and R. K. Smoot took Wilkes's place. Gooch was elected president pro tempore on January 12, 1881; on March 31, 1881, Francis M. Martin was chosen to serve in that capacity for the called session.

Finances occupied top place on the legislative calendar and became the focus of heated controversy when a conference committee deadlocked over the appropriations bill. Governor Roberts ruffled a few feathers when, in an interview published in the *Galveston News* on March 13, 1881, he boasted:

> [The legislature] had better look out what they are doing. Why, sir, I can ignore them; I can call a convention; I can disorganize the government, sir; but I don't want any fuss; and I don't want to be ruled by a mob. I haven't made up my mind to call them together. If they pass no appropriation bill, I can get along without them; and I will let them go home, to tell their people what they have not done.

Before the end of the regular session, the legislature did fall in line, largely because of pressure from Roberts. The governor's control was due primarily to the fact that his program for fiscal retrenchment worked. By the end of Roberts's four years, the public debt had decreased by more than $1 million, the annual interest burden had been reduced by one-third, and there was a surplus in the state treasury. Much of this improvement in the financial condition of the state government was due to a return of general prosperity to Texas—the tax rolls reflected an almost threefold increase in the total wealth of the state between 1875 and 1890—but the Democrats claimed the triumph as their own. The increase in funds enabled the Seventeenth Legislature to reduce taxation on property, undercutting the Greenbacker protest against high taxes. Although ad valorem taxes were reduced during the regular session, to four-tenths of 1 percent, most occupation taxes were increased and poll taxes were doubled to $2.00, with one-half of the revenue being reserved for public schools. During the called session, ad valorem taxes were further reduced, to three-tenths of 1 percent; poll taxes were reduced to $1.50 (with a dollar going to schools and 50 cents going into general revenue); and even some occupation taxes were lowered—not, however, those on persons selling alcoholic beverages. Over $1.8 million of the bonds authorized by the Sixteenth Legislature, along with the 1870 bonds for supporting the International Railroad signed by Governor Edmund J. Davis, were burned through an act signed on May 4, 1882.

The Senate gave its endorsement to a number of relief bills that also increased public support for the Democrats. Senator Harris introduced a bill to push back the deadline for the reclamation of land confiscated by the state for delinquent taxes until twelve months after the bill was signed. Harris's bill did not pass, but a similar House bill did pass and was signed on February 5, 1881. This new deadline was also extended for another year by an act adopted during the called session on April 20, 1882. Through a House bill, fifty-eight tax-paying entities (including businesses) in Savoy, Texas, which had been leveled by a tornado, were exempted from state and county taxes for 1880, and the same was done for all tax-paying entities in Cameron County, where a "tempest" had destroyed houses, fences, and crops. A fire in Plano on August 27, 1881, destroyed all the businesses except one and "nine-tenths of the dwelling houses," so the fire victims there were exempted from taxation in 1881.

Much of the financial burden of the state, especially in public education and construction, was being transferred to the local level. County commissioners were authorized to issue bonds at not more than 8 percent, to come due in fifteen years or less, for building courthouses. If the commissioners availed themselves of this form of financing, they were to levy an annual ad valorem tax to establish a sinking fund for repayment of the bonds. The first county to take advantage of this authorization was Robertson, whose finances were in such a condition that it was imperative that the bill take effect immediately after Governor Roberts signed it on February 11, 1881. A second bill, signed on April 6, 1881, permitted counties to issue 6 percent twenty-year bonds to retire outstanding debts.

The prohibition movement, with Senator Homan its main advocate, was a major influence on tax reform. The awkward "bell-punch law" passed by the Sixteenth Legislature, which had generated much public opposition and had become a campaign issue for the Greenbackers in 1880, was repealed. Through a bill introduced in the House, occupation taxes levied by the state on all retailers of alcoholic beverages were increased. In addition, commissioners courts and municipalities could each levy a tax equal to half the level of the state's imposition, and all these taxes were to be paid in advance each year; furthermore, anyone selling liquor, beer, or wine in quantities less than a quart had to post a bond of one thousand dollars. Thus the tax for selling alcoholic beverages could double for a saloonkeeper in an incorporated town or city, and he was forced to post a hefty bond to boot. Local taxes as well as local ordinances became potent weapons in the hands of those who favored restricting the sale of alcoholic beverages, including organizations such as the Women's Christian Temperance Union, which was established in Texas in 1881.

The legislature continued to receive numerous petitions demanding a statewide prohibition law, so the Senate passed a joint resolution to amend the constitution to ban the sale, exchange, or gift of any alcoholic beverage in Texas other than wines or malt liquors, except for "medicinal purposes." The resolution failed to pass the House, and a later Senate bill by Homan to enact prohibition by statute was not accepted by his Senate colleagues. While Homan championed the prohibition cause, the opposition was led by Terrell, who wrote in regard to the proposed constitutional amendment: "I am opposed to all sumptuary laws of any character. When governments begin to prohibit to man the right to determine what he shall eat, drink, or wear, it will end, if not checked, by its invasion of domestic life, and prescribing the forms of prayer." The joint resolution had passed the Senate by a vote of twenty-three to seven. A few days later there was a heated exchange on the floor between Homan and Terrell after the latter publicly ridiculed the evangelistic nature of the former's religion.

On another occasion, faced with a vote on the bill to increase the taxation of businesses that served alcohol, Terrell—the only senator who opposed passage—said, "It submits every man's personal right to drink a beverage in a licensed house, whether he be a drunkard or not, to the caprice of his female relatives, without regard to whether their relations to each other are friendly or hostile."

The only real losers in these exchanges and in the resulting mandate for local option laws to prohibit the sale of alcoholic beverages were the retailers, many of whom had paid their taxes in good faith. During the called session, a House bill provided for an appropriation to compensate those who had bought licenses but had been put out of business by local option laws. It was guided through the Senate by Terrell and signed without protest by Governor Roberts.

With the crime rate in Texas rising, the caseloads in the Supreme Court and in the Court of Appeals had become overwhelming. To ease the problem, the Commission of Appeals was created, through an act introduced by Senator Gooch, to preview petitions remanded to the superior tribunals. The commission was not able to decide a case independently, but submitted its final opinion and a synopsis of the case back to the court responsible for the appeal, which would deliver a judgment. If the opinion of the commission was adopted, it would be printed just as in any other decision. Roberts, a former chief justice of the Texas Supreme Court, endorsed Gooch's bill and signed it on February 9, 1881. In addition, a joint resolution was passed proposing a constitutional amendment to expand the Supreme Court to a chief justice and six associate justices, who would organize into two tribunals for business, but the resolution lost in the popular election. A Senate bill was passed empowering district courts, instead of the legislature, to hear petitions for the removal of minority status for those over the age of nineteen, but through another Senate bill the administration of the estates of deceased persons and the guardianship of minors, persons of unsound mind, and habitual drunkards were transferred from the district to the county courts, in order to clear the dockets of the former for criminal cases. Several judicial districts were reorganized.

Due to the prohibitionist fervor, laws were amended to provide stricter penalties for crimes involving alcohol. A bill introduced by Senator Buchanan of Wood and amended by Senator Homan provided that henceforth

> neither intoxication, nor temporary insanity of mind produced by the voluntary recent use of ardent spirits, shall constitute any excuse for the commission of crime, nor shall intoxication mitigate either the degree or the penalty of crime, but evidence of temporary insanity produced by such use of ardent spirits may be introduced by the defendant in any criminal prosecution in mitigation of the penalty attached to the offense for which he is being tried, and in case of murder for the purpose of determining the degree of murder of which the defendant may be found guilty.

The bill became law on February 17, 1881.

Attempts at gun control legislation were another response to the crime problem. Senator Homan introduced a bill to restrict the carrying of deadly weapons. Only ordinary army-size and navy-size revolvers were to be carried, and they had to be outside of all clothing and fully exposed to view. The bill was reported favorably out of committee but never passed the Senate. Another bill by Homan, one to restrict the import and sale of certain deadly weapons, passed the Senate but not the House. Senator Wynne introduced a bill that would have doubled the penalty for crimes committed with prohibited weapons, but this legislation also failed to become law, despite easy passage in the Senate.

Atrocities within the penitentiary system in Texas had given rise to horrific anecdotes and at least one petition from outraged citizens. One such document from Harris County related how convicts jailed for minuscule fines were hired out for just a penny a day until their account had been paid in full; those who protested were cruelly lashed. The Penitentiary Board was created through a bill introduced in the House. Its members included the governor, the state treasurer, and the superintendent of the state penitentiaries, who at the time was Thomas J. Goree. The superintendent served as the sole executive officer and was aided by assistant superintendents who resided at each of the prisons.

The Penitentiary Board would oversee the administration of all the state prisons and all contracts for convict labor. Two "inspectors of penitentiaries" would supervise the employment of any convicts outside the prison facilities, although the legislature would have to approve all contracts for convict labor. The provisions for the humane treatment of convicts adopted by the Sixteenth Legislature were amended to exclude the use of stocks as well as head shaving and starvation; and an earlier mandate that whipping could be administered only by special order in "aggravated and particular cases" was restated. Provisions were made for early parole for good behavior and for outright pardons in the event of especially meritorious conduct. If a female convict had an infant, the child could remain with her until it was four years of age, when the Penitentiary Board would have to determine its custody. Each penitentiary retained a physician and a chaplain under the new regulations.

There were also some purely symbolic gestures to attack perceived evils, some of which were occurring overseas. Senator Homan introduced, and both houses passed, a resolution expressing sympathy for the people of Ireland as they faced the "oppressive system of British landlordism." The Senate also adopted a House resolution, with amendments, to instruct the Texas congressmen to do what was best "to relieve the Jews from oppression in Germany." There was some argument over this, however, as the resolution voted on referred to "the Hebrew race" as "the exponent of our religion." Some senators, namely Gooch, Martin of Cooke, Harris, Hightower, Buchanan of Wood, and Martin of Navarro, objected to the religious references, especially the claim by a governmental body that it adhered to a particular religion. Henderson and Duncan also objected on the grounds that the resolution was purely sentimental and therefore inappropriate. The resolution as amended failed to pass the House.

Railroad corporations were the primary focus of civil law reform. Senator Swain championed the idea of a state regulatory board for railroads but was opposed by a majority led by Ross, who thought competition was the best regulator. During the course of debate, railroad financier Jay Gould made a timely visit to Texas, where he spoke against regulation and suspended work on a vital extension of the Missouri, Kansas and Texas until the bill for a railroad commission, introduced in the Senate by Davenport, had been defeated.

Gould's victory proved only temporary, however, as the called session would produce several new regulatory measures. The rates to be charged by railroads for transporting people were reduced to three cents per mile, and a requirement was imposed that one hundred pounds of luggage was to be admitted free of charge. An act signed into law on May 6, 1882, prohibited railroad companies from levying "excessive charges" for the transport of freight and from demanding more than the bill of lading stipulated. Despite a politely but strongly worded petition from the "Colored Men's Convention" at Waco in April, 1882, the segregation of railway cars was not prohibited nor were equal facilities required, even though black passengers were frequently charged first-class fares for substandard accommodations.

Senator Terrell introduced a bill prohibiting future land grants for the construction of railroads, but the senators unanimously adopted instead a House bill that was similar but also precluded donations for builders of canals and irrigation ditches; the bill was signed by Governor Roberts on April 22, 1882. The act stated that the "public domain subject to location by the owners of these certificates has been exhausted," but in fact, commitments to railroad companies alone already exceeded—by a mere eight million acres (12,500 square miles)—the amount of land set aside for that purpose. Terrell insisted that the pledges made by the state in the past were contingent upon the availability of land and were not hard-and-fast obligations, and that therefore the state could not be sued for failing to provide each company with the grants they had been promised. This legal construct was a flimsy one, and the threat of a suit hung over later legislation.

Some of the financial burden of internal improvements continued to be passed on to the federal government. For example, the legislature sent Congress a joint resolution, introduced by Senator Powers, relating to the dredging of the harbor at Galveston, as well as a second joint resolution concerning the attainment of a large draft of water on the bars at Port Aransas, Sabine Pass, Brazos de Santiago, Pass Cavallo, and the mouths of the Brazos River and Buffalo Bayou.

Overcommitment did not slow land grants by the Seventeenth Legislature to those believed to be deserving. Donations to veterans of the Texas Revolution and the signers of the Texas Declaration of

Independence, or their widows and heirs, were increased from 640 to 1,280 acres through a bill authored by Lightfoot which also expanded the original act to include the few survivors of the Dawson Massacre, perpetrated by Mexican troops in 1842. The bill by Senator Cooper mentioned earlier granted 1,280 acres to Texas soldiers, servants who had attended such soldiers, or the widows of such soldiers, if the soldiers had been wounded and permanently disabled in Confederate service and had less than one thousand dollars total in property. This measure was the first enacted by any state that conferred aid in such a practical form upon those who had fought for the Confederacy.

The Senate's vital interest in public education also belied the fiscal conservatism demonstrated in other areas. Lieutenant Governor Sayers, in his final opening address to the Senate on January 11, demanded an increase in support for public education. Schools in counties organized in the future would benefit from the reservation of three hundred leagues of the public domain, to be surveyed and granted in plats of four leagues apiece to each county. The budget again included an increase in the appropriation for public education at the constitutional limit of one-fourth of the general revenues, but the tax rate on property was lowered and part of the general fund was diverted to the Sam Houston Normal School, so the immediate impact was negligible. A Senate bill authorized the attendance of three students from each state senatorial district at the Agricultural and Mechanical College of Texas free of charge, provided that half the students so selected would study agriculture and the other half mechanical arts or engineering.

The most significant achievement in education by the Seventeenth Legislature was the creation of the University of Texas. The university was established by a bill introduced by J. C. Buchanan, chairman of the Senate Committee on Educational Affairs, and was shepherded through the Senate by Gooch, Stubbs, Terrell, and Wynne. A few senators balked at such a large financial commitment, but they were pressured into voting for the bill by Governor Roberts, who signed it on March 30, 1881. The university's location, as well as that of a separate medical department as provided in an amendment added on a motion by Senator Stubbs, was determined by popular election on September 6, 1881. The vote for the location of the university provided choices for where to put the entire university and where to put the main campus and the medical center if the two were split. Although Tyler beat out Austin in votes for the location of the main plant, it was decided that the main plant should be located in Austin because that city garnered the greatest total if the votes for the location of the entire university and the votes for the location of the main plant were added together. Galveston, as Stubbs had planned, was chosen as the site for the medical facility.

The organization of the university, as outlined in the organic act, was essentially that submitted to Roberts by Dr. Oscar H. Cooper of the Texas State Teachers Association and forwarded by him to the legislature. Senator Gooch introduced one major amendment to specifically permit both males and females to attend. A bill was introduced during the called session providing for the survey of two million acres for the support of the university; the measure passed the Senate but failed in the House.

The state constitution mandated that there be a branch of the University of Texas for blacks, and an election was ordered for its location in an act signed at the close of the called session on May 5, 1882, but such an institution never opened. This was a serious disservice to a group that constituted the largest ethnic minority in Texas. The "Colored Men's Convention" at Waco decried the poor educational opportunities for blacks, and funds were set aside through a House bill to recompense Prairie View Normal Institute for damages sustained in a storm and to purchase a library. However, the facilities there remained much poorer than those available at the University of Texas and the Agricultural and Mechanical College of Texas, which blacks were not allowed to attend. Other requests for a second normal school or college offering blacks instruction in engineering and agriculture went unheeded.

Conservation of natural resources became a concern of many Texans in the late nineteenth century as the state emerged from its frontier stage of abundant land and wildlife. Senator Stubbs introduced a measure for the conservation of fish and oysters in the tidal waters of the state, but his bill was replaced by a broader act introduced in the House that prohibited seining for fish in all of the public waters of Texas from February through June each year. The act also banned seining with a mesh less than two and one-half inches square, setting fish traps or fixed nets, and poisoning fish with any substance. Deer hunting and trapping were restricted to June

Colonial Capitol, 1853–81. Courtesy Austin History Center, Austin Public Library, # C00244.

through November of each year, and anyone found in possession of fresh venison at least one day before the season opened or ten days after it was closed would be fined. The season for wild turkey was closed from mid-May until the end of August; for prairie chickens from March through July; and for quail and partridges from March until the end of August. The netting of partridges was prohibited, and killing a nongame bird was made a misdemeanor.

Provisions for the enforcement of conservation laws were quickly set. An appropriation was made to employ a fish commissioner on March 31, 1881, and J. H. Dinkins, who had previously served in that capacity for two years without any compensation, became the first state fish commissioner to receive a salary. In addition to his salary, Dinkins was given five thousand dollars to preserve and distribute fish in the public waterways of Texas. Dinkins was killed in December, 1881, when a train crushed his leg while he was journeying to Washington on state business. Under his successor, R. R. Robertson, many shad, German carp, and Japanese goldfish were introduced into the waters of Texas within the first year of operation. Many of these were supplied by the U.S. Fish Commission, and they thrived in the warm waters of Texas.

Several vital issues prompted the special session that met from April 6 through May 5, 1882, including replacement of the old Capitol (which had burned on November 9, 1881), apportionment of congressional districts, and utility improvements for several underserved public institutions. Expansion of the Lunatic Asylum and construction of the University of Texas required some upgrading of the utilities supplied to state buildings in Austin. But even without the construction projects, the state government would have had plenty of inducement to improve its water facilities. An inadequate supply of water was the reason much of the old Capitol could not be saved. During this called session, on April 13, fire also destroyed one of the insane asylum buildings, leaving forty-six inmates without shelter. Despite the initiative for reducing public obligations, funds were appropriated for the Lunatic Asylum, the university, and the state penitentiaries. The Senate endorsed an additional three million dollars to facilitate completion of a new Capitol. A reapportionment of congressional districts was hastily passed, as five more seats in Congress had been allotted to Texas after the 1880 census. The Senate convened for the special session in the Armory Hall, which was down the block from Millet's Opera House, the meeting place for the House of Representatives.

At the end of his administration, Roberts could point with pride to a number of achievements in the areas of state budgeting and tax reduction. These achievements had been made at a high cost, however, because the public domain was rapidly disappearing into the hands of private speculators, and services—particularly education—were operating at a minimal level. Additional lands were not set aside for the Agricultural and Mechanical College of Texas, despite proposals to that effect, or for a reservation for the Tonkawa Indians, on whose behalf numerous citizens of Shackelford and Young counties had petitioned the legislature. Despite repeated re-

Firefighters battling Colonial Capitol fire, November 9, 1881.
Courtesy Austin History Center, Austin Public Library, # C00231.

quests from Governor Roberts, the Seventeenth Legislature failed to provide for a state board of health, more normal schools, or an immigration bureau. Laws were passed to quarantine diseased sheep but not cattle infected with the deadly Texas fever tick. Most of the blame for the legislature's failure to address the governor's requests, though, lay with the House, not the Senate, a fact which gave Texas newspaper editors much political grist for their literary mills.

These shortcomings, of course, were not enough to threaten the Democrats' stranglehold on either chamber of the legislature. A clear indication of their dominance came during the balloting for the U.S. Senate seat of Samuel Bell Maxey, whose term would expire on March 4, 1881. Maxey was an "ultra-simon-pure-secession-anti-reconstruction-Democrat," but the campaign between him and

Throckmorton was a race between two very similar Democrats. In the Senate, Stewart nominated Maxey, and Shannon nominated former governor Throckmorton; there were no other candidates, and Maxey defeated Throckmorton for the Senate's nomination by a vote of twenty-two to eight. The race was closer in the House, where Throckmorton got thirty-four votes to Maxey's fifty-one, but on January 26, 1881, the votes were counted in joint session and Maxey was declared the victor.

Concerned Greenbackers allied themselves with the Republicans in 1882—together the two parties had polled 37 percent of the popular vote in 1880—and temporarily rallied opposition to the Democrats for the election of 1882. The Democrats, nevertheless, swept almost every precinct in the state in that election, and Texas took another step toward the era of the "Solid South" of the early twentieth century.

CHAPTER 11

The Senate of the Eighteenth Legislature, 1883–84

The Eighteenth Legislature convened for its regular session on January 9, 1883. A predominantly Democratic assembly, it quickly fell in line with the tight-fisted policies of Democrat John Ireland of Seguin, who was inaugurated as governor on January 16, 1883. Ireland was a former Know-Nothing from Kentucky who had served as a colonel in the Confederate Army. Often called "Ox-Cart John" as a popular tribute to his opposition to land grants for railroads, he had a reputation as an intelligent politician dedicated to conservative fiscal and social reforms. He was not personable, however, and had almost lost the 1882 campaign to colorful George W. Jones of Bastrop (a former Unionist from Texas who also had been a Confederate colonel), who challenged the Democrats by running for office as an independent. Jones's loss to Ireland underscored the fact that—like the Republicans third parties and independents posed little threat to the established Democratic rule. This point was reinforced when Ireland substantially increased his margin of victory in a repeat campaign against Jones in 1884.

As governor, Ireland continued the retrenchment begun under his predecessor, Oran M. Roberts, but added such touches as opposing the sale of public lands and advocating the purchase by the state of its own bonds at high prices to hasten the extinction of the public debt. Ireland opposed Roberts's policy of freely selling public lands at low prices to the first bidder, preferring instead to reserve them for future homesteaders. The Eighteenth Legislature continued a program of economy in government, but Texas voters broke ranks with this policy in August, 1883, by approving new constitutional amendments to authorize special state and local school taxes. While the Eighteenth Legislature continued to provide funds sparingly for education and other matters, it proved to be unlike the previous legislature in actively seeking tangible solutions to the pressing problems of the state: the excessive selling of public lands, an ailing education system, and overcrowded prisons and asylums. Continuing conflicts over land and the implementation of the new constitutional amendments made a special session imperative in January, 1884, but the legislators did not adjourn the regular session until several lasting measures for law enforcement and education in Texas had been enacted.

Nine members of the Senate of the Seventeenth Legislature returned to their seats for the Eighteenth: John C. Buchanan, S. Bronson Cooper, William O. Davis, John Y. Gooch, Andrew J. Harris, Augustus W. Houston, Samuel C. Patton, William R. Shannon, and Alexander W. Terrell. This small cadre provided the necessary leadership; Houston served as president pro tempore during the regular session and Cooper during the called session. The remaining twenty-two seats were taken by newcomers, seven of whom had previously served in the House: Frank L. Johnston in the Fourteenth and Sixteenth legislatures; Lochlin J. Farrar in the Fourteenth; Alvah Chesley in the Fifteenth; Norman G. Collins in the Sixteenth; and Avery L. Matlock, John A. Peacock, and John H. Traylor during the Seventeenth. Fifteen senators were legislative neophytes: William A. Evans, James R. Fleming, J. Peter Fowler, William H. Getzendaner, Barnett Gibbs, John Johnson, James W. Jones, E. A. King, Rudolph Kleberg, John Alfred Martin, James S. Perry, George Pfeuffer, William H. Pope, Mansel Y. Randolph, and Asa E. Stratton, Jr. Despite the overall lack of political experience, or perhaps because of it, the Senate of the Eighteenth Legislature earned plaudits for its activism.

Except for one lonely independent, Stratton, the Senate of the Eighteenth Legislature was solidly Democratic; the Republicans and Greenbackers still fielded candidates in many races, but increasingly the Democratic primaries determined election outcomes. The composition of the Senate reflected the flood of immigrants into Texas (only King, Kleberg, and Peacock were native Texans). The state needed these settlers to help replace men lost in the war and to populate the vast empty areas in the west. Most of the new Texans in the Senate had been born in the states of the Confederacy, but seven came from Kentucky and one from Germany; and there were two Yankees, Chesley and Collins. The overwhelming majority were lawyers, with a couple of bankers, merchants, and farmers for leavening. The newcomers tended to hold the values of the societies from which they had come rather than the prewar frontier ethic of Texas. A sea change came over state government; retrenchment and caution replaced the old push to conquer the frontier.

On the second day of the regular session, the senators drew lots to determine the length of their terms following the redistricting which incorporated the results of the 1880 census. The senators drawing four-year terms were Davis, Evans, Farrar, Fowler, Getzendaner, Houston, Johnson, Jones, Kleberg, Peacock, Perry, Pfeuffer, Randolph, Shannon, Stratton, and Traylor. Those drawing two-year terms were Buchanan, Chesley, Collins, Cooper, Fleming, Gibbs, Gooch, Harris, Johnston, King, Martin, Matlock, Patton, Pope, and Terrell.

One of the two Yankees in the Senate, Alvah Chesley was from New Hampshire. Chesley came to Texas in 1859 at the age of twenty-eight and settled in Bellville, where he set up a law practice in June, 1861. Shortly thereafter, he went into the Confederate Army as a private. After serving in the Texas House of Representatives during the Fifteenth Legislature, he ran for the Senate of the Eighteenth as a Democrat and defeated W. M. Burton and John C. Cain, both black Republicans.

Norman G. Collins of Duval County was the other Senate Yankee. He was born in 1829 at New Woodstock, New York, and received his education in that state, choosing dentistry as his profession. When he was a young man he moved to Kentucky and from there to Texas, arriving in Bonham at about the age of twenty-two. He practiced dentistry for a few years but gave it up and became a general merchandiser in San Diego, Duval County. From that occupation he moved "largely and successfully" into the stock business. Livestock raising suited him well, and he amassed a considerable fortune. Collins was elected to the Texas House in the Sixteenth Legislature and was sent to the Senate for the Eighteenth. His wife,

Anna Hoffman, was born in Barringen, Austria, in 1837; she became Mrs. Collins in 1868 and lived in San Diego until she died in 1906. The senator died on November 20, 1899.

Senator William A. Evans of Bonham was one of the immigrants from Kentucky. In 1861 when he was thirty-one and a graduate of Cumberland Law School in Tennessee, he took his young wife and two little sons from Bowling Green, Kentucky, to Texas. They traveled down the Mississippi River, overland to Jefferson, and then north to Bonham, where they built a log home and lived the rest of their lives. Evans was an enrolling officer in the Confederate Army during the war, and at its close he established himself as a lawyer and newspaper editor in Bonham. "Through the years in spite of war, hostile Indians and many hardships, the Evans reared seven children, and, in addition, helped to care for half-brothers, sisters, nieces and nephews who came to visit and after lingered." Evans was presiding justice of Fannin County from 1873 to 1876, and after that was county judge until 1878. His biographer claims that he never had a case reversed on appeal during his whole term of office. His local popularity was such that, even though he was not a candidate, he was elected to the Senate of the Eighteenth Legislature and drew a four-year term by a majority of 6,811 votes. Evans died in 1916, leaving seven children and many friends to mourn him.

Lochlin J. Farrar from Groesbeck in Limestone County was a Georgian by birth who was educated in Atlanta and came to Texas in 1858 when he was twenty-one years old. The youthful immigrant settled in Austin and began to read law with Judge G. W. Paschal, author of *Paschal's Digest*. On January 4, 1859, he was admitted to the bar in Austin. He soon headed north to Limestone County, where he settled in Springfield on February 14. His fledgling law practice, like everything else, was interrupted by the war, which Farrar rushed to join during the early part of 1861. The company he raised in Limestone County disbanded because its members wanted to get into the field as soon as possible, without pesky organizational squabbles. So Farrar entered Parsons' Brigade as a private, rising eventually to major and serving with the brigade until the end of the war. He was mustered out at Hempstead in 1865.

Back in Limestone County, Farrar taught school until 1866, when he was elected district attorney. He acted in this capacity until he was removed from office in 1867 by General Granger as an impediment to Reconstruction. Farrar then pursued the general practice of law until 1874, when he was elected to the House of Representatives of the Fourteenth Legislature. Then he and all the other "impediments" cheerfully began the dismantling of the Republican government of Texas. Major Farrar played an active role in the Senates of the Eighteenth and Nineteenth legislatures.

In addition to practicing law, Major Farrar founded and presided over the First National Bank of Groesbeck. He married Miss Mattie Starley in July, 1869, and they had two children. Farrar died in 1901.

One of seven native Kentuckians in the Senate, James Richard Fleming of Cisco was born in Graves County, Kentucky, on September 10, 1848, but soon moved to Tennessee. Fleming went to school in Tennessee until August 17, 1861, when, only thirteen years old, he "played hooky" to join the Confederate Army under General Nathan Bedford Forrest. He managed to survive the entire war in Forrest's cavalry and was honorably discharged at Gainesville, Alabama, in May, 1865, a combat veteran at the age of seventeen.

Fleming came to Texas in 1867, settling in Columbus, where he studied law and was admitted to the bar on March 16, 1870. He moved on to Comanche in 1874 and in 1875 was elected as the Democratic nominee to the constitutional convention. The following year he was elected judge of the Twelfth Judicial District, a position he held for four years. Fleming resigned the judgeship in 1880 when he moved again, this time to Cisco in Eastland County, where he was elected to the Senate in November, 1882, without opposition.

John Peter Fowler of Bastrop came to Texas in 1854 at age two from Laurens District in South Carolina. The family settled in Travis County, and young John went to school there until 1868, when he entered the law department of Columbia College in Washington, D.C. He graduated with high honors in 1871 and established himself as a lawyer in Bastrop that same year. The next year he found a bride, Miss Cornelia Morgan Maynard, with whom he eventually had seven children. Fowler developed a prosperous practice and was elected mayor of Bastrop in 1864. In 1880 he was chosen county attorney, and in 1882 he was elected senator from the Thirteenth District by a majority of over two thousand votes. He had run as an independent against the regular Democratic nominee but called himself a Democrat and always supported the party ticket, except when his friend G. W. Jones ran for governor.

Fowler also served in the Nineteenth Legislature and was chairman of the Committee on Judicial Districts and the Committee on Enrolled Bills. After his four-year term, he returned to his position as senior partner in the firm of Fowler and Maynard, which had the reputation of being the largest and most lucrative practice in Bastrop County.

Senator William H. Getzendaner was regarded as a founding father of his Texas home city, Waxahachie. He had arrived there in 1859 as a twenty-five-year-old immigrant from Frederick County, Maryland; his people were farmers of Swiss extraction who had been in Frederick County since 1730. When William was nineteen he left the farm to attend Frederick Academy and then went to Dickinson College in Carlisle, Pennsylvania, to complete his education, graduating in 1858. He studied law both in school and in the office of W. J. Ross in Frederick; in late 1858 he moved to Huntsville, Texas. The following year he moved to Waxahachie and, after being admitted to the Texas bar at Tyler, began to practice law. The war interrupted the tranquil progression of his practice. He recruited and organized Company E, 12th Texas Cavalry, for the Confederate Army in 1861; he was a lieutenant in this company but was later assigned to duty as quartermaster of the regiment with the rank of captain. Later still he served as adjutant general of Parsons' Brigade and fought in more than thirty engagements, being wounded twice. He tried to farm for a few years after the war but gave it up and moved back to Waxahachie in 1867, where his fellow townsmen elected him the city's first mayor in 1872. As mayor, he organized the city corporation, drafted the ordinances, and mobilized the infant municipal machinery. After a year of this hard work, his health failed and he resigned the office. Meanwhile, in 1865 he had married Mrs. Willie Neal, the widow of a former state senator; they eventually had two children. On July 1, 1868, Captain Getzendaner, with his law partner J. W. Ferris, founded Waxahachie's first bank under the name "Ferris & Getzendaner, Attorneys-at-Law and Bankers." This bank prospered and later, in 1884, became Citizen's National Bank of Waxahachie, the city's first nationally chartered bank.

Despite being a banker, "a very heavy weight to carry in a popular election," Captain Getzendaner was handily elected after he was persuaded to run for the Texas Senate in 1882, and he drew a four-year term. Captain Getzendaner's biographer states, "partly as a lesson to young men who may read this biography," that when the captain arrived in Waxahachie he had only five dollars and was forty dollars in debt; by 1892 he owned so much property that he was arguably the biggest taxpayer in Ellis County in addition to being the town's most prosperous banker.

Freshman senator Barnett Gibbs of Dallas was at the start of a long and successful career in state government when he came to the legislature in 1883. Born in Yazoo City, Mississippi, on May 19, 1851, Gibbs arrived in Texas in August, 1873. Three years later he married Sallie Haynes, and they had a family of four children. Gibbs had earned a degree from Spring Hill College in Mobile, Alabama, in 1868 and graduated from the University of Virginia two years later. He received his law degree from Cumberland University in Tennessee and moved to Dallas, where he served as city attorney from 1877 to 1883 before taking his seat in the Senate representing Dallas, Kaufman, and Rockwall counties. In 1884 Gibbs was elected lieutenant governor and the following year acted as governor for several months during the absence of Governor Ireland. After his term as lieutenant governor, he retired to private practice. He left the Democrats in 1896 for the Populists but was defeated in his attempts to gain a seat in Congress and to be elected governor of Texas in 1898.

When Gibbs first served as lieutenant governor he was thirty-three years old—the youngest lieutenant governor Texas had ever had as well as the youngest acting governor. He was also at one time the youngest grand master of the Order of Odd Fellows in the state, and he was a member of the Knights of Pythias. His skills as a public speaker were avidly sought, and he was an effective worker in the lobbying effort that resulted in securing funds from Congress for the development of harbors on the Texas coast. Gibbs was a major builder in Dallas and had large landed interests in Texas and New Mexico. He died on October 5, 1904.

Senator John Johnson of McKinney, at sixty-three the oldest member of the Senate, was born in Ashe County, North Carolina,

Barnett Gibbs, lieutenant governor, 1885–86, in Nineteenth Legislature, senator in Eighteenth Legislature. Reproduced from holdings of Texas State Archives.

in 1820; he came to Texas from De Kalb County, Missouri, in 1861 with his wife and family. Johnson's early life is a fascinating tale of triumph over adversity.

John Johnson's father died when he was thirteen, leaving a penniless widow, two daughters, and a younger son six years old, all of whom became John's dependents. They moved to Johnson County, Missouri, where the boy split rails for thirty cents a hundred rails to feed his family. They stayed in Johnson County for five years, then moved to Platte County, where Johnson took a preemption claim, worked it for two years, and sold it for four hundred dollars before moving to Buchanan County. Here he preempted eighty acres, farmed them for eight years, and sold out again—this time for three thousand dollars. He then moved to De Kalb County, purchased another farm, and sold out in 1861 for forty-two thousand dollars. Meanwhile, his mother had died, and he had married Polly Kimsey. Miss Kimsey's father had forbidden the match, not realizing that his daughter's suitor had faced greater obstacles undeterred. Sure enough, the pair eloped on horseback with the bride-to-be wrapped in a quilt. Mrs. Johnson was an educated woman and helped her husband overcome his lack of formal schooling.

Johnson had become a slaveholder, and when Missouri opted against secession, he decided to come to Texas and settled in McKinney. He left behind in Missouri not only his newly built home but also a political career, having represented De Kalb County in the Missouri Legislature in 1856. When he reached McKinney he purchased two hundred acres four miles east of town. He farmed, raised stock, and drove cattle to Missouri, becoming one of the wealthiest men in the county.

Johnson was a member of the Constitutional Convention of 1875, and in 1882 he was elected to the Senate of the Eighteenth Legislature by a large majority. His Senate service was distinguished by his zeal in supporting farming interests, and he was chairman of the Senate Committee on Agriculture during the Nineteenth Legislature. He had an enviable record. He was responsible for collection of the revenue from thirty-five million acres of land on which taxes had not been paid for thirty years; he successfully defended his homestead bill against John H. Reagan, preventing the encumbrance of a homestead by mortgage or any other means; he stood for legislative control of railroad rates; and he strove for a constitutional prohibition against interest rates higher than 12 percent. Senator Johnson was known as "Rutabaga" and was recognized for his "blunt, honest speech, straightforward ways and primitive simplicity of dress and manner." He was a Democrat, a member of the Primitive Baptist Church, a prominent Mason, and a member of the Grange. A contemporary description of the personnel of the state government calls him "advanced in years, but . . . a doughty and staunch old warrior whose blows fall right and left in the interest of people with telling effect."

Frank L. Johnston from Buena Vista in Shelby County was born in Madison County, Mississippi, on October 1, 1840, and came to Texas four years later, when his family settled in Shelby County. On February 5, 1862, he enlisted as a private in the 11th Texas Infantry under Colonel O. M. Roberts (Randall's Brigade, Walker's Division) and served until the end of the war. He returned to the comparative peace of Shelby County and began to practice law in 1866. Johnston was elected to the House of Representatives of the Fourteenth and Sixteenth legislatures. In 1882 he was elected to the Senate of the Eighteenth Legislature as a Democrat and served a two-year term.

Senator James Warren Jones of Harris County was born in Tennessee in 1844. He was a thirty-nine-year-old Houston lawyer when elected from the Ninth Senatorial District to the Texas Senate for the Eighteenth Legislature. Jones had a strong record in the upper house. He was chairman of the Committee on Penitentiaries and a member of the committees on the Judiciary, Education, Internal Improvements, Finance, the Treasurer's and Comptroller's Offices, the Rules, and Commerce and Manufactures during the Nineteenth Legislature.

One of the few native Texans in the Senate, E. A. King from Pittsburg in Camp County was listed as "merchant" in Will Lambert's *Pocket Directory of the Eighteenth Legislature of Texas*, but it seems that he was in fact another lawyer on a Senate roster teeming with lawyers. Senator King was born on March 17, 1851, in Cass County but grew up in Hunt County, where his parents moved in 1856. He was schooled at the Odd Fellows' College of Greenville and read law with Judge J. F. Bohanan of Pittsburg. Admitted to the bar in Upshur County in 1874, he began to practice in Pittsburg and was elected county attorney of Camp County in 1876. In 1882 he married Laura Towns of Titus County. He was elected to the Senate that same year and served a two-year term. When Pittsburg was incorporated in 1891, E. A. King was the city's first mayor, and he was also prominent as the owner of the town's second bank.

Rudolph Kleberg, the first native Texan of German descent to be elected to the Texas Senate, was born in Austin County in 1847 and moved along with his family to Cuero in DeWitt County in 1848. His father had come from Germany and had fought in the Texas Revolution; in 1886 he was said to be a crusty old Texian veteran eighty-six years of age. In 1864 Rudolph left his father's farm to join General Tom Green's Brigade in Louisiana. When the war was over, he completed his general education and studied law; he was admitted to the bar in 1872 at San Antonio and went back to Cuero to practice. In 1873 he established the first newspaper in DeWitt County, the *Cuero Star*. This was during Radical rule in Texas, when the Sutton-Taylor feud was raging in DeWitt County; the civil authorities were powerless as men were murdered daily. Kleberg's paper ran bold articles about this lawlessness and by exposing the perpetrators did much to restore peace. For a time he "carried his life in his hand," but he was never discouraged from printing what he thought was right and gained a strong reputation for bravery and ability. He was elected county attorney of DeWitt County in 1876 and again in 1878. In 1882, he was elected to the Texas Senate, where he made a fine record during his terms in the Eighteenth and Nineteenth legislatures. Kleberg resigned before the end of his term. He was appointed U.S. attorney for the Western District of Texas by President Cleveland and served in that office from 1885 until 1896, when he was elected to the U.S. Congress, serving there until 1903. After his congressional service, he came back to Cuero and resumed his law practice. In 1905 he received an appointment as official reporter for the Court of Criminal Appeals in Austin and held that position until his death on December 28, 1924. His widow, the former Mathilde Eckhardt, and five children survived him.

Senator John Alfred Martin was born in Charleston, South Carolina, on May 31, 1846, and was raised and educated in that city. In the spring of 1864 he joined the Confederate Army as a private and served until the end of the war. After the war he attended Charleston College, where he graduated with first honors in 1869. He set out for Texas that same year and taught school at Nelsonville in Austin County until the spring of 1870. He then moved to Waco and took a job as assistant engineer for the Waco Tap Railroad; he located the line from Marlin to Waco and was appointed engineer of construction. The following year, Martin moved to Marlin and began to read law under Judge L. W. Goodrich, and he would serve four years as deputy surveyor for Falls County. In 1873 he was admitted to the bar and began his successful practice of law. He was elected to the Senate of the Eighteenth Legislature and served a four-year term but declined to run for reelection in 1886 and went back to his law practice and other business pursuits. He was active in real estate, founded the Falls County Fair Association, and served as president of the Marlin Oil Company and as a director of the First National Bank of Marlin. Martin married Miss Alla Slater of Alabama on May 5, 1874, and they had six children. He was a devout Presbyterian and a member of the Masons.

Avery L. Matlock of Montague was born on April 22, 1852, in Tennessee, where he attended Ewing and Jefferson College and graduated in the class of 1870; he went on to law school in Lebanon, Tennessee, graduating and gaining admission to the bar in 1872. He set up practice in Loudon, Tennessee, but a year later moved to Montague, Texas, where he soon made a name for himself as an able lawyer. He served as county attorney for Montague County from 1875 to 1878. As county attorney he received credit for convicting "some of the worst criminals that have infested the State." In 1880 he was elected to the Texas House of Representatives, where he was chairman of the Land Committee. He was elected to the Senate in 1882 and drew a two-year term. During his legislative service he authored the bill prohibiting fence cutting and also the legislation which repealed the law granting to the railroads sixteen sections of land per mile of track laid. Matlock resigned from the Senate on September 24, 1884. Later that year he was one of the electors from Texas when Grover Cleveland was elected president, and he was chairman of the Clark faction in the Clark-Hogg gubernatorial campaign of 1892. In 1890 he moved from Montague to Fort Worth, and in 1906 he moved again, this time to San Antonio, where he continued the practice of law.

One of three native Texans in the Senate, John Atlas Peacock was born on November 23, 1845, in Titus County. Peacock was educated in private schools and first appears in public service as alderman of Daingerfield in 1870. He was elected justice of the peace, assessor of taxes, and county commissioner, respectively, before his election as county judge of Morris County after that county was organized in 1875. He was elected county attorney in 1876 and again in 1878 but resigned in 1879 to serve in the House of Representatives of the Seventeenth Legislature. He had won his seat as a Democrat in a four-way race against two Greenbackers and one independent Democrat. His senatorial race in 1882 was less dramatic; he defeated the independent candidate, James H. Culberson, for a four-year term. Senator Peacock later moved to Fort Worth, where he was a prominent member of the local bar association.

James Samuel Perry of Rockdale was born in Scott County, Kentucky, September 5, 1835, but spent nine of the next eighteen years in Lafayette County, Missouri, before he and his parents moved to Travis County, Texas, in 1853. They moved again in 1858 to Independence in Washington County. James attended Baylor University from 1858 until 1861, when, like most of his compatriots, he joined the Confederate Army, enlisting in Company F, 10th Texas Infantry, known as Nelson's Regiment. He was taken prisoner along with his brigade at the fall of Arkansas Post in 1863 but was later exchanged. He was with Generals Braxton Bragg and then J. E. Johnston and John Bell Hood in the Chattanooga and Georgia campaigns until Atlanta, when in the second day's fight under Hood he was wounded and lost the thumb and two fingers of his left hand. Thus disabled, he was placed in the detective service until the end of the war. After he returned to Texas, he read law, was admitted to the bar in 1866 at Brenham, and set up practice in Millican and Bryan. He was elected county judge of Brazos County in 1866 but was removed in 1867 as an impediment to Reconstruction and went back to practicing law until 1872. In that year he moved to Cameron in Milam County, where he was elected county judge; in 1874 he moved to Rockdale, where he became interested in banking as well as law. He was elected to the Senate in 1882 as a Democrat, defeating an independent Greenbacker and a Republican, and drew a four-year term. After serving in the Eighteenth and Nineteenth legislatures, Perry returned to Rockdale, where he was president of the Rockdale Cotton Oil Mills, a promoter of water works and electricity, a farmer, a stockman, a banker, and mayor. He had married Miss Annie Hubert of Bryan in 1869 and they had five children.

George Pfeuffer of New Braunfels had come to Texas at the age of fifteen, along with his parents and five siblings, from Obernbreit in the Kingdom of Bavaria, where he was born on October 17, 1830. The family reached Galveston without event, but when they embarked for Indianola they were shipwrecked and lost nearly all their possessions. They nonetheless managed to get to New Braunfels and the father was able to buy some land there. George went to work as a clerk in John F. Torrey's store in New Braunfels, and when the Mexican War came along he moved to Corpus Christi. He met and married Susan Gravis in Corpus Christi in 1855 and lived in that city until the outbreak of the Civil War led him to take his wife and their several small children to the relative safety of New Braunfels. He joined the firm of William Mann & Company in San Antonio, but the business lost heavily because of the depreciation of Confederate money, and he sold out to start over again. Back in New Braunfels, he and his brother opened a very profitable merchandising business, and he bought property, made investments, and so broadened his business interests that he became owner of a sawmill in Northeast Texas. He established lumberyards along the International and Great Northern Railroad and made a fortune, even extending his interests into Mexico.

In 1877 Pfeuffer was appointed county judge of Comal County to fill an unexpired term, and he was unanimously elected to the office in 1880. The county judge was ex officio the superintendent of the public schools, and Pfeuffer, himself the beneficiary of excellent schooling before he left Germany, set out to build up the county's schools. He found good teachers for each school, lengthened the school year to include all twelve months, and became known as "the Sage of Comal." In 1880 Governor Oran Roberts appointed him a director of the Agricultural and Mechanical College of Texas and he discovered his life's work. Pfeuffer believed ardently in the mission of the college and realized that substantial state support was essential to its operation. When he got to the Senate in 1883, he began at once to advocate placing the college on an equal basis with other educational institutions. Early in the session he raised a storm of protest when he introduced a bill to entitle the college to a portion of the school fund. Pfeuffer was accused of being the enemy of education and of trying to destroy the state university, and university students threatened to hang him in effigy. The senator endured all sorts of vilification until the final day of the session, when he answered his critics in a speech that lasted more than an hour and taught his opponents a few things about vitriolic language. Senator Pfeuffer accomplished his aim; the Agricultural and Mechanical College of Texas received state aid, which put it on a strong financial foundation, and the success of Texas A&M University is due in large part to his efforts. Pfeuffer served as chairman of the Senate Committee on Finance in the Eighteenth Legislature and as chairman of the Committee on Education in the Nineteenth but lost the Democratic nomination for the state senatorial race in 1886 and died of apoplexy in Austin on September 15 of that year.

When William Henry Pope of Marshall was sworn in as senator from the Third District, it was the beginning of a ten-year career in the Senate. Senator Pope was born February 15, 1847, in Wilkes County, Georgia, and came to Texas along with his family in 1858. The family settled in Marshall, where young William studied at Marshall University. The institution was in fact not a college but a secondary school. Pope enlisted in the Confederate Army in 1863 and served with Terry's Scouts and Wharton's Cavalry until the end of the war, after which he studied law at the University of Virginia. Back home in Marshall, he read law with his father and, after being admitted to the bar in 1868, began his thirty-year active practice of law in Marshall. He was elected county and district attorney from 1870 to 1879. In 1872 he married Fannie Stedman. Pope was a popular orator and enjoyed an excellent reputation as a lawyer. His years in the legislature were spent in the active presentation of Texas' claim against the United States for frontier services rendered by the Texas Rangers. Governor Sul Ross appointed him agent for the collection of frontier claims, and he spent four years in Washington, D.C., in pursuit of the money. His efforts resulted in the recognition and payment of $1.5 million of the claims. Pope was appointed to a railroad receivership which entailed his moving to Beaumont, where he was elected judge of the Fifty-eighth Judicial District in 1902 and again in 1906 and 1910. He died in Waco on February 15, 1913, and was buried in Marshall.

Mansel Yules Randolph of Madisonville was born in Jefferson County, Alabama, June 6, 1848, and came to Texas two years later. His family settled at Huntsville, where he was educated and where he graduated from Austin College. In 1870 Randolph began to practice law and was elected city attorney of Huntsville the same year. He moved to Madisonville the following year and set up his practice there. He was asked to run for the Senate several times but did not accept until 1882. He was elected over a Republican by a majority of 6,150 votes and served a four-year term. During the Nineteenth Legislature he chaired the Committee on State Affairs. Randolph was a member of the Methodist Episcopal Church, South, and the International Order of Odd Fellows.

Asa E. Stratton, Jr., of Brazoria was the only non-Democrat in the Senate. He had run as an independent against M. S. Munson, a Democrat from Brazoria County, and drew a four-year term but resigned following the called session of the Eighteenth Legislature. Senator Stratton was born in Panola County, Mississippi, January 13, 1844, and came to Texas with his father, Major A. E. Stratton, on a visit when he was fifteen years old. His father left him at Soule University in Washington County and brought the rest of the family from Mississippi the next year, settling in Brazoria County in 1861.

Young Asa enlisted in the Confederate Army in Colonel Joseph Bates's Regiment, serving in Texas and Louisiana; later he was orderly sergeant of Company G and sergeant major of Brown's Regiment. After the war Stratton returned to South Texas, read law in Matagorda, and got his law license in 1869. He served as county surveyor, county attorney, and county judge of Brazoria County before he was elected to the Senate in 1882.

John H. Traylor of Granbury was one of two former Virginians in the Senate of the Eighteenth Legislature. He was born in Traylorsville, Virginia, on March 27, 1839, but was raised and educated in Troup County, Georgia, so that when he joined the Confederate Army, it was in the 4th Georgia Regiment, Company B, that he enlisted. His regiment served in the Army of Northern Virginia throughout the war, and Traylor was engaged in most of the bloodiest battles of the conflict; he was wounded at Warrenton, Spotsylvania Courthouse, and Chancellorsville, where his only brother was killed and where he was within a few yards of Stonewall Jackson when the general received his fatal wound. Later he was appointed quartermaster of ordnance of General Early's corps.

Traylor came to Texas in 1867 and settled in Jefferson, where he tried his hand at merchandising and in 1869 married Miss Pauline Lockett. Four years later the couple moved to Granbury in Hood County, where John located and sold lands until 1875. This was not so tame a pursuit as it might seem: the thousands of acres he surveyed in Hood, Parker, Palo Pinto, and other counties farther west were subject to raids by Comanche and Kiowa horse-rustling bands, and surveyors went armed and slept lightly. Traylor was elected sheriff and tax collector of Hood County in February, 1876, and was reelected in November, 1878. He served in the House of Representatives of the Seventeenth Legislature, where he was said to have introduced and seen through to passage more bills than any other member but one. In the next election he was chosen senator for the Thirtieth District by a large majority. During his service in the Senate of the Eighteenth Legislature his knowledge of surveying and land laws was useful in the settlement of the problems of sale, lease, and disposition of state lands. Senator Traylor was also active in opposing the leasing of convicts by the state, proposed solutions to the fence-cutting problems which the special session attempted to address, and served on the conference committee that reported out the fence war legislation that passed. During the Nineteenth Legislature he was chairman of the Senate Committee on Finance and served on the committees on Public Lands, Public Debt, Penitentiaries, Internal Improvements, Constitutional Amendments, Frontier Protection, and Enrolled Bills. In 1887 Traylor moved to Dallas, where he was a successful businessman and was elected mayor in 1898. He died in San Antonio on March 19, 1925, at the age of eighty-six.

The Senate of the Eighteenth Legislature, conscious of the need for economy, elected only a bare-bones roster of officers and clerks: William N. Ramey, secretary; C. M. Boynton, first assistant secretary; W. M. Hunter, second assistant secretary; John H. Kerby, calendar clerk; Fergus Kyle, sergeant-at-arms; A. A. Burck, assistant sergeant-at-arms; A. M. Belvin, engrossing clerk; J. E. Kaufman, enrolling clerk; and R. K. Smoot, chaplain. William "Old Bill" Fitzhugh, who listed his regular occupation as "bee hunter," served as doorkeeper during the regular session but died at the age of sixty-five after the regular session adjourned. The loss of Fitzhugh was a sad occasion for the Senate. An unusually distinguished officer, he not only had served as the doorkeeper for the Constitutional Convention of 1875 and for the Senate for nearly a decade, but also was a veteran of the Seminole War in Florida, the Mormon War in Missouri, the Mexican War, several campaigns against the Indians as a captain in the Texas Rangers, and the Civil War as a colonel in the Confederate Army. The senators took time from debate to draft several resolutions in honor of this stalwart old warrior. Fitzhugh was succeeded by W. A. Squires for the called session.

Debate over land sales began as soon as the Senate convened. Lieutenant Governor Leonidas J. Storey delivered a brief address to the Senate on the first day of the session before surrendering the office to Francis M. Martin, who had been a senator in the Eighth, Sixteenth, and Seventeenth legislatures. The focus of Storey's speech was a request to halt the sale of public lands and to institute a system of leases instead. An act approved on January 22 rescinded the law of July 14, 1879, which had provided for the sale of the unappropriated public domain at fifty cents an acre. These lands were not returned to the public domain—they remained set apart pending a final disposition by the legislature—but this measure effectively halted the sale of immense blocks of public land. On February 3, 1886, Governor Ireland signed a bill introduced by Senator Pfeuffer that suspended sales of all school, university, and asylum land, which had been made available for sale for one and two dollars an acre.

Most of the public land was later sold at auction for minimum prices of from one to three dollars an acre. An act approved on April 12, 1883, provided for the creation of a State Land Board, which consisted of the governor, comptroller, treasurer, attorney general, and commissioner of the General Land Office. This board classified the remaining public tracts into categories according to their timber resources and the availability of water, then offered them for sale at prices ranging from two to five dollars. Settlers resident on a parcel since before January 1, 1883, were given six months in which to file for buying no less than 160 acres nor more than 640 acres for a homesite. After the land was placed on the market by the board to be sold at public auction, sales were limited to one section

Francis Marion Martin, lieutenant governor, 1883–85, in Eighteenth Legislature, senator in Eighth, Sixteenth, and Seventeenth legislatures. Reproduced from holdings of Texas State Archives.

of watered land or seven sections of unwatered land. Land for agriculture would be sold only to actual settlers; no person could buy more than three sections within five miles of the geographical center of a county, and no corporation could buy more than one section in any one county. A separate act approved on April 14, 1883, reserved all mineral rights for the benefit of the funds for which the land was designated, and a constitutional amendment approved in August, 1883, provided for the investment of revenue derived from the sale of school lands and vested all rights in school lands in the respective county governments, which would dispose of any income generated by their sale or lease.

Much of the legislation restricting land sales reflected public disaffection with corporate speculation and corruption, but not a few innocent homesteaders were the real losers in the rush to conserve public lands. For instance, the act of April 9, 1881, which granted 1,280 acres to disabled Confederate veterans or their unmarried widows was repealed on February 2, 1883, due to the "exhaustion" of the vacant public domain. The repeal bill, which had been introduced by Senator Davis, became law without Governor Ireland's signature. A second Land Board to investigate alleged land frauds and instigate suits on behalf of the state was established through a bill that originated in Senate Judiciary Committee Number 1, chaired by Terrell. The three appointed commissioners, who served along with the governor and the comptroller as ex officio board members, were also to investigate the operations of the General Land Office and report any improprieties to the attorney general.

Because Ireland urged more consistent enforcement of criminal laws and pledged to follow a less liberal policy on pardons than had Roberts, immediate action had to be taken to provide for an increase in the state penitentiary capacity. In November, 1882, five-year leases had been signed with private contractors who could exercise nearly exclusive control over the convicts; the leases required the approval of the Senate before final enactment, but the contractors' lobby was powerful and—though he remained officially silent on the issue—Ireland was known to favor ratifying the contracts. A bill introduced by Senator Fleming to provide for enlarging the penitentiaries so that prisoners would only be employed within their walls was reported adversely from the Senate Committee on Penitentiaries, chaired by Johnston, and it appeared a foregone conclusion that the leases would be ratified despite general public opposition.

A number of incidents combined to reverse the initial support for the prison contractors in the Senate. Fleming, Jones, Kleberg, and Pfeuffer submitted a strong dissent to Johnston's majority report. They declared that it was "utterly inconsistent with the genius of our institutions and government" that the "unfortunate criminals of the country, should be continually paraded before the public and employed with the laboring classes of the country in their daily work"; that the Democratic party had pledged to employ all convicts within prison walls, but the present accommodations afforded "not even a pretext for the redemption of this pledge"; and that the employment of convicts posed unfair competition for free labor and prevented "redemption and reformation of the offender." They argued that if the prison expansion bill did not pass the existing penal laws should be amended to prevent the "parodic farce" of sentencing offenders to "hard labor in the State penitentiary" when a judge should instead say "hard labor in convict camps and on Brazos bottom farms." In a separate address, Terrell endorsed their stand and added that prison reform was necessary to protect the general populace: between 1849 and 1870 only 75 convicts had escaped from state prison; but 2,034 slipped their bonds between 1873 and 1882 under the lease system.

The turning point came when *Texas Siftings*, an Austin news magazine, reported that lobbyists for the prison contractors had paid legislators to vote in favor of their clients. Senators Johnston and Pope served on a joint committee that investigated the charges of bribery and visited the state penitentiaries at Huntsville and Rusk, where they found the prisoners idle, and an outlying camp, whose conditions appalled them. If the committee report was not enough to sway the legislators, the revelation that the state's share of the profits from convict labor would decrease under the new contracts, while the contractors' share would increase substantially, undermined support for prison contracting, and the Senate refused to ratify the leases for convict labor.

The Penitentiary Board was reorganized through a bill signed on April 18, 1883. Henceforth, the board would consist of the governor and two commissioners of state penitentiaries appointed by the governor with the advice and consent of the Senate; the commissioners would serve for two years. The act clearly stated that "no lease of the penitentiaries, or either of them, shall henceforth be made, and the State shall resume control thereof." The employment of convicts would be controlled by the board. Convicts could not be engaged in "mechanical labor" outside the prison but could work within the walls either for the state or for private operators to whom the state leased shops; they could not be employed on public works other than the construction of reformatories or other prisons but could be hired out in gangs to railroad construction foremen. The Huntsville textile industries, however, were not successful, and the iron foundry at Rusk proved to be a white elephant. The act did provide for the purchase of a prison farm, which became the mainstay of the convict labor system after everything else had failed.

Many of the county jails, as well as the two state prisons, were crowded with persons who suffered from mental illness. These people were not criminally insane, but the asylum at Austin was overcrowded and there was nowhere else to put them. A House bill to establish a branch of the State Lunatic Asylum in North Texas was endorsed by the Senate and signed by Ireland on February 16, 1883. The act provided for an appointed board of three commissioners to select a site and appropriated two hundred thousand dollars for its purchase. The branch opened at Terrell in 1885; like the Lunatic Asylum, Blind Asylum, and Deaf and Dumb Asylum in Austin, it operated under the supervision of a five-member board of managers appointed by the governor under reorganization acts approved by the Eighteenth Legislature in 1883.

Support for public education in Texas was the subject of several proposed amendments to the state constitution that were debated by the Senate. The delinquent school poll taxes in 1882 amounted to over ninety-two thousand dollars, a substantial sum. A joint resolution introduced by Senator Terrell would have required the payment of a poll tax before one could vote, but it was reported unfavorably by the Senate Committee on Constitutional Amendments. Seven members (Terrell, Fleming, Johnston, Peacock, Pfeuffer, Stratton, and Gibbs, who chaired the committee) protested the adverse majority report, pointing out—to no avail—that their amendment discarded existing property qualifications in favor of a small poll tax that everyone could pay. A majority of the legislators preferred to continue support for public education through ad valorem taxes, which ideally would distribute the financial burden on the basis of ability to pay. Texas voters endorsed this method by approving two constitutional amendments in a referendum held in August, 1883.

On January 8, 1884, Governor Ireland convened a called session to consider many pressing issues. First among the topics at hand was support for public schools under the constitutional amendments, which proposed to provide for both education and a reduction of state property taxes in line with Ireland's recommendation after reduction of the state debt had made it feasible to cut taxes.

During the called session, the legislature passed a pair of education bills, introduced by Senators Buchanan and Pfeuffer, which became law without Ireland's signature. The acts revised the existing public education system by providing for an elected state superintendent of instruction who exercised limited supervisory power over public schools, which were placed under the immediate supervision of the county judges. Furthermore, the new law required all teachers, except those who had graduated from normal schools in Texas, to have certificates issued by a board of examiners appointed by the county judge, who also was to institute a system of registers and reports. Schools were to be open seven hours a day, five days a week, for not less than twenty days per month, exclusive of certain holidays, during five months of every year.

The weakest aspects of Buchanan's and Pfeuffer's bills were the provisions dealing with funding. All but fifty-three sparsely populated counties were subdivided into school districts that had the privilege of voting on a local ad valorem tax of up to 0.20 percent to fund their schools as well as electing three trustees. Further provisions from the constitutional amendments were incorporated, setting aside for the schools one-fourth of the state revenue from occupation taxes, all of the revenue from a one-dollar poll tax on all males aged twenty-one to sixty years, and proceeds from a state ad valorem tax of as much as 0.20 percent in addition to that levied through local referendums. Terrell and Johnson opposed the amendment to permit state levies of up to 0.20 percent, arguing that the figure was extravagant. Their view prevailed, and the state ad valorem rate for public education approved by the Eighteenth Legislature was 0.12 percent.

The new law shifted responsibility for public education from the state as a whole to local communities. Proceeds from land sales did ensure some measure of state support for schools, but it was not enough. Higher education suffered disproportionately from the dearth of financial support. Legislative parsimony prevented passage of several bills to establish more normal schools for the education of Texas teachers. To salve their consciences for their neglect of education, in lieu of cash the legislators provided the schools with an abundance of land: Ireland signed a House bill setting aside a million acres for an endowment for the University of Texas and another million for public schools in the state. These tracts proved to be unsalable and returned little or no money initially to either the university or the public schools.

The Eighteenth Legislature did repay part of the state's debt to the public education coffers, emptied during the Civil War to pay for military expenditures. On February 23, 1883, Ireland signed a bill introduced by Senator Davis appropriating $256,273 to redeem the state's debt to the university fund and another $582,074 to replenish the common school fund. Again, this was only enough to reassure legislators that they had done their part for education, when in fact the labors of the Eighteenth Legislature would not bear fruit for the university until the 1920s, when oil was discovered under its barren West Texas tracts. The continued influx of immigrants and the reluctance of voters to approve local taxes unfortunately ensured that education at all levels remained limited in poor communities and in many cases advanced only sporadically in larger towns and cities.

The question of race also impeded improvement of education in Texas. Under the new laws, separate schools were to be provided for the "white and colored children," but "impartial provision" was to be made for each. The board of three trustees to be elected in every school district was to be duplicated wherever a colored school was established: three whites for a white school, three coloreds for a colored school. "Colored" was redefined to include anyone with as little as one-eighth Negro blood. All children aged eight to sixteen years regardless of race were entitled to the "benefit of the public school fund," but public school funds would be withheld from schools where both races attended together. A vital provision in the act hedged on equal division of the public school fund, declaring that the "colored children shall receive the benefit as far as practicable of the public school fund," and this provided a loophole for a growing disparity in public school facilities. The branch of the University of Texas for black students mentioned in several acts that were passed during this period was never built.

The unsold school lands, as well as the rest of the public domain in Texas, need not have been a problem, because the new laws restricting their sale also made them available for lease on a competitive basis. The 300 leagues of public land set aside for schools on March 16, 1882, was increased to 325 leagues through an act introduced by Senator Fleming and signed by Ireland on April 7, 1883. This land was opened for lease at five cents an acre yearly through an act introduced during both the regular and called sessions by Senator Gibbs and approved on February 6, 1884. Individuals could lease as large a parcel as they wished for a term of from five to seven years, but land was not to be leased to corporations. Senator Fleming protested the fact that no limit was placed on the amount that could be leased, insisting that a few cattlemen would soon dominate the state, deflecting the "tide of population" from Texas to other states and depreciating the worth of public lands. Fleming's counterproposal to lease or sell land in parcels no larger than 640 acres, and only to settlers who would live on the land for three years before transferring ownership, was ignored by the Senate, to its later chagrin.

The new laws for leasing large parcels encouraged the development of huge ranches, enclosed by a new invention that was just gaining popularity—barbed wire. "Bob war" had been introduced into Texas in 1875, and its use spread quickly. During the early 1880s wealthy cattlemen began enclosing thousands of acres that they owned or "intended" to purchase or lease. Left out were those who could not afford to make even a pretense of buying or leasing land: "landless gentry" who owned large herds but no land and smallholders who had some land but not enough for all their livestock. By 1883 the fencing of the whole state was almost an accomplished fact, and the stage was set for a clash of colossal proportions.

A drought during the summer of 1883 sparked one of those peculiarly Texan violent problem-solving episodes known as the "fence-cutting wars," as stock owners discovered that many watering holes had been enclosed by fences. Other contributing factors were the continuing quest for free grass and open range and the hatred of corporatism of which the large enclosed areas were a symbol. Conversely, fence cutting was pejoratively attributed to communistic influences. On a more practical note, fences impeded travel—one drift fence in the Panhandle was 127 miles long. When no gate was available, such fences were often cut. In 1883 fence cutting erupted into open warfare, as fences were cut in more than half the counties in the state. Some people were killed in the disputes, and Texas gained a reputation for lawlessness. Property depreciated, immigration declined, and a business depression ensued as capital shied away. Ireland made a personal tour of some of the more turbulent counties, and the called session was inundated with petitions from both sides.

Dozens of bills were introduced, ranging from making the shooting of a fence cutter a justifiable homicide to strict herd laws for the state. Terrell, who introduced a moderate compromise on the first day of the called session, estimated that if the more than thirty million acres of school land that remained unsold were leased for as little as four cents an acre annually, $1.2 million would be raised to support education. The senator declared that the state policy of "free grass" benefited "favored classes" whose selfish use of public lands provoked "acts of lawlessness in the indiscriminate destruction of fences"; on the other hand, "free grass" also encouraged a "spirit of communism destructive of property rights." Terrell's bill provided for smallholders, exempting from penalty those who turned loose for grazing no more than twenty-five head, but it also restricted large ranchers by requiring them to own or lease ten acres for every head of livestock they turned loose to graze. Ranchers were also prohibited from grazing stock on private property, from fencing public land without paying an annual fee of four cents an acre, and from enclosing public water. Ten "commissioners of pasturage" were to be employed to police public lands with the aid of a new patrol force, and the governor could invoke martial law if necessary to enforce these provisions. Penalties for improperly grazing livestock included a fine of up to $500 and two years in jail—the same as that for damaging a fence—plus a dollar a head for having more than one hundred loose livestock over the permitted limit.

The Terrell bill was approved by a majority of the Senate Committee on Stock and Stockraising (Collins, Kleberg, Matlock, and Traylor), but Fleming, Houston, and Shannon protested that the bill would create a "landed aristocricy [*sic*]" and would provide further inducements for the "war now carried on against property rights in Texas." They claimed that by protecting grass on private property the bill encouraged land speculators to purchase more property, which could then be leased or sold more profitably, because public and private lands would no longer be open for grazing. Since crops had to be fenced from trespass, they argued that grass also should be enclosed or be free for the taking. They did not believe that a distinction should be drawn between private and public lands for purposes of grazing restrictions; the poor man would still be the loser. The minority also portrayed the provisions for the commissioners as "dictatorial powers" and said they would be enforced through "military despotism."

The protests against Terrell's bill prevented its passage, but the principle of "free grass" did not remain inviolate. Two House bills mandating stiff penalties for fencing or allowing livestock to graze on public land or on private land other than one's own were passed after long debate and approved by Ireland on February 7, 1884. The voting in the Senate was close. Although Shannon voted in favor, Houston and Fleming remained steadfast in their opposition, and Kleberg, Matlock, and Collins, along with six others, joined them. The new law designated fines for illegal enclosure ranging up to a dollar an acre monthly until the offending fence was removed or a prison term of up to two years in the county jail. Half of the fines collected would be awarded to the person who informed on the trespasser. Those who already had fences in place had just six months in which to obtain a lease or written permission from the owner whose land they had enclosed; those who allowed their stock to roam freely on public lands could be fined up to one hundred dollars a section for each year that they did so. A House bill signed on April 11, 1883, aided in the enforcement of the last provision, requiring that all cattle and horses be branded with a distinctive "county brand," in addition to private brands, to help in the identification of strays.

No exception was made for the smallholder. In fact, while illegal enclosure remained a misdemeanor, fence cutting was made a felony and penalties were increased to a maximum of five years in prison through an act introduced by Senator Jones and signed on February 6, 1884. The next day, Ireland approved a bill introduced by Senator Shannon providing for prison terms of up to five years for anyone burning grass on public or private land not his own. The original bill had condemned the burning of grass as a "wide spread communistic raid against property in the form of fencing and pasture," but this language was deleted in its final form. A final measure on the subject of fencing was successfully proposed by Senator Gibbs. It required that an unlocked gate be installed for every three miles of fence. Fines could be as much as two hundred dollars a day until a gate was built.

Although many thousands of acres were enclosed, without effective laws to enforce the collection of leases, such as that proposed by Terrell, the state received little money. Efforts to achieve competitive bidding on state-owned ranch leases continued throughout the 1880s. But the primary result was a three-way quarrel among the governor, the land board created by the Eighteenth Legislature to regulate land sales, and the ranchers. Suits to force the latter to pay leases and to abandon land held illegally were of little use; most of the cases were tried before "West Texas cowboy juries" controlled by the ranchers themselves. The laws passed during the called session quickly ended the fence-cutting wars but did little to relieve the plight of the small herder.

One undeniable benefit of the fencing laws was an improvement in public roads through the removal of obstructing wires. Roads and other public works were also the beneficiaries of more direct action. Although the Eighteenth Legislature did not set aside funds for roadways, it did expand the authority of county commissioners to contract for public works and authorized additional local bond issues. The situation was similar for Texas' waterways. No state funds were appropriated for their improvement, but a bill signed on April 7, 1883, permitted municipal authorities in towns along the coast to use funds raised through previous bond issues, originally sold for other purposes, to improve harbors. A joint resolution introduced by Senator Cooper during the called session urged the Texas congressional delegation to secure federal funds to dredge Sabine Pass, and another joint resolution originating in the House requested federal aid to improve Galveston harbor according to a plan proposed by James B. Eads. Finally, railroads became the responsibility of the state engineer, an appointive office re-created through a bill signed on April 10, 1883. The state engineer would inspect tracks, rolling stock, and all facilities affecting the "safety and proper accomodation [*sic*] of the public" and was responsible for compiling information on freight and passenger rates. Companies guilty of discrimination in rates could be fined as much as five hundred dollars for each offense, in addition to damages.

The Eighteenth Legislature did find the money to facilitate enforcement of new laws for quarantine against contagious disease, primarily the dreaded "Yellow Jack," or yellow fever, which had ravaged Brownsville in 1882. Among the expenditures was the purchase of a steam tugboat to patrol the coast. During the debate over the appropriations bill that funded the tug, Senator Gibbs proposed a sarcastic amendment that "between epidemics" the boat was to be at the service of state officials "for fishing excursions, on invitation of the Senator from Galveston district," but Gibbs was ruled out of order. On a more serious note, strict penalties were provided for those who violated quarantine laws: up to five years in prison. Pfeuffer's bill to provide for a quarantine against the spread of smallpox, however, did not pass the Senate, as the general reorganization of the quarantine statutes was thought to be sufficient. Senator Collins introduced a joint resolution that was approved on April 14, 1883, asking the Texas delegation in Congress to secure federal intervention to persuade Mexico to cooperate in the quarantine. On another issue, following submission of a petition from the State Medical Association, the duties of the state health officer were expanded to include enforcement of new statutes against the adulteration of food and drugs or the sale of such substances. Each offense could incur a fine of up to five hundred dollars.

Before adjourning, the Eighteenth Legislature had to tie up a lot of loose ends left from other sessions. Claims for expenses incurred by Texas in border defense had never been paid by the federal government. Following an act of Congress inviting the submission of petitions, a board consisting of Governor Ireland, the comptroller, and the adjutant general was to present Texas' case. Later, Senator Pope was appointed by Governor Lawrence S. Ross to lobby Congress, and he eventually succeeded in having about $1.5 million in claims recognized and paid. The legislature also endorsed a joint resolution introduced by Senator Stratton urging that the Texas delegation press Congress to settle claims stemming from the burning of the town of Brenham on September 7, 1866, by U.S. troops. On a related topic, the legislature allowed the State Fireman's Association of Texas, through an act introduced by Senator Gibbs, to build a monument on the grounds of the new Capitol to those firemen who had lost their lives in the discharge of their duties. In other matters, the legislature created a county, Reeves, and revived the "Blue Law" against conducting business on Sunday, but it rejected yet another proposal for statewide prohibition. With the disposal of these and numerous more mundane topics, the Senate of the Eighteenth Legislature adjourned for good on February 6, 1884.

CHAPTER 12

The Senate of the Nineteenth Legislature, 1885

The Nineteenth Legislature met for one brief session, from January 13 to March 31, 1885. John Ireland had been reelected governor in the fall of 1884, campaigning as a Democrat on a platform that promised economic retrenchment, the regulation of railroad companies, and the restriction of corporate landholdings. Conservative agrarian leaders in the Democratic party also ensured the election of former state senator Barnett Gibbs as Texas' youngest lieutenant governor up to that time: he was just thirty-three years old. His youth, and that of many of the newly elected legislators, became the basis for sardonic commentaries by influential Democratic editors who attacked the Nineteenth Legislature for failing to provide quick and easy solutions to the complex problems that plagued Texas as the state entered the second year of an economic depression. These editors, who had supported Ireland and the Democratic platform, had revered the Eighteenth Legislature but consigned the members of the Nineteenth to a political purgatory. Although the members of the new Senate earned praise for their accomplishments, it was what they failed to enact, as well as the melodrama of scandal in the Senate, that became topics of retrospectives after adjournment. Acrimonious debates, the stabbing of a reporter by an officer of the Senate, and an inability to legislate on several pressing issues reflect the tension in the Senate as it tried to deal with the persistent economic depression.

Some tension was perhaps inevitable because the Senate was undertaking a difficult and ambitious agenda. Ireland and his supporters were determined to cut state expenses; assist the settler, the small farmer, and the small cattleman; and regulate big corporations and railroads. They had already pushed all the easier pieces of their program through the Eighteenth Legislature. With the possible exception of the profitable sector of wool growers, about which little was said except in acts to "protect the wool growing interest of Texas," all regions and classes in Texas were under stress, and the usual conflicts between their respective needs were heightened. The Senate factions which championed such diverse interests could seldom garner a majority, but they could frequently stalemate one another. Perhaps even elder statesmen would have found no better compromises.

Editors at the time of the Nineteenth Legislature said that Democrats held a majority in the House but not in the Senate. This statement seems puzzling because Republican senatorial victories, such as that of J. O. Terrell, were few and far between and third parties did not run for the Senate in 1884. What could the other senators be if not Democrats? Apparently the answer lies in the variety of groups within the democracy and the fact that the party merged around the edges with a cloud of quasi-independents who were neither Democrats nor exactly non-Democrats. What the editors meant was that the majority of senators were neither "Ireland Democrats" nor supporters of the party platform. The Democratic platform was obviously much influenced by the demands of farmers and by a need to respond to the frustration, anger, and growing influence of the Populists. But the railroad industry also had to be considered in the platform because the nationwide depression caused by overspeculation had drastically reduced railway building, and the state had virtually ceased its own road-building programs in the interests of economy. The last things businessmen from the cities and cattlemen in West Texas wanted were cutbacks in the development of Texas' infrastructure, including legislation that might threaten the railway construction that would bring more goods to them, despite the fact that rates were currently too high to ship much cargo by rail. The Senate was willing to endorse measures to ensure the fiscal responsibility of the railroads but was hesitant to go further, especially since Congress was taking some steps in the direction of regulation. In keeping with the pro-business platform, editors, legislators, and businessmen exhorted Texas' representatives in Washington to press again for federal assistance to deepen Galveston harbor.

The charges of youth and inexperience leveled at the Senate by the newspapers in 1885 did not, in fact, apply to most of the members. Sixteen of them had served in the Senate of the Eighteenth Legislature: William O. Davis (who began his Senate service in the Seventeenth Legislature), William A. Evans, Lochlin J. Farrar, John Peter Fowler, William H. Getzendaner, Augustus W. Houston (who was first elected to the Senate of the Sixteenth Legislature), John Johnson, James W. Jones, Rudolph Kleberg, John A. Peacock, James S. Perry, George Pfeuffer, William H. Pope, Mansel Y. Randolph, William R. Shannon (who had served three terms in the House prior to his Senate service during the Eleventh, Sixteenth, Seventeenth, and Eighteenth legislatures), and John H. Traylor. During the Nineteenth Legislature, these senators demonstrated many of the same leadership abilities as well as personal quirks that had surfaced during the previous session, but the issues they now faced were much less open to compromise, and occasionally they completely stymied the legislators.

Several of the freshman senators were veteran legislators with as much experience as any member returning from the Eighteenth Legislature. William L. Douglass had served in the House of the Seventeenth and Eighteenth legislatures. Caleb J. Garrison, a native of Georgia, had served as the second assistant secretary of the Senate of the Fifth Legislature, engrossing clerk of the Senate of the Sixth, court clerk for the Rusk County Court, quartermaster for the Frontier Regiment, state superintendent of public works along the Sabine River, and representative in the Fifteenth, Sixteenth, and Eighteenth legislatures. Constantine B. Kilgore had been a delegate to the Constitutional Convention of 1875, and even the cantankerous editor of the *Austin Democratic Statesman* admitted during the Nineteenth Legislature that "Senator Kilgore in point of ability and good looks is the peer of any member of the legislature." Senator John Woods had served in the House during the Eighteenth Legislature.

Some of the other new members had served previously in lesser offices and would compile distinguished records after they left the Texas Legislature. Charles K. Bell, a native of Tennessee, had taken up permanent residence in Texas in 1874. Prior to his election as a state senator, he had been county attorney of Hamilton County and district attorney for the Twenty-ninth District. After two terms in the Texas Senate, he returned to private practice but went on to serve in the U.S. Congress from 1893 to 1897 and as attorney general under Governor Joseph D. Sayers from 1901 to 1904. James H. Calhoun, a Georgia native who moved to Texas in 1871, had been county judge of Eastland County and district attorney of the Twelfth Judicial District. In 1903 he was elected judge of the Forty-second District.

Three freshman senators had been born into prominent families and weaned on Texas politics: Temple Lea Houston, George Washington Glasscock, Jr., and John L. Camp, Jr.

Temple Lea Houston was the son of Sam Houston and was born in the Governor's Mansion on August 12, 1860, during his father's last administration. The family moved to Independence in Washington County after Governor Houston's resignation. The last child born to his father, Temple Lea was very young when his father died. After his father's death, his mother, Margaret M. Lea Houston, bought a house in Independence, but she died when Temple was only seven, and he was taken in by relatives. Named after his maternal grandfather, Colonel Temple Lea of Alabama, Temple Lea preferred reading to hunting and fishing yet grew up to be a man who seemed to be made for the frontier, combining his law practice with enjoyment of a strenuous outdoor life. As an adult he took up hunting and fishing, and his favorite reading was history and archaeology. His essay on the Mound Builders was considered a literary jewel.

During his mid-teens, Temple served three terms as a page in the U.S. Senate, studying law in his spare time. At seventeen, he enrolled at Baylor University, which at that time was located in Independence. He graduated from Baylor in 1881 and was recognized by Dr. William Crane, then president of the university, as one of the best students ever to have come out of the three states in which Dr. Crane had taught. In February, 1882, Houston married Laura Cross, with whom he had three children. He read law in Washington County and was admitted to the bar at nineteen. The young couple then moved to Mobeetie, where Houston was appointed to fill out the remainder of the term of District Attorney J. N. "Honest

Jim" Browning for the Thirty-fifth Judicial District. The district attorney and the judge journeyed far and wide over the Panhandle to dispense justice. Known for his eccentric attire, Houston dressed in high-heeled boots, white California trousers, a white Stetson (occasionally exchanged for black), a white shirt with rattlesnake tie, and a long Prince Albert coat. He enjoyed his reputation as a brilliant speaker and formidable trial lawyer.

There are numerous tales of how quick, accurate, and dangerous a gunslinger young Houston could be. In the courtroom on one occasion, in defense of a farmer who had prudently shot an outlaw before the outlaw drew, Houston demonstrated, with two guns, how ineffectual an ordinary fellow would be against a killer with a fast draw: one gun blazed in the direction of the judge, the other in the direction of the jury. Although Houston's guns were loaded with blanks, the judge rose from behind the bench having turned a decidedly peculiar color. When, despite his little demonstration, the jury found his client guilty, Houston petitioned for a new trial. "Why?" the judge asked. Temple Lea responded that the rules required that the jury must not be separated during the trial, and when he had fired his guns, the jury had scattered in all directions. He got the new trial, and his client was acquitted. On a more somber occasion, during the course of a trial in which Houston and an opposing lawyer would have come to a fistfight in the courtroom had not the bailiff gotten between them, Houston entered a saloon where the rival lawyer and his two brothers were drinking. Houston saw the man start for his gun and warned him not to. It was said that Houston was so fast that in spite of the other lawyer's head start, Houston still drew and fired before the other man got his shot off. The reckless attorney fell lifeless to the floor, and one of his brothers who then drew on Houston was shot in the shoulder. Houston was tried and acquitted on the grounds of self-defense.

In spite of Houston's youth—he was twenty-four when elected to the Senate—his stature among his fellow members was such that he would preside over the dedication of the new state Capitol in 1888. But Houston served only a single term in the Texas Legislature and never held another elective office.

He was from Mobeetie in Wheeler County and represented twelve organized and forty-four unorganized counties in the Panhandle. He did not remain in that region, however, deciding instead to make the "run" into the Cherokee strip, along with a horde of others. The move to Oklahoma proved successful, and Houston lived out the rest of his life there, dying on August 15, 1905, at the age of forty-five.

George Washington Glasscock, Jr., of Georgetown, was born in Travis County to a distinguished family. His father, G. W. Glasscock, Sr., had been a partner of Abraham Lincoln when the two men ran a flatboating business on the Sangamon River in Illinois. The father moved to Texas in 1834 and was in business partnership with prominent Texians. He was with Chesshire's Company in the Grass Fight and at the siege of Bexar. Glasscock County and the city of Georgetown were named in honor of the senior Glasscock.

George Glasscock, Jr., was getting started on a good education when the Civil War broke out. The family was Unionist, but when the war finally came, George enlisted in the Confederate Army at age seventeen as a member of the 33rd Texas Cavalry. The remainder of his education was gained through personal reading. At war's end he married Jane H. Boatner of Anderson County, Texas, and the young couple settled in Navasota, where Glasscock engaged in mercantile affairs and from whence he maintained close ties to Austin. An epidemic of yellow fever in 1867 forced him to move his business from Navasota to Austin. In 1872 he began to read law in the firm of Walker and Terrell, and in October, 1873, he was admitted to the bar. He practiced in Austin until 1879, when he relocated to Georgetown and was appointed county attorney of Williamson County. Again, he maintained close ties to Austin, and he practiced law in both towns while continuing to build up his business affairs, which eventually assumed "gigantic proportions." Later in his life, Glasscock successfully added farming to his enterprises. His election to the Senate of the Nineteenth Legislature was the beginning of a long legislative career. He went on to serve in the Twentieth, Twenty-first, Twenty-second, Twenty-ninth, and Thirtieth legislatures. An important member of the Senate, he served on all the major Senate committees at one time or another.

The Glasscocks did not have children, and George found time to be active in a wide number of Masonic endeavors, including service as Grand Patron of the Eastern Star of Texas in 1910. He was an active Odd Fellow and served in all the order's offices, becoming

Grand Master of the Texas Order. Glasscock continued to practice law in Georgetown until his death on May 15, 1911.

The father of Senator John L. Camp, Jr., had been a delegate to the Texas Constitutional Convention of 1866 and a senator in the Fourteenth Legislature, and Camp County was named in his honor. The younger Camp was elected to the Senate from Upshur County, where he had been county attorney since 1876. After his tenure in the Senate during the Nineteenth and Twentieth legislatures, he continued the family tradition of public service: for seventeen years, beginning in 1897, Camp presided over the Forty-fifth District Court, then accepted an appointment as U.S. district attorney for the Western District of Texas.

A native of Gilmer, Upshur County, John Camp, Jr., was born on September 23, 1855, and was educated at Trinity University and at the Texas Military Institute in Austin. He practiced law in Gilmer up to his election to the legislature and married Mary Lamartine Felder in 1881. Following Camp's Senate service, the couple and their nine children moved to Tyler. In 1890 the family moved to San Antonio, where Camp died on August 10, 1918.

Charles Keith Bell of Hamilton was born in Chattanooga, Tennessee, on April 8, 1853, and came to Texas in 1871. He returned to Tennessee in 1873 to read law and qualified for the bar in 1874. The new lawyer returned to Texas and began his practice in Hamilton. In 1876 Bell began his career in public service with his election as county attorney of Hamilton County. He went on to become district attorney of the Twenty-ninth District in 1880 and 1882. Elected to the Senate in 1884, he served on important committees during the brief session of the Nineteenth Legislature and returned to the Senate for the Twentieth, where he played a prominent role. Bell was elected to the U.S. Congress in 1892 and reelected in 1894; he moved to Fort Worth in 1893. While in Congress he authored an important minority report which led to the federal government's recovering over $100 million in loans to the Union and Southern Pacific railroads. When the attorney general of Texas died in office, Governor Sayers appointed Bell to the position in March, 1901, and the following year he was elected to the office. Bell's tenure as attorney general was a period of antitrust prosecution; his office recovered over $120,000 and more than 200,000 acres of land for the state and revoked the permits of more than forty corporations, both foreign and domestic.

Bell was an unsuccessful candidate for governor in 1906, after which he retired from politics. He was an Episcopalian and a Mason; he served as chairman of the Young Men's Christian Association of Fort Worth and, at one time, as chairman of the Anti-State-Wide Prohibition Association. Married to Florence Smith in 1906, he was father to one son. Bell died on April 23, 1913, and was buried with Masonic ceremonies in the East Oakwood Cemetery in Fort Worth.

Following his participation in the brief deliberations of the Senate of the Nineteenth Legislature, James Henry Calhoun of Eastland played a prominent role in the drought-relief bill passed during his term in the Senate of the Twentieth. Calhoun was born in La Grange, Georgia, on January 17, 1849. Graduated from Homer College in Louisiana in 1870, he moved to Waco in 1871 and was admitted to the bar in 1873. He was engaged in the land business until 1876, when he was elected county judge; from 1881 to 1884 he was district attorney for the Twelfth Judicial District. After his Senate service, Calhoun was elected judge of the Forty-second District. He had married Jennie Connor of Eastland in 1882, and they had three children. The family moved to Cisco in 1903, where Judge Calhoun died and was buried in 1919.

William Levi Douglass of Beaumont was born in Mississippi in 1853 and moved to Texas after the close of the war. Douglass was a successful lawyer and served in the House during the Seventeenth and Eighteenth legislatures and in the Senate during the Nineteenth and Twentieth. In the Senate of the Nineteenth Legislature, he served as chairman of the Committee on Military Affairs and was a member of numerous other committees including the Committee on the Judiciary Number 1, the Committee on Privileges and Elections, the Committee on Public Health, and the Committee on Internal Improvements. Douglass was a conservative.

For much of his adult life Caleb Jackson Garrison, of Glen Fawn in Rusk County, had a solid career in public service. He was born in 1827 in Carroll County, Georgia, where he received a liberal education. He moved in February, 1851, to Glen Fawn. He engaged in the mercantile business for two years, during which time he read law. After being admitted to the bar in late 1853 or early 1854, he began to practice, but around 1856 he earned his livelihood largely as a planter. Garrison was elected second assistant secretary of the Senate during the Fifth Legislature and was engrossing clerk of that body during the regular session of the Sixth. During the Civil War he served the Confederacy in General Ector's Brigade and was a staff officer in the Army of Tennessee. In the postwar years he was clerk of the Rusk County Court for two years and was appointed by Governor Runnels to the position of superintendent of public works on the Sabine River. He was elected to the House of the Fifteenth Legislature and was reelected to the Sixteenth as the Democratic nominee (beating out a Republican-Greenback opponent and an independent Democrat); he later returned as a member of the House of the Eighteenth. Garrison served in the Senate of the Nineteenth and Twentieth legislatures and was president pro tempore during part of the regular session of the Twentieth. Subsequently, he was considered a strong candidate for state comptroller but was unsuccessful in his bid. Garrison belonged to the Methodist Episcopal Church, South, and was a Mason. He died about 1901 and was buried at Jacksonville.

E. F. Hall was born in New York and came to Texas in 1863, settling at Laredo. The scanty biographical information available about him does not mention Confederate sympathies. It is known that he was educated at Columbia College in New York and that he was a devout Catholic noted for his assistance to the needy. Hall was about thirty-seven when he was elected to the Senate of the Nineteenth Legislature and was considered one of the best educated and most intellectual members of the upper house. He was chairman of the Committee on Rules and Regulations and a member of other important committees: the Committee on the Judiciary Number 2, the Committee on Finance, the Committee on State Affairs, the Committee on the General Land Office, the Committee on Frontier Protection, the Committee on Public Health, and the Committee on Private Land Claims. Hall died in office on April 28, 1886.

Richard Henry Harrison of Waco was only twenty-seven when he defeated William Reagan, the brother of the famous John H. Reagan, for the Senate seat from Falls and McLennan counties. Harrison was of distinguished lineage, his father being Brigadier General James E. Harrison, a descendant of the historic Harrison family of Virginia. After the Civil War, the general and his family had resumed life on their fertile plantation in the Brazos bottomlands and were beginning to recoup their fortunes when the father died. The family's twice-reduced circumstances meant that Richard could obtain only a local education in Salado. He took up farming and kept at it until 1877, when he joined the Texas Rangers under the command of Major John B. Jones and began riding out on those harsh adventures, which he continued to take part in until the fall of 1879. He returned to McLennan County and for a year took over the management of the farming interests of his uncle, General Thomas Harrison. He decided, however, that farming was not to his taste, even though he excelled at it and made a profit for his uncle out of the venture. Over the protests of his family and friends, Harrison decided to study law and proceeded to save every penny he could to go to school. At night he read law and English history in preparation for his matriculation, and in 1880 he entered the junior law class at Cumberland University in Tennessee. Much praised for his devotion to his studies, he graduated in February, 1881, and was admitted to the bar at Waco a month later. He immediately gained a fair practice there.

By the summer of 1884 a petition was in circulation asking Harrison to run for the Senate. Nominated by acclamation at the Democratic nominating convention, he was opposed in the polls by Reagan, who presumably also ran as a Democrat, and defeated him by a majority of twenty-five hundred votes, a remarkable margin. Harrison served in the Senates of the Nineteenth and Twentieth legislatures, and during that time his abilities attracted the attention of James S. Hogg, who was then the attorney general. Following the regular session of the Twentieth Legislature, Harrison was appointed assistant attorney general and resigned his seat in the Senate on April 20, 1887. He was succeeded by Waller S. Baker, who was sworn during the called session of the Twentieth.

Harrison soon earned a reputation as an aggressive litigator. The Texas courts were inundated with matters that had been neglected for years, as well as with a remarkable number of suits resulting from Hogg's making full use of recent legislation to regulate corporations. During these fierce legal battles, Harrison recovered some public lands for counties. A description by a contemporary biographer described his speaking style: "His very earnestness and vehemence command attention. His style is rugged, nervous and impassioned. He never selects any but the strongest Saxon words to express his meaning; and when denouncing any measure or person that he conceives to be mean, despicable or tainted with fraud, his speeches are logic on fire."

Harrison was married at Salado on November 14, 1882, to Mary S. Robertson, daughter of Colonel E. Sterling C. Robertson. As was noted at the time, "In this marriage, two of the oldest and most historic families of the country were united, Mrs. Harrison being a descendant of General James Robertson, of revolutionary fame, and founder of Tennessee, and granddaughter of Major Sterling C. Robertson, of Texian fame." As of 1890, the couple had one child, James M. Harrison. Senator Harrison was a member of the Missionary Baptist Church and was described as singularly chaste and abstemious.

W. M. Jerdone of Galveston was born in Charles City, Virginia, on November 8, 1849. During the Civil War young Jerdone participated in some heavy fighting around Richmond with Company 4, 24th Regiment, Army of Northern Virginia. Jerdone was a graduate of the Military Institute of Virginia. He came to Texas on September 3, 1871. He first lived in Austin, then went to the frontier; he moved to Galveston in 1874 and was admitted to the bar there the same year. He was soon elected district attorney and became prominent in Galveston's legal fraternity. During his term in the Senate, Jerdone was chairman of the Committee on Public Health and a member of the committees on Public Lands, Federal Relations, Commerce and Manufactures, and Public Buildings and Grounds.

One of the strong figures to emerge from the Senate in the Nineteenth Legislature was Constantine Buckley Kilgore of Wills Point in Van Zandt County. The town of Kilgore, founded by the Missouri-Pacific Railroad Line in 1872, was named for him. Kilgore was born on February 20, 1835, in Newnan, Coweta County, Georgia. In 1846, when he was eleven years old, his parents brought him to Rusk County, Texas, where he received a common school education and academic training. Kilgore entered the Confederate Army during the Civil War as a private and by 1862 was serving as adjutant general of Ector's Brigade. He was severely wounded at Chickamauga and was captured and confined as a prisoner in Fort Delaware in 1864. Kilgore began his political life as justice of the peace in 1869, after he had been admitted to the bar and had practiced law in Rusk County. In 1874 the family moved to Gregg County and resided there three years, then moved to Wills Point. Kilgore was a member of the Constitutional Convention of 1875; in 1880 he was chosen as a presidential elector on the Democratic ticket and voted for Hancock and English. He was elected to the Texas Senate in 1884 for a term of four years and served as president pro tempore ad interim of the Nineteenth Legislature but resigned on October 23, 1885. Kilgore was elected as a Democrat to the Fiftieth through the Fifty-third congresses, serving from March 4, 1887, to March 3, 1896. President Cleveland appointed him U.S. judge for the Southern District of the Indian Territory on March 20, 1895, the position he held at his death in Ardmore, Indian Territory, on September 23, 1897, at the age of sixty-seven.

Born in 1835 in the province of Silesia in the Kingdom of Prussia, Hermann Knittel came to Texas in 1852 as part of the wave of immigration from Central Europe, which was particularly intense during the 1850s. He settled in Burton, Washington County, and went into business. At the beginning of the Civil War, Knittel plunged in vigorously on the Confederate side, becoming a second lieutenant in Waul's Texas Legion and earning a considerable reputation as an intrepid officer. As a senator in the Nineteenth and Twentieth legislatures, he was known as a hard worker. He was described as short and of fair complexion, with blue eyes and dark hair turning silver. He was a member of the Southern Church and was a Mason of the Order of A. F. & A. M.

Born in Hunt County on April 11, 1852, Samuel David Stinson lived at Gilmer in Upshur County during the first thirteen years of his life, then moved permanently to Greenville in the county of his birth. Graduated from the law school at Trinity University, he was admitted to the bar in 1878 and elected district attorney of Hunt County in 1880. Stinson was elected to the Senate for the Nineteenth Legislature without opposition. He served as chairman of the Committee on Public Lands in the Nineteenth Legislature and as chairman of the Committee on Public Buildings and Grounds in the Twentieth. Stinson was a member of the Independent Order of Odd Fellows. He was described as being five feet ten inches in height, weighing 150 pounds, and having light hair, blue eyes, and a complexion fair and ruddy.

One of the rare Republicans still able to win office, J. O. Terrell was a banker, a lawyer, and a cattle breeder who was much admired for his leading work in improving the Jersey strain in Texas. Terrell was born in Kaufman County on April 6, 1856, the son of Jonathan W. Terrell, a merchant who had come to Texas from Virginia, and his wife, Amelia Love, a member of a pioneer Texas family. The Terrells were an old and prominent Virginia family. J. O. Terrell attended Texas public schools and later entered Trinity University. Following his graduation, he read law in a private office in Kaufman; he was admitted to the bar at age twenty or twenty-one and built up an extensive practice. Later he moved to Terrell, Texas, a town named in honor of his family. He was elected to the Senate of the Nineteenth Legislature at the age of twenty-eight, where he served for four years. At one point he was an unsuccessful Republican candidate for governor. Presidents Theodore Roosevelt and Taft were his personal friends, and he numbered the governors of many states among his close acquaintances.

In 1897 Terrell moved to San Antonio, where he lived until his death. By the time of his last move, he was already one of the foremost members of the Texas bar and a leader in other areas of Texas life. In San Antonio he and his son Marshall first put the Terrell and Terrell law firm on a sound footing, having switched from criminal to civil law. A third member of the family, his son Dick, joined the firm, and then the father and Marshall went on to found another Jersey cattle breeding farm, the Saint Cloud Farm, which, according to the *American Biography*, became the foremost in the world, surpassing Terrell's first famous farm, the Valley Stock Farm, established when he was in his early twenties. Part of his herd came from the island of Jersey itself.

Terrell was enthusiastic about the development of San Antonio and played an important role in building the city. One of his more notable ventures was the establishment of the Central Trust Company in 1910. It later merged and became the City Central National Bank. Terrell was president and in 1918 built the City National Bank Building. His three sons were active with him in the family's varied legal, financial, and cattle interests.

J. O. married Mattie Simpson, the daughter of a Methodist Episcopal minister in Kaufman County, at Terrell in 1877; the couple had six children, of whom two died in childhood and four survived into adulthood. Among those four the most notable, Chester H., also died young. Chester served in the Texas House as a Democrat and was the youngest speaker elected by that body. The son had attracted the friendship of Warren G. Harding and other men prominent on the national stage, and it was generally acknowledged that he stood on the threshold of a brilliant career. His death in 1920 was considered a great loss. The father, J. O., by then in his mid-sixties, died in San Antonio only three years later, on June 28, 1923, and was much missed by the citizens of his city and state.

John Woods had served for three years as district attorney of Lavaca County and had been a member of the House of Representatives in the Eighteenth Legislature. Born in Alabama, Woods came to Texas and settled in Lavaca County in 1853 and received his education in Texas. He married Mary E. Ricinger of Fayette County, and the couple had two children. He was a Mason and an Odd Fellow. Senator Woods introduced Senate Bill 8, which forbade the sale of lands to corporations for purposes of speculation, a bill which was received with great favor. He also supported public highways and advocated, unsuccessfully, the construction of a juvenile house of corrections. Woods was a calm, analytical type who tended to use figures rather than rhetoric to carry his point. He was thirty-eight at the time of the session.

The relative youth and inexperience of a handful of the senators of the Nineteenth Legislature did provide some basis for the harsh criticism leveled at them. Although J. O. Terrell, a Texas native in his late twenties, was holding his first elective office, he became chairman of one of the Senate judiciary committees. John Woods, who had served without distinction in the House during the Eighteenth Legislature, introduced important legislation in the Senate of the Nineteenth, with mixed results. Woods did not return to public office after he left the Senate. Several of the freshmen—for example, E. F. Hall, Richard H. Harrison, W. M. Jerdone, Hermann Knittel, and Samuel D. Stinson—achieved little distinction. In fact, Jerdone barely escaped expulsion after he was implicated in a scandal involving Senate calendar clerk Alexander Sampson, who conspired with House clerks to prevent a bill to prohibit speculation in commodity futures from reaching the Senate floor for a vote. Sampson was dismissed by the Senate after he stabbed the reporter responsible for his exposure, but Jerdone weathered the investigation conducted by a committee composed of Senators Temple Lea

Houston, Mansel Y. Randolph, and Augustus W. Houston. Although the measure to prohibit futures trading went on to pass both chambers by a two-thirds vote, the unseemly affair lent weight to partisan editors' condemnation of the Senate.

Apart from the volatile Sampson, the officers of the Senate proved to be good selections. Secretary William N. Ramey, First Assistant Secretary Charles M. Boynton, and Chaplain Richmond K. Smoot had held their positions during the Eighteenth Legislature. The new officers included A. P. Finlay, engrossing clerk; Yancey Lewis, enrolling clerk; W. T. Brewer, sergeant-at-arms (after fourteen ballots); J. A. Stuart, assistant sergeant-at-arms; and Andrew J. Dorn, doorkeeper (despite Temple Houston's eloquent speech in favor of the opponent). The officers of this Senate established an important historical precedent: at Chaplain Smoot's suggestion, Rabbi Joseph Silverman of Dallas presided over the Senate on March 4, 1885, the first Jewish religious leader to do so.

Governor Ireland's message, which was read in full in the Senate on the second day of the session, began on a note of optimism. The chief executive pointed out that Texas was free from internal strife and from the "external and illegal interference of our federal agency in the choice of her public servants and the administration of her affairs." He asserted that, despite two consecutive poor harvests and a persistent drought, the aggregate wealth and population of the state had continued to increase. Ireland attributed the depression that afflicted important sectors of the state's economy primarily to oppressive federal and state taxation, declaring that taxes had "absolutely locked up and withdrawn from circulation" a third of the national currency. He also placed part of the blame on railroad companies, which he insisted had been developed with predominately foreign capital, contributing to a drain of funds from the United States to pay the principal and interest on large foreign loans. Finally, he decried the "rapid and unparalleled accumulation of vast fortunes in the hands of a few persons, aided in various ways by favoritisms by governments."

Ireland demanded that the Nineteenth Legislature fulfill the campaign promises which the Democratic party had made in the fall of 1884: continued retrenchment in government and regulation of corporate interests. He spoke with pride of the reduction in the state surplus effected by the Eighteenth Legislature, which had retired many debts and authorized important projects, such as the North Texas Insane Asylum, while reducing taxes. He insisted that the remaining surplus, which he identified as "several hundred thousand dollars" lying idle in the state treasury, "should be unlocked in some way." At the same time, he said, more funds could be left in the hands of the people if greater reductions were made in state government agencies and salaries. He spoke against a plan to pay the boarding fees of normal school students at Sam Houston and Prairie View and said that funds for the Agricultural and Mechanical College of Texas should come from the endowments of the University of Texas. As there was a surplus in the public school fund, he asked for a reduction in the tax to nine or ten cents.

Among Ireland's specific recommendations in his opening address was the liquidation of the sinking fund that had been set aside for the repayment of state bonds at maturity. Annual revenues provided more than enough for the early retirement of those issues. The *Austin Democratic Statesman* reported in January that Senator Traylor had "been on a still hunt in the treasury office" and had found "some fifty or sixty thousand dollars that had been lying idle in the vaults for years." Traylor introduced a bill that mandated the transfer of not only the sinking fund but also several other funds providing for the settlement of special debts, thus returning an aggregate of $46,636 to the general revenue. Ireland gladly signed Traylor's measure on January 31.

Ireland assured the legislators that exigencies should be covered through bonds issued by Texas agencies rather than through foreign sources. On February 13, 1885, he signed a second bill introduced by Senator Traylor that authorized the issuance of $200,000 worth of 6 percent bonds that would mature in only five years. These were to be offered to the Board of Education in exchange for the funds the board was authorized to invest. The bill stipulated that, if the board accepted the bonds, they could not be sold or transferred, and if it refused to accept the issue, the certificates were to be destroyed at once. For Ireland it was a perfect solution to an unexpected shortfall in revenues, but many businessmen in Texas argued that it was financial nepotism that could only lead to disaster, as it depended on future increases in state revenues for redemption.

For the immediate future, however, the patchwork of bills permitted another reduction in state taxes—but at the cost of a decrease in state services. Through a House bill signed by Ireland on the last day of the session, the ad valorem tax for general revenue on real and personal property was reduced to 25 cents per $100 and that for public education to 12.5 cents per $100. The ceiling on county taxes for the support of schools was lowered to 20 cents per $100. County revenue taxes were set at one-fourth of 1 percent and road and bridge taxes at 15 cents per $100. Many of the financial burdens of state government were reduced or else shifted to local authorities. For example, the pension program for veterans and widows of veterans of the Texas Revolution, which was plagued with charges of fraud, was reorganized, and annual payments were reduced to $150 per year. The legislature also reduced state expenditures by conveying possession of the Alamo, purchased with funds authorized by the Eighteenth Legislature, to the city of San Antonio, in return for the city's pledge to keep the Alamo in "good order and repair at no cost to the state." An act introduced in the House allowed municipal officials to levy a tax of 25 cents per $100 to support public works such as the restoration of the Alamo, which had so quickly proven to be a liability to the state.

The debate over the adjustments in the taxes levied for the support of public schools was overshadowed by another public education issue: Senator Pfeuffer's bid to formalize the claim of the Agricultural and Mechanical College of Texas to a portion of the endowment which the State Constitution set aside for the University of Texas. Pfeuffer had been president of the board of directors of the Agricultural and Mechanical College, and it was rumored that the entire purpose of his career in the Senate was to increase support for that institution at the expense of the University of Texas. Governor Ireland supported his bill to put the Agricultural and Mechanical College, the University of Texas, a medical school to be built in Galveston, and a college for blacks at Austin into a single system under the control of the State Board of Education. Ireland's endorsement, however, could not drive Pfeuffer's bill through the Senate, which was besieged by influential University of Texas lobbyists who demonstrated to the senators that the university actually had a much smaller budget than the Agricultural and Mechanical College and, in fact, needed more financial support, not a further partitioning of its endowment.

Besides tax reduction, Ireland pushed for assessments reform, as it was widely known that special interests, especially ranchers with large herds, were not paying their fair share. A wealthy cattleman in North Texas had boldly told the governor during the special session of the Eighteenth Legislature that the bulk of his property had not been assessed or taxed for seven years. Ireland recalled that admission in his own speech to the Nineteenth Legislature and declared, "The little farmer or small stock man remembers to a head the number of cattle or stock he has, and renders them. If he should forget, his neighbors remind him." By way of further example, Ireland pointed out that the tax rolls of Wichita County recorded only about seven thousand head, but in reality the county had more than one hundred thousand. The Senate endorsed tax reforms only after amending them to ensure more equitable assessments.

Cattlemen also came under fire for obstructing public land sales. After the Eighteenth Legislature passed the enclosure acts, cattlemen began fencing off vital watering holes in dry regions, confirming the Land Board's worst fears. The ranchers had also balked at paying leases on public land after the board increased the rate from four cents per acre to eight. Ranchers continued to use the land, discouraging settlers, without paying for it.

Although the Land Board created by the Eighteenth Legislature had sold more than 2.1 million acres of public land and had leased over 1.8 million additional acres, more than 24.5 million acres in the public domain remained unsold. Sales of public land had failed to meet expectations because much of the land was in arid West Texas or was of otherwise poor quality. The public lands included tracts reserved for the support of the public schools, the University of Texas, the Blind Asylum, the Deaf and Dumb Asylum, the Insane Asylum, and the Orphan Asylum. The board had deliberately refrained from selling many sections that contained permanent water sources because often they served many surrounding acres.

Governor Ireland in his opening address urged the members of the Nineteenth Legislature to enact measures permanently to dedicate the remaining water holes as public land, with a right-of-way no less than two hundred yards in width leading to and around each water hole. If a constitutional amendment was necessary to create this public easement, he pledged his full support, as preserving access to water sources for all would stimulate the sale and leasing of arid tracts. Coupled with his pledge was a request that a time limit of six years be placed on all leases and that half the unsold public land in each county be reserved from leasing to encourage sales to settlers.

The legislature considered several bills to amend earlier provisions for the sale and lease of public lands. Three such measures passed both chambers; but all were vetoed by Governor Ireland, who objected because the proposals allowed the leasing of unlimited amounts of land, permitted the restriction of transit, gave purchasers a leasing advantage over others, and priced watered lands at only two dollars an acre (Ireland believed that ranchers could afford more). The governor did sign a measure, introduced by Senator Johnson, that prohibited the posting of parcels larger than two thousand acres from hunting and fishing. The controversy between the Ireland-appointed Land Board and cattlemen continued to simmer and became a factor in the 1886 gubernatorial election.

The only bill for the encouragement of public land sales signed by Ireland held little promise of immediate revenue for the state but was designed to encourage immigration by poor settlers. Introduced by Senator Augustus Houston of Bexar, the act required purchasers to make a down payment of only one-thirtieth of the purchase price. The remainder would be paid in twenty-nine annual installments on January 1 of each year, with 5 percent annual interest on the unpaid principal payable on March 1. If a payment was not made before the deadline of August 1, the land could be reclaimed by the state after a twelve-month grace period. The purchaser generally could not retire the debt earlier than seven years, but if a settler made improvements on the land, he would be allowed to pay the note in full after three years. A second bill introduced by Senator Shannon and passed unanimously by both chambers clarified the point that failure to meet the yearly August 1 deadline did not mean a forfeiture of rights; a purchaser still had a year in which to meet the obligation. To expedite land sales in vast West and Southwest Texas, three new counties (Midland, Webb, and Val Verde) were created, as well as three new land districts (Nolan, Hardeman, and Webb).

Texas was still receiving immigrants, but land speculation and the harsh climate in the west hindered their prospects. Many who had failed in the semiarid regions were trying desperately to get the means for one more try elsewhere. New settlers, however, continued to arrive in Texas even as others left, complicating the immigration picture. Ireland's faction was sympathetic to their plight and strongly supported measures to restrict large corporations from acquiring more public lands and water sources, wishing to reserve them for settler families and small ranchers; but the only measure the legislature could agree on was a modest restraint of corporate land speculation that was easy to circumvent.

The conflict over public land was intertwined with the most dramatic issue dividing the state, one which was to be the subject of countless western novels and films—the fight over open range, or "free grass" versus barbed wire. Discussions of the subject omit the fact that in Texas open range first developed and continued to function in the plains area of the northeastern counties well into modern times. In West Texas, however, large cattle corporations owned by Europeans or other out-of-state investors paid no taxes, and huge operations of Texas cattlemen were underassessed. Smaller outfits, which were often fully assessed, struggled for survival; and their access to the range and to water was often inadequate. The legislature passed a bill to address this inequity in taxation.

In Ireland's view, free grass merely meant that the strongest competitor drove out everyone else and monopolized vast areas of range and water, but proponents of free grass believed that it benefited the pocket rancher as well as the big operators. Siding with the governor, the Nineteenth Legislature provided penalties for those who threatened, frightened, or forced legitimate settlers off previously public lands. Whether such legislation could be enforced was questionable.

It was not the issue of free grass but the dull-sounding question of abolishing the position of commissioner of insurance, statistics and history that pushed the Senate to the brink of violence. The *Galveston News* reported on March 15 that Temple Houston took the floor to assert that it was the responsibility of the commissioner "to preserve Texas history" and that to discontinue the office was to do a great injury to the preservation of near-sacred information on the state. Senator Davis retorted that the history of Texas was contained largely in the newspapers and that a low-paid file clerk could sort and store newspapers just as well as a highly paid commissioner. The two opponents traded personal insults on the Senate floor, and soon

> the Senate chamber was a perfect bedlam . . . shouting and denouncing from all quarters of the chamber. Pistols were passed around as cards are dealt at a whist-table. Messengers were dispatched for pistols, knives were taken out and opened, and for a while everyone was certain that bloodshed was imminent. . . . The Senate is the laughing stock of the town tonight, the members of the House being especially free with their wit. . . . Mr. Houston has been very generally dignified, and not until to-day has he been guilty of any untoward conduct.

The editors saw Davis, who was often sarcastic, as the instigator of the hostilities.

The next day, the *San Antonio Daily Express* observed with amusement, "In the Senate lobby today, there was an unusual number of corpulent people observed. Your correspondent, on elbowing among them, discovered that this corpulency was artificial. Visitors had padded themselves with books, boiler iron, plowshares, and other impenetrable articles of virtue in order to be prepared for any of the usual senatorial methods of arguing a measure. Ladies are afraid to venture in the chamber at all."

Several controversial measures were being debated that March 16, the hottest of which was the contract for the new state Capitol building. The Capitol cornerstone had been laid on March 2, Texas Independence Day, amid much festivity and celebration, although construction arrangements aroused frustration and opposition in many. Some felt that the contract was a bad one and that the foundation was not being laid well, and they distrusted the quality of the stone. During the debate on the sixteenth, the galleries were filled with mechanics, members of the stonecutters guild, and members of the Knights of Labor, all there to protest that convict labor was being used to build the Capitol, rather than working men from the private sector.

Despite the controversy that surrounded the operation of the Land Board, it survived the retrenchment push of the Nineteenth Legislature unscathed. The complaints of Davis, the only senator who challenged the methods of Land Commissioner W. C. Walsh, were rejected after a Senate investigation. Senator Evans had more success with his bill to abolish the office of fish commissioner and to dispose of all fishponds and other property belonging to the fish department; the bill became law without Ireland's signature. The department's property was turned over to the superintendent of

Partially completed limestone foundation and basement of the new Capitol building. Reproduced from holdings of Texas State Archives.

public buildings and grounds. The primary function of the fisheries office had been to supervise the introduction of fish species that would reproduce rapidly when introduced into the waterways of Texas and provide both food and sport. German carp, which the editor of the *Austin Democratic Statesman* referred to as a "vegetable fish," had been the most successful; and the final draft of Evans's bill contained an amendment by Senator Terrell which reserved some fish to the state by requiring that five hundred carp be transferred to the ponds on the grounds of the North Texas Insane Asylum before the remaining stock and facilities of the commission were sold or leased. In another wildlife matter, Senator Randolph filed legislation that provided a penalty for deer hunting at night by firelight. The bill received an adverse committee report, but Randolph called it up anyway; the measure passed only after being amended to exempt three-fourths of the state.

Senator Davis unsuccessfully introduced a bill which would have allowed the defendant in a criminal trial to speak in his own defense. Davis introduced thirteen bills, none of which succeeded. He was not alone. Most bills introduced in the Senate died in that chamber, while the House passed a much larger percentage of its bills. However, House legislation sent to the Senate quickly perished there, and only a small number of bills reached Ireland's desk.

The *Austin Democratic Statesman* also advocated the abolition of the post of commissioner of insurance, statistics and history. Despite the notorious debate between Temple Houston and Davis in which Houston made his impassioned plea to save the office, Senator Johnson's proposal to abolish the post passed the Senate when Shannon broke a tie in favor of the measure, but it failed in the House. An attempt to abolish the state police force, by now known as the Texas Rangers, failed despite strong backing in the legislature. Popular support for disbanding the Rangers increased when a detachment assigned to patrol the Mexican border lost its entire complement of horses to bandits in early February, 1885. In the opinion of those in frontier and border counties, however, Ireland and Senate cost cutters were wrong to suggest reducing the strength of the Texas Rangers—they had plenty of work to keep them occupied. Granted, violence had been reduced overall during the preceding decade, but "members who live in the eastern and central portion of the state, where there has been no frontier for fifty years, imagine there is no more frontier and are in favor of cutting down the ranger force." The Rangers survived the challenge to both their existence and their pride, but their budget, like those of the Commission of Insurance, Statistics and History and many other state agencies, was substantially reduced.

The state penitentiary provided many opportunities for retrenchment and reform. Ireland reported that Texas' system, built to hold no more than 1,600 convicts, contained 2,632 in January, 1885. In his message to the legislature the governor asked for four basic reforms. First, lesser grades of punishment than imprisonment in the state system should be provided for some minor crimes. Second, because "the wisdom of allowing juries to inflict [i.e., to have the discretion to impose only] the penalty of confinement in the penitentiary for life [instead of capital punishment] for deliberate murder is not apparent," Ireland urged that "the man who wilfully takes life should no longer be permitted to annoy society or government."

Third, a "house of corrections" should be provided for boys "and others rendered harmless by reason of age or other conditions." Finally, the restrictions placed by the Eighteenth Legislature on the employment of convicts should be relaxed, as there was no evidence that convict labor displaced free labor. On the contrary, convicts were used outside the walls for tasks that free men would not perform, but those at work in the prisons worked at industries that did compete with free labor, such as textiles and machine shops.

The Nineteenth Legislature took little action on the governor's suggestion for easing prison overcrowding. The penalty for gambling was actually increased, and new punishments were imposed for those who vandalized telephone equipment. As for the idea of capital punishment for murder, it too was rejected. The last two items on Ireland's agenda received more support. Senator Woods's bill to set aside funds for the construction of a reformatory for convicts under eighteen years of age passed the Senate but failed in the House. On the other hand, a House bill passed by the Senate and signed by Ireland on March 31, 1885, deleted the restrictions on the outside employment of convicts contained in the act passed by the Eighteenth Legislature; the same bill removed the governor from the Penitentiary Board (in accordance with Ireland's request that the chief executive be relieved of serving on so many boards) and provided for three commissioners and a financial agent to be appointed by the governor with the advice and consent of the Senate. The senators passed the bill despite receiving petitions of protest from such influential organizations as the Knights of Labor. The growing power of the Knights, who claimed to have thirty thousand members in Texas, and rival labor groups such as the dockworkers' union led by black Republican boss Norris W. Cuney in Galveston got the attention of the Senate, especially after statewide strikes in March, 1885, led to bloodshed. As a sop to Cuney, the senators endorsed a House bill forbidding the employment of foreign sailors and crews in rolling cotton, handling cargo, or laboring on the wharves or levees of Texas ports. Although Governor Oran M. Roberts had vetoed a similar bill, Ireland signed this measure on March 26, 1885.

Another labor-related topic sparked lively debate. Senator Evans introduced a bill to require the comptroller, the land commissioner, and the treasurer to employ females as clerks in their offices. Senator Randolph, chairman of the Committee on State Affairs, to which the measure was referred, issued a strong report against its passage, but Evans, as a member of the committee, delivered an influential dissenting speech before a gallery that he had strategically filled with women. The ladies greeted senators who argued in favor of the bill with warm applause and withered those who spoke in opposition with cold stares. Randolph stated his case against the employment of females eloquently but "failed to overcome the subtle influence of the many bright eyes sparkling in the Senate chamber." When the bill was debated in the House, the galleries again overflowed with women. Evans was not allowed to speak in favor of his bill, but the Senate adjourned so that members could attend the debate. The House passed the bill with one major amendment—the women were required to have lived in Texas for a year—and sent the bill back to the Senate. Governor Ireland, however, had let it be known that he would not sign the bill, so its support in the Senate dissipated. When the House asked to be allowed to reconsider its amendments, the Senate refused to return the bill. House leaders protested, but Lieutenant Governor Gibbs ruled that the Senate could lawfully refuse to send the bill back.

Railroad strikes in Texas bolstered Ireland's demand for stricter regulation of the industry. Railroad companies, Ireland said, had been justifying their differentials in rates and their lack of service, which contributed to public resentment, with the claim that railroads in Texas could not pay their expenses out of their revenues. The governor contested this, recalling that he and others had had to stand on his last trip from Fort Worth to Dallas by rail because every seat on the train was occupied. "I would not see these roads crippled," he declared, "unless it be that requiring them to fulfill their duty to the people is crippling them." Stricter regulation would not "make capital timid," the governor asserted, because the "excellent men" managing the railroads in Texas could not object to "reasonable regulations."

Proposals for a state commission to effectively police railroad rates were defeated after considerable lobbying by the railroads, but several measures were enacted to curtail the careless business practices and sloppy record keeping that made it difficult to assess taxes. The Senate endorsed a House bill, signed by Ireland on March 17, 1885, requiring railroad companies to deliver annual statements of their rolling stock and facilities to be assessed for taxes. Another

House bill signed by Ireland on March 28 required accounts of all real and personal property held by a company as well. The governor also signed a House bill requiring railroad companies to keep crossings "in proper use for the traveling public." A fine of ten dollars per week would be levied until the companies complied.

Many railroad companies had avoided Texas law by not opening an office in the state. A House bill signed on March 28, 1885, required every railroad company operating in Texas to maintain a public office in the state where open records were to be kept for inspection by stockholders, by "any officer or agent of the State whose duty it may be to inspect such books," and by the legislature whenever it was felt necessary. The directors of every railroad company were to hold at least one meeting annually at their Texas office and to publicize it for thirty days beforehand in local newspapers. The president or superintendent of every railroad company in the state was to report annually under oath to the governor or comptroller on the condition of his operation. Noncompliance would cost a railroad company a thousand dollars a month until it met the act's requirements; a company already in operation had six months to comply.

Complementing the act requiring railroads to maintain public offices within the state was an act introduced by Senator Kleberg and signed on March 31, 1885, which fixed the venue for suits against railroad companies in the county where their public office was located. A bill written by Senator Pope and signed on March 28 required the attorney general to initiate an investigation of railroads and other corporations operating in violation of the Texas Constitution.

Against the passage of these laws, the railroad lobbies argued that Texas railroads were not making money. But the legislature, in its effort to ensure more responsible practices by the railroad companies, held firm against an industry whose rates were still unregulated. The only direct result of the pleading was Ireland's endorsement of Senator Terrell's bill that waived the deadline on previous contracts which several railroad companies had with the state for the completion of their roadbeds. The effective date for computing the charters' deadlines for completion was moved to January 1, 1887, because of the depression, which had hindered new construction.

The legislative debate over railroad regulation briefly shed more light on the condition of blacks in Texas. In his opening remarks to the Nineteenth Legislature, Ireland had declared that he would not challenge the policy of segregation on trains but asked whether it might not be proper to require a fare reduction for blacks, as they were forced to ride in second-class cars. A petition from the Colored Men's State Convention held in Houston in August, 1884, and received by the Senate in January, 1885, added to the list of black issues requests for reforms in jury law, county convict farms, houses of correction, and facilities at Prairie View. The Senate Committee on State Affairs, chaired by Randolph, rejected every one of the proposals except those pertaining to county convict farms; the proposals on convict farms were referred to the Senate Committee on the Judiciary Number 2, chaired by Davis, where they were allowed to lay on the table. Plans to build a branch of the University of Texas for blacks, as required by the state constitution, were tabled in the wake of Senator Pfeuffer's legislative fiasco. The Nineteenth Legislature also chose to ignore the escalating violence against blacks and poor whites at the polls, contributing to the development of a closed political system in Texas by the turn of the century.

The end of the session brought a flood of editorial invective against the Nineteenth Legislature. Although the members had passed a number of important bills, they had failed to enact many portions of the Democratic campaign platform in a satisfactory manner. Reductions in taxes had been accompanied by unpopular decreases in services, especially in education. The problems of corporate landholdings in Texas had scarcely been addressed, and efforts to establish a permanent organization with more substantial authority to regulate railroads had come to naught. The feisty editor of the *Austin Democratic Statesman* accused the legislators of "intellectual constipation" and asserted that, even if they all went back to school, only one in ten might comprehend "great public questions." His claim that the Nineteenth Legislature would be remembered as "the most incompetent legislative body ever assembled in Texas" can certainly be dismissed as hyperbole, but the fact remains that the Senate had disappointed many in the state. Resentment and rumors of scandal became the legacy of this abbreviated session, which left many tasks unfinished.

CHAPTER 13

The Senate of the Twentieth Legislature, 1887–88

The Twentieth Legislature met for a regular session from January 11 to April 4, 1887, and returned for a called session from April 16 to May 15, 1888. The legislators convened under the administration of Governor Lawrence Sullivan "Sul" Ross but quickly proceeded beyond his simple, conservative platform to enact legislation touching on many areas of importance to Texans.

Sul Ross was a genuine military hero who had led the Ranger company that recaptured Cynthia Ann Parker from the Comanches and had commanded a brigade during a Civil War career that included participation in over 135 engagements. As a delegate to the 1875 Constitutional Convention he had argued forcefully in favor of economic retrenchment, and he had championed that cause again as a senator in the Seventeenth Legislature. In the 1886 elections Ross had emerged from a field of five candidates to easily win the governorship. While serving as governor he remained keenly interested in fiscal conservatism but also concerned himself with public lands, education, and railroad regulation.

Ross's lieutenant governor was Thomas Benton Wheeler. Wheeler was born June 7, 1840, in Alabama and came to Texas along with his family in 1854. He served the Confederacy in Company A, Peter C. Woods's Regiment. Wheeler moved to Austin after the war and became the county attorney for Travis County in 1867. Federal officials removed him from office for interfering with Reconstruction, so he ran for mayor of Austin and served in that capacity from 1872 to 1877. In 1877 he moved to Breckenridge, where he practiced law, then served as judge of the Twelfth Judicial District from 1880 to 1886, resigning to run for lieutenant governor. After serving two terms as lieutenant governor, he returned to Breckenridge but soon moved to Aransas Pass and would promote the locating of harbor facilities there. Wheeler married Kitty G. Manor in 1866; after her death in 1881 he married Ida de Berry. He died in San Antonio on February 2, 1913.

The Senate of the Twentieth Legislature benefited from the leadership of the senatorial veterans among its members. Thirteen senators retained their seats from the tempestuous Nineteenth Legislature: Charles Keith Bell; James H. Calhoun; John L. Camp, Jr.; William L. Douglass; Caleb J. Garrison; George W. Glasscock, Jr.; Richard H. Harrison; Temple Lea Houston; Hermann Knittel; William H. Pope; Samuel D. Stinson; J. O. Terrell; and John Woods. Also among those elected to the Senate in the fall of 1886 was William Henry Burges, who had served in the Senate of the Seventeenth Legislature and now returned in place of George F. Pfeuffer, who had failed to be renominated and then died suddenly of apoplexy on September 15, 1886. Burges had practiced law with John Ireland and had served as county and district attorney for Guadalupe County.

Three former state representatives were elected to the Senate in 1886. William Thomas Armistead of Jefferson had served in the House during the Eighteenth and Nineteenth legislatures. Armistead was born in Georgia on October 25, 1848. After enlisting at age sixteen, he served in the 2nd Regiment of Georgia state troops under Generals Johnston, Hood, and Hardee and was promoted to captain. He was wounded at Jonesboro and captured at the end of the war. After the war, Armistead returned to school and graduated from the University of Georgia in 1871. He then moved to Douglassville, in Cass County, Texas, where he taught school until he was admitted to the bar. He became the law partner of the prominent politician David Browning Culberson in Jefferson. Armistead was a delegate to every state Democratic convention from 1874 to 1889. He served in the Senate during the Twentieth and Twenty-first legislatures and returned to the House for the Twenty-fourth. In the words of one source, "In politics he is a Democrat, in religion a

Lawrence Sul Ross, governor of Texas, 1887–91.
Reproduced from holdings of Texas State Archives.

Thomas Benton Wheeler, lieutenant governor, 1887–91, in Twentieth and Twenty-first legislatures, mayor of Austin, 1872–79. Reproduced from holdings of Texas State Archives.

Baptist and is a member in good standing of the A. F. & A. M., Legion of Honor, and United Workmen Lodges." William Thomas Armistead died on September 1, 1920, in Jefferson.

William Wallace Davis of Augusta in Houston County had served briefly in the House of the Fourteenth Legislature, succeeding a representative who had resigned. Davis's parents had come to Texas from Mississippi in 1828, and he was born March 15, 1831, in Houston County. William was the only son and the youngest of four children. The children were orphaned young and were raised by their maternal grandmother, and William had little formal education. In 1850 the nineteen-year-old William married Lucy Margaret Penick, a Missouri native. They had four children, John, Elizabeth, Alice, and William. Before being elected to the legislature, Davis was a farmer, merchant, and soldier. He served in Sibley's Brigade and participated in the battles of Mansfield and Pleasant Hill, Louisiana, "and others less sanguinary"; later biographical sketches refer to him as Colonel Davis. He was elected to the Senate of the Twentieth Legislature from the Eighth District by a majority of eight thousand votes; one source says that he was unopposed. Davis served as chairman of the Committee on Retrenchment and Reform. He remained in the Senate through the Twenty-first Legislature. He rarely spoke on the floor, reserving his succinct and persuasive arguments for private conversations. Davis died July 22, 1910.

Freshman senator Louis Napoleon Frank of Stephenville had served in the House during the Eighteenth Legislature. Frank was born in Louisiana on December 22, 1849, and came to Texas at age twenty-four. He resided in South Texas for one year, then settled in Erath County in 1874. He read law, was licensed in 1875, and began to practice the following year in Stephenville. Frank was a senator in the Twentieth through the Twenty-second legislatures and chaired the Committee on Penitentiaries; he served as president pro tempore during the called session of the Twenty-second Legislature.

Twelve of the other fourteen freshman senators who began the twentieth session of the legislature, and Waller S. Baker, who replaced Senator Harrison for the called session, had nonlegislative political experience or were attorneys. Leonard Anderson Abercrombie was born on December 1, 1832, in Alabama. He was admitted to the Alabama bar in 1854 but then moved to Madison County,

Texas, where he established himself in a partnership with Henderson Yoakum, the historian, and a Mr. Branch. In 1856 he moved to Huntsville, his residence until his final illness. Abercrombie was elected prosecuting attorney for the district in 1860 and was chosen a delegate to the Secession Convention. In 1861 he resigned his office to join the army and served in Gillespie's Company of Nichols's Regiment throughout the war, rising to the rank of lieutenant colonel. Abercrombie was a tireless worker, a Mason, and a patriot. He married Lavinia Chilton on January 1, 1860; and they had seven children: Mary, Lavinia, Ella Haden, Corinne R., Francis A., Leonard A., and William Chilton. The Abercrombies were known for their hospitality and their care in providing their children with the finest educations. Abercrombie served in the Senates of the Twentieth and Twenty-first legislatures. He died in Philadelphia on December 23, 1891, and was buried at Huntsville.

Robert Henry Burney of Kerrville, who was born on October 22, 1854, in McNairy County, Tennessee, had come to Texas along with his family in 1856. Burney enlisted in the Texas Rangers at the age of twenty. He married Mattie Prather of Palestine on September 13, 1879, and they made their home in Kerrville. Burney opened a law office in 1881 after graduating from Southwestern University in Georgetown, Texas, and studying law at Vanderbilt University. He served in the Senates of the Twentieth through the Twenty-second legislatures, representing the Twenty-eighth Senatorial District, which was at the time the state's largest, containing sixteen counties and extending from San Antonio to El Paso. In the Twentieth Legislature he was chairman of the joint select committee charged with investigating the conduct of the Comptroller's Office. Burney wrote the committee's report, which formed the basis of the legislation authored by Senator Jarvis requiring monthly statements from the tax collectors. Senator Burney was also chairman of the Committee on Public Printing and was the author of legislation regarding furnishing the new Capitol and clearing and ornamenting the grounds. In the Twenty-first Legislature he chaired the Committee on Education; in the Twenty-second, he was chairman of the Committee on State Asylums and was elected ad interim president pro tempore. Burney presided for many years over the judicial district composed of Bandera, Edwards, Kendall, Kerr, Medina, Real, and Zavala counties, serving from 1904 until his death in 1926.

John M. Claiborne of Galveston, who was born on February 27, 1839, had come to Texas from Tennessee with his family in 1846 at the age of seven. The family settled in Bastrop County, where John was educated at the Texas Military Institute, Austin; he later attended Baylor University. Claiborne read law with his father but much preferred farming. In his long career, he held various administrative, political, and military positions. He was a clerk for the comptroller in 1860 and 1861; district and county clerk for Bastrop County after the Civil War; chairman of the state Democratic executive committee for two years; and aide-de-camp to Governor Roberts. Claiborne began his military service as a private in Terry's Texas Rangers in 1861 and rose to the rank of brevet colonel. In 1864 General John Bell Hood placed him in the secret service and promoted him for gallantry. He was seriously wounded three times, slightly wounded twice, and had four horses killed under him, but he remained active and served as a major general of the Texas Volunteer Guards after Reconstruction.

In 1865 Claiborne married Sue M. Phillips of Kentucky. They had three children: R. Sidney, Tom Jack, and Hattie Overton. Although his district had a Republican majority, Claiborne handily won his seat in the Senates of the Twentieth and Twenty-first legislatures. His platform emphasized equal treatment under the law and governmental restraint. He chaired the Committee on Commerce and Manufactures and was vice-chair of the Committee on Military Affairs. Claiborne resigned his seat in the Twenty-first Legislature on February 19, 1890. Mrs. Claiborne died in 1900, and in 1902 the senator married Ella Holbrook. General Claiborne pursued his love of agriculture and wrote noted papers on hedges suitable for the Texas climate. He died on April 20, 1909.

Scott Field of Calvert in Robertson County was born in Mississippi on January 26, 1847, and served in the army in Alabama, Georgia, and Tennessee from the age of sixteen. He attended the University of Virginia, then returned to Mississippi, where he taught school and studied law. Field moved to Calvert in 1872, soon after being admitted to the bar, and was prosecuting attorney for Robertson County from 1878 to 1882. He served in the Senates of the Twentieth and Twenty-first legislatures, chairing the Committee on the Treasurer's and Comptroller's Offices, the Committee on Enrolled Bills, and, in the Twenty-first session, the Committee on

Mining, Irrigation, and Agriculture. He was a delegate to the Democratic National Convention in 1892 and served in the Fifty-eighth and Fifty-ninth congresses from 1903 to 1907, then returned to a lucrative private practice and farming in Texas. Field was married three times: first to Victoria Luckey of Mississippi, who died two years after the marriage; then, in 1878, to Lucy Garrett Randolph, with whom he had three sons, Thomas, Scott, and Eugene; and, finally, to Maude Green. Senator Field began losing his sight toward the end of his life and was completely blind by 1923.

Alexander White Gregg of Palestine was born in Centerville, Texas, on January 30, 1854. He began his education in the public schools of Texas, then graduated from King's College, Tennessee, in 1874. After studying law at the University of Virginia, he was admitted to the bar in 1878 and returned to Texas to practice in Palestine. Gregg served in the Senate only during the Twentieth Legislature, chairing the Committee on Internal Improvements. He was later elected to the Fifty-eighth Congress and remained in office from March 4, 1903, until March 3, 1919. He died on April 30, 1919, in Palestine.

James Jones Jarvis of Fort Worth had been district attorney for the Sixth Judicial District and county judge of Wood County. Born on April 30, 1831, in Surry County, North Carolina, Jarvis had lived in Tennessee and in Illinois, where he was educated and studied law. Abraham Lincoln was one of his bar examiners. Soon after being admitted to the bar, Jarvis took a steamboat to New Orleans, then went on to Shreveport. With only one hundred dollars cash in hand, he began his walk to Texas, traveling as far as the East Fork of the Trinity River but returning from that edge of civilization to Quitman in Wood County in 1857. Jarvis's reputation for philanthropy perhaps began there, when he loaned most of his remaining sixty dollars to a friend and started a law practice with only five dollars. In addition to practicing law, he published the *Quitman Herald* for two years. In 1861 he enlisted in the 10th Texas Cavalry and served as major and adjutant. He was wounded and returned home shortly before the end of hostilities. During his public service in Wood County he met and married Ida Van Zandt.

In 1872 the Jarvises moved to Tarrant County, and Major Jarvis became associated with the firm of Smith & Hendricks, soon to be Smith, Jarvis & Hendricks, then Smith & Jarvis, which became quite prominent. This practice was located in the young city of Fort Worth, which Jarvis predicted would flourish as a railroad center; he would later invest in real estate and also raise shorthorns and thoroughbreds. A "man of sterling worth and strict integrity," he bought and donated to the Christian Church the property of Add-Ran College at Thorp Spring and became a trustee of the school, renamed Add-Ran Christian University. The institution relocated to Waco in 1895, became Texas Christian University in 1902, and moved to Fort Worth in 1910. The former property in Thorp Spring continued to serve as the site of Jarvis Institute, later known as Add-Ran Jarvis College. The Jarvises also donated 465 acres to found Jarvis Christian College, a four-year school for Negroes, at Hawkins, Texas. James Jarvis died in Fort Worth on January 20, 1914.

During his service in the Senates of the Twentieth and Twenty-first legislatures, Major Jarvis was chairman of the Finance Committee. By shepherding through an act in the regular session requiring monthly reports of tax assessors and collectors, he contributed significantly to the treasury surplus that had accumulated by the called session.

Jonathan Lane of La Grange, born on October 15, 1855, was the youngest member of the Senate. On December 28, 1880, he married Alma Harrison, and they adopted a son. Lane became a member of the bar in 1882 and began to practice law in 1885 in La Grange. In the Senate of the Twentieth Legislature he was chairman of the Committee on Insurance, Statistics and History, and in the Senate of the Twenty-first he served as chairman of the Committee on Public Roads and Bridges. At the end of his term, Lane and his family moved to Houston, where he became quite a tycoon, serving as president or a director of banking, railroad, insurance, irrigation, rice milling, and lumber companies. Lane remained politically active and chaired the state Democratic convention of 1892. Senator Lane—a Knight Templar, Mason, Shriner, and Knight of Pythias—died on May 27, 1916, at Port Aransas.

Henry D. McDonald of Paris was a Texas native and an attorney. The circumstances of his election to the Senate were peculiar. The Third District was composed of three counties—Lamar, Red River, and Fannin. The delegates to the Democratic convention had long agreed that the office would rotate among the counties, and for the 1886 election the nominee was to be from Lamar County. But the delegates from Fannin and Red River refused to support the Lamar selection, County Attorney Richard Wooldridge; they said they would vote for any other Lamar man. The delegates from Lamar, however, had their instructions and thus were prevented from offering alternates. Finally, the other delegates decided upon McDonald.

Senator McDonald was too young to have served in the war. He was educated at McKenzie Institute and read for the bar, earning admission in 1868 at an early age. He is said to have been striking in appearance, his "person [being] the worthy casket of his mind." In the Senate of the Twentieth Legislature he was chairman of the Judicial Districts Committee; during the Twenty-first Legislature he served as chairman of Judiciary Committee Number 1 and, during the regular session, as president pro tempore. McDonald announced for the governorship in 1890 but inexplicably withdrew. He died in Paris in 1925.

Francis E. MacManus of Corpus Christi was born in Leitram County, Ireland, on February 20, 1830. He attended Louisiana University in New Orleans beginning in 1860 and moved to Texas in 1865. He was a district attorney and a special judge and made his home in Corpus Christi. MacManus served only in the Senate of the Twentieth Legislature and was chairman of the Committee on Stock and Stockraising.

Eldred James Simkins of Corsicana was born on October 13, 1839, in South Carolina. He served the Confederacy in his home state in Hampton's Legion and the 1st Confederate Artillery Regiment. For such loyalty to their state, he and his family had to forfeit all of their property under the second Confiscation Act, passed by Congress in July, 1862. Simkins moved to Florida in 1867 and practiced law at Monticello with his brother. He was also chairman of the county Democratic executive committee and editor of the local paper.

In 1871 Simkins moved to Corsicana, where he opened a law office and later edited the newspaper; he served as district attorney from 1872 to 1876. He was chairman of the Democratic party in Navarro County until 1876 and was a regent for the University of Texas from 1882 to 1896. Simkins served in the Senates of the

Twentieth, Twenty-first, and Twenty-second legislatures, resigning on April 30, 1892. He was chairman of the Federal Relations Committee and, in the Twenty-second Legislature, of the Committee on Constitutional Amendments. He was principally an advocate of higher education but during the Twenty-second Legislature also played a prominent role in the establishment of the railroad commission. Simkins was considered highly polished and scholarly and was a member of the Episcopal Church and the Masonic Grand Lodge. He married Eliza Trescott (or Trescote or Trescot), and they had five children who survived infancy. In 1892 Governor James S. Hogg appointed Simkins associate justice of the Court of Criminal Appeals, on which he would serve two years before returning to private practice in Corsicana, where he died on June 25, 1903.

Samuel Crockett Upshaw of Hillsboro was born on January 31, 1840. He came to Texas from Arkansas, having spent the first ten years of his life in the Chickasaw Nation, where his father served as agent for the tribe under President Van Buren. The younger Upshaw was educated in public schools and completed his studies at Cumberland University in Lebanon, Tennessee, in 1861. He entered the army as a second lieutenant and fought at Bull Run. He then returned to Texas and joined Waul's Legion; while serving with this unit, he was captured at Vicksburg. After his parole, Upshaw came back to Texas, studied law, and was admitted to the bar in 1866 at Brenham. In 1870 he moved to Corsicana, where he was appointed district attorney; he served in that capacity until his removal two years later under Reconstruction. Upshaw served in the Senates of the Twentieth and Twenty-first legislatures. In the former he chaired the Committee on Roads and Bridges, and in the latter, the Committee on Constitutional Amendments. He was a Knight Templar and a Mason. Senator Upshaw died on January 20, 1901.

William H. Woodward of Port Lavaca, a Kentucky native born on August 30, 1817, had practiced law since 1849. In 1852 he moved to Indianola, Texas, where he served as a county judge. Woodward had also been a farmer for a short time. He volunteered to serve his adopted state and became a brigadier general with the 24th Brigade operating along the coast. Long after the Civil War, the hurricane of August 20, 1886, destroyed every house in Indianola, which was never rebuilt, and Woodward moved to Port Lavaca. He served as chairman of the Committee on Military Affairs in the Senate of the

Twentieth Legislature and on the Committee on Counties and County Boundaries in the Senate of the Twenty-first. He was married to Penelope R. Woodward of Christian County, Kentucky.

Another native Kentuckian, Waller Saunders Baker, the chairman of the Democratic executive committee in McLennan County, took the place of Senate veteran Richard H. Harrison, who resigned before the called session. Taking over for Harrison included assuming the chairmanships of the Committee on Private Land Claims and the Committee on Counties and County Boundaries. Baker, born on March 30, 1855, in Lexington, Kentucky, had come to Texas in 1859. He was educated at Baylor University, studied law, and was licensed at the age of twenty-one; he married Mary Mills in 1886. The called session of the Twentieth Legislature was the only session in which he served. In 1892 he was a delegate to the Democratic convention and was campaign manager for James S. Hogg. Baker died on September 9, 1913, while on vacation in San Francisco. An associate would say of that event, "His falling into the arms of death, like the falling of a mighty oak in the forest, left a gap in the sky and a chasm in the earth amidst the membership of the Waco bar."

The membership of the new Senate included two political neophytes who were not lawyers. William Allen, yet another Kentucky native, had tried his hand at a number of callings, including teacher, author, farmer, and Methodist deacon and elder; he was also a Mason and an army chaplain. Allen was born on March 18, 1835, and came to Texas in 1855. In 1866 he established a school at Bethel and married Abbie Mayes. They had no children but raised several orphans. Allen served in the Twentieth and Twenty-first legislatures. He was chairman of the Committee on Agricultural Affairs. The Allens lived in Denton County until 1904, then moved to Frisco, Texas, where William died on August 12, 1908. A philanthropist, he gave a large portion of his estate, including over twelve hundred acres of land near Frisco, to Southwestern University in Georgetown, of which he was a trustee, and to Southern Methodist University in Dallas.

Elbridge Geary Douglass of Sherman, another political novice, was a farmer from Missouri. Elbridge Douglass had come to Texas at the age of fourteen and was forty-two when elected to the Senate of the Twentieth Legislature, where he would serve as chairman of the Committee on Privileges and Elections. He contributed little to

Senate debates and resigned on January 23, 1889, early in the Twenty-first Legislature.

The election of officers for the Senate of the Twentieth Legislature resulted in several personnel changes—not all of them fortunate. William N. Ramey and Charles M. Boynton were again elected secretary and first assistant secretary for the regular session, but Boynton succeeded Ramey—who had been appointed assistant superintendent of the penitentiary and placed in charge of the facility at Rusk by Governor Ross—as secretary for the called session. W. E. Donley then became first assistant secretary. Wiley M. Imboden had worked as second assistant secretary during the Nineteenth Legislature, but as that position was now abolished, he served as journal clerk for the Twentieth. Rufus G. Childress took the place of tempestuous Alexander Sampson as calendar clerk. H. J. Huck, Jr., served as engrossing clerk, and William P. Williams as enrolling clerk. Andrew J. Dorn returned as doorkeeper, Richmond K. Smoot as chaplain, and J. A. Stuart as assistant sergeant-at-arms, but newcomer Pat H. Hennessy took over as sergeant-at-arms. Hennessy was arrested in March, 1887, on charges of forgery brought by several members of the Senate. A special committee was appointed to investigate the affair, and its resolution in favor of his dismissal was adopted unanimously on March 11, 1887. W. T. Brewer served as acting sergeant-at-arms for the balance of the regular session and for the called session.

The Twentieth Legislature proved to be slow in organizing, and the first week of the regular session passed without substantive activity. Outgoing governor Ireland's message on the first day, which was read to the senators by a clerk, consisted primarily of a review of the accomplishments of his administration; Ireland offered few guidelines for the future. Governor Ross delivered a lengthy inaugural address to a joint session of the legislature six days later, on January 18. He, too, avoided specific recommendations, offering instead general admonishments to reduce taxes and provide for the safety and development of Texas. On January 20 he finally sent a substantial written message to the legislature outlining his expectations for the session. Ross desired greater equity in taxation, especially in assessments; relief for those suffering from the drought; and more funds for state institutions. It was not an inspired mandate, but it provided a good starting point.

The problem of taxation was put aside for the time being, in light of the need for immediate relief for disaster-stricken areas of the state. A severe drought had oppressed the western counties since June, 1885, temporarily halting the westward migration of farmers who had surged forward with the coming of the railroads. Numerous petitions from western counties requesting drought relief were submitted to the Senate, some in the name of the new Farmers' Alliance. Most of the victims were farmers who had recently settled on public school lands, spending all of their money on improvements. The Senate voted to appropriate one hundred thousand dollars, to be distributed by a committee of three appointed by the governor, to commissioners courts in afflicted counties for the purchase of corn, flour, and meal for destitute families.

The drought measure, which had been introduced by Senator Frank, passed with a simple majority on January 26. Senators Camp, Terrell, Davis, and Abercrombie immediately changed their votes from negative to affirmative so that the bill would receive the two-thirds majority it required in order to take effect immediately. The four senators explained in a communication they had entered into the *Senate Journal:* "While we believe that the aid should not have been granted, we recognize the fact that the bill has a majority of the Senate in its favor, and if aid is to be given at all, it should be given at once." When Senator Houston returned to the chamber, he requested and received permission to register an affirmative vote, even though he had been absent during the original balloting. The legislation allowed the committee in charge of the relief effort only forty days to investigate conditions in the drought district, which covered an area larger than all of New England. The railroads generously donated transportation of the supplies, and newspapers raised a fund to purchase seeds. Eventually the committee disbursed $93,462.50 for the relief of 28,750 people in thirty-seven stricken counties, about $3.25 per capita.

The drought was not the only calamity facing Texans in the mid-1880s. The Indianola hurricane of August 20, 1886, had wiped out the town, and Senator Woodward introduced a bill for the relief of his former neighbors. Although Armistead, as chairman of the Committee on Finance, reported against the bill, a strong minority report from Glasscock proved to be more influential, and Governor Ross signed the measure on March 25, 1887. The Senate also passed—with only one dissenting vote—a second bill from Woodward which permitted railroads to abandon tracks that led to termini in coastal county seats that had been destroyed by a storm, as long as the companies then built a line leading to the new county seat. The legislation was endorsed unanimously by the House, and Ross signed it on February 16, 1887. The Senate in turn unanimously approved a House bill, which was signed on March 8, 1887, to provide relief for ninety-three citizens who had lost homes or businesses when a "most terrific, terrible and destructive cyclone and flood from the Gulf, such as has never occurred before within the memory of the oldest inhabitant," flattened Sabine Pass City on October 12, 1886.

The Twentieth Legislature responded in a timely fashion to Governor Ross's requests for reform of charitable state institutions. A state orphan asylum was created through a Senate bill introduced by Bell and signed on April 4, 1887. Its primary support came from the sale of public lands, but several private organizations in Austin also contributed to its development. A House bill approved on April 5, 1887, provided for the construction of a Deaf and Dumb and Blind Asylum for Colored Youth. Like the orphan asylum, its site was selected near Austin by a board of three commissioners appointed by the governor. The institution for blacks did not share the revenue from public land sales; instead, fifty thousand dollars was set aside for its construction.

Many of the private charitable organizations in Texas during this period, including the major contributor to the new orphan asylum, were directed by women. A married woman, however, was not allowed to incorporate or to serve as an officer of a corporation without the consent of her husband. Senator Terrell introduced a bill, signed on April 2, 1887, which repealed this old provision. The incident that drew his attention to the discrimination was the attempt to organize a "Home for Sick Women" in Dallas, which had been blocked by the law.

Any progress the state's prison system made during this period was scarcely due to legislative appropriations. A legislative committee investigated the facilities of the state penitentiary system and determined that they were in satisfactory condition. The committee recommended, however, that the convicts be employed within the walls of the prisons as soon as possible, and because that was expensive, it also asked for and obtained increased appropriations to better equip the outlying prison farms and camps. In keeping with the goal of making the prisons self-supporting, a bill introduced by Senator Camp and approved on March 1, 1887, authorized the employment of county convicts who had been jailed for defaulting on the payment of the fine or costs adjudged against them. Such convicts could be used in county road construction, on the county farm, or under contract to private companies until their fines had been worked off. A convict's labor, regardless of the contract price, would be valued at twenty-five cents a day, including Sunday, and could continue for up to two years unless the fine and costs were finally discharged earlier.

A House bill endorsed by the Senate and signed on March 29, 1887, did provide funds for the construction of a reformatory for "youthful convicts"—inmates of the penitentiaries who were under sixteen years of age and whose unexpired sentences were five years or less and newly convicted felons under sixteen who were sentenced to five years or less. A panel of three commissioners appointed by the governor would select a site distant from the two state prisons and farther than two miles from any incorporated town or city. The legislation stipulated that the land could not cost more than ten thousand dollars, while another forty thousand dollars could be spent to build the new facility. The institution would operate under the supervision of three trustees appointed by the governor, who were to see to it that the young inmates were taught "habits of industry and sobriety, some useful trade, and to read and write, and are also supplied with suitable books." The trustees were to provide for the "reformation, education, and discipline" of the convicts and also for their "profitable employment" in "mechanical industries" to be founded by the trustees in connection with the reformatory. Finally, they were to be especially careful that the "white and colored inmates shall be kept, worked, and educated separately."

Prison expansion was accompanied by some reform of the judicial system. A bill introduced by Senator Frank and signed on March 30, 1887, provided for the organization of a commission of appeals, consisting of three members to be appointed by the governor for two-year terms beginning April 1, 1887. The commission would review and pronounce awards in civil cases pending before the Supreme Court if the parties consented to the referral of the case. The commission's conclusions would be reported back to the Supreme Court and would become the judgment of the court, along with such other orders as might be necessary. At the same time, the Senate endorsed a sweeping reorganization of the lower courts.

Unfortunately, reorganization did not solve the pervasive problem of corruption in the Texas judiciary, and the Senate of the Twentieth Legislature failed to follow through on its reform initiative in this field. The House on March 1, 1887, transmitted a joint resolution to remove Judge Frank Willis of the Thirty-first Judicial District from office. A Senate committee of three—McDonald, Simkins, and Camp—was appointed to investigate the judge.

The investigation of Judge Willis was prompted by the following facts. Over 6.1 million acres of public land had been reserved for the support of schools, the university, and asylums in that district, of which about 1.3 million had been unlawfully enclosed by ranchers and livestock corporations. By January, 1887, these interests owed the state $123,353 for the use of the public lands, assessed at four cents per acre annually. Judge Willis had cooperated in the organization of a grand jury that returned eighty-six bills of indictment against the Panhandle Stock Association for illegal use of public lands, including six each against jury foreman Charles Goodnight, who was president of the association, and five other members of the grand jury. Fifty-six cases were tried in four days in January, 1886, by a district attorney who was on a retainer from the association and before petit juries composed primarily of employees of the accused and of the accused themselves. Not surprisingly, the result in every case was an acquittal.

After a lengthy investigation, the Senate committee recommended that Judge Willis be removed from office, as the House requested. The senators agreed to let each side present its case once more to the Senate as a whole before they voted. Attorney General James S. Hogg spoke for an hour and forty-five minutes in favor of removal. Willis, who had not been allowed to speak before the House, delivered a moving speech that lasted more than two hours and snatched victory from the jaws of defeat. An informal poll just days before had shown that two-thirds of the Senate was ready to remove him, but on the day of the final vote, Senator Houston spoke against adoption of the resolution of removal, and the vote was twenty-two to five in Willis's favor. MacManus explained in an opinion entered in the *Senate Journal* that the time to impeach Willis had been during the term in which the offense was committed. Although he had been reelected, Willis was "not the same judge by virtue of a continuous and uninterrupted tenure of that office, and the present official cannot lawfully be punished for alleged offenses of his predecessor in office, whether the present official be the same man or not."

Revisions in law accompanied the halting reforms in the judicial system. Governor Ross signed a House bill on February 24 that increased the penalty for carrying a deadly weapon to a maximum of two hundred dollars or sixty days in jail and approved another House measure on February 25 that more clearly defined the offense of rape. A bill from the House raised the penalty for bigamy to a maximum of five years. A Senate bill introduced by Calhoun and approved on March 8, 1887, stipulated that no one could be convicted of murder unless the body of the deceased, or "portions of it," were found and identified as the alleged victim. Penalties were also increased for the illegal sale of liquor or the operation of gaming tables. Senator Frank introduced a bill that updated the provisions for local option on prohibition, which Ross signed April 1, 1887, but a proposed amendment to the state constitution for statewide prohibition was not approved by the voters in an August, 1887, referendum.

The debate over gambling took on a comical aspect early in the Senate's deliberations. On January 14 an angry Senator MacManus hastily introduced a resolution that the sergeant-at-arms be ordered to remove a blackboard from the front of the temporary Capitol on which bets were being posted on the election of a U.S. senator by the Texas Legislature. The resolution was adopted but, on a motion of Senator William Douglass of Beaumont, the vote was reconsidered. Senator Glasscock offered a substitute calling for the removal of the person who had placed the blackboard in front of the statehouse. But, on a motion of Senator Houston, the substitute and resolution were tabled. Although the blackboard eventually was removed, the betting pools continued to thrive. The Crystal Saloon in Austin, following the news that caucuses had been held for John Ireland, Samuel Bell Maxey, John H. Reagan, and Alexander W. Terrell, organized a pool in which Ireland was the favorite, Maxey a distant second, and Reagan dead last, behind "the field."

The Twentieth Legislature's balloting for U.S. senator proved unpredictable, and many customers of the Crystal Saloon must have lost their wagers. Four ballots were taken in a joint session on January 26, with no clear victor, then six ballots the next day with the same result. Maxey won the first balloting, then lost ground to Reagan, while Ireland corralled a handful of swing votes. Thirteen more ballots were taken on January 28, 29, and 31, again with no one winning a majority. The senators voted evenly in their support for Maxey and Ireland, but a minority held out for Reagan. On February 1, the sixth day of voting, Senator Pope stated that Ireland had wanted his name removed from nomination five days earlier, but his friends and supporters had kept it in despite his wishes. Pope formally withdrew Ireland from contention, but Representative E. Taylor Moore nominated Terrell. On the seventh ballot of the day, Moore withdrew Terrell's name, and Reagan then won by a majority of one, with the last Senate tally showing sixteen votes for Reagan, twelve for Maxey, one for Ireland, and two for Oran M. Roberts, who watched from the gallery.

The public campaign against gambling extended to speculation as well, especially in commodities futures. The law against selling futures passed by the Nineteenth Legislature had sparked a protest, both over the circumstances of its hasty passage—after the stabbing of a Saint Louis reporter by the calendar clerk of the Senate—and its poor phrasing. Senator McDonald successfully sponsored a better-written bill that increased the penalty for trading in commodities futures to a maximum fine of five hundred dollars for each offense, with each day of such conduct being a separate offense, or thirty days to six months in jail. The Senate received many petitions protesting the adoption of any law against commodity speculation, which caused some delay in their consideration of McDonald's proposal, but the bill passed on a split vote. The Senate did not endorse a proposed joint resolution from the House that would have instructed the Texas delegation in Congress to work for passage of federal laws against speculation in grain and cotton futures, electing instead to leave such decisions to those lawmakers.

Governor Ross's interest in railroad regulation was reflected in the number of bills on the topic that were submitted during the Twentieth Legislature. State regulations for railroads were amended through a bill introduced by Senator Harrison to ensure that the freight or passengers transferring from one railroad to another be accepted without delay or discrimination in rates or service. Another Senate bill, introduced by Gregg, made it unlawful for railroads to discriminate in the rates or services they offered to express companies. Ross approved both bills on April 2, 1887. Two days later, he signed two more acts. One, introduced by Senator Harrison, provided substantial penalties for consolidating parallel railroads, which was prohibited under the state constitution. The other required railway companies to supply requested freight cars within a reasonable time. However, a proposal by Senator Upshaw to establish a three-man railroad commission was not passed. Among those who lobbied against the bill were representatives of the Knights of Labor, who maintained that the current legal system was sufficient. Railroad companies were pleased with that development, as well as with the repeal of an 1879 law that had required trains to pause at the boundaries of Texas.

Several railroad regulation bills were designed to answer the complaints of farmers and ranchers. Through a bill introduced by Senator Lane and signed on March 23, 1887, railroads which fenced their rights-of-way were required to have an opening and crossing at least thirty feet wide each mile and a half, with every enclosure, regardless of size, required to have at least one opening and crossing. The placement of a crossing could be determined by the petition of two citizens who lived or owned land within five miles of the enclosed right-of-way. If the company failed to comply within thirty days, it would have to pay five hundred dollars a month to each of the petitioners until it did comply. A House bill approved on March 26 required that railroad companies provide double-decked cars for the shipment of sheep, goats, hogs, and calves and charge the same per-car price as that for a single-decked carload of cattle or horses. If they did not want to provide double-decked cars, they could ship the smaller livestock on single-decked cars but could only charge half price. The fine for noncompliance was five hundred dollars. This bill had failed to pass the Nineteenth Legislature, but in the wake of violence against the railroads across the state the Twentieth Legislature took definite steps to dispel agrarian unrest.

Labor strikes against the railroads also had some clear impact. The Senate endorsed a House bill strengthening provisions giving prior liens to mechanics, operatives, and laborers who performed work for railroads. A Senate bill introduced by Harrison and approved on March 14 provided that railroad companies had to give thirty days' notice before reducing the wages of employees. At the same time, a bill proposed by Senator Elbridge Douglass of Sherman and signed on March 8 provided that a conviction for obstructing railroad tracks or tampering with railroad facilities in a manner that endangered life could result in a prison sentence of up to seven years. If such tampering led to loss of life, the charge was to be murder. A House bill further provided that anyone who detained a train by threatening the engineer or other railroad employees could be fined from one hundred to five hundred dollars and jailed for up to one year; vandalizing railroad engines or cars to prevent their operation could be punished by a fine of up to one hundred dollars and a sentence of from three to twelve months in jail.

Governor Ross did not propose any specific remedies for the corruption and inefficiency of the Land Board in his opening messages to the Twentieth Legislature, but the editor of the *Austin Weekly Statesman* opined that when the legislature was through with the board "there won't be enough of it left to make a grease spot." His remark would prove correct. A measure introduced by Senator McDonald and signed by Ross on April 1, 1887, provided for the sale or lease of lands set aside for public schools, asylums, and the university. The land was to be classified and valued by the commissioner of the General Land Office according to use—pasture, agriculture, or timber—and sold to actual settlers only in parcels of 160 acres and multiples thereof, with a maximum of 640 acres. No mention was made of the Land Board, which was allowed to quietly expire.

The land legislation reflected the influence of agrarian lobbies and several years of legislative squabbling. No sales were to be made to a corporation, either foreign or domestic, and transfers of land by a settler to a corporation brought the cancellation of the original sale by the state. Settlers also had to reside on the land for three consecutive years or the sale was void. Tracts were to be sold at no less than two dollars an acre, with those having permanent water to be sold at no less than three dollars an acre; timberland was to be sold at no less than five dollars an acre. Settlers had to pay one-fortieth of the purchase price down, with another fortieth, plus 5 percent annual interest, every August 1 until the amount was paid off. After three consecutive years of occupying the land, a settler could retire the entire debt. Land could also be leased at four cents an acre, to be paid in advance each year, but leases for more than five years were not permitted. Grazing land under lease could not be sold by the state, but agricultural land could be sold out from under the lessee unless he had made improvements worth more than one hundred dollars. The legislation restricted the number of stock animals that could be turned loose on lands leased from the state. Using public lands without leasing them could earn one up to a one-thousand-dollar fine and two years in jail for each day of unauthorized use, but the Senate already had observed—as in the scandal involving Judge Willis—that convictions would be difficult to obtain.

These provisions were retained in subsequent land legislation. A bill introduced by Senator Bell and passed during the regular session of the Twentieth Legislature provided for the sale of unappropriated public domain to settlers at two dollars an acre, in parcels no larger than 640 acres, on the same terms as McDonald's measure. Unfortunately, rather than encouraging genuine settlers, these laws, according to the 1908 report of Commissioner John J. Terrell, gave rise to "untold perjury." Despite the rigid provisions, land sales in western counties greatly outnumbered the number of settlers, and the greater part of the public domain came under the control of ranchers. One avenue for land speculation was eliminated, however, with repeal of the statute adopted by the Seventeenth Legislature granting certificates for 1,280 acres of land to Texas veterans. Senator Harrison, responding to frequent reports of fraud, introduced the bill, which was signed on February 15, 1887.

Two more acts concerning land provided for the relief of drought victims, while at the same time ensuring a maximum return to the state on some public land sales. Under a House bill endorsed by the Senate, the period of time for repaying the principal owed to the state for school lands purchased under the 1874 acts was extended for ten years, but the 10 percent annual interest still accrued during the extension. The state benefited by extending the period of the original notes because the interest on them was higher than that which could be obtained for new ones. A second House bill, approved on March 10, 1887, allowed those whose land had been sold for taxes by the state a right of redemption by paying their back taxes within twelve months of the effective date of the act, thereby salvaging sales for the state while again providing farmers and ranchers time to recover from the drought.

The drought combined with federal legislation provided the impetus for creation of the state Bureau of Agriculture. A House bill was approved on April 1, 1887, placing the bureau within the reorganized Department of Agriculture, Insurance, Statistics, and History. It was to operate in conjunction with the U.S. Department of Agriculture in research and extension work to improve farming methods across the state. A Senate bill proposed by McDonald and signed on April 2, 1887, provided for the establishment of an Agricultural Experiment Station at the Agricultural and Mechanical College of Texas, pursuant to a grant of fifteen thousand dollars from Congress through the Hatch Amendment to the Morrill Act of 1862.

The drought had not completely suspended immigration into Texas, and many new areas of settlement needed to be formally organized. In central and western Texas, the Senate endorsed the creation of Mills and Brewster counties and established the western boundary of Edwards County. The western portion of Tom Green County became seven counties: Crane, Ector, Glasscock, Loving, Upton, Ward, and Winkler. Buchel, Foley, and Jeff Davis counties were carved from Presidio County; the bill dividing Presidio, which originated in the House, initially called for the creation of four new counties (Albion, Hayne, Prentiss, and Jeff Davis), but it was amended by Senator Burney before its final passage. Sutton and Schleicher counties were carved from Crockett County, again through a House bill. Senator Houston introduced a bill to create Willie County from parts of Williamson and Bell counties, but it failed to pass after numerous petitions against division were submitted to the Senate. To facilitate land sales, the legislature authorized the land districts of Crosby, Knox, Martin, and Scurry.

The Senate did not neglect the wildlife resources of Texas, which were under considerable pressure from professional hunters. The fine for taking fish with poison or explosives was increased to a maximum of $150 through a House bill approved on March 15, 1887. Another House bill signed ten days later prohibited the hunting of quail and partridges from April through September and banned the netting of these game birds altogether. A Senate bill introduced by

Claiborne and approved on April 2, 1887, provided regulations for saltwater netting. Henceforth, all smaller fish that customarily had been dumped from nets or pots onto land or into shallow water to perish would have to be released in water of sufficient depth to ensure their survival. Only the lowly croaker was excepted. The staking of oyster beds 538 yards square was authorized, but the taking of oysters less than an inch and a half in length was prohibited, as was the taking of any free oysters from May 1 to August 25. Only mature shrimp and crabs could be taken; immature ones were protected under the regulations for small fish. Predatory animals did not receive similar consideration from the senators; in fact, they endorsed MacManus's bill, signed on April 2, increasing the bounties for bobcat and coyote scalps to fifty cents; wolf scalps to one dollar; and panther, tiger, leopard, and "Mexican Lion" scalps to two dollars.

Governor Ross called the Twentieth Legislature into special session in April, 1888, to deal with several topics, including the disposition of a surplus in the state treasury, completion and inspection of the new Capitol, tax reform, settlement of the boundary dispute involving Greer County, and support for public schools. The senators had bowed to the "Piney Woods" faction in the House near the close of the regular session and endorsed a "mossback" economy, and the governor's call to dispose of a budget surplus provided an opportunity for them to redeem themselves. Several bills were passed quickly, including legislation for the direction and support of public schools. The Senate endorsed a House bill to lower the state ad valorem tax rate for general revenue to ten cents per one hundred dollars for 1888, but only after it had been amended to provide that the rate would be twenty cents per one hundred dollars for succeeding years. During the regular session, the House had killed Senator Simkins's bill to employ a state geologist, a proposal favored by agrarian interests in the state. Simkins had his revenge during the called session when fifteen thousand dollars was set aside to fund a state geological and mineralogical survey.

The crowning achievement of the called session was a supplemental appropriation devised to eliminate the state budget surplus. Among other things, the appropriation provided ten thousand dollars for the purchase of paintings and statues of men prominent in the history of Texas to be used to decorate the new Capitol,

Dedication parade along Congress Avenue for new Capitol, 1888.
Reproduced from holdings of Texas State Archives.

which first opened for public inspection on San Jacinto Day, 1888. Through a motion introduced by Senator Burney, five senators (Bell, Burges, Burney, Davis, and McDonald) were appointed, along with five members of the House, to inspect the new Capitol and to provide estimates of the cost of landscaping and furnishings. The Senate subsequently endorsed a House bill providing $140,000 for that purpose. Much of the material for the new Capitol had been furnished at little or no cost to the state—the granite had been donated, then cut by convict labor, and the iron foundry at the Rusk prison provided all of the columns, pedestals, and castings—so the legislators did not protest the cost of decoration. On the afternoon

Convicts at work on granite columns for new Capitol.
Reproduced from holdings of Texas State Archives.

of May 10, 1888, the Senate endorsed a concurrent resolution from the House for the removal of the Twentieth Legislature to the new Capitol. The senators recessed so that their furniture could be transferred, then met in their new chamber for the first time at half past eight that night. Senator Woods presided as president pro tempore, and Chaplain R. K. Smoot blessed the new hall with a prayer for peace, rain, and legislative wisdom.

The supplemental appropriation included the substance of many bills introduced on behalf of special interests who wanted a piece of the pie. A "loan" of $125,000 went to the available fund of the University of Texas, to be repaid at no interest by January 1, 1910. The disbursal was made "in full payment and satisfaction of all claims of the University of Texas against the State of Texas for moneys drawn from the University fund by said State." The amount had been set by a joint committee appointed to discuss details of the budget, on which Senators Armistead, Glasscock, Jarvis, Lane, and McDonald—some of the university's most ardent supporters—served. The university in Austin had originally received no appropriation for 1888–89, beyond the proceeds of the endowment it shared with the Agricultural and Mechanical College of Texas. A legislative attack by proponents of the latter institution was shattered by a proposal, made only half in jest, that if the college really were a branch of the university, it should relocate to Austin so the buildings in College Station could be used to house a division of the university for black students.

Other institutions also benefited from the supplemental budget. Fifty thousand dollars of the "loan" to the university was reserved for building a medical branch in Galveston; that city had already agreed to donate land, and the administrators of the John Sealy estate had pledged to construct a teaching hospital. The wording for this provision, appended in the House, was essentially that of Senator Claiborne, who had sought, unsuccessfully, to have the original Senate bill for the loan to the university amended in the same manner. The Agricultural and Mechanical College of Texas requested \$100,000 in additional appropriations and received \$41,500; Prairie View Normal School requested \$35,000 and got \$25,000. The new orphan asylum was given an additional \$15,000 with which to begin construction near Corsicana, and the reformatory received \$25,890.

A separate measure submitted by Terrell and approved unanimously by the Senate provided \$150,000 to build two new wings onto the North Texas Insane Asylum at Terrell, Texas. Debate then centered on funding the construction of another asylum for the insane in southwestern Texas. The appropriations bill passed both chambers, but on May 15 the president of the Senate gave notice that as the speaker of the House had refused to sign it, he would not do so either. A hot debate ensued on printing the entire bill in the *Senate Journal*. Those who supported the motion to print the measure won, and the Twentieth Legislature adjourned *sine die* at 11:30 that night.

The senators of the Twentieth Legislature redeemed themselves with their actions during the called session. Despite lackluster leadership by Governor Ross, in the end they had passed substantial legislation. The one subject they had avoided—typical for their times—was race relations. Senator Field's bill to build an addition to the State Lunatic Asylum in Austin for use by black patients had failed to pass the House during the called session. And in spite of several petitions on the topic, the Twentieth Legislature steadfastly refused to provide an appropriation to carry out the mandate of the Fifteenth to construct an agricultural and mechanical school for blacks. Senator Claiborne had introduced a bill to construct such an institution which received a favorable report from committee, but the matter progressed no further. It is interesting to note that Claiborne in the regular session introduced an unsuccessful joint resolution to amend the state constitution to require payment of a poll tax before voting. He described his position in the minority report by saying:

> I do not desire to tax a man for the privilege of casting his vote, but submit the fact that a man who does not contribute something to carry on the government, whose immunities and protection he enjoys, is not a suitable person to elect legislators to pass laws, or men to administer the affairs of State. The object is not so much to gain revenue as [to] make the ballot pure.

With the support of blacks restricted to such paternalism and with conservatives such as Ross consolidating their hold on the Democratic party, the future course of politics in Texas was already clear.

CHAPTER 14

The Senate of the Twenty-first Legislature, 1889

At its state convention in the fall of 1888, the Democratic party, responding to the protest of a few increasingly powerful agrarian interest groups, called for stricter railroad and antitrust legislation. About half the members of the Twenty-first Legislature were farmers and ranchers, the highest proportion of agriculturists in any representative body in Texas since the 1875 constitutional convention, and this group would add an element of agrarianism to the deliberations, especially over the regulation of transportation rates. Although none of the members of the Twenty-first Legislature identified themselves as non-Democrats, Democratic U.S. senator Richard Coke, who was reelected unanimously in January, 1889, estimated that at least seventeen were allied with dissident political factions. Governor Lawrence S. "Sul" Ross and Lieutenant Governor Thomas B. Wheeler had been reelected easily in the fall of 1888, and the Democratic domination of Texas politics remained intact through 1889. But public discontent over corruption in government and business, that would split the party within a few years was already evident in the debates of the Twenty-first Legislature, which met for only one session, from January 8 to April 6, 1889.

Eighteen members of the Senate of the Twenty-first Legislature retained their seats from the previous session: Leonard A. Abercrombie; William Allen; William T. Armistead; William H. Burges; Robert H. Burney; John M. Claiborne; William W. Davis; Elbridge G. Douglass; Scott Field; Louis N. Frank; George W. Glasscock, Jr.; James J. Jarvis; Jonathan Lane; Henry D. McDonald; William

H. Pope; Eldred J. Simkins; Samuel C. Upshaw; and William H. Woodward. Because the majority of the newcomers to the Senate in 1889 were comparatively young and inexperienced, the veterans were able to dominate the activities of that body more than in previous sessions.

The editor of the *Austin Democratic Statesman* noted the youth of the new senators but added, "They seem earnest, able and ready men, well equipped for the duties demanding their thought and action." Not all of the newcomers were serving their first term in the legislature; four of them had previously served in the House.

Marcus Henry Townsend of Columbus was in the Texas House of Representatives during the Eighteenth Legislature; his election in 1882 to the House's Sixty-seventh District was the first by a Democratic party nominee in Colorado County, a Republican party stronghold, since the start of Reconstruction. Townsend was born on March 26, 1858, in Colorado County; he was raised on a farm and educated in the common schools. He attended lectures in the law department at Baylor University at Independence and was admitted to the bar in 1880. Townsend set up practice at Columbus in 1881. Following his service in the House during the Eighteenth Legislature, he was elected to the Senate's Eleventh District seat in 1888 and served one term during the Twenty-first and Twenty-second legislatures. Townsend's family was involved in a long-standing feud in Columbus known locally as the "Townsend-Reese feud." In 1899 Townsend was arrested for manslaughter in a case involving the death of a member of the Reese clan. The charge was dismissed and Townsend relocated to San Antonio. His interest in his home county continued, though, and he later helped found the town of Garwood in Colorado County. Townsend died of cancer in 1915.

Edwin Augustus Atlee, Sr., of Laredo had served in the House of the Nineteenth Legislature. Atlee was born in Athens, McMinn County, Tennessee, on March 16, 1846. He attended East Tennessee Wesleyan University and, following graduation in 1870, became a member of the faculty there, teaching Latin and Greek. In 1873 he moved to Corpus Christi, where he taught school and studied law. The following year he was admitted to the bar and became the county attorney for Nueces County. He served in that position until 1879, when he moved to Laredo; he was elected to the House of

Representatives the next year. Following this first legislative service, Atlee became mayor of Laredo, a position he held from 1885 until the beginning of his tenure in the Senate in 1889. In the election of 1888 he won the Twenty-seventh District Senate seat as a Democrat. He served in the Senate through the Twenty-sixth Legislature and was ad interim president pro tempore during the Twenty-third. Atlee died in 1910. Edwin A. Atlee, Jr., served several terms in the Texas House of Representatives after his father's death.

Like Atlee, Robert Snead Kimbrough of Mesquite in Dallas County had served in the House during the Nineteenth Legislature. Kimbrough was born on September 19, 1851, in Monroe County, Tennessee. He came to Texas in 1874 and first settled in Clay County; eighteen months later he moved to Mesquite, where he established a mercantile business. In 1884 Kimbrough was elected to represent Dallas County in the House. Four years later he was elected to the Senate for one term and served in the Twenty-first and Twenty-second legislatures representing Dallas, Kaufman, and Rockwall counties.

William Cone Johnson of Tyler began his political career in 1886 when he was elected as a Democrat to represent Smith and Gregg counties in the House of the Twentieth Legislature. Johnson was born in Dawsonville, Georgia, on June 11, 1860. He studied at Emory College in Oxford, Georgia, and at Peabody Normal College in Nashville, Tennessee, before receiving his bachelor's degree from the University of Nashville in 1880. Johnson moved to Tyler in December of that year and taught at East Texas University. He studied law while he taught and was admitted to the bar in 1885. Following his one term in the House, Johnson was elected to the Senate and represented Smith, Wood, Rains, Gregg, and Upshur counties in the Twenty-first and Twenty-second legislatures. In 1910 he was an unsuccessful candidate for governor in a race won by Oscar B. Colquitt. A noted orator and Democratic party loyalist, Johnson would be involved in politics for many years. He attended the 1912 Democratic National Convention, where he, along with other members of the Texas delegation, helped secure the nomination of Woodrow Wilson. President Wilson appointed him to the position of solicitor for the State Department in Washington, D.C. Johnson later became a member of the Smith County Highway Commission and in 1927 was appointed by Governor Dan Moody to serve as a member of the Texas State Highway Commission. He died on March 17, 1933.

Some of the new senators had previously been elected to lesser public offices. Robert H. Morris of Rusk, a self-taught attorney, had won recognition for his prosecutions as a county and district attorney in Nacogdoches County; he had also served as a judge of the county court. Born in Gadsden, Florida, in 1846, Morris came to Texas with his parents in 1866 and settled in Nacogdoches. His first job was as a farm laborer, but he educated himself at home and later became a schoolteacher. During his stint as a teacher Morris studied law; he was admitted to the bar in 1876. After moving to Rusk he ran for the Senate in 1888 as a Democrat and represented Cherokee, Anderson, Henderson, and Van Zandt counties. Morris did not complete his term as senator; he resigned on principle on July 9, 1890, over the constitutional amendment to establish a railroad commission. He had been such a strong opponent of a commission that his resignation was required, as one biographer stated, in order to give "his constituents an opportunity to elect a State Senator thoroughly in sympathy with them on this question."

Prior to his service in the Senate, Kennan Ben Seale had served as the attorney for Jasper County and for the First Judicial District. Seale was born in Jasper on March 4, 1855. He was educated at Waco University and later studied law before opening his practice in Jasper. He was thirty-three when he was elected to the Senate in the fall of 1888 as a Democrat to represent ten East Texas counties. Seale would serve one term as a senator through the Twenty-second Legislature.

Two of the newly elected senators would go on to become U.S. congressmen. John Walter Cranford of Sulphur Springs was born in Grove Hill, Alabama, on July 28, 1859. At the close of the Civil War, he moved with his family to Hopkins County, Texas, settling at Sulphur Springs. Cranford was admitted to the bar in 1880. He was elected to the Senate in November, 1888, as a Democrat and represented Camp, Delta, Franklin, Hopkins, and Hunt counties. He continued his service in the Senate during the Twenty-second and Twenty-third legislatures, serving as president pro tempore during the Twenty-second. In 1896 he ran for the U.S. Congress and served as a representative from March 4, 1897, until his untimely death in March, 1899.

In contrast to Cranford's tragically short tenure in the U.S. Congress, John Hall Stephens of Montague served five terms in that body. Stephens was from an old Texas political family; his grandfather was James Truit, who had been a member of the Congress of the Republic of Texas and a state senator for many years. Stephens was born in Shelby County on December 22, 1847. He was educated at Mansfield College in Tarrant County and graduated from the law department of Cumberland University in Lebanon, Tennessee, in 1872. Following law school, he set up practice in Montague County, which at the time was as far as civilization reached in northwest Texas. Stephens began his political career in 1888 when he ran for the Senate as a Democrat and was elected to represent the Nineteenth District, a huge district stretching from Montague County westward. He served one term in the Twenty-first and Twenty-second legislatures. In 1892 he moved to Vernon in Wilbarger County and continued the practice of law. Stephens was elected to the U.S. Congress in 1896 to represent the Thirteenth Congressional District and served in Congress from 1897 until 1917. Following his congressional service he moved to Monrovia, California, where he died in 1927. His body was returned to Texas for burial in Vernon.

Another new senator who was also a native Texan from a political family was George W. Tyler of Belton, whose father had served in the Texas House of Representatives during the Tenth Legislature. Tyler was born in Coryell County on October 31, 1851. He moved to Salado in 1864 and graduated from Salado College in 1871. He then attended the University of Virginia for one year and graduated from law school in Lebanon, Tennessee, in 1874; he began the practice of law that same year in Belton. Tyler was active in Democratic politics and was regularly a delegate at the Democratic state convention. He represented Bell, Coryell, Hamilton, and Lampasas counties in the Twenty-first and Twenty-second legislatures. Following his Senate service, he was for many years president of the board of trustees of the Belton public schools. He also served on the board of regents of the University of Texas. Tyler was a Mason and served as Grand Master of Texas in 1890. He retired from the practice of law in 1912 to devote time to the study and writing of history; he died on October 11, 1927. Tyler's *The History of Bell County*, edited by Charles W. Ramsdell, was published posthumously in 1936.

The rest of the newcomers came from a variety of backgrounds. John Hampton Harrison was born in Monroe County, Mississippi, on November 3, 1842. In 1858 his family moved to Texas and settled in McLennan County. Harrison attended Baylor University at Independence and was a sophomore there when the Civil War began. He enlisted in the Confederate Army and served in Hood's Texas Brigade and Green's Brigade of Texas Cavalry. After the war he returned to McLennan County and engaged in farming. In 1888 he was elected to the Senate as a Democrat and represented McLennan and Falls counties in the Twenty-first and Twenty-second legislatures. Harrison studied law and was admitted to the bar during his legislative service in 1891. He later served as U.S. postmaster in Waco during the second Cleveland administration.

Another Confederate veteran among the new senators was James Melville Ingram of Hemphill, who was born in Randolph County, Georgia, on December 7, 1840. Ingram came to Texas in 1857 when his family settled at Sexton in Sabine County. He was three months from graduating from Emory College in Oxford, Georgia, when the Civil War began and he enlisted in the Confederate Army. Ingram served in the infantry through several campaigns and later saw service in the cavalry and was captain of Company C of Whitfield's Legion. He was elected without opposition to the Senate in 1888 and served one term through the Twenty-second Legislature.

Henry Taylor Sims of Coleman was born in Talladega County, Alabama. He lived in both Alabama and Georgia as a child before coming to Texas with some schoolmates in 1870; he located at Harmony Hill in Rusk County and went into the grocery business. Sims sold his store after eight months and moved to Sherman in Grayson County, where he clerked in a store and began reading the law. He returned to Alabama in 1873 to complete his law studies and was admitted to the bar in Alabama in that year. He soon came back to Texas and eventually set up practice in Coleman County. In 1888 he was elected to the Senate as a Democrat without opposition and represented a large district consisting of Coleman and the surrounding counties. His official biographies during his legislative service contain no birth date, but he was reported to be "about thirty-six years of age" when elected. Sims served one term in the Senate, holding office during the Twenty-first and Twenty-second legislatures.

One exception to the general youth of the new senators was Ernst Gustav Maetze of Bellville, who had been a retired teacher before his election to the Senate in 1888 at the age of seventy-two. He had founded the first public school in Millheim in Austin County after immigrating there from his native Silesia in the Kingdom of Prussia. Maetze was born in Glogan, Silesia, on September 20, 1817. He was a graduate of the University of Breslau, where he studied Protestant theology. After receiving his degree, he became headmaster of an intermediate school. He participated in the German revolutionary movement of 1848 before coming to Texas in the 1850s. Maetze served in the Senate during the Twenty-first and Twenty-second legislatures and was the president pro tempore of the Senate at the time of his death on October 12, 1891. He was succeeded as senator by William W. Searcy for the called session of the Twenty-second.

John Wesley Finley of Sherman entered the Senate two months into the session, when he replaced Elbridge Douglass on March 5, 1889. Douglass had resigned early in the session on being appointed assistant superintendent of penitentiaries by Governor Ross. Prior to his service in the Senate, Finley had been the city attorney for Sherman.

John Finley was born in Monroe County, Tennessee, on January 19, 1847. He entered the Confederate Army when he was only fourteen and served with the 5th Tennessee Cavalry and the 63rd Tennessee Infantry. He attended the University of Kentucky at Lexington in 1871 and 1872. His family moved to Georgia for a time before coming to Texas in 1873. He had been admitted to the bar in Georgia in 1873 and was admitted to the Texas bar at Sherman in 1874. Finley held no further legislative office after his service in the Senate during the Twenty-first Legislature.

Seven of the Senate officers of the Twenty-first Legislature had served during the previous session. Charles M. Boynton returned as secretary, as did W. E. Donley as assistant secretary, Rufus G. Childress as calendar clerk, William P. Williams as enrolling clerk, W. T. Brewer as sergeant-at-arms, Andrew J. Dorn as doorkeeper, and Richmond K. Smoot as chaplain. Newly elected were Samuel H. Johnson as journal clerk, Sterling P. Strong as engrossing clerk, H. E. Henderson as assistant sergeant-at-arms, and George W. Fitzhugh as assistant doorkeeper. W. W. Works was chosen to fill the new position of assistant journal clerk, created on January 12,

1889. Veteran senator McDonald was elected president pro tempore without a dissenting vote.

The legislature was holding its first full regular session in the new Capitol, and the process of adjusting to the new surroundings took some time. On January 10, the *Galveston News* reported that the Senate elevators were operational, but "so far most of the members shy at it." On January 15, in ceremonies held in the House chamber with the floor and the galleries packed with spectators, Governor Ross became the first governor inaugurated in the new structure. At the time of the convening of the session, the chambers lacked their permanent carpeting and furniture, and the newspapers reported frequently on when the delivery of these items was expected. After taking a long weekend to allow for installation, on Tuesday, February 19, the Senate met in its chambers for the first time with its new furniture and carpeting in place. The temporary Capitol building, which had housed the legislature from 1881 to 1888, was leased to the directors of the John B. Hood Camp of United Confederate Veterans through legislation passed by the Twenty-first Legislature.

The dominant theme in Governor Ross's opening address to the Twenty-first Legislature on January 10, 1889, was economy in government. Although the previous legislature had founded several new state institutions—the Reformatory, the Deaf and Dumb and Blind Asylum for Colored Youth, and the State Orphan's Asylum—Ross recommended parsimony in considering requests for operating funds. The Senate responded by enacting a series of bills to shift the responsibility for public services elsewhere. The power of municipal authorities to levy taxes, issue bonds, and provide for public works was augmented through a series of measures introduced in both the House and Senate, and new, broader charters were adopted for many cities, including Dallas, El Paso, Fort Worth, Galveston, Houston, San Antonio, and Waco. Similarly, the legislature extended the authority of commissioners courts to provide for road and bridge construction and other public works projects. Many local-level conventions had adopted resolutions calling for public road improvements, and these actions of the Twenty-first Legislature were offered in response.

The legislature sought a more permanent solution to the threat of drought than relief programs could provide. A House bill authorized the operation of irrigation ditches and provided for the forma-

Lieutenant governor's reception room, Capitol building, circa 1888.
Reproduced from holdings of Texas State Archives.

tion of private companies to build such facilities. Irrigation projects were already under way in many western states, but they would not reach fruition until after the turn of the century when the federal government provided substantial financial aid.

Budget deliberations reflected a similar concern for economy. Senator Burney introduced a bill to provide more stringent guidelines for veterans' pensions, which were only $150 a year, and just $120,000 was set aside for Texas veterans for the 1889–91 biennium. In higher education, Sam Houston Normal School received $80,000 and the Agricultural and Mechanical College got $47,900 plus the interest earned on the state bonds it held, but Prairie View

The Senate met in its new chambers for the first time on February 19, 1889. Senate chamber, Capitol building, circa 1894. Reproduced from holdings of Texas State Archives.

Normal School had to make do with $25,000 and the University of Texas got only an appropriation for constructing and furnishing a building at the medical branch in Galveston. Senator Tyler's bill to accept the donation of Salado College to the state, to be reopened as "Peabody Normal School," failed to pass because the state would have had to pay to refurbish the facility. The failure of this measure must have wounded Senator Tyler deeply because he had attended Salado College and was an avid supporter of education.

The University of Texas was expected to rely on its endowments. Both chambers unanimously passed a House bill, signed on March 21, 1889, authorizing the university to accept donations of money

Temporary Capitol burning, 11th and Congress, 1899. Courtesy Austin History Center, Austin Public Library, # PICA 06185.

and property from individuals for the purpose of establishing endowed professorships; as a state institution the university had previously been unable to accept such donations. An identical bill, except for a provision that the bill would take effect immediately, was introduced in the Senate by McDonald. The second bill passed unanimously, received a four-fifths vote in the House, and was signed by Ross on March 27, 1889, six days after the first. A measure introduced by Senator Armistead, passed unanimously by both chambers and signed by the governor on April 2, 1889, provided that any surplus in the university permanent fund over five thousand dollars could be exchanged for state bonds bearing 5 percent inter-

Austin, 1880–89. View of Capitol looking north from south of the Colorado River. Courtesy Austin History Center, Austin Public Library, # PICA 01089.

est, which was higher than that afforded by previous bonded investments. Despite the fact that its lands remained the primary source of funding for the University of Texas, bills introduced in both chambers to cede all control over university lands to the regents failed, as they had in previous sessions. Senator Simkins, as a current member of the university's board of regents during this time, must have been disappointed.

Despite Ross's admonition to the contrary, the Twenty-first Legislature did provide for one new state facility. The establishment of a branch asylum for the treatment of the insane in southwest Texas had been a heated issue during the previous session. That legislature had failed to provide for one, but the Twenty-first, through a House bill, set aside $150,000 for the purchase and development of a facility located west of the Colorado River to house at least five hundred patients. But that was as far as the legislature's generosity went. Senator Glasscock's bill to build a state penitentiary in the same region of the state was rejected outright.

Glasscock made his proposal because the Democratic convention had again demanded that all state prisoners be confined within penitentiary walls, but as before, the parsimony of the legislature precluded such action. The state prisons and farms were filled nearly to capacity, and even a joint investigation committee chaired by Senator Davis was at a loss to suggest means by which the Democratic initiative could be carried out economically. The committee reported that a board of pardons should be established to visit the prisons periodically—the committee suggested every three months—to select and recommend to the governor the names of prisoners who should be paroled.

The majority report of the investigating committee painted a rosy picture of the Texas prison system, but this view was challenged by a minority report which claimed that some of the guards were "brutal and cruel" and that the conditions at outlying stations were often deplorable. Mortality among prisoners at the state-run sugar plantations, the minority report asserted ironically, would "eventually solve the vexed convict question" by substantially reducing the number of convicts held. In two years, of the 498 men held at the farms located in Fort Bend County, 27 escaped and 57 died. The report concluded that the state prison farm system was "barbarous, impolitic, inhuman and a relic and prototype of slavery in its worst conditions and features," adding that the whipping post would be preferable to such punishment. Expanding on the majority's recommendation that a board of pardons be established, the minority report proposed reductions in some criminal sentences, such as that for petty theft, and the expansion and improvement of the prisons.

The lack of response by the legislators to the minority's impassioned appeal must be considered within the context of the times. The editor of the *Austin Democratic Statesman* provided an insight on public opinion when he printed an article demanding that the reformatory be made self-sustaining. The author insisted that the young inmates "must be put to work of the hardest description on the farm, otherwise negro youths of 15, and white ones for that matter, will consider it a sort of paradise and flock thither." The article concluded, "Hard work must be the rule inside. Away with sentimental measures." With public sentiment in favor of such draconian measures, the legislature had little reason to proceed further in prison reform.

The legislators were not, however, totally unsympathetic to pleas for reform. In a bill introduced by Senator Upshaw, the compensation for county convicts hired out for labor was doubled to fifty cents a day, their contracts were restricted to work on public roads and streets or on the county farm, and the length of individual contracts was restricted to one year, half the previous permissible length. This measure, proposed in response to allegations of unfair practices with regard to the use of county convicts, passed the Senate unanimously, received only two votes in opposition in the House, and was signed by Governor Ross on March 7, 1889.

With a surplus in the state treasury, the Twenty-first Legislature was not pressed to find a way to supplement revenues. It did, however, endorse several bond issues for specific purposes. A forty-year bond issue initiated on August 5, 1870, had contained a provision that made the 7 percent bonds redeemable at the pleasure of the state after twenty years. In his opening address, Governor Ross suggested that these old bonds be exchanged for a new bond issue with a lower interest rate, thereby saving some money for the state. Through a bill introduced by Senator Ingram, an issue of new thirty-year bonds at 5 percent interest was authorized, to be exchanged for the old bonds or sold to redeem those of holders who did not wish to swap. These new bonds could be redeemed at the pleasure of the state five years after their date of issuance.

Despite protests from agrarian groups that the taxing power of the commissioners courts was too broad, the courts were permitted to issue twenty-year, 6 percent interest–bearing bonds to fund their indebtedness through a bill introduced by Senator Stephens and signed on April 4, 1889. These bonds could be redeemed in two years by the county, which was authorized to levy a tax of twenty-five cents for each one hundred dollars in taxable property to pay the annual interest and amortize not less than 2 percent of the principal of the bonds each year.

Anticorporatism had been pushed to the forefront of Texas politics by the development of agrarian protest groups. The most influential of these was the Farmers' Alliance, which weathered a tempestuous convention in 1886 to emerge the following year as a strong political organization with a nationwide constituency. Farmers in Texas, as elsewhere in the South, were trapped by the expansion of a one-crop economy; as the price of cotton declined in the latter half of the 1880s, so did farmers' fortunes. In 1887, 1.6 million bales of cotton grown in Texas sold for about $88 million; three years later, Texas farmers produced 2 million bales but received only $68 million for their crop. Farmers blamed the easiest targets: corporations for charging too much for their products and driving up interest rates; middlemen for taking too large a share of the profits; and railroad companies for manipulating transport rates.

The real villains, in the eyes of Texas farmers and their allies, were the trusts and monopolies. Five House bills were combined into one omnibus measure against the formation and operation of trusts in Texas. The final version of the bill was the result of a collaboration between Attorney General James S. Hogg, Representative Alvin C. Owsley, and Commissioner of Insurance, Statistics and History L. L. Foster, who modeled their legislation after a bill introduced by John H. Reagan in the U.S. Senate. The measure adopted unanimously by the Texas Legislature forbade price-fixing, restraint of trade, restriction of competition, and setting of transportation rates through illegal combinations. Any company that disregarded these provisions immediately would have to surrender its state charter; foreign corporations found to be in violation would be denied the privilege of continuing to do business in Texas. Individuals could be fined up to five thousand dollars and jailed for up to ten years for each day of infringement of the antitrust act.

The Twenty-first Legislature also played an active role in interstate antitrust activities. In response to an invitation from the Kansas Legislature, which had passed the first antitrust law in the United States on March 2, 1889, the Texas lawmakers adopted a concurrent resolution on March 6 authorizing a delegation of three senators and five representatives to attend an antitrust convention in Saint Louis. The resolution asserted that trusts were "operating in many dark devious ways in the state of Texas to the almost utter destruction of the stock interests in this state." The popularly accepted villains were the meatpacking trusts in Chicago and Kansas City, commonly referred to as "the beef and pork combines," who were, it was believed, manipulating prices for beef, cattle, and hogs in the West.

Senators Atlee, Stephens, and Upshaw attended the Saint Louis convention along with the members of the Texas House and delegates from many other western states. Atlee was largely responsible for the convention's adoption of a resolution, which was sent to the president to be laid before the next Congress, asking for the construction of a deepwater port in Texas for the benefit of all the West. The resolution adopted by the convention also called on the federal government to enact antitrust legislation and to amend the Interstate Commerce Act so that it could be used, along with federal antitrust law, to control illegal trust activities among railroads. The convention delegates also voted unanimously to recommend to their state legislatures the passage of a uniform law defining illegal business combinations and punishing those engaged in such practices. The omnibus antitrust bill discussed previously was Texas' fulfillment of this recommendation.

On March 29, 1889, a concurrent resolution was adopted by the legislature in response to recommendations made by the Interstate Deep Harbor Convention held in Denver, Colorado, in August of 1888. Joining Texas delegates at this convention were representatives from the states of Colorado, Nebraska, Missouri, Iowa, Arkansas, California, Nevada, and Kansas and from the Indian Territory and the territories of New Mexico, Wyoming, Dakota, and Arizona. The resolution requested the Texas delegation in Congress to support the convention's demand for a deepwater port in the state; it was thought that developing an alternative access to the western states would encourage greater competition in the meatpacking industry and reduce the influence of existing trusts. The project would require the support of the federal government. Senator Burney introduced a bill to set aside three million acres of Texas' public domain to support construction of a deepwater port, but the bill did not pass the Senate.

Agrarian anticorporatism collided head-on with the introduction of modern industry into Texas. By the late 1880s the state boasted successful enterprises in meatpacking, some textiles, and lumber.

Oil production on a limited scale had begun in Nacogdoches County in 1886, although that industry would not mature until after the turn of the century. Senator Lane introduced a bill to exempt from taxation for twenty years any person or association investing at least $100,000 in the manufacture of textiles, metals, or other products of the state, but the bill did not become law. A majority of the Senate Committee on State Affairs reported in favor of the measure, but a minority of two committee members, Cranford and Abercrombie, proved more persuasive in their protest that the proposed law would "help the rich and powerful corporation to oppress and strangle the smaller manufacturing establishments of our State." The two senators called the measure the "worst species of class legislation" and successfully campaigned against its adoption.

The Senate of the Twenty-first Legislature did demonstrate some interest in fostering the development of mining in Texas, primarily because that industry had brought such fabulous wealth to other western states. A House measure, signed by Governor Ross on March 29, 1889, reserved from sale all school, university, and asylum lands containing valuable mineral deposits, specifically gold, silver, cinnabar, lead, tin, and copper, as well as other metals. These tracts were declared open to public prospecting. Claims were to be no more than 25 acres in area and were to be sold at twenty-five dollars an acre. In order to keep a claim, the owner had to open and operate a mine for the recovery of mineral deposits. Placer claims could be had for ten dollars an acre, not to exceed 40 acres per person or 320 for a corporation.

The bill provided that those interested in recovering less glamorous minerals would receive more generous terms from the state. Miners who located and wished to recover deposits of iron ore, coal, kaolin, salt, marble, baryta, fire clays, valuable building stone, oil, or natural gas could claim up to 160 acres for an individual or 320 for an association, although any corporation that expended more than five thousand dollars in improvements could double the latter figure again. The cost was ten dollars an acre for land situated more than ten miles from a completed railroad but twice that amount for tracts within ten miles of an operating railway. By the turn of the century, profitable ventures had been established in coal, iron ore, salt, limestone, and granite. Although prospectors in the state failed to uncover significant deposits of precious metals such as gold or silver, they found evidence of oil, which in the following century would become a bonanza for landowners.

Railroad companies did not escape the attention of legislative trustbusters. The members of the Twenty-first Legislature, like their immediate predecessors, considered a bill to create a commission to regulate railroad transport. The railroad commission bill had passed the House but was introduced in the Senate by Johnson in heavily amended form as a substitute for his own bill on the topic. Many of the senators questioned whether the 1876 constitution permitted the legislature to delegate its authority in such a manner. A majority of them agreed that the Democratic platform adopted in the fall of 1888 had pledged more railroad regulation, but they argued that the pledge did not imply that a commission would be created. When the House gave notice that it would not accept the amended version of its bill championed by Johnson, the Senate adopted a measure introduced by Lane that provided for stricter oversight—without a commission—through freight-rate regulation. The House killed this legislation on April 1, near the end of the session.

Frustrated proponents of a railroad commission refused to admit defeat, even after the House closed ranks to defeat legislation proposed by Senator Pope providing for the appointment of a single railroad commissioner whose office would be attached to the attorney general's office—a weak measure described by Claiborne as a "political lightning rod" designed "to ward off the indignation of the people in the future, but without the proper insulators." Instead, the advocates of a commission threw their support behind a joint resolution introduced in the Senate to amend the constitution through a plebiscite to provide for the organization of a railroad regulatory agency. Attorney General Hogg adopted the issue as his own during his successful campaign for governor in the fall of 1890, in which both he and the joint resolution to establish a railroad commission received overwhelming support from the voters of Texas.

The debate over a railroad commission brought out the worst in several senators. Pope attacked Johnson's bill, which he bitterly opposed, with a barrage of ridicule and sarcasm. At one point Pope took the floor to deliver a poem castigating Senator Claiborne, who admitted that, in his zeal to have a railroad commission established, he had presented petitions which contained names taken from tombstones. Entitled "Pope's Essay on Claiborne," the poem began:

Hark, from the tomb, a doleful sound,
John Claiborne, hear the cry.
Why do you trespass on the ground
Where men sleep when they die?

Far better had you ne'er been bred,
My dear, my General John,
Than to live to filch the names of the dead
To build a railroad on.

The state press duly noted Pope's inflammatory humor and the fact that the railroad commission had been killed by the "House of Lords." Claiborne resigned in February, 1890, and no one was elected to complete his term.

Pope became notorious for his use of sarcasm to belittle his opponents. Early in the session the editor of the *Austin Democratic Statesman* had remarked that "few of the senators can equal Senator Pope in repartee, and he generally scores his point very forcibly." Only a few weeks later, the journalist would refer to Pope as the "satirist of the House of Lords," as many in the Texas press had come to call the Senate, and he added that the senator "can make a man feel meaner in three minutes than any well developed case of yellow jaundice." While discussing a measure that would have banned firearms and other weapons from specific places such as churches and saloons and certain social assemblies, Senator Pope sarcastically moved to have "cornshucking" and "sheepshearing" included on the list of protected activities. Pope's amendment to this weapons bill failed, as did one from Senator Upshaw to permit the carrying of pistols into churches where the sermon was over forty minutes in length. The whole measure failed, however, and was replaced by a weaker compromise weapons bill that established the maximum penalty at two hundred dollars or thirty days in a county jail. This bill, which was introduced by Senator Morris, did pass and was signed on January 30, 1889.

Although most of the railroad legislation proposed during the Twenty-first Legislature failed to pass, a few notable bills to regulate the carriers were adopted. Through a measure introduced in the House, all points where railroads intersected were defined as "depots," and companies were required to provide public "passenger houses" that were warmed and well lighted. This bill made no mention of segregated facilities, but that was the focus of a bill signed during this same session. Senator Pope, who would later be known as the "Jim Crow Senator," introduced a bill to require railroad companies to provide separate cars for black passengers. The measure passed in the Senate but failed in the House, its opponents arguing that it would be too much of a financial burden on the railroad companies. A House bill to "authorize" rather than "require" railroad companies to provide separate coaches or compartments for black passengers passed the Senate with only one dissenting vote and became law without Governor Ross's signature.

The segregation measure adopted by the Twenty-first Legislature required that the separate railroad accommodations be of "equal character as to comfort, etc.," and be clearly designated by signs. Black leaders in Texas stridently opposed legislative efforts to segregate railroad cars, arguing that blacks would not be provided equal facilities. As one explained, he would support measures to establish different rates for first-class and second-class accommodations, as that would accomplish the same thing in a more straightforward fashion. The editor of the *Democratic Statesman* spelled out the leader's rationale: "When colored folks are forced into second-class cars, he wants the companies forced to haul them at second-class rates." The protest failed, and the Twenty-second Legislature would amend the act to *require* separate cars and impose a fine of up to twenty dollars on a person of either race who attempted to ride in the prohibited accommodation.

Racism also tainted the arguments over eliminating corruption in Texas politics. Although a bill by Senator Seale to require a poll tax for suffrage was unsuccessful, a resolution introduced by Senator Kimbrough to amend the state constitution to provide for a property qualification for suffrage passed the Senate with only one dissenting vote. The nay vote was cast by Cranford, who had his protest entered in the *Senate Journal.* The senator concluded, "In my opinion the right of free suffrage is one of the fundamental principles of free democratic government, and the slightest abridgement of this right is contrary to the spirit and genius of our institutions, and is dangerous in practice and wrong in theory." The resolution failed to pass the House, but suffrage restriction remained a vital concern of Texas lawmakers, who finally passed such restrictions after the turn of the century.

Much of the opposition to suffrage restrictions in the Senate of the Twenty-first Legislature can be attributed to the agrarian challenge: such measures would affect poor whites as well as blacks. Agrarianism also influenced other legislative action. A landlord's prior lien on the property of his tenants was restricted to one year through a bill introduced in the Senate by Field and signed March 28, 1889. Mechanic's liens were strengthened through a measure introduced by Kimbrough and signed April 5, 1889. A House bill signed on April 3, 1889, conferred on the owner or keeper of any stallion, jack, or bull a lien on its progeny. However, a bill introduced by Glasscock which would have given a lien to owners of pastures on stock placed there to graze for a fee failed to pass the Senate.

Land legislation in 1889 reflected a mix of agrarian concerns and fiscal restraint. The laws providing for preemptions were repealed through a Senate bill introduced by Stephens and signed on March 7, 1889. Following the effective date of this act, "scrap lands," or parcels of 640 acres or less, would be sold to settlers only after they filed a petition. A House bill, signed on April 8 after passing the Senate unanimously, provided for the sale of school and other appropriated lands in parcels as small as 80 acres but no larger than 640 acres. It was recommended that timberland be sold at five dollars an acre and other land at two dollars an acre. All public lands could be leased for four cents an acre per year except university lands, which could be leased for three cents. A separate bill introduced by Stephens and signed by Ross on April 8 authorized the leasing of school lands at two cents an acre in eight unorganized counties in West Texas: Andrews, Bailey, Cochran, Dawson, Grimes, Hockley, Lamb, and Martin. Leases on land in central and eastern Texas could be signed only for six years, but West Texas land could be leased for ten years. As with previous legislation, agricultural land could be sold to settlers out from under a lease.

The Twenty-first Legislature acted to resolve two vexing legal problems involving land in Texas, one of which did not turn out the way the legislators had planned. Pursuant to Governor Ross's recommendation in his opening day address, all legitimate sales and issues of patents by the defunct Land Board were validated through a House bill signed on March 12, 1889 (the state Supreme Court had declared the board's actions illegal because it had often disregarded or exceeded its legislative mandate). The validation of these contracts was accompanied by many individual petitions for redress, each of which had to be considered on its own merits by the legislature in a laborious process that took up many hours of the session.

On February 23, Governor Ross signed a more controversial House measure that provided for the organization of a three-man board of arbitration to determine the validity of Texas' claim to Greer County. This county, created by the legislature in 1860 and formally organized in 1886, lay east of the 100th meridian of longitude between the northern and southern forks of the Red River. Texas contended that its boundary with federal territory lay on the northern fork, while the federal government argued that the true boundary was the southern fork. The Twenty-first Legislature hoped that Congress, which was considering the bill to organize the Oklahoma Territory, would agree to this arbitration, but instead Congress in 1890 ordered the U.S. attorney general to file suit against Texas. Six years later the U.S. Supreme Court declared that Greer County was not part of Texas, thereby severing from the state more than 1.5 million acres of land, much of which had already been filed upon by Texas veterans and other settlers.

The balance of the Senate calendar was occupied by a variety of bills covering a broad spectrum of issues. A measure introduced by Senator Claiborne and signed on April 4, 1889, provided for stricter penalties against owners of a "disorderly house" or a theater or saloon where "any prostitute, lewd woman, or woman of bad reputation for chastity" conducted herself in a "lewd, lascivious, or indecent manner." On a more pedestrian note, a bill by Senator Tyler designated February 22 as Arbor Day in Texas, commemorated for the first time in 1889. In contrast to the Arbor Day designation, the cause of conservation was set back when a House bill was passed exempting a long list of counties from the fish and game laws enacted by the Twentieth Legislature; included in the list were two new counties, Coke and Irion, which were carved from Tom Green County by the Twenty-first Legislature. In an attempt to deal with the growing problem of "whimsically explosive" illuminating oil, as one editor described it, the Senate endorsed a House bill to establish the office of "state inspector of oils," who would test petroleum products for quality and standardization in illumination. Licensing boards for pharmacists and dentists were created in separate bills, the one concerning dentists being introduced by Senator Harrison. Finally, through a bill introduced in the Senate by Simkins and signed on March 29, 1889, Jewish rabbis were authorized to perform marriages in Texas—they had not previously been so authorized.

In the eighty-nine days of the Twenty-first session, the legislature considered 1,070 separate bills, exclusive of resolutions, and enacted 147 laws. Members of the Senate had introduced 393 bills. In spite of this deluge of legislation, the legislature had failed to address many of the demands being made by Texans. Abusive railroad practices, electoral fraud, judicial corruption, the poor condition of public roadways, and the lack of an industrial base led to a public outcry for a new state constitution. Numerous petitions to redress the imbalance between taxation and services garnered little response from the legislature. Indeed, a House bill increased occupation taxes at a time when state services were being reduced.

Clearly, the Democrats did not yet realize the depth of public dissatisfaction, and they seriously underestimated the agrarian challenge. However, economic conditions and difficulties faced by farmers (and ignored by their government) had forced farmers to organize to seek reform. The continued growth and influence of these agrarian organizations, particularly the Farmers' Alliance, and their plea for government regulation of railroads and trusts and an expansion of the money supply—as well as the threat of third parties—caused some Democrats to move from the traditionalist view favoring a spare and weak government to a position in favor of a more active role for government.

The persistent and increasingly vocal demands of the agrarian groups would lead in 1890 to the nomination for governor of James Stephen Hogg, an advocate of railroad regulation and a proponent of the establishment of a railroad commission. With the election of Hogg and legislators filled with reformist zeal, the elections of 1890 evidenced a dramatic shift within the Democratic party. While the adjournment of the Twenty-first Legislature ended a session that failed to come to grips with a growing public outcry, the convening of the Twenty-second would witness the emergence of the Progressive movement in Texas—well before it emerged as a force nationwide.

Appendix A

MEMBERS OF THE NINTH LEGISLATURE*

Regular Session, November 4, 1861–January 14, 1862
First Called Session, February 2–March 7, 1863

Governor Francis R. Lubbock
Lieutenant Governor John M. Crockett

Senate

Member	*District Number*	*Address*	*Home County*	*Counties Comprising District*
Andres, James W.[1]	2	Livingston	Polk	Hardin, Jasper, Newton, Orange, Polk, Tyler
Batte, William C.	8	Mount Pleasant	Titus	Red River, Titus
Beasley, Stephen W.[2]	6	Gilmer	Upshur	Harrison, Upshur
Boyd, John	19	Tehuacana	Limestone	Ellis, Freestone, Limestone, Navarro
Branch, Anthony M.[3]	17	Huntsville	Walker	Grimes, Montgomery, Walker
Burnett, John H.[4]	11	Crockett	Houston	Anderson, Houston, Trinity
Burney, George E.[5]	28	Waco	McLennan	Bosque, Brown, Callahan, Coleman, Comanche, Coryell, Eastland, Ellis, Hamilton, Hill, McLennan, Runnels, Taylor
Casey, Lewis F.	4	Shelbyville	Shelby	Panola, Sabine, Shelby
Cook, Henry C.	33	El Paso	El Paso	El Paso, Presidio
Cooper, Leroy W.[4]	11	Crockett	Houston	Anderson, Houston, Trinity
Crawford, Anderson F.[1]	2	Jasper	Jasper	Hardin, Jasper, Newton, Orange, Polk, Tyler
Crawford, John F.[6]	14	Bonham	Fannin	Fannin, Hunt
Darden, Stephen H.[7]	25	Gonzales	Gonzales	Caldwell, Gonzales, Guadalupe
Davis, James B.[6]	14	Bonham	Fannin	Fannin, Hunt
Dickson, David C.[3]	17	Montgomery	Montgomery	Grimes, Montgomery, Walker

Dickson, J. J.[8]	15	McKinney	Collin	Collin, Grayson
Durant, John W.	18	Centerville	Leon	Brazos, Burleson, Leon, Madison, Robertson
Erath, George B.[5]	28	Waco	McLennan	Bosque, Brown, Callahan, Coleman, Comanche, Coryell, Eastland, Ellis, Hamilton, Hill, McLennan, Taylor, Runnels
Finlay, George P.[9]	24	Lavaca	Calhoun	Calhoun, DeWitt, Jackson, Lavaca, Victoria
Ford, Spencer[7]	25	Lockhart	Caldwell	Caldwell, Gonzales, Guadalupe
Graham, Robert H.	21	Decatur	Wise	Archer, Baylor, Buchanan, Clay, Cooke, Denton, Hardeman, Haskell, Jack, Jones, Knox, Montague, Shackelford, Throckmorton, Wichita, Wilbarger, Wise, Young
Guinn, Robert H.	10	Rusk	Cherokee	Cherokee
Harcourt, John T.	22	Columbus	Colorado	Colorado, Fayette, Matagorda, Wharton
Hartley, Rufus K.	1	Galveston	Galveston	Chambers, Galveston, Jefferson, Liberty
Hord, Edward R.[10]	32	Rio Grande City	Cameron	Cameron, Duval, Encinal, Hidalgo, Starr, Webb, Zapata
Houston, John N.	27	Belton	Bell	Bell, Burnet, Lampasas, Milam, Williamson
Jordan, A. N.[12]	16	Houston	Harris	Brazoria, Fort Bend, Harris
Lair, William D.[8]	15	Melissa	Collin	Collin, Grayson
Lea, Pryor	29	Goliad	Goliad	Bee, Dimmit, Goliad, Karnes, La Salle, Live Oak, McMullen, Nueces, Refugio, San Patricio
Locke, Matthew F.[2]	6	Lafayette	Upshur	Harrison, Upshur
Maxey, Rice[13]	9	Paris	Lamar	Hopkins, Lamar
Maxey, Samuel B.[13]	9	Paris	Lamar	Hopkins, Lamar
Mitchell, N. A.[11]	30	San Antonio	Bexar	Bexar
Moore, A. W.[14]	26	Bastrop	Bastrop	Bastrop, Hays, Travis
Moore, John W.	7	Linden	Davis (Cass)	Bowie, Davis, Marion
Obenchain, Alfred T.[15]	20	Weatherford	Parker	Erath, Johnson, Palo Pinto, Parker, Tarrant
Parsons, Jesse H.	5	Henderson	Rusk	Rusk
Quayle, William[15]	20	Norton's Grove	Tarrant	Erath, Johnson, Palo Pinto, Parker, Tarrant

Reed, Erastus	31	Boerne	Blanco	Atascosa, Bandera, Blanco, Comal, Concho, Dawson, Frio, Gillespie, Kerr, Kinney, Llano, McCulloch, Mason, Maverick, Medina, Menard, San Saba, Uvalde, Zavala
Scarborough, Edwin B.[10]	32	Brownsville	Cameron	Cameron, Duval, Encinal, Hidalgo, Starr, Webb, Zapata
Selman, Benjamin T.	12	Tyler	Smith	Smith, Van Zandt, Wood
Shelley, Nathan G.[14]	26	Austin	Travis	Bastrop, Hays, Travis
Shepard, Chauncy B.	23	Long Point	Washington	Austin, Washington
Weatherford, Jefferson	13	Pleasant Run	Dallas	Dallas, Henderson, Kaufman
Wheeler, M. W.	3	Homer	Angelina	Angelina, Nacogdoches, San Augustine
White, S. Addison[9]	24	Victoria	Victoria	Calhoun, DeWitt, Jackson, Lavaca, Victoria

*Journals and election records for this wartime legislature are fragmentary, and some members undoubtedly left for military service without a formal resignation.

1. Andres, sworn February 2, 1863, succeeded Anderson F. Crawford, who resigned.
2. Beasley, sworn December 16, 1861, succeeded Matthew F. Locke, who resigned.
3. David C. Dickson, sworn February 2, 1863, succeeded Anthony M. Branch, who resigned.
4. Cooper, sworn February 2, 1863, succeeded John H. Burnett, who resigned.
5. Burney, sworn February 2, 1863, succeeded George B. Erath, who resigned.
6. Davis, in special election on October 24, 1863, succeeded John F. Crawford, who resigned September 21, 1863.
7. Ford, sworn February 2, 1863, succeeded Stephen H. Darden, who resigned.
8. Lair, sworn February 2, 1863, succeeded J. J. Dickson, who resigned.
9. White, sworn February 2, 1863, succeeded George P. Finlay, who resigned.
10. Hord, sworn February 11, 1863, succeeded Edwin B. Scarborough, who was murdered on October 7, 1862.
11. Mitchell did not attend the 1st Called Session.
12. Jordan did not attend the 1st Called Session until February 27, 1863.
13. Rice Maxey, by special election on August 4, 1862, succeeded his son, Samuel B. Maxey, member-elect, who had joined the Confederate Army on May 25, 1861, leaving District 9 without representation during the Regular Session.
14. A. W. Moore, sworn February 2, 1863, succeeded Nathan G. Shelley, who resigned April 1, 1862.
15. Quayle, sworn February 3, 1863, succeeded Alfred T. Obenchain, who resigned February 15, 1862.

Appendix B

MEMBERS OF THE TENTH LEGISLATURE

Regular Session, November 2–December 16, 1863
First Called Session, May 9–May 28, 1864
Second Called Session, October 17–November 15, 1864

Governor Pendleton Murrah*
Lieutenant Governor Fletcher S. Stockdale**
Provisional Governor Andrew Jackson Hamilton***

Senate

Member	*District Number*	*Address*	*Home County*	*Counties Comprising District*
Beasley, Stephen W.	6	Gilmer	Upshur	Harrison, Upshur
Burney, George E.	28	Waco	McLennan	Brown, Bosque, Callahan, Coleman, Comanche, Coryell, Eastland, Falls, Hamilton, Hill, McLennan, Runnels, Taylor
Charlton, Napoleon B.	2	Woodville	Tyler	Hardin, Jasper, Newton, Orange, Polk, Tyler
Cooley, A. O.	31	Fredericksburg	Gillespie	Atascosa, Bandera, Blanco, Comal, Concho, Dawson, Edwards, Frio, Gillespie, Kerr, Kimble, Kinney, Llano, McCulloch, Mason, Maverick, Medina, Menard, San Saba, Uvalde, Zavala
Davis, James B.	14	Bonham	Fannin	Fannin, Hunt
Dickson, David C.	17	Anderson	Grimes	Grimes, Montgomery, Walker
Durant, John W.	18	Centerville	Leon	Brazos, Burleson, Leon, Madison, Robertson
Ford, Spencer[1]	25	Lockhart	Caldwell	Caldwell, Gonzales, Guadalupe

Guinn, Robert H.	10	Rusk	Cherokee	Cherokee
Harcourt, John T.	22	Columbus	Colorado	Colorado, Fayette, Matagorda, Wharton
Hartley, Rufus K.	1	Galveston	Galveston	Chambers, Galveston, Jefferson, Liberty
Haskell, J. A.	27	Cameron	Milam	Bell, Burnet, Lampasas, Milam, Williamson
Holland, Spearman[2]	4	Carthage	Panola	Panola, Sabine, Shelby
Hord, Edward R.	32	Brownsville	Cameron	Cameron, Duval, Encinal, Hidalgo, Starr, Webb, Zapata
Jordan, A. N.	16	Houston	Harris	Brazoria, Fort Bend, Harris
Jowers, William G. W.	11	Palestine	Anderson	Anderson, Houston, Trinity
Kinsey, Henry M.[3]	3	San Augustine	San Augustine	Angelina, Nacogdoches, San Augustine
Knox, William B.[4]	30	San Antonio	Bexar	Bexar, Wilson
Lea, Pryor	29	Goliad	Goliad	Bee, Dimmit, Goliad, Karnes, La Salle, Live Oak, McMullen, Nueces, Refugio, San Patricio
Magoffin, James W.[5]	33	El Paso	El Paso	El Paso, Presidio
Maxey, Rice	9	Paris	Lamar	Hopkins, Lamar
Mitchell, N. A.[4]	30	San Antonio	Bexar	Bexar, Wilson
Montague, Daniel	21	Gainesville	Cooke	Archer, Baylor, Clay, Cooke, Denton, Hardeman, Haskell, Jack, Jones, Knox, Montague, Shackelford, Stephens, Throckmorton, Wichita, Wilbarger, Wise, Young
Moore, A. W.[6]	26	Bastrop	Bastrop	Bastrop, Hays, Travis
Moore, John W.	7	Linden	Davis (Cass)	Bowie, Davis
Neal, Thomas C.[7]	19	Wilton	Ellis	Ellis, Freestone, Limestone, Navarro
Parsons, Jesse H.	5	Henderson	Rusk	Rusk
Peck, William M.[7]	19	Fairfield	Freestone	Ellis, Freestone, Limestone, Navarro
Quayle, William[8]	20	Norton's Grove	Tarrant	Erath, Johnson, Palo Pinto, Parker, Tarrant
Selman, Benjamin T.	12	Tyler	Smith	Smith, Van Zandt, Wood
Shepard, Chauncy B.[9]	23	Brenham	Washington	Austin, Washington
Throckmorton, James W.	15	McKinney	Collin	Collin, Grayson
Weatherford, Jefferson[10]	13	Lancaster	Dallas	Dallas, Henderson, Kaufman
White, S. Addison	24	Victoria	Victoria	Calhoun, DeWitt, Jackson, Lavaca, Victoria

Wilson, William C.[7]	19	Fairfield	Freestone	Ellis, Freestone, Limestone, Navarro
Wootten, Gilbert H.	8	Clarksville	Red River	Red River, Titus

*Murrah, on or before June 12, 1865, abandoned office at the end of Confederate civil and military government in Texas and died in exile on August 4, 1865.

**Stockdale became governor upon departure of Murrah, but was not sworn, delivering keys of state offices to Andrew Jackson Hamilton on August 2, 1865.

***Hamilton was appointed provisional governor by President Andrew Johnson June 17, 1865.

1. Ford resigned June 2, 1865.

2. Holland did not attend the 1st Called Session.

3. Kinsey's death was reported on February 10, 1865.

4. Knox, chosen in a special election on April 25, 1864, was sworn May 9, 1864; he succeeded N. A. Mitchell, who died after Regular Session.

5. Magoffin, sworn May 9, 1864, did not attend the Regular Session.

6. A. W. Moore did not attend the 2nd Called Session and resigned May 1, 1865.

7. Wilson, sworn November 5, 1863, succeeded Thomas C. Neal, who died on September 13, 1863. Peck, sworn May 17, 1864, succeeded William C. Wilson, who resigned April 23, 1864.

8. Quayle did not attend the 2nd Called Session.

9. Shepard did not attend the 1st Called Session.

10. Weatherford did not attend the 2nd Called Session.

Appendix C

MEMBERS OF THE ELEVENTH LEGISLATURE

Regular Session, August 6–November 13, 1866

Governor James W. Throckmorton*
Lieutenant Governor George W. Jones*
Provisional Governor Elisha M. Pease**

Senate

Member	*District Number*	*Address*	*Home County*	*Counties Comprising District*
Blount, J. M.	21	Denton	Denton	Archer, Baylor, Buchanan, Cooke, Clay, Denton, Hardeman, Haskell, Jack, Jones, Knox, Montague, Shackelford, Throckmorton, Wichita, Wilbarger, Wise, Young
Boyd, James B.	18	Owensville	Robertson	Brazos, Burleson, Leon, Madison, Robertson
Braswell, Samuel N.	8	Mount Pleasant	Titus	Red River, Titus
Brown, John G.	5	Camden	Rusk	Rusk
Bumpass, John K.	15	Farmersville	Collin	Collin, Grayson
Burney, George E.	28	Waco	McLennan	Bosque, Brown, Callahan, Coleman, Comanche, Coryell, Eastland, Ellis, Falls, Hamilton, Hill, McLennan, Runnels, Taylor
Cook, Richard V.	22	Columbus	Colorado	Colorado, Fayette, Matagorda, Wharton
Cooley, A. O.	31	Fredericksburg	Gillespie	Atascosa, Bandera, Blanco, Comal, Concho, Dawson,

				Edwards, Frio, Gillespie, Kendall, Kerr, Kinney, Llano, McCulloch, Mason, Maverick, Medina, Menard, San Saba, Uvalde, Zavala
Coppedge, C. C.	6	Marshall	Harrison	Harrison, Upshur
Dalrymple, William C.	27	Georgetown	Williamson	Bell, Burnet, Lampasas, Milam, Williamson
Foscue, Frederick F.	1	Liberty	Liberty	Chambers, Galveston, Jefferson, Liberty
Gentry, Abram M.	16	Houston	Harris	Brazoria, Fort Bend, Harris
Guinn, James W.[1]	3	Homer	Angelina	Angelina, Nacogdoches, San Augustine
Guinn, Robert H.	10	Rusk	Cherokee	Cherokee
Jowers, William G. W.	11	Parkersville	Anderson	Anderson, Houston, Trinity
Knox, William B.	30	San Antonio	Bexar	Bexar
Lane, Robert H.[2]	14	Bonham	Fannin	Fannin, Hunt
Littleton, John T.	29	Helena	Karnes	Bee, Dimmit, Goliad, Karnes, La Salle, Live Oak, McMullen, Nueces, Refugio, San Patricio
McDade, James M.	23	Hempstead	Austin	Austin, Washington
Nelson, Hudson W.	9	Bright Star	Hopkins	Hopkins, Lamar
Neyland, William M.	2	Jasper	Jasper	Hardin, Jasper, Newton, Orange, Polk, Tyler
Parker, Francis J.	32	Brownsville	Cameron	Cameron, Duval, Encinal, Hidalgo, Starr, Webb, Zapata
Randolph, Benton	17	Huntsville	Walker	Grimes, Montgomery, Walker
Record, J. K. P.	13	Dallas	Dallas	Dallas, Henderson, Kaufman
Reid, Jacob B.	24	Victoria	Victoria	Calhoun, DeWitt, Jackson, Lavaca, Victoria
Saufley, William P.	7	Jefferson	Marion	Bowie, Davis, Marion
Selman, Benjamin T.	12	Tyler	Smith	Smith, Van Zandt, Wood
Shannon, William R.	20	Buchanan	Johnson	Erath, Johnson, Palo Pinto, Parker, Tarrant
Shelley, Nathan G.	26	Austin	Travis	Bastrop, Hays, Travis
Stell, James W.	25	Gonzales	Gonzales	Caldwell, Gonzales, Guadalupe
Truit, James A.	4	White Cottage	Shelby	Panola, Sabine, Shelby
Voight, Frederick[1]	3	Nacogdoches	Nacogdoches	Angelina, Nacogdoches, San Augustine
Warren, Henry	33	El Paso	El Paso	El Paso, Presidio
Yarbro, John C.	19	Fairfield	Freestone	Ellis, Freestone, Limestone, Navarro

*July 30, 1867, Special Orders No. 105 from Major General Philip Henry Sheridan, commander of the Fifth Military District, removed Throckmorton and Jones as impediments to Reconstruction.

** Pease, appointed provisional governor in the orders that removed Throckmorton and Jones, was sworn August 7, 1867. During his term there were no lieutenant governor and no legislature.

1. Voight, sworn October 8, 1866, succeeded James W. Guinn, who died August 18, 1866.

2. Lane resigned October 31, 1866, with no successor.

Appendix D

MEMBERS OF THE TWELFTH LEGISLATURE

Provisional Session, February 8—February 24, 1870*
Called Session, April 26—August 15, 1870
Regular Session, January 10—May 31, 1871
Adjourned Session, September 12—December 2, 1871

Governor Edmund J. Davis**
Lieutenant Governor James W. Flanagan***

Senate

Member	*District Number*	*Address*	*Home County*	*Counties Comprising District*
Alford, E. L.[1]	26	La Grange	Fayette	Bastrop, Fayette
Baker, Thomas H.	27	Lockhart	Caldwell	Caldwell, Gonzales, Guadalupe
Bell, John G.	13	Bellville	Austin	Austin, Fort Bend, Wharton
Bowers, Marmion H.	28	Austin	Travis	Bell, Brown, Coleman, Comanche, Concho, Coryell, Hamilton, Hays, Lampasas, McCulloch, San Saba, Travis, Williamson
Broughton, E. Thomas	22	Sherman	Grayson	Baylor, Clay, Cooke, Denton, Grayson, Hardeman, Haskell, Jack, Knox, Montague, Throckmorton, Wichita, Wilbarger, Wise, Young
Campbell, Donald***	8	Jefferson	Marion	Bowie, Davis, Marion
Clark, Amos[2]	2	Nacogdoches	Nacogdoches	Angelina, Nacogdoches, Sabine, San Augustine, Shelby, Trinity
Cole, David W.	10	Black Jack Grove	Hopkins	Hopkins, Hunt, Wood
Dillard, James E.[3]	3	Rusk	Cherokee	Cherokee, Houston
Dohoney, Ebenezer L.	11	Paris	Lamar	Fannin, Lamar
Douglas, James P.	6	Tyler	Smith	Smith, Upshur

Evans, Andrew J.[4]	19	Waco	McLennan	Falls, Limestone, McLennan
Evans, Samuel[5]	21	Fort Worth	Tarrant	Collin, Dallas, Tarrant
Flanagan, Webster***	5	Henderson	Rusk	Panola, Rusk
Ford, S. W.	19	Waco	McLennan	Falls, Limestone, McLennan
Foster, Abner K.[6]	25	Hallettsville	Lavaca	Colorado, Lavaca
Fountain, Albert J.	30	El Paso	El Paso	Atascosa, Cameron, Dimmit, Duval, El Paso, Encinal, Frio, Hidalgo, Karnes, Kinney, La Salle, Live Oak, McMullen, Maverick, Medina, Nueces, Presidio, Starr, Uvalde, Webb, Zapata, Zavala
Gaines, Matthew (Black)	16	Brenham	Washington	Washington
Hall, Phidello W.	18	Calvert	Robertson	Freestone, Leon, Robertson
Hertzberg, Theodore[7]	29	Menard	Menard	Bandera, Bexar, Blanco, Burnet, Comal, Edwards, Gillespie, Kendall, Kerr, Kimble, Llano, Mason, Menard, Wilson
Hillebrand, Reinhard[1]	26	La Grange	Fayette	Bastrop, Fayette
Latimer, Henry R.	9	Clarksville	Red River	Red River, Titus
Mills, John S.	15	Navasota	Grimes	Grimes, Madison, Walker
Parsons, W. H.[8]	14	Montgomery	Montgomery	Harris, Montgomery
Pettit, E.[9]	4	Palestine	Anderson	Anderson, Henderson, Van Zandt
Pickett, Edward B.	1	Liberty	Liberty	Chambers, Hardin, Jasper, Jefferson, Liberty, Newton, Orange, Polk, Tyler
Pridgen, Bolivar J.	24	Prices Creek	DeWitt	Bee, Calhoun, DeWitt, Goliad, Jackson, Refugio, San Patricio, Victoria
Priest, Mijamin[3]	3	Rusk	Cherokee	Cherokee, Houston
Pyle, William H.	20	Kaufman	Kaufman	Ellis, Hill, Kaufman, Navarro
Rawson, Henry	7	Marshall	Harrison	Harrison
Ruby, George T. (Black)	12	Galveston	Galveston	Brazoria, Galveston, Matagorda
Saylor, William A.	17	Bryan	Brazos	Brazos, Burleson, Milam
Shannon, George R.	23	Burleson	Johnson	Bosque, Callahan, Eastland, Erath, Hood, Johnson, Jones, Palo Pinto, Parker, Shackelford, Stephens, Taylor
Swift, William H.[2]	2	Nacogdoches	Nacogdoches	Angelina, Nacogdoches, Sabine, San Augustine, Shelby, Trinity
Tendick, Robert P.[6]	25	Columbus	Colorado	Colorado, Lavaca

* Legislative members eligible to subscribe the qualifying oath were ordered to convene on February 8, 1870, to ratify the 14th and 15th amendments to the United States Constitution, as a condition of readmission of Texas to the Union, and to elect two U.S. senators. Both houses were required to adjourn from day to day until all members had qualified.

** Special Orders No. 6, Fifth Military District, of January 8, 1870, announced the election of Davis and Flanagan as governor and lieutenant governor and appointed them provisional governor and provisional lieutenant governor, effective immediately.

*** Flanagan presided as president of the Senate in Provisional Session and was elected U.S. senator, vacating his state office. Flanagan's successor, Donald Campbell, "President of the Senate for the time being," was elected April 27, 1870. He died November 6, 1871, and was succeeded by Webster Flanagan, elected November 13, 1871.

1. Hillebrand, in a special election of November 28 through December 1, 1870, was sworn on February 17, 1871, succeeding E. L. Alford, who was expelled for resisting arrest during call of the Senate.

2. Swift, chosen in a special election of October 3 through 6, 1871, succeeded Amos Clark, who died on February 18, 1871.

3. Dillard ran second to Priest in the District 3 election for Provisional Session and was putative successor to Priest when the latter was declared ineligible by the military government on February 17, 1870. However, the resolution granting the seat to Dillard was tabled on February 22. Priest, qualified and sworn in the Called Session, resigned August 15 and was succeeded in a special election of November 28 to December 1 by Dillard, who was sworn January 10, 1871. Dillard then was declared ineligible and the seat declared vacant on April 10. In a special election of October 3 through 6, Dillard won again and was sworn October 31.

4. Ford, sworn February 16, 1870, succeeded Andrew J. Evans, who had been sworn February 10, 1870. Evans was unseated in an election contest.

5. Samuel Evans refused to qualify on February 8, 1870, qualified February 10, 1870, and did not attend the Called Session until May 28, 1870, when he again qualified.

6. Tendick, sworn January 10, 1871, succeeded Abner K. Foster, who died March 9, 1870.

7. Hertzberg resigned on December 2, 1871.

8. Parsons resigned on December 4, 1871.

9. Pettit, sworn April 26, 1870, did not attend the Provisional Session.

Appendix E

MEMBERS OF THE THIRTEENTH LEGISLATURE

Regular Session, January 14—June 4, 1873

Governor Edmund J. Davis
President of the Senate Edward B. Pickett*

Senate

Member	*District Number*	*Address*	*Home County*	*Counties Comprising District*
Avinger, Hamilton J.	8	Hickory Hill	Cass	Bowie, Cass, Marion
Baker, Thomas H.	27	Lockhart	Caldwell	Caldwell, Gonzales, Guadalupe
Ball, Andrew J.	23	Weatherford	Parker	Bosque, Callahan, Eastland, Erath, Hood, Johnson, Jones, Palo Pinto, Parker, Shackelford, Stephens, Taylor
Broughton, E. Thomas	22	Sherman	Grayson	Baylor, Clay, Cooke, Denton, Grayson, Hardeman, Haskell, Jack, Knox, Montague, Throckmorton, Wichita, Wilbarger, Wise, Young
Cole, David W.	10	Black Jack Grove	Hopkins	Hopkins, Hunt, Wood
Dillard, James E.	3	Rusk	Cherokee	Cherokee, Houston
Dohoney, Ebenezer L.	11	Paris	Lamar	Fannin, Lamar
Evans, Samuel	21	Fort Worth	Tarrant	Collin, Dallas, Tarrant
Finlay, George P.	24	Lavaca	Calhoun	Bee, Calhoun, DeWitt, Goliad, Jackson, Refugio, San Patricio, Victoria
Flanagan, Webster	5	Henderson	Rusk	Panola, Rusk
Ford, S. W.	19	Waco	McLennan	Falls, Limestone, McLennan
Fountain, Albert J.	30	El Paso	El Paso	Atascosa, Cameron, Dimmit,

				Duval, El Paso, Encinal, Frio, Hidalgo, Karnes, Kinney, La Salle, Live Oak, McMullen, Maverick, Medina, Nueces, Presidio, Starr, Uvalde, Webb, Zapata, Zavala
Franks, Francis G.	13	Wharton	Wharton	Austin, Fort Bend, Wharton
Gaines, Matthew (Black)	16	Brenham	Washington	Washington
Hall, Phidello W.	18	Calvert	Robertson	Freestone, Leon, Robertson
Henry, John L.	6	Tyler	Smith	Smith, Upshur
King, Henry C.	29	Boerne	Kendall	Bandera, Bexar, Blanco, Burnet, Comal, Edwards, Gillespie, Kendall, Kerr, Kimble, Llano, Mason, Menard, Wilson
Latimer, Henry R.	9	Clarksville	Red River	Red River, Titus
Pickett, Edward B.*	1	Liberty	Liberty	Chambers, Hardin, Jasper, Jefferson, Liberty, Newton, Orange, Polk, Tyler
Pyle, William H.	20	Kaufman	Kaufman	Ellis, Hill, Kaufman, Navarro
Randle, Edward T.	15	Huntsville	Walker	Grimes, Madison, Walker
Rawson, Henry	7	Marshall	Harrison	Harrison
Ruby, George T. (Black)	12	Galveston	Galveston	Brazoria, Galveston, Matagorda
Sayers, Joseph D.	26	Bastrop	Bastrop	Bastrop, Fayette
Saylor, William A.	17	Bryan	Brazos	Brazos, Burleson, Milam
Shelley, Nathan G.	28	Austin	Travis	Bell, Brown, Coleman, Comanche, Concho, Coryell, Hamilton, Hays, Lampasas, McCulloch, San Saba, Travis, Williamson
Swift, William H.	2	Nacogdoches	Nacogdoches	Angelina, Nacogdoches, Sabine, San Augustine, Shelby, Trinity
Tendick, Robert P.	25	Columbus	Colorado	Colorado, Lavaca
Tracy, James G.	14	Houston	Harris	Harris, Montgomery
Word, Thomas J.	4	Palestine	Anderson	Anderson, Henderson, Van Zandt

* Pickett was elected president of the Senate for the time being on January 15, 1873.

Appendix F

MEMBERS OF THE FOURTEENTH LEGISLATURE

First Regular Session, January 13—May 4, 1874
Second Regular Session, January 12—March 15, 1875

Governor Richard Coke
Lieutenant Governor Richard B. Hubbard

Senate

Member	*District Number*	*Address*	*Home County*	*Counties Comprising District*
Allison, Robert D.	21	McKinney	Collin	Collin, Denton, Wise
Baker, William R.	14	Houston	Harris	Harris, Montgomery
Ball, Andrew J.	23	Weatherford	Parker	Callahan, Eastland, Erath, Haskell, Hill, Hood, Jack, Johnson, Jones, Palo Pinto, Parker, Shackelford, Stephens, Taylor, Throckmorton, Young
Bradley, L. D.	9	Fairfield	Freestone	Freestone, Limestone, Navarro
Bradshaw, Amzi	20	Waxahachie	Ellis	Dallas, Ellis, Tarrant
Burton, Walter M. (Black)	13	Richmond	Fort Bend	Austin, Fort Bend, Wharton
Camp, John L., Sr.[1]	6	Gilmer	Upshur	Smith, Upshur
Craven, N. S.[2]	22	Whitesboro	Grayson	Archer, Baylor, Clay, Cooke, Grayson, Hardeman, Knox, Montague, Wichita, Wilbarger
Culberson, David B.[3]	7	Jefferson	Marion	Bowie, Cass, Marion
Davenport, Jewett H.	17	Belton	Bell	Bell, Falls, Milam
Davidson, T. G.[4]	16	Caldwell	Burleson	Burleson, Washington
Dillard, James E.	3	Rusk	Cherokee	Angelina, Cherokee, Houston, Trinity
Dwyer, Joseph E.	29	San Antonio	Bexar	Atascosa, Bandera, Bexar, Comal, Edwards, Gillespie, Kendall,

				Kerr, Kimble, Mason, Menard, Wilson
Ellis, Olinthus	25	Hallettsville	Lavaca	Colorado, Lavaca
Erath, George B.	19	Waco	McLennan	Bosque, Brown, Coleman, Comanche, Coryell, Hamilton, McLennan, Runnels
Flanagan, Webster	5	Henderson	Rusk	Harrison, Rusk
Franklin, Benjamin C.[5]	12	Galveston	Galveston	Brazoria, Galveston, Matagorda
Friend, William R.	24	Clinton	DeWitt	Aransas, Bee, Calhoun, DeWitt, Goliad, Jackson, Karnes, Live Oak, Refugio, San Patricio, Victoria
Hobby, Edwin	1	Woodville	Tyler	Chambers, Hardin, Jasper, Jefferson, Liberty, Newton, Orange, Polk, Tyler
Ireland, John	27	Seguin	Guadalupe	Caldwell, Gonzales, Guadalupe, Hays
Joseph, Thomas M.[5]	12	Galveston	Galveston	Brazoria, Galveston, Matagorda
Ledbetter, William H.	26	La Grange	Fayette	Bastrop, Fayette
Moore, William E.	11	Blossom	Lamar	Fannin, Lamar
Morris, Joseph	10	Greenville	Hunt	Delta, Hopkins, Hunt, Rains, Wood
Parker, Cader A.	8	Lone Star	Titus	Red River, Titus
Randle, Edward T.	15	Huntsville	Walker	Grimes, Madison, San Jacinto, Walker
Russell, William H.	30	Brownsville	Cameron	Bexar, Cameron, Dimmit, Duval, El Paso, Encinal, Frio, Hidalgo, Kinney, La Salle, McMullen, Maverick, Medina, Nueces, Pecos, Presidio, Starr, Uvalde, Webb, Zapata, Zavala
Shepard, Seth[4]	16	Brenham	Washington	Burleson, Washington
Stirman, Winfield B.	4	Athens	Henderson	Anderson, Henderson, Kaufman, Rockwall, Van Zandt
Swift, William H.	2	Nacogdoches	Nacogdoches	Nacogdoches, Panola, Sabine, San Augustine, Shelby
Trolinger, William H.[2]	22	Whitesboro	Grayson	Archer, Baylor, Clay, Cooke, Grayson, Hardeman, Knox, Montague, Wichita, Wilbarger
Westfall, William H.	28	Burnet	Burnet	Blanco, Burnet, Concho, Lam-

				pasas, Llano, McCulloch, San Saba, Travis, Williamson
Wood, William D.	18	Centerville	Leon	Brazos, Leon, Robertson

1. Camp resigned March 13, 1875.

2. Craven, sworn January 25, 1875, succeeded William H. Trolinger, who resigned.

3. Culberson resigned March 3, 1875.

4. Shepard, selected in a special election held February 17, 1874, was seated March 26, 1874. He succeeded T. G. Davidson, who refused to qualify on January 14, 1874.

5. Joseph, sworn March 19, 1874, succeeded Benjamin C. Franklin, member-elect who died on December 25, 1873.

Appendix G

MEMBERS OF THE FIFTEENTH LEGISLATURE

Regular Session, April 18—August 21, 1876

Governor Richard Coke*
Lieutenant Governor Richard B. Hubbard**

Senate

Member	*District Number*	*Address*	*Home County*	*Counties Comprising District*
Ball, Thomas	23	Jacksboro	Jack	Clay, Jack, Montague, Parker, Tarrant, Wise, Young
Blassingame, William	11	Sandusky	Grayson	Cooke, Grayson
Brady, John T.	18	Houston	Harris	Harris, Montgomery
Brown, William M.	21	Marlin	Falls	Bell, Falls, Milam
Burnett, James R.[1]	16	Anderson	Grimes	Grimes, Madison, Trinity, Walker
Burton, Walter M. (Black)	17	Richmond	Fort Bend	Fort Bend, Waller, Wharton
Carroll, John W.	20	Caldwell	Burleson	Austin, Burleson, Washington
Crain, William H.[2]	28	Indianola	Calhoun	Aransas, Atascosa, Bee, Calhoun, DeWitt, Goliad, Jackson, Karnes, Refugio, Victoria, Wilson
Douglas, James P.	7	Tyler	Smith	Camp, Gregg, Smith, Upshur
Edwards, Peyton F.	2	Nacogdoches	Nacogdoches	Angelina, Houston, Nacogdoches, San Augustine, Sabine
Ford, John S.	29	Brownsville	Cameron	Cameron, Dimmit, Duval, Encinal, Frio, Hidalgo, Kinney, La Salle, Live Oak, McMullen, Maverick, Medina, Nueces, San Patricio, Starr, Uvalde, Webb, Zapata, Zavala
Francis, Christopher C.	8	Rusk	Cherokee	Anderson, Cherokee, Henderson

Grace, Charles D.	9	Bonham	Fannin	Delta, Fannin, Lamar
Guy, Robert S.	13	Lancaster	Dallas	Dallas, Ellis
Henry, Francis M.	5	Linden	Cass	Bowie, Cass, Marion, Morris
Henry, John R.	14	Mexia	Limestone	Freestone, Limestone, Navarro
Hobby, Edwin	1	Woodville	Tyler	Chambers, Hardin, Jasper, Jefferson, Liberty, Newton, Orange, Polk, San Jacinto, Tyler
Lane, Ellsberry R.[2]	28	Goliad	Goliad	Aransas, Atascosa, Bee, Calhoun, DeWitt, Goliad, Jackson, Karnes, Refugio, Victoria, Wilson
Ledbetter, William H.	26	La Grange	Fayette	Bastrop, Fayette, Lee
McCormick, Andrew P.	19	Brazoria	Brazoria	Brazoria, Galveston, Matagorda
McCulloch, Thomas J.	15	Jewett	Leon	Brazos, Leon, Robertson
McLeary, James H.	30	San Antonio	Bexar	Bandera, Bexar, Comal, Concho, Crockett, Edwards, El Paso, Gillespie, Kendall, Kerr, Kimble, Mason, Menard, Pecos, Presidio, Tom Green
Martin, B. D.	10	Greenville	Hunt	Hunt, Kaufman, Rains, Rockwall, Wood, Van Zandt
Moore, John W.	22	Granbury	Johnson	Hill, Johnson, McLennan
Motley, John W.	3	Henderson	Rusk	Panola, Rusk, Shelby
Piner, Finis E.	12	Denton	Denton	Collin, Denton
Ripetoe, Walter (Black)	4	Marshall	Harrison	Harrison
Smith, Tillman[1]	16	Navasota	Grimes	Grimes, Madison, Trinity, Walker
Stephens, John D.	24	Comanche	Comanche	Bosque, Brown, Callahan, Coleman, Comanche, Coryell, Eastland, Erath, Hamilton, Hood, Jones, Palo Pinto, Runnels, Shackelford, Somervell, Stephens, Taylor
Storey, Leonidas J.	31	Lockhart	Caldwell	Blanco, Caldwell, Guadalupe, Hays, Llano, McCulloch, San Saba
Terrell, Alexander W.	25	Austin	Travis	Burnet, Lampasas, Travis, Williamson
Thompson, Wells[3]	27	Columbus	Colorado	Colorado, Gonzales, Lavaca
Wortham, William A.	6	Sulphur Springs	Hopkins	Franklin, Hopkins, Red River, Titus

* Governor Coke resigned on December 1, 1876, to become United States senator.

** Lieutenant Governor Hubbard took an "indefinite leave of absence" from his duties as president of the Senate as of August 9, 1876, and succeeded Coke as governor on December 1, 1876.

1. Burnett, sworn in the 16th Legislature, succeeded Tillman Smith, who resigned on November 19, 1876.

2. Lane, sworn in the 16th Legislature, succeeded William H. Crain, who resigned on August 20, 1877.

3. Thompson, elected president pro tempore on April 19, 1876, presided as president of the Senate when Hubbard retired from those duties as of August 9.

Appendix H

MEMBERS OF THE SIXTEENTH LEGISLATURE

Regular Session, January 14—April 24, 1879
First Called Session, June 10—July 9, 1879

Governor Oran M. Roberts
Lieutenant Governor Joseph Draper Sayers

Senate

Member	*District Number*	*Address*	*Home County*	*Counties Comprising District*
Blassingame, William	11	Sandusky	Grayson	Cooke, Grayson
Brown, William M.	21	Marlin	Falls	Bell, Falls, Milam
Buchanan, John C.	10	Mineola	Wood	Hunt, Kaufman, Rains, Rockwall, Van Zandt, Wood
Buchanan, John T.[1]	16	Anderson	Grimes	Grimes, Madison, Trinity, Walker
Burnett, James R.[1]	16	Anderson	Grimes	Grimes, Madison, Trinity, Walker
Burton, Walter M. (Black)	17	Richmond	Fort Bend	Fort Bend, Waller, Wharton
Davenport, Jewett H.	24	Eastland	Eastland	Bosque, Brown, Callahan, Coleman, Comanche, Coryell, Eastland, Erath, Hamilton, Hood, Jones, Palo Pinto, Runnels, Shackelford, Somervell, Stephens, Taylor
Duncan, John M.	7	Longview	Gregg	Camp, Gregg, Smith, Upshur
Edwards, Peyton F.[2]	2	Nacogdoches	Nacogdoches	Angelina, Houston, Nacogdoches, Sabine, San Augustine
Ford, John S.[3]	29	Brownsville	Cameron	Cameron, Dimmit, Duval, Encinal, Frio, Hidalgo, Kinney, La Salle, Live Oak,

				McMullen, Maverick, Medina, Nueces, San Patricio, Starr, Uvalde, Webb, Zapata, Zavala
Gooch, John Y.	8	Palestine	Anderson	Anderson, Cherokee, Henderson
Grace, Charles D.	9	Bonham	Fannin	Delta, Fannin, Lamar
Guy, Robert S.	13	Lancaster	Dallas	Dallas, Ellis
Hobby, Edwin[4]	1	Livingston	Polk	Chambers, Hardin, Jasper, Jefferson, Liberty, Newton, Orange, Polk, San Jacinto, Tyler
Homan, William K.[5]	20	Caldwell	Burleson	Austin, Burleson, Washington
Houston, Augustus W.	30	San Antonio	Bexar	Bandera, Bexar, Comal, Concho, Crockett, Edwards, El Paso, Gillespie, Kendall, Kerr, Kimble, Mason, Menard, Pecos, Presidio, Tom Green
Lair, William D.	12	Melissa	Collin	Collin, Denton
Lane, Ellsberry R.	28	Goliad	Goliad	Aransas, Atascosa, Bee, Calhoun, DeWitt, Goliad, Jackson, Karnes, Refugio, Victoria, Wilson
Ledbetter, William H.	26	La Grange	Fayette	Bastrop, Fayette, Lee
McCormick, Andrew P.[6]	19	Brazoria	Brazoria	Brazoria, Galveston, Matagorda
McCulloch, Thomas J.[7]	15	Jewett	Leon	Brazos, Leon, Robertson
Martin, Francis M.	14	Corsicana	Navarro	Freestone, Limestone, Navarro
Moore, John W.	22	Granbury	Johnson	Hill, Johnson, McLennan
Motley, John W.	3	Overton	Rusk	Panola, Rusk, Shelby
Patton, Samuel C.	27	Hallettsville	Lavaca	Colorado, Gonzales, Lavaca
Ripetoe, Walter (Black)	4	Marshall	Harrison	Harrison
Shannon, William R.	23	Weatherford	Parker	Clay, Jack, Montague, Parker, Tarrant, Wise, Young
Stewart, Charles	18	Houston	Harris	Harris, Montgomery
Storey, Leonidas J.	31	Lockhart	Caldwell	Blanco, Caldwell, Guadalupe, Hays, Llano, McCulloch, San Saba
Street, Robert G.[6]	19	Galveston	Galveston	Brazoria, Galveston, Matagorda
Swain, William J.	6	Clarksville	Red River	Franklin, Hopkins, Red River, Titus
Terrell, Alexander W.	25	Austin	Travis	Burnet, Lampasas, Travis, Williamson
Tilson, William H.	5	Texarkana	Bowie	Bowie, Cass, Marion, Morris

1. John T. Buchanan, in a special election of February 17, 1880, succeeded James R. Burnett, who resigned on October 9, 1879.

2. Edwards resigned October 18, 1879.

3. Ford resigned August 30, 1879.

4. Hobby resigned July 10, 1879.

5. Homan resigned on July 9, 1879, and succeeded himself in a special election held on February 17, 1880.

6. Street, sworn June 10, 1879, succeeded Andrew P. McCormick, who resigned on April 12, 1879.

7. McCulloch resigned September 3, 1879.

Appendix I

MEMBERS OF THE SEVENTEENTH LEGISLATURE

Regular Session, January 11—April 1, 1881
First Called Session, April 6—May 5, 1882

Governor Oran M. Roberts
Lieutenant Governor Leonidas J. Storey

SENATE

Member	*District Number*	*Address*	*Home County*	*Counties Comprising District*
Brown, Lucas H.[1]	28	Helena	Karnes	Aransas, Atascosa, Bee, Calhoun, DeWitt, Goliad, Jackson, Karnes, Refugio, Victoria, Wilson
Buchanan, John C.	10	Mineola	Wood	Hunt, Kaufman, Rains, Rockwall, Van Zandt, Wood
Buchanan, John T.[2]	16	Anderson	Grimes	Grimes, Madison, Trinity, Walker
Burges, William H.	31	Seguin	Guadalupe	Blanco, Caldwell, Guadalupe, Hays, Llano, McCulloch, San Saba
Burton, Walter M. (Black)	17	Richmond	Fort Bend	Fort Bend, Waller, Wharton
Cooper, S. Bronson	1	Woodville	Tyler	Chambers, Hardin, Jasper, Jefferson, Liberty, Newton, Orange, Polk, San Jacinto, Tyler
Davenport, Jewett H.	24	Hamilton	Hamilton	Bosque, Brown, Callahan, Coleman, Comanche, Coryell, Eastland, Erath, Hamilton, Hood, Jones, Palo Pinto, Runnels, Shackelford, Somervell, Stephens, Taylor

Davis, William O.[3]	11	Gainesville	Cooke	Cooke, Grayson
Duncan, John M.	7	Longview	Gregg	Camp, Gregg, Smith, Upshur
Gooch, John Y.	8	Palestine	Anderson	Anderson, Cherokee, Henderson
Harris, Andrew J.	21	Belton	Bell	Bell, Falls, Milam
Henderson, John N.	15	Bryan	Brazos	Brazos, Leon, Robertson
Hightower, Robert L.	4	Elysian Fields	Harrison	Harrison
Homan, William K.	20	Caldwell	Burleson	Austin, Burleson, Washington
Houston, Augustus W.	30	San Antonio	Bexar	Bandera, Bexar, Comal, Concho, Crockett, Edwards, El Paso, Gillespie, Kendall, Kerr, Kimble, Mason, Menard, Pecos, Presidio, Tom Green
Lair, William D.	12	McKinney	Collin	Collin, Denton
Lane, Ellsberry R.[1]	28	Goliad	Goliad	Aransas, Atascosa, Bee, Calhoun, DeWitt, Goliad, Jackson, Karnes, Refugio, Victoria, Wilson
Lightfoot, Henry W.	9	Paris	Lamar	Delta, Fannin, Lamar
McDonald, James G.[2]	16	Anderson	Grimes	Grimes, Madison, Trinity, Walker
McLane, Charles A.[4]	29	Brownsville	Cameron	Cameron, Dimmit, Duval, Encinal, Frio, Hidalgo, Kinney, La Salle, Live Oak, McMullen, Maverick, Medina, Nueces, San Patricio, Starr, Uvalde, Webb, Zapata, Zavala
Martin, Francis M.	14	Corsicana	Navarro	Freestone, Limestone, Navarro
Martin, J. M.[3]	11	Gainesville	Cooke	Cooke, Grayson
Moore, A. W.	26	Bastrop	Bastrop	Bastrop, Fayette, Lee
Patton, Samuel C.	27	Hallettsville	Lavaca	Colorado, Gonzales, Lavaca
Powers, Stephen[4]	29	Brownsville	Cameron	Cameron, Dimmit, Duval, Encinal, Frio, Hidalgo, Kinney, La Salle, Live Oak, McMullen, Maverick, Medina, Nueces, San Patricio, Starr, Uvalde, Webb, Zapata, Zavala
Rainey, Anson	13	Waxahachie	Ellis	Dallas, Ellis
Ross, Lawrence S.	22	Waco	McLennan	Hill, Johnson, McLennan
Shannon, William R.	23	Weatherford	Parker	Clay, Jack, Montague, Parker, Tarrant, Wise, Young
Stewart, Charles	18	Houston	Harris	Harris, Montgomery
Stubbs, James B.	19	Galveston	Galveston	Brazoria, Galveston, Matagorda

Swain, William J.	6	Clarksville	Red River	Franklin, Hopkins, Red River, Titus
Terrell, Alexander W.	25	Austin	Travis	Burnet, Lampasas, Travis, Williamson
Tilson, William H.	5	Texarkana	Bowie	Cass, Bowie, Marion, Morris
Weatherred, William W.	2	Hemphill	Sabine	Angelina, Houston, Nacogdoches, Sabine, San Augustine
Wynne, Richard M.	3	Henderson	Rusk	Panola, Rusk, Shelby

1. Brown, sworn April 6, 1882, succeeded Ellsberry R. Lane, who resigned February 1, 1882.
2. McDonald, sworn April 6, 1882, succeeded John T. Buchanan, who died January 29, 1882.
3. Davis, sworn April 6, 1882, succeeded J. M. Martin, who died March 9, 1882.
4. McLane, sworn April 6, 1882, succeeded Stephen Powers, who died after the Regular Session.

Appendix J

MEMBERS OF THE EIGHTEENTH LEGISLATURE

Regular Session, January 9—April 13, 1883
First Called Session, January 8—February 6, 1884

Governor John Ireland
Lieutenant Governor Francis M. Martin

Senate

Member	*District Number*	*Address*	*Home County*	*Counties Comprising District*
Buchanan, John C.	6	Mineola	Wood	Gregg, Rains, Smith, Upshur, Wood
Chesley, Alvah	12	Bellville	Austin	Austin, Burleson, Fort Bend, Waller, Washington
Collins, Norman G.	27	San Diego	Duval	Cameron, Dimmit, Duval, Encinal, Frio, Hidalgo, Kinney, La Salle, Maverick, Nueces, Starr, Uvalde, Webb, Zapata, Zavala
Cooper, S. Bronson	1	Woodville	Tyler	Chambers, Hardin, Jasper, Jefferson, Liberty, Newton, Orange, Polk, San Jacinto, Tyler
Davis, William O.	18	Gainesville	Cooke	Cooke, Grayson
Evans, William A.	31	Bonham	Fannin	Fannin, Lamar, Red River
Farrar, Lochlin J.	15	Groesbeck	Limestone	Freestone, Limestone, Navarro
Fleming, James R.	29	Cisco	Eastland	Andrews, Borden, Brown, Callahan, Coleman, Comanche, Concho, Dawson, Eastland, Fisher, Gaines, Howard, Jones, McCulloch, Martin, Mitchell, Nolan,

				Runnels, San Saba, Scurry, Shackelford, Stephens, Taylor
Fowler, John P.	13	Bastrop	Bastrop	Bastrop, Fayette, Lee
Getzendaner, William H.	21	Waxahachie	Ellis	Ellis, Hill, Johnson
Gibbs, Barnett	16	Dallas	Dallas	Dallas, Kaufman, Rockwall
Gooch, John Y.	7	Palestine	Anderson	Anderson, Cherokee, Henderson, Van Zandt
Harris, Andrew J.	23	Belton	Bell	Bell, Coryell, Hamilton, Lampasas
Houston, Augustus W.	28	San Antonio	Bexar	Bandera, Bexar, Crockett, Edwards, El Paso, Gillespie, Kerr, Kimble, Mason, Medina, Menard, Pecos, Presidio, Tom Green
Johnson, John	17	McKinney	Collin	Collin, Denton
Johnston, Frank L.	2	Buena Vista	Shelby	Nacogdoches, Panola, Rusk, Sabine, San Augustine, Shelby
Jones, James W.	9	Houston	Harris	Harris, Montgomery, Trinity, Walker
King, E. A.	5	Pittsburg	Camp	Camp, Delta, Franklin, Hopkins, Hunt
Kleberg, Rudolph	26	Cuero	DeWitt	Aransas, Atascosa, Bee, Calhoun, DeWitt, Goliad, Jackson, Karnes, Live Oak, McMullen, Refugio, San Patricio, Victoria, Wilson
Martin, John A.	22	Marlin	Falls	Falls, McLennan
Matlock, Avery L.[1]	19	Montague	Montague	Archer, Armstrong, Bailey, Baylor, Briscoe, Carson, Castro, Childress, Clay, Cochran, Collingsworth, Cottle, Crosby, Dallam, Deaf Smith, Dickens, Donley, Floyd, Garza, Gray, Greer, Hale, Hall, Hansford, Hardeman, Hartley, Haskell, Hemphill, Hockley, Hutchinson, Kent, King, Knox, Lamb, Lipscomb, Lubbock, Lynn, Montague, Moore, Motley, Ochiltree, Oldham, Parmer, Potter,

				Randall, Roberts, Sherman, Stonewall, Swisher, Terry, Throckmorton, Wheeler, Wichita, Wilbarger, Yoakum, Young
Patton, Samuel C.	11	Hallettsville	Lavaca	Colorado, Gonzales, Lavaca, Wharton
Peacock, John A.	4	Daingerfield	Morris	Bowie, Cass, Marion, Morris, Titus
Perry, James S.	14	Rockdale	Milam	Brazos, Milam, Robertson
Pfeuffer, George	25	New Braunfels	Comal	Blanco, Caldwell, Comal, Guadalupe, Hays, Kendall, Llano
Pope, William H.	3	Marshall	Harrison	Harrison
Randolph, Mansel Y.	8	Madisonville	Madison	Angelina, Grimes, Houston, Leon, Madison
Shannon, William R.	20	Weatherford	Parker	Jack, Parker, Tarrant, Wise
Stratton, Asa E., Jr.[2]	10	Brazoria	Brazoria	Brazoria, Galveston, Matagorda
Terrell, Alexander W.	24	Austin	Travis	Burnet, Travis, Williamson
Traylor, John H.	30	Granbury	Hood	Bosque, Erath, Hood, Palo Pinto, Somervell

1. Matlock resigned September 24, 1884.
2. Stratton resigned May 14, 1884.

Appendix K

MEMBERS OF THE NINETEENTH LEGISLATURE

Regular Session, January 13—March 31, 1885

Governor John Ireland
Lieutenant Governor Barnett Gibbs

Senate

Member	*District Number*	*Address*	*Home County*	*Counties Comprising District*
Bell, Charles K.	23	Hamilton	Hamilton	Bell, Coryell, Hamilton, Lampasas
Calhoun, James H.	29	Eastland	Eastland	Andrews, Borden, Brown, Callahan, Coleman, Comanche, Concho, Dawson, Eastland, Fisher, Gaines, Howard, Jones, McCulloch, Martin, Mitchell, Nolan, Runnels, San Saba, Scurry, Shackelford, Stephens, Taylor
Camp, John L., Jr.	6	Gilmer	Upshur	Gregg, Rains, Smith, Upshur, Wood
Davis, William O.	18	Gainesville	Cooke	Cooke, Grayson
Douglass, William L.	1	Beaumont	Jefferson	Chambers, Hardin, Jasper, Jefferson, Liberty, Newton, Orange, Polk, San Jacinto, Tyler
Evans, William A.	31	Bonham	Fannin	Fannin, Lamar, Red River
Farrar, Lochlin J.	15	Groesbeck	Limestone	Freestone, Limestone, Navarro
Fowler, John P.	13	Bastrop	Bastrop	Bastrop, Fayette, Lee
Garrison, Caleb J.	2	Glen Fawn	Rusk	Nacogdoches, Panola, Rusk, Sabine, San Augustine, Shelby

Getzendaner, William H.	21	Waxahachie	Ellis	Ellis, Hill, Johnson
Glasscock, George W., Jr.	24	Georgetown	Williamson	Burnet, Travis, Williamson
Hall, E. F.[1]	27	Laredo	Webb	Cameron, Dimmit, Duval, Encinal, Frio, Hidalgo, Kinney, La Salle, Maverick, Nueces, Starr, Uvalde, Webb, Zapata, Zavala
Harrison, Richard H.	22	Waco	McLennan	Falls, McLennan
Houston, Augustus W.	28	San Antonio	Bexar	Bandera, Bexar, Crockett, Edwards, El Paso, Gillespie, Kerr, Kimble, Mason, Medina, Menard, Pecos, Presidio, Tom Green
Houston, Temple L.	19	Mobeetie	Wheeler	Archer, Armstrong, Bailey, Baylor, Briscoe, Carson, Castro, Childress, Clay, Cochran, Collingsworth, Cottle, Crosby, Dallam, Deaf Smith, Dickens, Donley, Floyd, Garza, Gray, Greer, Hale, Hall, Hansford, Hardeman, Hartley, Haskell, Hemphill, Hockley, Hutchinson, Kent, King, Knox, Lamb, Lipscomb, Lubbock, Lynn, Montague, Moore, Motley, Ochiltree, Oldham, Parmer, Potter, Randall, Roberts, Sherman, Stonewall, Swisher, Terry, Throckmorton, Wheeler, Wichita, Wilbarger, Yoakum, Young
Jerdone, W. M.	10	Galveston	Galveston	Brazoria, Galveston, Matagorda
Johnson, John	17	McKinney	Collin	Collin, Denton
Jones, James W.	9	Houston	Harris	Harris, Montgomery, Trinity, Walker
Kilgore, Constantine B.[2]	7	Wills Point	Van Zandt	Anderson, Cherokee, Henderson, Van Zandt
Kleberg, Rudolph[3]	26	Cuero	DeWitt	Aransas, Atascosa, Bee, Calhoun, DeWitt, Goliad, Jackson, Karnes, Live Oak, McMullen,

				Refugio, San Patricio, Victoria, Wilson
Knittel, Hermann	12	Burton	Washington	Austin, Burleson, Fort Bend, Waller, Washington
Peacock, John A.	4	Daingerfield	Morris	Bowie, Cass, Marion, Morris, Titus
Perry, James S.	14	Rockdale	Milam	Brazos, Milam, Robertson
Pfeuffer, George[4]	25	New Braunfels	Comal	Blanco, Caldwell, Comal, Guadalupe, Hays, Kendall, Llano
Pope, William H.	3	Marshall	Harrison	Harrison
Randolph, Mansel Y.	8	Madisonville	Madison	Angelina, Grimes, Houston, Leon, Madison
Shannon, William R.	20	Weatherford	Parker	Jack, Parker, Tarrant, Wise
Stinson, Samuel D.	5	Greenville	Hunt	Camp, Delta, Franklin, Hopkins, Hunt
Terrell, J. O.	16	Terrell	Kaufman	Dallas, Kaufman, Rockwall
Traylor, John H.	30	Granbury	Hood	Bosque, Erath, Hood, Palo Pinto, Somervell
Woods, John	11	Hallettsville	Lavaca	Colorado, Gonzales, Lavaca, Wharton

1. Hall died April 28, 1886.
2. Kilgore resigned October 23, 1885.
3. Kleberg resigned September 9, 1886.
4. Pfeuffer died September 15, 1886.

Appendix L

MEMBERS OF THE TWENTIETH LEGISLATURE

Regular Session, January 11—April 4, 1887
First Called Session, April 16—May 15, 1888

Governor Lawrence Sullivan Ross
Lieutenant Governor Thomas Benton Wheeler

Senate

Member	*District Number*	*Address*	*Home County*	*Counties Comprising District*
Abercrombie, Leonard A.	9	Huntsville	Walker	Harris, Montgomery, Trinity, Walker
Allen, William	17	Rock Hill	Collin	Collin, Denton
Armistead, William T.	4	Jefferson	Marion	Cass, Bowie, Marion, Morris, Titus
Baker, Waller S.[1]	22	Waco	McLennan	Falls, McLennan
Bell, Charles K.	23	Hamilton	Hamilton	Bell, Coryell, Hamilton, Lampasas
Burges, William H.	25	Seguin	Guadalupe	Blanco, Caldwell, Comal, Guadalupe, Hays, Kendall, Llano
Burney, Robert H.	28	Kerrville	Kerr	Bandera, Bexar, Crockett, Edwards, El Paso, Gillespie, Kerr, Kimble, Mason, Medina, Menard, Pecos, Presidio, Tom Green
Calhoun, James H.	29	Eastland	Eastland	Andrews, Borden, Brown, Callahan, Coleman, Comanche, Concho, Dawson, Eastland, Fisher, Gaines, Howard, Jones, McCulloch, Martin, Mitchell, Nolan,

				Runnels, San Saba, Scurry, Shackelford, Stephens, Taylor
Camp, John L., Jr.	6	Gilmer	Upshur	Gregg, Rains, Smith, Upshur, Wood
Claiborne, John M.	10	Galveston	Galveston	Brazoria, Galveston, Matagorda
Davis, William W.	8	Augusta	Houston	Angelina, Grimes, Houston, Leon, Madison
Douglass, Elbridge G.	18	Sherman	Grayson	Cooke, Grayson
Douglass, William L.	1	Beaumont	Jefferson	Chambers, Hardin, Jasper, Jefferson, Liberty, Newton, Orange, Polk, San Jacinto, Tyler
Field, Scott	14	Calvert	Robertson	Brazos, Milam, Robertson
Frank, Louis N.	30	Stephenville	Erath	Bosque, Erath, Hood, Palo Pinto, Somervell
Garrison, Caleb J.	2	Henderson	Rusk	Nacogdoches, Panola, Rusk, Sabine, San Augustine, Shelby
Glasscock, George W., Jr.	24	Georgetown	Williamson	Burnet, Travis, Williamson
Gregg, Alexander W.	7	Palestine	Anderson	Anderson, Cherokee, Henderson, Van Zandt
Harrison, Richard H.[1]	22	Waco	McLennan	Falls, McLennan
Houston, Temple L.	19	Mobeetie	Wheeler	Archer, Armstrong, Bailey, Baylor, Briscoe, Carson, Castro, Childress, Clay, Cochran, Collingsworth, Cottle, Crosby, Dallam, Deaf Smith, Dickens, Donley, Floyd, Garza, Gray, Greer, Hale, Hall, Hansford, Hardeman, Hartley, Haskell, Hemphill, Hockley, Hutchinson, Kent, King, Knox, Lamb, Lipscomb, Lubbock, Lynn, Montague, Moore, Motley, Ochiltree, Oldham, Parmer, Potter, Randall, Roberts, Sherman, Stonewall, Swisher, Terry, Throckmorton, Wheeler, Wichita, Wilbarger, Yoakum, Young
Jarvis, James J.	20	Fort Worth	Tarrant	Jack, Parker, Tarrant, Wise

Knittel, Hermann	12	Burton	Washington	Austin, Burleson, Fort Bend, Waller, Washington
Lane, Jonathan	13	La Grange	Fayette	Bastrop, Fayette, Lee
McDonald, Henry D.	31	Paris	Lamar	Fannin, Lamar, Red River
MacManus, Francis E.	27	Corpus Christi	Nueces	Cameron, Dimmit, Duval, Encinal, Frio, Hidalgo, Kinney, La Salle, Maverick, Nueces, Starr, Uvalde, Webb, Zapata, Zavala
Pope, William H.	3	Marshall	Harrison	Harrison
Simkins, Eldred J.	15	Corsicana	Navarro	Freestone, Limestone, Navarro
Stinson, Samuel D.	5	Greenville	Hunt	Camp, Delta, Franklin, Hopkins, Hunt
Terrell, J. O.	16	Terrell	Kaufman	Dallas, Kaufman, Rockwall
Upshaw, Samuel C.	21	Hillsboro	Hill	Ellis, Hill, Johnson
Woods, John	11	Hallettsville	Lavaca	Colorado, Gonzales, Lavaca, Wharton
Woodward, William H.	26	Port Lavaca	Calhoun	Aransas, Atascosa, Bee, Calhoun, DeWitt, Goliad, Jackson, Karnes, Live Oak, McMullen, Refugio, San Patricio, Victoria, Wilson

1. Baker, chosen in a special election held June 4, 1887, and sworn April 16, 1888, succeeded Richard H. Harrison, who resigned on April 20, 1887.

Appendix M

MEMBERS OF THE TWENTY-FIRST LEGISLATURE

Regular Session, January 8—April 6, 1889

Governor Lawrence Sullivan Ross
Lieutenant Governor Thomas Benton Wheeler

Senate

Member	*District Number*	*Address*	*Home County*	*Counties Comprising District*
Abercrombie, Leonard A.	9	Huntsville	Walker	Harris, Montgomery, Trinity, Walker
Allen, William	17	Rock Hill	Collin	Collin, Denton
Armistead, William T.	4	Jefferson	Marion	Bowie, Cass, Marion, Morris, Titus
Atlee, Edwin A., Sr.	27	Laredo	Webb	Cameron, Dimmit, Duval, Encinal, Frio, Hidalgo, Kinney, La Salle, Maverick, Nueces, Starr, Uvalde, Webb, Zapata, Zavala
Burges, William H.	25	Seguin	Guadalupe	Blanco, Caldwell, Comal, Guadalupe, Hays, Kendall, Llano
Burney, Robert H.	28	Kerrville	Kerr	Bandera, Bexar, Crockett, Edwards, El Paso, Gillespie, Kerr, Kimble, Mason, Medina, Menard, Pecos, Presidio, Tom Green
Claiborne, John M.[1]	10	Galveston	Galveston	Brazoria, Galveston, Matagorda
Cranford, John W.	5	Sulphur Springs	Hopkins	Camp, Delta, Franklin, Hopkins, Hunt
Davis, William W.	8	Augusta	Houston	Angelina, Grimes, Houston, Leon, Madison

Douglass, Elbridge G.[2]	18	Sherman	Grayson	Cooke, Grayson
Field, Scott	14	Calvert	Robertson	Brazos, Milam, Robertson
Finley, John W.[2]	18	Sherman	Grayson	Cooke, Grayson
Frank, Louis N.	30	Stephenville	Erath	Bosque, Erath, Hood, Palo Pinto, Somervell
Glasscock, George W., Jr.	24	Georgetown	Williamson	Burnet, Travis, Williamson
Harrison, John H.	22	Harrison	McLennan	Falls, McLennan
Ingram, James M.	2	Hemphill	Sabine	Nacogdoches, Panola, Rusk, Sabine, San Augustine, Shelby
Jarvis, James J.	20	Fort Worth	Tarrant	Jack, Parker, Tarrant, Wise
Johnson, William C.	6	Tyler	Smith	Gregg, Rains, Smith, Upshur, Wood
Kimbrough, Robert S.	16	Mesquite	Dallas	Dallas, Kaufman, Rockwall
Lane, Jonathan	13	La Grange	Fayette	Bastrop, Fayette, Lee
McDonald, Henry D.	31	Paris	Lamar	Fannin, Lamar, Red River
Maetze, Ernst G.	12	Bellville	Austin	Austin, Burleson, Fort Bend, Waller, Washington
Morris, Robert H.[3]	7	Rusk	Cherokee	Anderson, Cherokee, Henderson, Van Zandt
Pope, William H.	3	Marshall	Harrison	Harrison
Seale, Kennan B.	1	Jasper	Jasper	Chambers, Hardin, Jasper, Jefferson, Liberty, Newton, Orange, Polk, San Jacinto, Tyler
Simkins, Eldred J.	15	Corsicana	Navarro	Freestone, Limestone, Navarro
Sims, Henry T.	29	Coleman	Coleman	Andrews, Borden, Brown, Callahan, Coleman, Comanche, Concho, Dawson, Eastland, Fisher, Gaines, Howard, Jones, McCulloch, Martin, Mitchell, Nolan, Runnels, San Saba, Scurry, Shackelford, Stephens, Taylor
Stephens, John H.	19	Montague	Montague	Archer, Armstrong, Bailey, Baylor, Briscoe, Carson, Castro, Childress, Clay, Cochran, Collingsworth, Cottle, Crosby, Dallam, Deaf Smith, Dickens, Donley, Floyd, Garza, Gray, Greer, Hale, Hall, Hansford, Hardeman, Hartley, Haskell,

				Hemphill, Hockley, Hutchinson, Kent, King, Knox, Lamb, Lipscomb, Lynn, Lubbock, Montague, Moore, Motley, Ochiltree, Oldham, Parmer, Potter, Randall, Roberts, Sherman, Stonewall, Swisher, Terry, Throckmorton, Wheeler, Wichita, Wilbarger, Yoakum, Young
Townsend, Marcus H.	11	Columbus	Colorado	Colorado, Gonzales, Lavaca, Wharton
Tyler, George W.	23	Belton	Bell	Bell, Coryell, Hamilton, Lampasas
Upshaw, Samuel C.	21	Hillsboro	Hill	Ellis, Hill, Johnson
Woodward, William H.	26	Victoria	Victoria	Aransas, Atascosa, Bee, Calhoun, DeWitt, Goliad, Jackson, Karnes, Live Oak, McMullen, Refugio, San Patricio, Victoria, Wilson

1. Claiborne resigned February 19, 1890.

2. Finley, seated March 5, 1889, succeeded Elbridge G. Douglass, who resigned on January 23, 1889.

3. Morris resigned July 9, 1890.

Bibliography

In addition to the entries under the individual chapters, the following primary and secondary sources were used extensively in the preparation of the entire book.

Primary sources included all of the *Senate Journals* for the time period involved, most of the *House Journals* for the time period, and all of the general and special laws printed by both state printers and private printers.

Among the most frequently consulted secondary sources were:

Richardson, Rupert N., Ernest Wallace, and Adrian N. Anderson. *Texas: The Lone Star State.* Englewood Cliffs, N.J.: Prentice-Hall, 1981.

Tyler, Ron, ed. *The New Handbook of Texas.* 6 vols. Austin: Texas State Historical Association, 1996.

Webb, Walter Prescott, ed. *The Handbook of Texas.* 3 vols. Austin: Texas State Historical Association, 1952–77.

CHAPTER 1

Acheson, Sam, and Julie Ann Hudson O'Connell, eds. "George Washington Diamond's Account of the Great Hanging at Gainesville, 1862." *Southwestern Historical Quarterly* 63, no. 3 (January 1963): 331–414.

Bentley, H. L., and A. J. Pilgrim. *The Texas Legal Directory for 1876–77.* Austin: *Democratic Statesman* Office, 1877.

Biographical Encyclopedia of Texas. New York: Southern Publishing Company, 1880.

Brown, John Henry. *Indian Wars and Pioneers of Texas.* Austin: L. E. Daniell, 1898; reprint, Austin: State House Press, 1988.

Clark, James Lemuel. *Civil War Recollections of James Lemuel Clark.* College Station: Texas A&M University Press, 1984.

Fehrenbach, T. R. *Lone Star: A History of Texas and the Texans.* New York: American Legacy Press, 1968.

History Book Committee of Houston County Historical Commission, ed. *History of Houston County, Texas, 1687–1979.* Tulsa, Okla.: Heritage Publishing Company, 1979.

History of Texas, Together with a Biographical History of the Cities of Houston and Galveston. Chicago: Lewis Publishing Company, 1895.

Hord, Arnold Harris. *Genealogy of the Hord Family.* Philadelphia: J. B. Lippincott Company, 1898.

Hughes, W. J. *Rebellious Ranger: Rip Ford and the Old Southwest.* Norman: University of Oklahoma Press, 1964.

McCaslin, Richard B. *Tainted Breeze—The Great Hanging at Gainesville, Texas, 1862.* Baton Rouge and London: Louisiana State University Press, 1994.

A Memorial and Biographical History of Navarro, Henderson, Anderson, Limestone, Freestone and Leon Counties, Texas. Chicago: Lewis Publishing Company, 1893.

Neville, Alexander White. *Backward Glances.* Paris, Tex.: Wright Press, 1983.

Procter, Ben, and Archie P. McDonald, eds. *The Texas Heritage.* 2d ed. Wheeling, Ill.: Harlan Davidson, 1992.

Raines, C. W. *Year Book for Texas.* 2 vols. Austin, Tex.: Gammel Book Company, 1901–1903.

Russell, Traylor. *History of Titus County, Texas.* 2 vols. Waco, Tex.: W. M. Morrison, 1965–66.

Sleeper, John, and J. C. Hutchins. *Waco and McLennan County, Texas.* Waco, Tex.: J. W. Galledge, 1876.

Speer, William S., ed. *The Encyclopedia of the New West.* Marshall, Tex.: United States Biographical Publishing Company, 1881.

Wallace, Ernest. *Texas in Turmoil.* Vol. 4 of *The Saga of Texas Series.* Austin: Steck-Vaughn Company, 1965.

CHAPTER 2

Acheson, Sam, and Julie Ann Hudson O'Connell, eds. "George Washington Diamond's Account of the Great Hanging at Gainesville, 1862." *Southwestern Historical Quarterly* 63, no. 3 (January 1963): 331–414.

Austin Tri-Weekly State Gazette. December 18, 1863.

Austin Weekly State Gazette. 1863–64.

Brown, Frank. "Annals of Travis County and of the City of Austin: From the Earliest Times to the Close of 1875." Austin: Texas State Library, Archives Division, n.d.

Calvert, Robert A., and Arnoldo De Leon. *The History of Texas.* 2d ed. Wheeling, Ill.: Harlan Davidson, 1996.

Casarez, Tomasa. "Magoffin, Founder of El Paso." *Junior Historian* 13, no. 5 (March 1953): 16–18.

Current, Richard N., T. Harry Williams, and Frank Freidel. *American History: A Survey.* 4th ed. New York: Knopf, 1975.

Fehrenbach, T. R. *Lone Star: A History of Texas and the Texans.* New York: American Legacy Press, 1968.

Fulmore, Z. T. *The History and Geography of Texas, as Told in County Names.* Austin: Steck Company, 1935.

Harnrow, Anne. "West Texas and the State Constitutional Convention of 1875." Master's thesis, Texas Technological College, 1933.

James, Vinton Lee. *Frontier and Pioneer Recollections of Early Days in San Antonio and West Texas.* San Antonio: Artes Gráficas, 1938.

Kinney, John M., ed. *Index to Applications for Texas Confederate Pensions.* Austin: Texas State Library, Archives Division, 1975.

"Ledger of the Senate Journal, Tenth Regular Legislative Session 1863." Austin: Texas State Library, Archives Division, 1863.

Linley, E. R. *A Biographical Directory of the Texas Conventions and Congresses, 1832–1845.* Austin: Book Exchange, 1941.

Spaw, Patsy, ed. *The Texas Senate.* Vol. 1. College Station: Texas A&M University Press, 1990.

Wooster, Ralph A. "An Analysis of the Membership of the Texas Secession Convention." *Southwestern Historical Quarterly* 62, no. 3 (January 1959): 322–35.

CHAPTER 3

Bates, Edmond Franklin. *History and Reminiscences of Denton County.* Denton, Tex.: McNitzky Printing Company, 1918.

Bell, William H. "Knights of the Golden Circle: Its Organization and Activities in Texas Prior to the Civil War." Master's thesis, Texas College of Arts and Industries, August 1965.

Bentley, H. L., and A. J. Pilgrim. *The Texas Legal Directory for 1876–77.* Austin: *Democratic Statesman* Office, 1877.

Brown, Frank. "Annals of Travis County and of the City of Austin: From the Earliest Times to the Close of 1875." Austin: Texas State Library, Archives Division, n.d.

Calvert, Robert A. "The Freedmen and Agricultural Prosperity." *Southwestern Historical Quarterly* 76, no. 4 (April 1973): 461–71.

Calvert Robert A., and Arnoldo De Leon. *The History of Texas.* 2d ed. Wheeling, Ill.: Harlan Davidson, 1996.

Colorado County Historical Commission, ed. *Colorado County Chronicles, from the Beginning to 1923.* 2 vols. Austin: Nortex Press, 1986.

Crouch, Barry A. "'All the Vile Passions': The Texas Black Code of 1866." *Southwestern Historical Quarterly* 97, no. 1 (July 1993): 12–35.

Ericson, Carolyn Reeves. *Nacogdoches—Gateway to Texas: A Biographical Directory, 1773–1849.* Fort Worth: Arrow/Curtis Printing Company, 1974.

Haley, J. Evetts. *Fort Concho and the Texas Frontier.* San Angelo, Tex.: *San Angelo Standard-Times,* 1952.

Hodge, Floy Crandall. *A History of Fannin County Featuring Pioneer Families.* Hereford, Tex.: Pioneer Publishers, 1966.

Kaufman County Historical Commission, comp. *A History of Kaufman County.* Dallas: Taylor Publishing Company, 1978.

Legislative Manual for the State of Texas, 1882–1883. Austin: E. W. Swindells, 1883.

"Letter from Governor J. W. Throckmorton addressed to Major General Charles Griffin, Commander of the Department of Texas, January 30, 1867." Executive Record Book, p. 253. Austin: Texas State Library, Archives Division.

Loughery, E. H. *Personnel of the Texas State Government for 1885.* Austin: L. E. Daniell, 1885.

McGraw, John. "The Texas Constitution of 1866." Ph.D. diss., Texas Technological College, 1959.

Members of the Texas Congress, 1836–1845; Members of the Texas Legislature, 1846–1992. 2 vols. Austin: Senate Engrossing and Enrolling and Senate Reproduction, 1992.

Parker, Richard Denny. *Historical Recollections of Robertson County, Texas.* Salado, Tex.: Anson Jones Press, 1955.

Ramey, William N., ed. *Texian Annual.* Austin: W. N. Ramey, 1886.

Ramsdell, Charles W. *Reconstruction in Texas.* New York: Longmans, Green and Company, 1910; reprint, Austin: University of Texas Press, 1970.

Shelby County Historical Commission, eds. *History of Shelby County, Texas.* Dallas: Curtis Media Corporation, 1988.

Shook, Robert. "Federal Occupation and Administration of Texas, 1865–1870." Ph.D diss., North Texas State University, 1970.

Smythe, H. *Historical Sketch of Parker County.* St. Louis, Mo.: Louis C. Lavat, Book and Job Printer, 1877.

Speer, William S., ed. *The Encyclopedia of the New West.* Marshall, Tex.: United States Biographical Publishing Company, 1881.

Walker County Genealogical Society and Walker County Historical

Commission, ed. *Walker County, Texas. A History.* Dallas: Curtis Media Corporation, 1986.
Wallace, Ernest. *Texas in Turmoil.* Vol. 4 of *The Saga of Texas Series.* Austin: Steck-Vaughn Company, 1965.
Yeary, Mamie, comp. *Reminiscences of the Boys in Gray, 1861–1865.* Dayton, Ohio: Morningside House, Inc., 1912.

CHAPTER 4

Constitution of the State of Texas. Adopted by the Constitutional Convention. Austin: J. G. Tracy, State Printer, 1871.
Current, Richard N.; T. Harry Williams; and Frank Freidel. *American History: A Survey.* 4th ed. New York: Knopf, 1975.
Fehrenbach, T. R. *Lone Star: A History of Texas and the Texans.* New York: American Legacy Press, 1968.
Ramsdell, Charles W. *Reconstruction in Texas.* New York: Longmans, Green and Company, 1910; reprint, Austin: University of Texas Press, 1970.
Wallace, Ernest. *Texas in Turmoil.* Vol. 4 of *The Saga of Texas Series.* Austin: Steck-Vaughn Company, 1965.

CHAPTER 5

Austin City Directory. 1872–73.
Avillo, Philip J., Jr. "Phantom Radicals: Texas Republicans in Congress, 1870–1873." *Southwestern Historical Quarterly* 77, no. 4 (April 1974): 431–44.
Baggett, James A. "Birth of the Texas Republican Party." *Southwestern Historical Quarterly* 78, no. 1 (July 1974): 1–20.
———. "The Constitutional Union Party in Texas." *Southwestern Historical Quarterly* 82, no. 3 (January 1979): 233–64.
Baker, J. W. *A History of Robertson County.* Waco, Tex.: Texian Press, 1970.
Barr, Alwyn. *Black Texans: A History of Negroes in Texas, 1528–1971.* Austin: Pemberton Press, 1973.
Barr, Alwyn, and R. A. Calvert, eds. *Black Leaders: Texans for Their Times.* Austin: Texas State Historical Association, 1981.
Barr, Amelia. *All the Days of My Life.* New York: Arno Press, 1913.
Baum, Dale. "Chicanery and Intimidation in the 1869 Texas Gubernatorial Race." *Southwestern Historical Quarterly* 97, no. 1 (July 1993): 37–54.
Bentley, H. L., and A. J. Pilgrim. *The Texas Legal Directory for 1876–77.* Austin: *Democratic Statesman* Office, 1877.
Biographical Directory of American Congress, 1774–1927. Washington, D.C.: U.S. Government Printing Office, 1950.
Biographical Directory of the Texan Conventions and Congresses. Austin: Book Exchange, 1941.

Biographical Encyclopedia of Texas. New York: Southern Publishing Company, 1880.

Biographical Souvenir of the State of Texas. Chicago: F. A. Battey and Company, 1889; reprint, Easley, S.C.: Southern Historical Press, 1978.

Brewer, J. Mason. *Negro Legislators of Texas.* Austin: Mathis Publishing Company, 1935.

Broaddus, J. Morgan, Jr. *The Legal Heritage of El Paso.* Edited by Samuel D. Myres. El Paso: Texas Western College Press, 1963.

Brockman, John M. "Railroads, Radicals, and the Militia Bill: A New Interpretation of the Quorum-Breaking Incident of 1870." *Southwestern Historical Quarterly* 83, no. 2 (October 1979): 105–22.

Brown, Frank. "Annals of Travis County and of the City of Austin: From the Earliest Times to the Close of 1875." Austin: Texas State Library, Archives Division, n.d.

Brown, John Henry. *History of Texas.* 2 vols. St. Louis, Mo.: L. E. Daniell, 1892–93.

Buenger, Walter. "Secession and the Texas German Community: Editor Lindheimer vs. Editor Flake." *Southwestern Historical Quarterly* 82, no. 4 (April 1979): 379–402.

Calvert, Robert A., and Arnoldo De Leon. *The History of Texas.* 2d ed. Wheeling, Ill.: Harlan Davidson, 1996.

Campbell, Randolph B. *An Empire for Slavery: The Peculiar Institution in Texas, 1823–1865.* Baton Rouge: Louisiana State University Press, 1989.

———. "Human Property: The Negro Slave in Harrison County, 1850–1860." *Southwestern Historical Quarterly* 76, no. 4 (April 1973): 384–96.

———. *A Southern Community in Crisis: Harrison County, Texas, 1850–1880.* Austin: Texas State Historical Association, 1983.

Cantrell, Gregg. "Racial Violence and Reconstruction Politics in Texas, 1867–1868." *Southwestern Historical Quarterly* 93, no. 3 (January 1990): 333–55.

Casdorph, Paul D. "The Bogus Texas Delegation to the 1860 Republican National Convention." *Southwestern Historical Quarterly* 65, no. 4 (April 1962): 480–86.

———. *A History of the Republican Party in Texas.* Austin: Pemberton Press, 1965.

"Certified copy of a letter from J. J. Reynolds, Brevet Major General U.S.A., commanding Fifth Military District, addressed to the Adjutant General, United States Army, March 10, 1870." In collections of the Texas State Library and Archives Commission, Austin.

Chabot, Frederick Charles. *Genealogies of Early San Antonio Families.* San Antonio: Artes Gráficas, 1937.

———. *With the Makers of San Antonio.* San Antonio: Artes Gráficas, 1937.

Cherokee County History. Jacksonville, Tex.: Cherokee County Historical Society, 1986.

Clark, T. D., ed. *Travels in the New South: A Bibliography.* Vol. 1 of *The Postwar South, 1865–1900: An Era of Reconstruction and Readjustment.* Norman: University of Oklahoma Press, 1961.

Colorado County Historical Commission, ed. *Colorado County Chronicles, from the Beginning to 1923.* 2 vols. Austin: Nortex Press, 1986.

Committee on Reconstruction, State of Texas, ed. *Affairs in Texas: Letters from Governor Pease and Hon. C. Caldwell in Regard to Affairs in the State of Texas.* N. p., 1868.

"Confederate Muster Rolls." Austin: Texas State Library, Archives Division, n.d.

Crouch, Barry A. "Hidden Sources of Black History: The Texas Freedmen's Bureau Records as a Case Study." *Southwestern Historical Quarterly* 83, no. 3 (January 1980): 211–26.

———. "'Unmanacling' Texas Reconstruction: A Twenty-year Perspective." *Southwestern Historical Quarterly* 93, no. 3 (January 1990): 275–302.

Current, Richard N.; T. Harry Williams; and Frank Freidel. *American History: A Survey.* 4th ed. New York: Knopf, 1975.

Daily Austin Republican. 1868–69.

Davis, E. J. "Letter Press, Outgoing, Records of the Governor." Austin: Texas State Library, Archives Division, n.d.

Degener, E. "Speech of Hon. E. Degener." *Daily Austin American,* July 22, 1868.

Dohoney, E. L. *An Average American.* Paris, Tex.: N. p., 1907.

———. *Man: Origin, Nature, and Destiny.* St. Louis, Mo.: John Burns Publishing Company, 1885.

Dwyer, Joseph. "Biographies of Leading Texans." 4 vols. Austin: Texas State Library, Archives Division, n.d.

Ellis, L. Tuffly. "The Round Bale Cotton Controversy." *Southwestern Historical Quarterly* 71, no. 2 (October 1967): 194–225.

Ericson, Carolyn Reeves. *Nacogdoches — Gateway to Texas: A Biographical Directory, 1773–1849.* Fort Worth: Arrow/Curtis Printing Company, 1974.

Evans, C. A., ed. *Confederate Military History.* 12 vols. Atlanta, Ga.: Confederate Publishing Company, 1899.

Evans, Lemuel D. "On the condition of Texas, and the formation of new States." Speech of Hon. L. D. Evans, delivered in the Constitutional Convention of Texas, Austin, January 6, 1869.

Evidence of Lawlessness in Limestone and Freestone Counties, Which Caused the Proclamation of Martial Law. Austin: Tracy and Siemering, 1871.

Farrow, M. H. *The Texas Democrats.* San Antonio: Naylor Company, 1944.

Fehrenbach, T. R. *Lone Star: A History of Texas and the Texans.* New York: American Legacy Press, 1968.

Ford, John S. *Rip Ford's Texas.* Edited by Stephen Oates. Austin: University of Texas Press, 1963.

Gage, Larry J. "The City of Austin on the Eve of the Civil War." *Southwestern Historical Quarterly* 63, no. 3 (January 1960): 428–38.

Galveston City Directory. 1868–69.

Galveston City Directory. 1872.

Galveston Flake's Bulletin. 1866–71.

"George T. Ruby." Austin: Texas State Historical Association, 1993.

Gibson, A. M. *The Life and Death of Col. Albert Jennings Fountain.* Norman: University of Oklahoma Press, 1965.

Greene, A. C. "The Durable Society: Austin in the Reconstruction." *Southwestern Historical Quarterly* 72, no. 4 (April 1969): 492–518.

Gregory, Thomas Watt. "Reconstruction and the Ku Klux Klan." Austin: Texas State Library, Archives Division, n.d.

Hayes, Charles W. *Galveston: History of the Island and the City.* Austin: Jenkins Garrett Press, 1974.

A History of Kaufman County. Terrell, Tex.: Kaufman County Historical Society, 1978.

History of Texas, Together with a Biographical History of Tarrant and Parker Counties. Chicago: Lewis Publishing Company, 1895.

Holbrook, Abigail Curlee. "Cotton Marketing in Antebellum Texas." *Southwestern Historical Quarterly* 73, no. 4 (April 1970): 431–55.

Hornsby, Alton, Jr. "The Freedmen's Bureau Schools in Texas, 1864–1870." *Southwestern Historical Quarterly* 76, no. 4 (April 1973): 397–417.

Houston City Directory. 1866.

Houston Telegraph. 1870–71.

Jefferson's Manual: Rules and Practice, House of Representatives. Washington, D.C.: U.S. Government Printing Office, 1931.

Johnson, Frank W. "The City of Austin from 1839 to 1865." *Quarterly of the Texas State Historical Association* 14, no. 2 (October 1910): 113–28.

———. *A History of Texas and Texans.* 5 vols. Edited and brought up to date by Eugene C. Barker, with the assistance of Ernest W. Winkler. Chicago: American Historical Society, 1916.

Johnson, Sidney Smith. *Texans Who Wore the Gray.* Tyler, Tex.: N. p., 1907.

Johnson County History Book Committee. *The History of Johnson County.* Dallas: Curtis Media Corporation, 1985.

Journal of the Reconstruction Convention Which Met at Austin, Texas, June 1, A. D. 1868. Austin: Tracy, Siemering Company, Printers, 1870.

Kelley, Dayton, ed. *The Handbook of Waco and McLennan County, Texas.* Waco, Tex.: Texian Press, 1972.

Kibart, Sylvia M., and Rita Adams, eds. *Pioneers of Hopkins County, Texas.* Sulphur Springs, Tex.: Hopkins County Genealogical Society, 1986.

Kinsey, W. L. "Negro Labor in Texas, 1865–1876." Master's thesis, Baylor University, 1965.

Kittrell, Norman Goree. *Governors Who Have Been, and Other Public Men of Texas.* Houston: Dealy-Adey-Elgin Company, 1921.

Malone, Ann Patton. "Matt Gaines: Reconstruction Politician." In *Black Leaders: Texans for Their Times*, edited by Alwyn Barr and Robert A. Calvert. Austin: Texas State Historical Association, 1981.

Marten, James. *Texas Divided: Loyalty and Dissent in the Lone Star State, 1856–1874.* Lexington: University Press of Kentucky, 1990.

Mason's Manual of Legislative Procedures. New York: McGraw-Hill, 1953.

McCrary, Peyton. *Abraham Lincoln and Reconstruction: The Louisiana Experiment.* Princeton, N.J.: Princeton University Press, 1978.

"Members of the Legislature of the State of Texas from 1846 to 1939." Austin: n. p., 1939.

Miller, Thomas L. "Texas Bounty Land Grants, 1835–1888." *Southwestern Historical Quarterly* 66, no. 2 (October 1962): 221–33.

Mills, W. W. *Forty Years at El Paso, 1858–1898.* El Paso, Tex.: Carl Hertzog, 1962.

Moneyhon, Carl H. "Edmund J. Davis in the Coke-Davis Election Dispute of 1874: A Reassessment of Character." *Southwestern Historical Quarterly* 100, no. 2 (October 1996): 131–51.

———. *Republicanism in Reconstruction Texas.* Austin: University of Texas Press, 1980.

Morris, Leopold. *Pictorial History of Victoria and Victoria County.* San Antonio: Clemens Printing Company, 1953.

Murphree, Nellie. *A History of DeWitt County.* N. p., n.d.

Nacogdoches County Families. Nacogdoches, Tex.: Nacogdoches County Genealogical Society, 1986.

Neville, A. W. *The History of Lamar County.* Paris, Tex.: North Texas Publishing Company, 1937.

Nunn, William Curtis. "Texas During the Administration of E. J. Davis." Ph.D. diss., University of Texas, 1938.

Paddock, B. B., ed. *A Twentieth-Century History and Biographical Record of North and West Texas.* Chicago: Lewis Publishing Company, 1906.

Parker, Richard Denny. *Historical Recollections of Robertson County, Texas.* Salado, Tex.: Anson Jones Press, 1955.

Parsons, W. H. "Speech on the logical results of the war, and the objects, aim, and constitutionality of the Militia Act: Delivered in the Senate of Texas, Austin, June 21, 1870." Center for American History, University of Texas at Austin.

Partlow, Miriam. *Liberty, Liberty County, and the Atascosita District.* Austin: N. p., 1974.

Pickett, Arlene. *Historic Liberty County.* Dallas: Tardy Publishing Company, 1936.

Pool, William C., Edward Triggs, and Lance Wren. *A Historical Atlas of Texas.* Austin: Encino Press, 1975.

"Population of the State of Texas." Secretary of State, 1880.

Porter, E. O. Review of *The Life and Death of Col. Albert Jennings Fountain,* by A. M. Gibson. In *Southwestern Historical Quarterly* 69, no. 2 (October 1965): 253–57.

Proceedings of the Republican State Convention, Assembled at Austin, August 12, 1868. Austin: Daily Republican Book and Job Office, 1868.

Proceedings of the Tax-Payers' Convention of the State of Texas, held at the City of Austin, Sept 22d, 23d, and 25th, 1871. Galveston: News Steam Book and Job Office, 1871.

Ramsdell, Charles W. *Reconstruction in Texas.* New York: Longmans, Green and Company, 1910; reprint, Austin: University of Texas Press, 1970.

Richardson, Thomas Clarence. *East Texas: Its History and Its Makers.* 4 vols. New York: Lewis Historical Publishing Company, 1940.

Roach, Hattie Joplin. *Hills of Cherokee: Historical Sketches of Life in Cherokee County, Texas.* Rusk, Tex.: N. p., 1952.

Russ, William A., Jr. "Radical Disenfranchisement in Texas, 1867–70." *Southwestern Historical Quarterly* 38, no. 1 (January 1934): 40–52.

Russell, Traylor. *History of Titus County, Texas.* 2 vols. Waco, Tex.: W. M. Morrison, 1965–66.

San Antonio Daily Express. 1870–71.

Shook, Robert. "Toward a List of Reconstruction Loyalists." *Southwestern Historical Quarterly* 76, no. 3 (January 1973): 315–20.

Smallwood, James. *Time of Hope, Time of Despair: Black Texans During Reconstruction.* Port Washington, N.Y.: Kennikat Press, 1981.

Smyrl, Frank H. "Texans in the Union Army, 1861–1865." *Southwestern Historical Quarterly* 65, no. 2 (July 1962): 234–50.

Sneed, Edgar P. "A Historiography of Reconstruction in Texas: Some Myths and Problems." *Southwestern Historical Quarterly* 72, no. 4 (April 1969): 435–48.

Soard's New Orleans Directory. 1876.

Soard's New Orleans Directory. 1879.

Somers, D. A. "James P. Newcomb: The Making of a Radical." *Southwestern Historical Quarterly* 72, no. 4 (April 1969): 449–69.

Sowell, A. J. *History of Fort Bend County.* Houston: W. H. Coyle, 1904.

Speer, William S., ed. *The Encyclopedia of the New West.* Marshall, Tex.: United States Biographical Publishing Company, 1881.

Spindler, Frank M. "The History of Hempstead and the Formation of Waller County, Texas." *Southwestern Historical Quarterly* 63, no. 3 (January 1960): 404–27.

"State Militia Reports, 1871." Austin: Texas State Library, Archives Division.

"Tabular Statements, 1870, Fifth Military District." 1869 voter returns by county. Austin: Texas State Library, Archives Division.

Texas Almanac, 1988–1989. Dallas: *Dallas Morning News,* 1987.

Texas Legislative Manual, 1879–80. Austin: E. W. Swindells, 1880.

Throckmorton's Final Report. Austin: John Cardwell, State Printer, 1873.

"U.S. Census, Texas, 1870." Austin: Texas State Library, Archives Division.

"Voter Registration Rolls, 1869–70." Austin: Texas State Library, Archives Division.

Wallace, Ernest. *Texas in Turmoil.* Vol. 4 of *The Saga of Texas Series.* Austin: Steck-Vaughn Company, 1965.

Waller, John L. *Colossal Hamilton.* El Paso: Texas Western Press, 1968.

Weyand, L. R., and Houston Wade. *An Early History of Fayette County.* La Grange, Tex.: *La Grange Journal,* 1936.

Wharton, Clarence R. *Wharton's History of Fort Bend County.* San Antonio: Naylor Company, 1939.

Whitney, N. A. *The History of Lamar County.* Paris, Tex.: North Texas Publishing Company, 1986.

Who's Who in Waco and Central Texas. Chicago: Forrister History Company, 1912.

"William H. Parsons." Austin: Texas State Historical Association, 1993.

Williams, M. L., ed. *Fayette County, Past and Present.* La Grange, Tex.: N. p., 1976.

Winfrey, Dorman H. "General Webster Flanagan." *Junior Historian* 4, no. 2 (November 1943): 5–8.

Woods, Randall B. "George T. Ruby: A Black Militant in the White Business Community." *Red River Valley Historical Review* 1, no. 3 (Autumn 1974): 269–80.

Yeary, Mamie, comp. *Reminiscences of the Boys in Gray, 1861–1865.* Dayton, Ohio: Morningside House, Inc., 1912.

CHAPTER 6

Arbingast, Stanley, et al. *Atlas of Texas.* 1976. Reprint, Austin: University of Texas at Austin, Bureau of Business Research, 1979.

Austin Daily State Journal. 1873.

Austin Democratic Statesman. 1872–73.

Baenziger, Ann Patton. "The Texas State Police During Reconstruction: A Reexamination." *Southwestern Historical Quarterly* 72, no. 4 (April 1969): 470–91.

Barkley, Mary Starr. *History of Travis County and Austin, 1839–1899.* Waco, Tex.: Texian Press, 1963.

Bentley, H. L., and A. J. Pilgrim. *The Texas Legal Directory for 1876–77.* Austin: *Democratic Statesman* Office, 1877.

Biesele, R. L. *The History of the German Settlements in Texas, 1831–1861.* Austin: Press of Von Boeckmann–Jones Company, 1930.

Biographical Encyclopedia of Texas. New York: Southern Publishing Company, 1880.

Biographical Files, Center for American History, University of Texas at Austin.

Brown, Frank. "Annals of Travis County and of the City of Austin: From the Earliest Times to the Close of 1875." Austin: Texas State Library, Archives Division, n.d.

Calvert, Robert A. "The Freedmen and Agricultural Prosperity." *Southwestern Historical Quarterly* 76, no. 4 (April 1973): 461–71.

———. "Nineteenth-Century Farmers, Cotton, and Prosperity." *Southwestern Historical Quarterly* 73, no. 4 (April 1970): 509–38.

Casdorph, Paul D. "Norris Wright Cuney and Texas Republican Politics, 1883–1896." *Southwestern Historical Quarterly* 68, no. 4 (April 1965): 455–64.

Chabot, Frederick Charles. *With the Makers of San Antonio.* San Antonio: Artes Gráficas, 1937.

The Citizen's Journal: Sixty Years in Cass County, 1879–1939. Atlanta, Tex.: N. p., 1939.

Conger, R. N. "Waco: Cotton and Culture on the Brazos." *Southwestern Historical Quarterly* 75, no. 1 (1971): 54–76.

Connelly, Thomas. "The American Camel Experiment: A Reappraisal." *Southwestern Historical Quarterly* 69, no. 4 (April 1966): 442–62.

Cox, James. *Historical and Biographical Record of the Cattle Industry and the Cattlemen of Texas and Adjacent Territory.* 1895. Reprint, with a new introduction by J. Frank Dobie, New York: Antiquarian Press, Ltd., 1959.

Current, Richard N.; T. Harry Williams; and Frank Freidel. *American History: A Survey.* 4th ed. New York: Knopf, 1975.

Daniell, L. E., comp. *Personnel of the Texas State Government, with Sketches of Distinguished Texans.* Austin: L. E. Daniell, 1889.

———. *Personnel of the Texas State Government, with Sketches of Representative Men of Texas.* San Antonio: Maverick Printing House, 1892.

———. *Texas: The Country and Its Men.* N. p., n.d.

———. *Types of Successful Men of Texas.* Austin: E. Von Boeckmann, 1890.

Davis, E. J. Papers. Center for American History, University of Texas at Austin.

Davis, Ellis A., and Edwin H. Grobe, eds. *The New Encyclopedia of Texas.* Dallas: Texas Development Bureau, 1929.

Ellis, L. Tuffly. "Maritime Commerce in the Far Western Gulf, 1861–1865." *Southwestern Historical Quarterly* 77, no. 2 (October 1973): 167–226.

———. "The Revolutionizing of the Texas Cotton Trade, 1865–1885." *Southwestern Historical Quarterly* 73, no. 4 (April 1970): 478–508.

———. "The Round Bale Cotton Controversy." *Southwestern Historical Quarterly* 71, no. 2 (October 1967): 194–225.

Evans, C. A., ed. *Confederate Military History, Extended Edition.* 17 vols. 1890. Reprint, Wilmington, N.C.: Broadfoot Publishing Company, 1989.

Evidence and Pleading in Six Cases of Impeachment Against Texas Judges. Austin: Texas Legislature, Joint Special Committee, 1873–74.

Ewell, Thomas T. *History of Hood County.* Granbury, Tex.: Frank Gaston, 1895; reprint, Granbury, Tex.: Junior Woman's Club, 1956.

Fehrenbach, T. R. *Lone Star: A History of Texas and the Texans.* New York: American Legacy Press, 1968.

Fleischer, M. B., ed. "Dudley G. Wooten's Comment on Texas Histories and Historians of the Nineteenth Century." *Southwestern Historical Quarterly* 73, no. 2 (October 1969): 235–42.

Ford, John S. *Rip Ford's Texas.* Edited by Stephen Oates. Austin: University of Texas Press, 1963.

Galveston Flake's Bulletin. 1872–73.

Glover, Robert W., ed. *Tyler and Smith County, Texas: An Historical Survey.* N.p.: American Bicentennial Committee of Tyler–Smith County, 1976.

Hart, Katherine, and the staff of the Austin-Travis County Collection, Austin Public Library. *Austin and Travis County, A Pictorial History, 1839–1939.* Austin: Encino Press, 1975.

Hodge, F. W., ed. *Handbook of American Indians.* Washington, D.C.: U.S. Government Printing Office, 1912.

Holbrook, Abigail Curlee. "Cotton Marketing in Antebellum Texas." *Southwestern Historical Quarterly* 73, no. 4 (April 1970): 431–55.

Hooper, William T. "Governor Edmund J. Davis, Ezra Cornell, and the A&M College of Texas." *Southwestern Historical Quarterly* 78, no. 3 (January 1975): 307–12.

Houston Telegraph. 1872–73.

Jackson, Pearl C. *Texas Governors' Wives.* Austin: E. L. Steck, 1915.

Jaynes, Nita M., and Willard G. Jaynes, comps. *History of Cass County, Texas.* Cass County Historical Society, 1972.

Johnson, Frank W. *A History of Texas and Texans.* 5 vols. Edited and brought up to date by Eugene C. Barker, with the assistance of Ernest W. Winkler. Chicago: American Historical Society, 1916.

Johnson, Sidney Smith. *Texans Who Wore the Gray.* Tyler, Tex.: N. p., 1907.

Kerr, Homer L. "Migration into Texas, 1860–1880." *Southwestern Historical Quarterly* 70, no. 2 (October 1966): 184–216.

Kindleberger, Charles Poor. *Manias, Panics, and Crashes: A History of Financial Crises.* New York: Basic Books, 1989.

Lindsley, P. *A History of Greater Dallas and Vicinity.* 2 vols. Chicago: Lewis Publishing Company, 1909.

Lynch, James D. *The Bench and Bar of Texas.* St. Louis, Mo.: Nixon-Jones Printing Company, 1885.

Marten, James. *Texas Divided: Loyalty and Dissent in the Lone Star State, 1856–1874.* Lexington: University Press of Kentucky, 1990.

M'Arthur, Niel J., and H. G. Wickes. *The Twenty-Seventh Legislature and State Administration of Texas, 1901.* Austin: Ben C. Jones and Company, Printers, 1901.

Mattick, Paul. *Economic Crisis and Crisis Theory.* White Plains, N.Y.: M. E. Sharpe, Inc., 1981.

McKenzie, Fred. *Avinger, Texas, USA.* Avinger, Tex.: Fred McKenzie, 1988.

Memorial and Genealogical Record of Southwest Texas. Chicago: Goodspeed Brothers, Publishers, 1894.

Moneyhon, Carl H. "Public Education and Texas Reconstruction Politics, 1871–1874." *Southwestern Historical Quarterly* 92, no. 3 (January 1989): 393–416.

———. *Republicanism in Reconstruction Texas.* Austin: University of Texas Press, 1980.

Newcomb, James. Papers. Center for American History, University of Texas at Austin.

Pitre, Merline. "Richard Allen: The Chequered Career of Houston's First Black State Legislator." *Houston Review* 7, no. 1 (1985): 79–87.

Pool, William C., Edward Triggs, and Lance Wren. *A Historical Atlas of Texas.* Austin: Encino Press, 1975.

Ramey, William N., ed. *Texian Annual.* Austin: W. N. Ramey, 1886.

Ramsdell, Charles W. *Reconstruction in Texas.* New York: Longmans, Green and Company, 1910; reprint, Austin: University of Texas Press, 1970.

Reese, James V. "The Evolution of an Early Texas Union: The Screwmen's Benevolent Association of Galveston, 1866–1891." *Southwestern Historical Quarterly* 75, no. 2 (October 1971): 158–85.

San Antonio Daily Express. 1872–73.

San Antonio Herald. 1872–73.

Smith, H. T., ed. *Austin: Its Architects and Architecture, 1836–1986.* Austin: Austin Chapter, American Institute of Architects, 1986.

Smith, Ralph. "The Cooperative Movement in Texas, 1870–1900." *Southwestern Historical Quarterly* 44, no. 1 (July 1940): 33–54.

Speer, William S., ed. *The Encyclopedia of the New West.* Marshall, Tex.: United States Biographical Publishing Company, 1881.

Texas Almanac, 1988–1989. Dallas: *Dallas Morning News,* 1987.

The Texas Almanac for 1869 and Emigrant's Guide to Texas. Galveston: W. & D. Richardson and Company, 1868.

Traxler, Ralph N. "The Texas and Pacific Railroad Land Grants: A Comparison of Land Grant Policies of the United States and Texas." *Southwestern Historical Quarterly* 61, no. 3 (January 1958): 359–70.

Tyler, Ronnie C. "Cotton on the Border, 1861–1865." *Southwestern Historical Quarterly* 73, no. 4 (April 1970): 456–77.

Wallace, Ernest. *Texas in Turmoil.* Vol. 4 of *The Saga of Texas Series.* Austin: Steck-Vaughn Company, 1965.

Webster, Michael G. "Intrigue on the Rio Grande: The Rio Bravo Affair, 1875." *Southwestern Historical Quarterly* 74, no. 2 (October 1970): 149–64.

White, Raymond E. "Cotton Ginning in Texas to 1861." *Southwestern Historical Quarterly* 61, no. 2 (October 1957): 257–69.

Woldert, Albert. *A History of Tyler and Smith County, Texas.* San Antonio: Naylor Company, 1948.

Woodfolk, George R. "Cotton Capitalism and Slave Labor in Texas." *Southwestern Social Science Quarterly* (June 1956): 43–52.

Woodman, Harold D. *King Cotton and His Retainers: Financing and Marketing the Cotton Crop of the South, 1800–1925.* Columbia: University of South Carolina Press, 1990.

Wooster, Ralph A. "Wealthy Texans, 1860." *Southwestern Historical Quarterly* 71, no. 2 (October 1967): 163–80.

———. "Wealthy Texans, 1870." *Southwestern Historical Quarterly* 74, no. 1 (July 1970): 24–35.

CHAPTER 7

American Council of Learned Societies. *Dictionary of American Biography.* 26 vols. New York: Scribner's, 1932.

Austin Daily Journal. 1873–74.

Austin Democratic Statesman. 1874.

Austin State Gazette. 1874.

Austin Weekly Democratic Statesman. 1873–74.

Bailey, E. E., ed. *Who's Who in Texas*. Dallas: Who's Who Publishing Company, 1931.

Baughman, James P., ed. "Letters from the Texas Coast, 1875." *Southwestern Historical Quarterly* 69, no. 4 (April 1966): 499–515.

Bentley, H. L., and A. J. Pilgrim. *The Texas Legal Directory for 1876–77*. Austin: *Democratic Statesman* Office, 1877.

Biographical Encyclopedia of Texas. New York: Southern Publishing Company, 1880.

Brewer, J. Mason. *Negro Legislators of Texas*. Austin: Mathis Publishing Company, 1935.

Brown, John Henry. *Indian Wars and Pioneers of Texas*. Austin: L. E. Daniell, 1898; reprint, Austin: State House Press, 1988.

Current, Richard N.; T. Harry Williams; and Frank Freidel. *American History: A Survey*. 4th ed. New York: Knopf, 1975.

Daily State Journal. 1874.

Daniell, L. E. *Personnel of the Texas State Government, with Sketches of Representative Men of Texas*. San Antonio: Maverick Printing House, 1892.

———. *Texas: The Country and Its Men*. N. p., n.d.

———. *Types of Successful Men of Texas*. Austin: E. Von Boeckmann, 1890.

Davenport, J. H. *The History of the Supreme Court of the State of Texas*. Austin: Southern Law Book Publishers, 1917.

Davis, Ellis A., and Edwin H. Grobe, eds. *The New Encyclopedia of Texas*. Dallas: Texas Development Bureau, 1929.

Dillon, Charles H. "The Arrival of the Telegraph in Texas." *Southwestern Historical Quarterly* 64, no. 2 (October 1960): 200–211.

Duncan, Merle Mears. "The Death of Senator Coke." *Southwestern Historical Quarterly* 63, no. 3 (January 1960): 385–403.

Dwyer, Joseph. "Biographies of Leading Texans." 4 vols. Austin: Texas State Library, Archives Division, n.d.

Evans, C. A., ed. *Confederate Military History*. 12 vols. Atlanta, Ga.: Confederate Publishing Company, 1899.

Fehrenbach, T. R. *Lone Star: A History of Texas and the Texans*. New York: American Legacy Press, 1968.

Ford, John S. *Rip Ford's Texas*. Edited by Stephen Oates. Austin: University of Texas Press, 1963.

Fulmore, Z. T. *The History and Geography of Texas, as Told in County Names*. Austin: Steck Company, 1935.

Galveston Daily News. 1873–74.

Galveston Tri-Weekly Civilian. 1873.

Gray, S. A., and W. D. Moore. *Mercantile and General City Directory of Austin, Texas—1872–73*. Austin: S. A. Gray, Book and Job Printer, 1872.

Hall, Claude. "The Fabulous Tom Ochiltree: Promoter, Politician, and Raconteur." *Southwestern Historical Quarterly* 71, no. 3 (January 1968): 347–76.

Henderson, Harry McCorry. *Texas in the Confederacy.* San Antonio: Naylor Company, 1955.

Henderson, Nat. Q., comp. *Directory of the Members and Officers of the Fourteenth Legislature of the State of Texas and Also the State Officers of the State of Texas.* Austin: Cardwell and Walker, 1874.

History of Texas, Together with a Biographical History of the Cities of Houston and Galveston. Chicago: Lewis Publishing Company, 1895.

Horton, Louise, ed. "Samuel Bell Maxey on the Coke-Davis Controversy." *Southwestern Historical Quarterly* 72, no. 4 (April 1969): 519–25.

Houston Telegraph. 1873–74.

Johnson, Frank W. *A History of Texas and Texans.* 5 vols. Edited and brought up to date by Eugene C. Barker, with the assistance of Ernest W. Winkler. Chicago: American Historical Society, 1916.

Johnson, Sidney Smith. *Texans Who Wore the Gray.* Tyler, Tex.: N. p., 1907.

Loughery, E. H. *Personnel of the Texas State Government for 1885.* Austin: L. E. Daniell, 1885.

Lynch, James D. *The Bench and Bar of Texas.* St. Louis, Mo.: Nixon-Jones Printing Company, 1885.

McKay, S. S. *Debates in the Texas Constitutional Convention of 1875.* Austin: University of Texas, 1930.

A Memorial and Biographical History of Navarro, Henderson, Anderson, Limestone, Freestone and Leon Counties, Texas. Chicago: Lewis Publishing Company, 1893.

Memorial and Genealogical Record of Southwest Texas. Chicago: Goodspeed Brothers, Publishers, 1894.

Moneyhon, Carl H. *Republicanism in Reconstruction Texas.* Austin: University of Texas Press, 1980.

Norvell, James R. "The Reconstruction Courts of Texas, 1867–1873." *Southwestern Historical Quarterly* 62, no. 2 (October 1958): 141–63.

Pennington, May A. *The History of Brenham and Washington County.* Houston: Standard Printing and Lithographing Company, 1915.

Pitts, Alice, comp. "Pecan Grove Cemetery Record." In *Collin County, Texas, Cemetery Inscriptions.* 2 vols. Fort Worth: Manney Company, 1975.

Ramsdell, Charles W. *Reconstruction in Texas.* New York: Longmans, Green and Company, 1910; reprint, Austin: University of Texas Press, 1970.

Rayburn, John C., and Virginia K. Rayburn, eds. *Century of Conflict.* Waco, Tex.: Texian Press, 1966.

Reese, James V. "The Early History of Labor Organizations in Texas, 1838–1876." *Southwestern Historical Quarterly* 72, no. 1 (July 1968): 1–20.

Rice, Lawrence D. *The Negro in Texas, 1874–1900*. Baton Rouge: Louisiana State University Press, 1971.

Richardson, Thomas Clarence. *East Texas: Its History and Its Makers*. 4 vols. New York: Lewis Historical Publishing Company, 1940.

Russell, Traylor. *History of Titus County, Texas*. 2 vols. Waco, Tex.: W. M. Morrison, 1965–66.

San Antonio Daily Herald. 1873–74.

San Antonio Express. 1873–74.

Shelley, George. "The Semicolon Court of Texas." *Southwestern Historical Quarterly* 48, no. 4 (April 1945): 449–68.

Shuffler, R. H. "Decimus et Ultimus Barziza." *Southwestern Historical Quarterly* 66, no. 4 (April 1963): 501–12.

Speer, William S., ed. *The Encyclopedia of the New West*. Marshall, Tex.: United States Biographical Publishing Company, 1881.

Stambaugh, J. Lee, and Lillian J. Stambaugh. *A History of Collin County, Texas*. Austin: Texas State Historical Association, 1958.

Summers, K. *The History of Grayson County, Texas*. Winston-Salem: Hunter Publishing, 1979.

Texas Almanac, 1988–1989. Dallas: *Dallas Morning News*, 1987.

Texas Legislative Manual, 1879–80. Austin: E. W. Swindells, 1880.

Thrall, Homer S. *The People's Illustrated Almanac, Texas Hand-Book and Immigrants' Guide for 1880*. St. Louis, Mo.: N. D. Thompson and Company, 1880.

———. *A Pictorial History of Texas*. St. Louis, Mo.: N. D. Thompson and Company, 1879.

Traylor, Russell. *History of Titus County, Texas*. Waco, Tex.: W. M. Morrison, 1965.

A Twentieth-Century History of Southwest Texas. 2 vols. Chicago: Lewis Publishing Company, 1907.

"U.S. Census, Texas, 1870." Austin: Texas State Library, Archives Division.

Wallace, Ernest. *Charles DeMorse: Pioneer Statesman and Father of Texas Journalism*. Paris, Tex.: Wright Press, 1985.

———. *Texas in Turmoil*. Vol. 4 of *The Saga of Texas Series*. Austin: Steck-Vaughn Company, 1965.

Weinert, W. M. *An Authentic History of Guadalupe County*. Seguin, Tex.: Seguin Conservation Society, 1976.

Wharton, Clarence R. *Wharton's History of Fort Bend County*. San Antonio: Naylor Company, 1939.

Winkler, E. W. *Platforms of Political Parties in Texas*. Austin: University of Texas, 1916.

Wood, W. D. "Reminiscences of Texas and Texans Fifty Years Ago." *Quarterly of the Texas State Historical Association* 5 (July 1901): 113–20.

Woodward, C. Vann. *Reunion and Reaction.* Boston: Little Brown, 1951.

Wooster, Ralph A. "Foreigners in the Principal Towns of Antebellum Texas." *Southwestern Historical Quarterly* 66, no. 2 (October 1962): 208–20.

———. "Wealthy Texans, 1860." *Southwestern Historical Quarterly* 71, no. 2 (October 1967): 163–80.

Wooten, Dudley G. *A Comprehensive History of Texas, 1685–1897.* 2 vols. Dallas: William G. Scarff, 1898.

Yeary, Mamie, comp. *Reminiscences of the Boys in Gray, 1861–1865.* Dayton, Ohio: Morningside House, Inc., 1912.

CHAPTER 8

Aldrich, Armistead Albert. *The History of Houston County, Texas.* San Antonio: Naylor Company, 1943.

Austin Democratic Statesman. July 25, 1876.

Biographical Encyclopedia of Texas. New York: Southern Publishing Company, 1880.

Brown, John Henry. *Indian Wars and Pioneers of Texas.* Austin: L. E. Daniell, 1898; reprint, Austin: State House Press, 1988.

Cardwell, John. *Fifteenth Legislature: Sketches of Legislators and State Officers, 1876–1878.* Austin: *Democratic Statesman* Steam Print, 1876.

Constitution of the State of Texas, 1875. Galveston: News Steam Book and Job Establishment, 1875.

Daniell, L. E. *Personnel of the Texas State Government, with Sketches of Representative Men of Texas.* San Antonio: Maverick Printing House, 1892.

Dwyer, Joseph. "Biographies of Leading Texans." 4 vols. Austin: Texas State Library, Archives Division, n.d.

Fulmore, Z. T. *The History and Geography of Texas, as Told in County Names.* Austin: Steck Company, 1935.

Grayson County Frontier Village. *The History of Grayson County, Texas.* N.p.: Hunter Publishing Company, 1979.

History of Texas, Together with a Biographical History of the Cities of Houston and Galveston. Chicago: Lewis Publishing Company, 1895.

Hodge, Floy Crandall. *A History of Fannin County Featuring Pioneer Families.* Hereford, Tex.: Pioneer Publishers, 1966.

Journal of the Constitutional Convention of the State of Texas, 1875. Galveston: News Office, 1875.

Kittrell, Norman Goree. *Governors Who Have Been, and Other Public Men of Texas.* Houston: Dealy-Adey-Elgin Company, 1921.

A Legislative Manual for the State of Texas, 1879–1880. Austin: E. W. Swindells, 1879.

Lynch, James D. *The Bench and Bar of Texas.* St. Louis, Mo.: Nixon-Jones Printing Company, 1885.

Martin, Charles L. "The Last of the Ranger Chieftains." *Texas Magazine* 4, no. 1 (January 1898): 33–41.

Memorial and Genealogical Record of Southwest Texas. Chicago: Goodspeed Brothers, Publishers, 1894.

Paddock, B. B., ed. *A Twentieth-Century History and Biographical Record of North and West Texas.* Chicago: Lewis Publishing Company, 1906.

Raines, C. W. *Year Book for Texas.* 2 vols. Austin: Gammel Book Company, 1901–1903.

Speer, William S., ed. *The Encyclopedia of the New West.* Marshall, Tex.: United States Biographical Publishing Company, 1881.

Yeary, Mamie, comp. *Reminiscences of the Boys in Gray, 1861–1865.* Dayton, Ohio: Morningside House, Inc., 1912.

CHAPTER 9

Austin Daily Democratic Statesman. 1878–79.

Austin State Gazette. 1878–79.

Austin Texas Capital. 1878–79.

Barr, Alwyn. *Reconstruction to Reform: Texas Politics, 1876–1906.* Austin: University of Texas Press, 1971.

Bentley, H. L., and A. J. Pilgrim. *The Texas Legal Directory for 1876–77.* Austin: *Democratic Statesman Office*, 1877.

Biographical Encyclopedia of Texas. New York: Southern Publishing Company, 1880.

Biographical Souvenir of the State of Texas. Chicago: F. A. Battey and Company, 1889; reprint, Easley, S.C.: Southern Historical Press, 1978.

Boethal, Paul C. *History of Lavaca County.* San Antonio: Naylor Company, 1936.

Braden, George D. *The Constitution of the State of Texas: An Annotated and Comparative Analysis.* Austin: State Agency Production, 1977.

Cardwell, John. *Fifteenth Legislature: Sketches of Legislators and State Officers, 1876–1878.* Austin: *Democratic Statesman* Steam Print, 1876.

Daniell, L. E. *Personnel of the Texas State Government, with Sketches of Representative Men of Texas.* San Antonio: Maverick Printing House, 1892.

Davis, Ellis A., and Edwin H. Grobe, eds. *The New Encyclopedia of Texas.* Dallas: Texas Development Bureau, 1929.

Evans, C. A., ed. *Confederate Military History.* 12 vols. Atlanta, Ga.: Confederate Publishing Company, 1899.

———. *Confederate Military History, Extended Edition.* 17 vols. 1890. Reprint, Wilmington, N.C.: Broadfoot Publishing Company, 1989.

Fehrenbach, T. R. *Lone Star: A History of Texas and the Texans.* New York: American Legacy Press, 1968.

Foote, Henry Stuart. *Texas and Texans.* Philadelphia: Thomas Cowperthwait, 1841.

Galveston Daily News. 1878–79.

Hardy, Dermot H., and Ingham S. Roberts, eds. *Historical Review of South-East Texas and the Founders, Leaders and Representative Men of Its Commerce, Industry and Civic Affairs.* Chicago: Lewis Publishing Company, 1910.

History of Texas, Together with a Biographical History of the Cities of Houston and Galveston. Chicago: Lewis Publishing Company, 1895.

History of the Texas Press and the Texas Press Association. Dallas: Harben-Spotts Company, 1929.

Hohes, Pauline Buck. *A Centennial History of Anderson County.* San Antonio: Naylor Company, 1936.

Johnson, Frank W. *A History of Texas and Texans.* 5 vols. Edited and brought up to date by Eugene C. Barker, with the assistance of Ernest W. Winkler. Chicago: American Historical Society, 1916.

Lang, Aldon S. "Financial History of Public Lands in Texas." *Baylor Bulletin* 35, no. 3 (July 1932): 1–262.

A Legislative Manual for the State of Texas, 1879–1880. Austin: E. W. Swindells, 1879.

A Legislative Manual for the State of Texas, 1882–1883. Austin: E. W. Swindells, 1883.

Love, Annie Carpenter. *History of Navarro County.* Dallas: Southwest Press, 1933.

Lynch, James D. *The Bench and Bar of Texas.* St. Louis, Mo.: Nixon-Jones Printing Company, 1885.

A Memorial and Biographical History of Navarro, Henderson, Anderson, Limestone, Freestone and Leon Counties, Texas. Chicago: Lewis Publishing Company, 1893.

Pitre, Merline. *Through Many Dangers, Toils and Snares: The Black Leadership of Texas, 1868–1900.* Austin: Eakin Press, 1985.

Ramey, William N., ed. *Texian Annual.* Austin: W. N. Ramey, 1886.

Richardson, Thomas Clarence. *East Texas: Its History and Its Makers.* 4 vols. New York: Lewis Historical Publishing Company, 1940.

Rogan, Charles. *Report of the General Land Office, State of Texas, November 1, 1899.* Austin: Von Boeckmann, Moore and Schutze, State Printers, 1899.

Speer, William S., ed. *The Encyclopedia of the New West*. Marshall, Tex.: United States Biographical Publishing Company, 1881.
Thrall, Homer S. *The People's Illustrated Almanac, Texas Hand-Book and Immigrants' Guide for 1880*. St. Louis, Mo.: N. D. Thompson and Company, 1880.
Weyand, L. R., and Houston Wade. *An Early History of Fayette County*. La Grange, Tex.: *La Grange Journal*, 1936.
Wood County, 1850–1900. Quitman, Tex.: Wood County Historical Society, 1976.

CHAPTER 10

Armstrong, Phebe Young. *From the Forks of Turkey Creek*. N.p.: P. Y. Armstrong, 1987.
Barker, Eugene C. *History of Texas*. Dallas: Southwest Press, 1929.
Barr, Alwyn. *Reconstruction to Reform: Texas Politics, 1876–1906*. Austin: University of Texas Press, 1971.
Bentley and Pilgrim. *The Texas Legal Directory for 1876–77*. Austin: *Democratic Statesman* Office, 1877.
Blair, E. L. *Early History of Grimes County*. Austin: N. p., 1930.
Brown, Frank. "Annals of Travis County and of the City of Austin: From the Earliest Times to the Close of 1875." Austin: Texas State Library, Archives Division, n.d.
Brown, John Henry. *Indian Wars and Pioneers of Texas*. Austin: L. E. Daniell, 1898; reprint, Austin: State House Press, 1988.
Campbell, Randolph B. *A Southern Community in Crisis: Harrison County, Texas, 1850–1880*. Austin: Texas State Historical Association, 1983.
Daniell, L. E. *Personnel of the Texas State Government, with Sketches of Representative Men of Texas*. San Antonio: Maverick Printing House, 1892.
Dwyer, Joseph. "Biographies of Leading Texans." 4 vols. Austin: Texas State Library, Archives Division, n.d.
Evans, C. A., ed. *Confederate Military History, Extended Edition*. 17 vols. 1890. Reprint, Wilmington, N.C.: Broadfoot Publishing Company, 1989.
Galveston Daily News. 1881–82.
Hardy, Dermot H., and Ingham S. Roberts, eds. *Historical Review of South-East Texas and the Founders, Leaders and Representative Men of Its Commerce, Industry and Civic Affairs*. Chicago: Lewis Publishing Company, 1910.
History of Texas, Together with a Biographical History of Tarrant and Parker Counties. Chicago: Lewis Publishing Company, 1895.
Johnson, Frank W. *A History of Texas and Texans*. 5 vols. Edited and brought

up to date by Eugene C. Barker, with the assistance of Ernest W. Winkler. Chicago: American Historical Society, 1916.

Johnson, Sidney Smith. *Texans Who Wore the Gray.* Tyler, Tex.: N. p., 1907.

Kelley, Dayton, ed. *The Handbook of Waco and McLennan County, Texas.* Waco, Tex.: Texian Press, 1972.

Kittrell, Norman Goree. *Governors Who Have Been, and Other Public Men of Texas.* Houston: Dealy-Adey-Elgin Company, 1921.

"Ledger, Senate and House Bills and Resolutions in the Senate in the Called Session of the Seventeenth Legislature." Austin: Texas State Library, Archives Division, 1882.

"Ledger, Senate and House Bills and Resolutions in the Senate in the Regular Session of the Seventeenth Legislature." Austin: Texas State Library, Archives Division, 1881.

Legislative Manual for the State of Texas, 1882–1883. Austin: E. W. Swindells, 1883.

Loughery, E. H. *Personnel of the Texas State Government for 1885.* Austin: L. E. Daniell, 1885.

Lubbock, Francis R. *Six Decades in Texas; or, Memoirs of Francis Richard Lubbock, Governor of Texas in War Time, 1861–1863.* Edited by C. W. Raines. Austin: Ben C. Jones and Company, 1900.

Manning, Wentworth. *Some History of Van Zandt County.* Des Moines: Homestead Company, 1919.

McDaniel, Robert Cecil. *Sabine County, Texas: The First One Hundred and Fifty Years (1836–1986).* Waco, Tex.: Texian Press, 1987.

A Memorial and Biographical History of Ellis County, Texas. Chicago: Lewis Publishing Company, 1892.

Neville, A. W. *The History of Lamar County.* Paris, Tex.: North Texas Publishing Company, 1937.

Norton, Frank Edgar. "The Major Administrative Policies of Oran Milo Roberts, with an Introduction to His Life." Master's thesis, University of Texas, 1925.

Paddock, B. B., ed. *A Twentieth-Century History and Biographical Record of North and West Texas.* Chicago: Lewis Publishing Company, 1906.

Raines, C. W. *Year Book for Texas.* 2 vols. Austin: Gammel Book Company, 1901–1903.

Richardson, Thomas Clarence. *East Texas: Its History and Its Makers.* 4 vols. New York: Lewis Historical Publishing Company, 1940.

Ruff, Nancy Blakeley. *Harrison County, Texas: Caucasian Residents in 1880.* Baltimore, Md.: Gateway Press, Inc., 1987.

Shanklin, Felda Davis. *Salado, Texas: Its History and Its People.* Belton, Tex.: Peter Hansbrough Press, 1960.

Speer, William S., ed. *The Encyclopedia of the New West.* Marshall, Tex.: United States Biographical Publishing Company, 1881.

Taylor, T. U. Collection. Vertical Files. Center for American History, University of Texas at Austin.

Thompson, James H. "A Nineteenth-Century History of Cameron County, Texas." Master's thesis, University of Texas, 1965.

Toole, Blanche Findley, comp. "1880 Population Census, Sabine County, Texas." N. p., 1978.

Tyler, George W. *The History of Bell County.* San Antonio: Naylor Company, 1936.

Yeary, Mamie, comp. *Reminiscences of the Boys in Gray, 1861–1865.* Dayton, Ohio: Morningside House, Inc., 1912.

CHAPTER 11

Brown, John Henry. *Indian Wars and Pioneers of Texas.* Austin: L. E. Daniell, 1898; reprint, Austin: State House Press, 1988.

Cardwell, John. *Fifteenth Legislature, Sketches of Legislators and State Officers, 1876–1878.* Austin: *Democratic Statesman* Steam Print, 1876.

Daniell, L. E., comp. *Personnel of the Texas State Government, with Sketches of Distinguished Texans.* Austin: L. E. Daniell, 1887.

———. *Personnel of the Texas State Government, with Sketches of Representative Men of Texas.* San Antonio: Maverick Printing House, 1892.

———. *Types of Successful Men of Texas.* Austin: E. Von Boeckmann, 1890.

Ellis County History Workshop. *History of Ellis County, Texas.* Waco, Tex.: Texian Press, 1972.

Evans, C. A., ed. *Confederate Military History, Extended Edition.* 17 vols. 1890. Reprint, Wilmington, N.C.: Broadfoot Publishing Company, 1989.

Ewell, Thomas T. *History of Hood County.* Granbury, Tex.: Frank Gaston, 1895; reprint, Granbury, Tex.: Junior Woman's Club, 1956.

Fannin County Folks and Facts: A Collection of Historical Sketches and Family Histories, Written by the Families and Friends of Fannin County. Dallas: Taylor Publishing Company, 1977.

Hall, Roy F., and Helen Gibbard Hall. *Collin County: Pioneering in North Texas.* Quanah, Tex.: Nortex Press, 1975.

History of Texas, Together with a Biographical History of Tarrant and Parker Counties. Chicago: Lewis Publishing Company, 1895.

Hodge, Floy Crandall. *A History of Fannin County Featuring Pioneer Families.* Hereford, Tex.: Pioneer Publishers, 1966.

Johnson, Sidney Smith. *Texans Who Wore the Gray.* Tyler, Tex.: N. p., 1907.

Lambert, Will, comp. *Pocket Directory of the Eighteenth Legislature of Texas.* Austin: Deffenbaugh and Company, 1883.

A Legislative Manual for the State of Texas, 1879–1880. Austin: E. W. Swindells, 1879.

A Legislative Manual for the State of Texas, 1882–1883. Austin: E. W. Swindells, 1883.

Loughery, E. H. *Personnel of the Texas State Government for 1885*. Austin: L. E. Daniell, 1885.

Memorial and Biographical History of Dallas County, Texas. Chicago: Lewis Publishing Company, 1892.

A Memorial and Biographical History of Ellis County, Texas. Chicago: Lewis Publishing Company, 1892.

A Memorial and Biographical History of McLennan, Falls, Bell and Coryell Counties, Texas. Chicago: Lewis Publishing Company, 1893.

A Memorial and Biographical History of Navarro, Henderson, Anderson, Limestone, Freestone and Leon Counties, Texas. Chicago: Lewis Publishing Company, 1893.

Men of Affairs of San Antonio. San Antonio: San Antonio Newspaper Artists' Association, n.d.

Ramey, William N., ed. *Texian Annual.* Austin: W. N. Ramey, 1886.

CHAPTER 12

American Biography: A New Cyclopedia. Vol. 43. New York: American Historical Society, Inc., 1930.

Austin Democratic Statesman. January–March, 1885.

Barr, Alwyn. *Reconstruction to Reform: Texas Politics, 1876–1906.* Austin: University of Texas Press, 1971.

Biographical Encyclopedia of Texas. New York: Southern Publishing Company, 1880.

Current, Richard N.; T. Harry Williams; and Frank Freidel. *American History: A Survey.* 4th ed. New York: Knopf, 1975.

Daniell, L. E., comp. *Personnel of the Texas State Government, with Sketches of Distinguished Texans.* Austin: L. E. Daniell, 1887.

———. *Personnel of the Texas State Government, with Sketches of Representative Men of Texas.* San Antonio: Maverick Printing House, 1892.

———. *Types of Successful Men of Texas.* Austin: E. Von Boeckmann, 1890.

Douglas, C. L. *Frontier Town.* Fort Worth, Tex.: Fort Worth Press, 1936.

Fehrenbach, T. R. *Lone Star: A History of Texas and the Texans.* New York: American Legacy Press, 1968.

Galveston Daily News. January–March, 1885.

Haley, J. Evetts. "The Grass Lease Fight and Attempted Impeachment of the First Panhandle Judge." *Southwestern Historical Quarterly* 38, no. 1 (July 1934): 1–27.

Hamner, Laura V. *Short Grass and Longhorns.* Norman: University of Oklahoma Press, 1943.

Hine, Darlene Clark. *Black Victory: The Rise and Fall of the White Primary in Texas.* Millwood, N.Y.: KTO Press, 1979.

Holden, W. C. "Law and Lawlessness on the Texas Frontier." *Southwestern Historical Quarterly* 44, no. 2 (October 1940): 188–203.

Jordan, Terry. "The Forgotten Texas State Census of 1887." *Southwestern Historical Quarterly* 85, no. 4 (April 1982): 401–408.

Langston, Mrs. George. *History of Eastland County, Texas.* Dallas: A. D. Aldridge and Company, 1904.

A Legislative Manual for the State of Texas, 1879–1880. Austin: E. W. Swindells, 1879.

Lewis, W. N. *Between Sun and Sod.* Clarendon, Tex.: Clarendon Press, 1938.

Loughery, E. H. *Personnel of the Texas State Government for 1885.* Austin: L. E. Daniell, 1897.

MacCallum, Henry D. "Barbed Wire in Texas." *Southwestern Historical Quarterly* 61, no. 2 (October 1957): 207–19.

A Memorial and Biographical History of McLennan, Falls, Bell and Coryell Counties, Texas. Chicago: Lewis Publishing Company, 1893.

Paddock, B. B., ed. *A History of Central and Western Texas.* 2 vols. Chicago: Lewis Publishing Company, 1911.

Parade of Progress: Hamilton County Centennial Edition, 1858–1958. N.p.: *Hamilton Herald News,* 1958.

Peterson, R. L. "Jay Gould and the Railroad Commission of Texas." *Southwestern Historical Quarterly* 58, no. 3 (January 1955): 422–32.

Porter, M. J. *Memory Cups of Panhandle Pioneers.* Clarendon, Tex.: Clarendon Press, 1945.

Raines, C. W. *Year Book for Texas.* 2 vols. Austin: Gammel Book Company, 1901–1903.

Ramey, William N., ed. *Texian Annual.* Austin: W. N. Ramey, 1886.

Randolph, H. C. *Panhandle Lawyers.* Amarillo, Tex.: Russell Stationery Company, 1931.

Richardson, Thomas Clarence. *East Texas: Its History and Its Makers.* 4 vols. New York: Lewis Historical Publishing Company, 1940.

Robertson, Pauline Durrett, and R. L. Robertson. *Panhandle Pilgrimage.* Amarillo, Tex.: Paramount Publishing Company, 1978.

San Antonio Daily Express. January–March, 1885.

Sandoz, Mari. *The Cattlemen.* New York: Hastings House, 1958.

"Temple Houston Tales." *Austin Statesman,* August 18, 1905.

Texas Almanac, 1988–1989. Dallas: *Dallas Morning News,* 1987.

Utley, Robert M. "The Range Cattle Industry in the Big Bend of Texas." *Southwestern Historical Quarterly* 69, no. 4 (April 1966): 419–41.

Wilson, James A. "Cattlemen, Packers, and Government: Retreating Individualism on the Texas Range." *Southwestern Historical Quarterly* 74, no. 4 (April 1971): 525–34.
Winfrey, Dorman H. *A History of Rusk County, Texas.* Waco, Tex.: Texian Press, 1961.

CHAPTER 13

Aldrich, Armistead Albert. *The History of Houston County, Texas.* San Antonio: Naylor Company, 1943.
Austin Daily Statesman. 1887–88.
Biographical Encyclopedia of Texas. New York: Southern Publishing Company, 1880.
Brown, John Henry. *Indian Wars and Pioneers of Texas.* Austin: L. E. Daniell, 1898; reprint, Austin: State House Press, 1988.
Cody, C. C., ed. *The Texas Methodist Historical Quarterly.* Georgetown, Tex.: Texas Methodist Historical Association, 1909–11.
Daniell, L. E. *Personnel of the Texas State Government, with Sketches of Distinguished Texans.* Austin: L. E. Daniell, 1887.
———. *Texas: The Country and Its Men.* N. p., n.d.
———. *Types of Successful Men of Texas.* Austin: E. Von Boeckmann, 1890.
Evans, C. A., ed. *Confederate Military History, Extended Edition.* 17 vols. 1890. Reprint, Wilmington, N.C.: Broadfoot Publishing Company, 1989.
Fehrenbach, T. R. *Lone Star: A History of Texas and the Texans.* New York: American Legacy Press, 1968.
Fitzgerald, Hugh Nugent, ed. *Texans and Their State: A Newspaper Reference Work.* Fort Worth, Tex.: Texas Biographical Association, 1918.
Galveston Daily News. 1887–88.
Geiser, Samuel Wood. *Horticulture and Horticulturists in Early Texas.* Dallas: Southern Methodist University Press, 1945.
Hill County Historical Commission, ed. *A History of Hill County, Texas, 1853–1980.* Waco, Tex.: Texian Press, 1980.
History Book Committee of Houston County Historical Commission, ed. *History of Houston County, Texas, 1687–1979.* Tulsa, Okla.: Heritage Publishing Company, 1979.
History of Texas, Together with a Biographical History of Tarrant and Parker Counties. Chicago: Lewis Publishing Company, 1895.
Hunter, J. Marvin. *Pioneer History of Bandera County: Seventy-five Years of Intrepid History.* Bandera, Tex.: Hunter's Printing House, 1922.
Jackson, George. *Sixty Years in Texas.* 2d ed. Dallas: Wilkinson Printing Company, 1908.
Johnson, Frank W. *A History of Texas and Texans.* 5 vols. Edited and brought

up to date by Eugene C. Barker, with the assistance of Ernest W. Winkler. Chicago: American Historical Society, 1916.

Johnson, Sidney Smith. *Texans Who Wore the Gray.* Tyler, Tex.: N. p., 1907.

Lotto, Frank. *Fayette County: Her History and Her People.* Schulenburg, Tex.: F. Lotto, 1902.

A Memorial and Biographical History of Johnson and Hill Counties, Texas. Chicago: Lewis Publishing Company, 1892.

A Memorial and Biographical History of McLennan, Falls, Bell and Coryell Counties, Texas. Chicago: Lewis Publishing Company, 1893.

Neville, A. W. *The History of Lamar County.* Paris, Tex.: North Texas Publishing Company, 1937.

Paddock, B. B., ed. *History of Texas: Fort Worth and the Texas Northwest Edition.* Chicago: Lewis Publishing Company, 1922.

———. *A Twentieth-Century History and Biographical Record of North and West Texas.* Chicago: Lewis Publishing Company, 1906.

Parker, Richard Denny. *Historical Recollections of Robertson County, Texas.* Salado, Tex.: Anson Jones Press, 1955.

Roach, Hattie Joplin. *A History of Cherokee County, Texas.* Dallas: Southwest Press, 1952.

Sowell, A. J. *Early Settlers and Indian Fighters of Southwest Texas.* New York: Argosy-Antiquarian Ltd., 1964.

Speer, William S., ed. *The Encyclopedia of the New West.* Marshall, Tex.: United States Biographical Publishing Company, 1881.

Stambaugh, J. Lee, and Lillian J. Stambaugh. *A History of Collin County, Texas.* Austin: Texas State Historical Association, 1958.

CHAPTER 14

Bentley, H. L., and A. J. Pilgrim. *The Texas Legal Directory for 1876–77.* Austin: *Democratic Statesman* Office, 1877.

Biographical Souvenir of the State of Texas. Chicago: F. A. Battey and Company, 1889; reprint, Easley, S.C.: Southern Historical Press, 1978.

Brown, John Henry. *Indian Wars and Pioneers of Texas.* Austin: L. E. Daniell, 1898; Austin: State House Press, 1988.

Chapman, Berlin B. "The Claim of Texas to Greer County." *Southwestern Historical Quarterly* 53, no. 1 (July 1949): 404–21.

Coleman County Historical Society, comp. *A History of Coleman County and Its People.* San Angelo, Tex.: Anchor Publishing Company, 1985.

Colorado County Historical Commission, ed. *Colorado County Chronicles, from the Beginning to 1923.* 2 vols. Austin: Nortex Press, 1986.

Cotner, Robert C. *James Stephen Hogg: A Biography.* Austin: University of Texas Press, 1959.

Crane, M. M. "Recollections of the Establishment of the Texas Railroad

Commission." *Southwestern Historical Quarterly* 50, no. 4 (April 1947): 478–86.

Daniell, L. E., comp. *Personnel of the Texas State Government, with Sketches of Distinguished Texans.* Austin: L. E. Daniell, 1889.

———. *Personnel of the Texas State Government, with Sketches of Representative Men of Texas.* San Antonio: Maverick Printing House, 1892.

———. *Types of Successful Men of Texas.* Austin: E. Von Boeckmann, 1890.

Evans, C. A., ed. *Confederate Military History, Extended Edition.* 17 vols. 1890. Reprint, Wilmington, N.C.: Broadfoot Publishing Company, 1989.

Fehrenbach, T. R. *Lone Star: A History of Texas and the Texans.* New York: American Legacy Press, 1968.

Finley, N. Webb. "An Address Containing a Brief Summary of the Fruits of Democratic Government in Texas." Delivered at Tyler, Tex., September 21, 1888.

Glover, Robert W., ed. *Tyler and Smith County, Texas: An Historical Survey.* N.p.: American Bicentennial Committee of Tyler–Smith County, 1976.

Kaufman County Historical Commission, comp. *A History of Kaufman County.* Dallas: Taylor Publishing Company, 1978.

Kelley, Dayton. *George W. Tyler of Texas and Some of His Achievements.* Waco, Tex.: Texian Press, 1969.

———. *The Handbook of Waco and McLennan County, Texas.* Waco, Tex.: Texian Press, 1972.

Loughery, E. H. *Texas State Government: A Volume of Biographical Sketches and Passing Comment.* Austin: McLeod and Jackson, Printers, 1897.

Lucas, Mattie Davis, and Mita Holsapple Hall. *A History of Grayson County, Texas.* Sherman, Tex.: Scruggs Printing Company, 1936.

Memorial and Biographical History of Dallas County, Texas. Chicago: Lewis Publishing Company, 1892.

A Memorial and Biographical History of McLennan, Falls, Bell and Coryell Counties, Texas. Chicago: Lewis Publishing Company, 1893.

Moore, Webb L. *The Greer County Question.* San Marcos, Tex.: Webb L. Moore, 1939.

Norton, Charles G., ed. *Men of Affairs of San Antonio.* San Antonio: San Antonio Newspaper Artists' Association, 1935.

Norvell, James R. "The Railroad Commission of Texas: Its Origin and History." *Southwestern Historical Quarterly* 68, no. 4 (April 1965): 465–80.

Paddock, B. B., ed. *A History of Central and Western Texas.* 2 vols. Chicago: Lewis Publishing Company, 1911.

———. *A Twentieth-Century History and Biographical Record of North and West Texas.* Chicago: Lewis Publishing Company, 1906.

Proceedings, Constitution, By-laws and Addresses of the Annual Reunion of the Texas Veterans. Austin: A. Deffenbaugh, 1888.

Reese, John Walter, and Lillian Estelle Reese. *Flaming Feuds of Colorado County.* Salado, Tex.: Anson Jones Press, 1962.

Watkins, Sue, ed. *One League to Each Wind.* Austin: Von Boeckmann–Jones, Printers, 1964.

Whisenhut, Donald W., and Vicki Betts, eds. *A Chronological History of Smith County, Texas.* Tyler, Tex.: Jack T. Greer Memorial Fund of the Smith County Historical Society, 1983.

Woldert, Albert. *A History of Tyler and Smith County, Texas.* San Antonio: Naylor Company, 1948.

Index